The SECRET CITY

The SECRET CITY

Woodlawn Cemetery *and the* Buried History of New York

FRED GOODMAN

BROADWAY BOOKS
NEW YORK

PRINTED IN THE UNITED STATES OF AMERICA

BROADWAY BOOKS and its logo, a letter B bisected on the diagonal, are trademarks of Random House, Inc.

Visit our website at www.broadwaybooks.com

First edition published 2004

The author and publisher gratefully acknowledge the following for the right to reprint material in this book:

"Incident" from *Color* by Countee Cullen. Copyright © 1925 by Harper & Brothers; copyright renewed 1953 by Ida M. Cullen. Reprinted by permission of GRM Associates, Inc., agents for the estate of Ida M. Cullen.

"You Brought a New Kind of Love to Me" by Sammy Fain, Irving Kahal, and Pierre Norman. Copyright © 1930 by Famous Music Corporation. All rights reserved. Reprinted by kind permission of Hal Leonard Corporation.

BOOK DESIGN BY DEBORAH KERNER / DANCING BEARS DESIGN
PHOTOGRAPHY BY GERALD HOWARD

LIBRARY OF CONGRESS CATALOGING-IN-PUBLICATION DATA
Goodman, Fred, 1955–
The secret city : Woodlawn Cemetery and the buried history of New York / Fred Goodman.—1st ed.
p. cm.
Includes bibliographical references (p. 380).
1. Woodlawn Cemetery (New York, N.Y.) 2. Celebrities—New York (State)—New York—Biography. 3. New York (N.Y.)—Biography. 4. New York (N.Y.)—Buildings, structures, etc. 5. Cemeteries—New York (State)—New York—History. I. Title.

F128.61.W8G66 2004
974.7'275—dc22
2003065428

ISBN 0-7679-0647-0

1   3   5   7   9   10   8   6   4   2

A book for

WARNE AND JOSHUA GOODMAN

and a love tape for

ELLIOT HORNE

CONTENTS

Failing to fetch me at first keep encouraged,

Missing me one place search another,

I stop somewhere waiting for you.

•

—WALT WHITMAN,
FROM "SONG OF MYSELF"

The past always looks better than it was.

It's only pleasant because it isn't here.

•

—FINLEY PETER DUNNE

The SECRET CITY

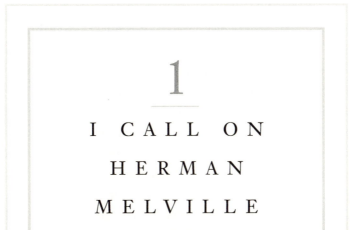

1

I CALL ON
HERMAN
MELVILLE

I first glimpsed Woodlawn through the window of a commuter express train. It was just another of the half-dozen Bronx stops I sped past twice each workday, and the concrete platforms and dull green signs of the Woodlawn station indicated nothing more than a disheveled collection of auto body shops, track yards, and overgrown lots framing an old, gray cemetery tucked against the city's northern border. It was, like so much of my native borough, just somewhere settled in some vague past and then left to its inevitable anonymous fade. If I happened to look up from my newspaper, I never gave the place a thought. And I certainly never imagined that some years later, in the wake of that terrible and inconceivable New York September, I would slip my moorings and drift out on the ocean of the city, floating without aim until the currents delivered me up to the ghosts of Woodlawn.

If I'm to be honest, I should say that I didn't even know I was drifting—just that I was suddenly having trouble sleeping. I live on a quiet street just beyond the fringe of the city these days and I'd never had a problem turning myself off before, even when I had an apartment across the street from the noisiest biker bar in Brooklyn. Back then, it fell to my girlfriend—bloodshot and bleary-eyed—to fill me in the next afternoon about the drag races which had shattered the sleep of everyone else at closing time. She would conjure malevolent chrome and black Harley choppers with glasspack-amplified exhaust systems roaring like rockets on a trajectory straight for either hell or Bay Ridge, whichever came first. For all I knew—blissful, unperturbed log that I was—she was making it up. Lately, however, I'd found myself dozing off earlier and earlier only to awaken at four, or two, or even midnight. The worst were the foggy or rainy nights when the nearby airport rerouted incoming jets right over my house. Then I'd snap awake with a sharp stab of panic at the ominous crescendo of enormous engines which, although actually high above, sounded as if they were about to crash through the roof and obliterate the house.

Nothing could lull me back to sleep, especially not the late-night news programs on the radio. If I went downstairs to reheat the coffee, just a glance at the day's spent grounds turned my stomach. The next morning on the train, exhausted and frazzled, I read my paper as I'd always done but without real comprehension, the words floating in the air before my red eyes like bits of disembodied ash that could never be put together again. And it wasn't just me. Everyone on the train, in the street, at work, lunch, or even just grabbing a smoke in front of the office buildings, was the same. That is, they were the same as they'd always been but different. Mourning hung like a gray cloud, yes, but it was more: a new uncertainty about things never questioned, a feeling of deep doubt akin to the first time you heard your father tell someone a lie. I don't know what others did, but I soon realized there were evenings when I needn't bother trying to get back to sleep. Instead, I surrendered and took to bicycling through the empty late-night streets of New York City.

Although my nocturnal sojourns were my own idea, I owed the original impetus for biking to my doctor. He's a nice guy, young and very low-key, and I like him despite the fact that he's conspicuously solemn in the manner of all modern doctors. As a kid I rode the bus with my grandmother for many of her frequent visits to a physician on the Grand Concourse—she had a heart condition—and I remember those appointments as something warm and congenial. After her exams, the doctor, a gray-haired man who favored vibrant silk ties and had a small pencil mustache like the urbane Manhattan gentlemen in Depression-era movies, would sit with her in his office and talk and laugh and share a smoke. Not something you'd want to see in your doctor today, of course. And perhaps as a seven-year-old I couldn't conceive of the approaching end that must have been the reason for all those exams, or decipher the subtle admonitions that I now suspect were the real meat of those seemingly casual conversations.

The tenor of my own trips to the doctor was all the proof I needed of how much times had changed, in general and for me. Somewhere along the line my annual physical had been magically transformed from the pro forma tests for infections and hernias that comprise back-to-school checkups into something a good deal more adult—and a great deal more anxiety-provoking. No more pencils, no more books: just stress tests, cardiograms, and the myriad nuances of the language of middle-aged blood with its lipids, glycerides, triglycerides, and omegas. "I know it seems a little humiliating," my nice doctor who doesn't smoke said sympathetically while snapping on the plastic glove for my first prostate exam. But I wasn't having any of his condescending crap. "Only one of us endured eight years of college to get to this moment," I shot back testily while exposing my best side, "and it wasn't me."

Maybe it was the glove, maybe it wasn't. But there's no doubt that there is a moment in midlife when you can feel death probing you and the inescapable fact of mortality finally comes to roost. No matter how good the rest of your day is it's always there when you get home, like the awful next-door neighbor who will never move away. That's certainly not the way it is when you are younger, when the people who die are suitably old—like, forty or fifty—or the victim of some rare disease or catastrophic event. Don't misunderstand me: I am grateful for a life blessedly free of such heartaches, for healthy children and a home. Still, you don't have to be as wretched as John Cheever to understand why all those straight-arrows with nice families, big houses, and rewarding jobs suddenly take lovers or get serious about their drinking or waste the better part of their afternoons watching the breeze shake the leaves out beyond their office windows, daydreaming about drifting away from the facts of their lives as lightly as a milkweed seed. But I'm the kind of coward who likes to do all of his running away close to home. So I bought a bicycle.

Growing up in the Bronx, my brothers and my friends and I all rode Huffys and Royce Unions from the Korvette's on the Boston Post Road— a fancy bike was a Schwinn and usually reserved for an only child or someone whose parents were getting divorced—and I can vividly remember my dad assembling my red and white Japanese three-speed in the living room of our apartment while keeping one eye on the first Nixon-Kennedy debate. When I took up riding again it was an unpleasant surprise to discover six-thousand-dollar bicycles. My childhood recollection is that bicycles were toys and that when you went to a bike shop the only adult was the owner. And it's the same on the roads now: you don't see kids with baseball gloves hanging from the handlebars on their way to the ball field, or hear baseball cards clicking against the spokes—it's middle-aged men and women with heart monitors tricked out any sunny Sunday morning in padded shorts and moisture-wicking socks, heading for Starbucks on expensive hybrids with oversized, prostate-friendly seats.

Like anyone who gets on a bicycle for the first time in twenty years, I was encouraged by the truism that riding is one of those things you never forget. But my first couple of weeks made me wish I had. They were bad. Real bad. Forget leg strength—I didn't have any—the shock was how winded I became at the first hint of a hill. And not just the big, obvious ones, either, because I made it a point to stay away from those, but the gentle rises you never notice in a car, the modest but steady slope of neighborhood streets normally noticed only by the children who have to walk to and from school every day. When I recall that first week, I don't picture myself on the bicycle. Usually I'm walking. Or kneeling alongside it, fixing a jammed chain, my hands coated in thick, black grease. Still, I stuck it out and was soon proficient enough not to drop the chain whenever I downshifted for a hill. Within a month my wind and endurance were much improved, my rides increasingly ambitious. Another month and I was averaging fifteen to twenty miles with longer rides on the weekends. The gains came faster and faster and soon I was looking to extend my territory like a neighborhood dog. Inspired, I picked up the pace and rode daily. I also changed my diet, giving up meat. When that made me feel even better, I also dropped cheese and whole milk. I had discovered The Brutal Inverse Law of Midlife Fitness: If you want to feel good as a man, you've got to run around like a boy and eat like a girl.

Before long, it wasn't uncommon for me to ride fifty miles at a clip, and when I tried my hand at centuries, organized hundred-mile rides, I was pleased to discover that, while I certainly wasn't at the front of the pack, I could do them without difficulty. I also began to glimpse another level in the distance: I was meeting bikers who rode more than twenty thousand miles a year over the hilliest routes they could find, athletes training for triathlons, and riders who participated in double centuries— a particularly grueling kind of insanity requiring roughly fourteen hours of nearly nonstop riding over two hundred miles. I wasn't sure how I felt about taking it to the next step.

Then something unanticipated happened: my satisfaction proved short lived. It was that same feeling you have when you go to bed tired and happy after a hard day only to find yourself suddenly wide awake two hours later, an elusive but profoundly unsettling thought skipping quickly away along the far edge of your consciousness. I was kidding myself—no matter how far I rode, no matter how many sprints I did, it was never going to be enough. I gave up oils, fats, and nuts. Then white flour and white rice. I rode twice a day.

So I can't just blame my nice doctor who doesn't smoke. He was only doing his job responsibly when he diagrammed my family's history of heart disease, or raised his eyebrows and tilted his head meaningfully when I recounted my long, sweet affair with tobacco (those good old pre-mortality days!), or when he sonorously listed the striking number of my close relatives who chew Lipitor like it is pez. Something else had happened. I had become superstitious.

At first it was an unspoken but increasingly strong conviction that a direct correlation existed between how many long, torturous miles I could ride and the length of my life. After all, isn't that the dynamic of exercise—something like putting money in the bank? The more I ride, the safer I'll be. But I had to get off the bike sometime, and that was the conundrum, the nameless nag. *This is a game you are going to lose.*

If my bicycle had subsequently languished in the garage, perhaps you can still understand why I reached for it once again on those late summer nights when every commuter plane sounded like a missle and Mars looked to come crashing down from the twilight sky. We were in a new world and I wasn't even sure that all the old streets—so quiet, so dark, and so empty—were still out there. I prayed the vibrations from the wheels of my bicycle would travel up my legs, make my body tingle with the rhythm of the city, and hum a familiar lullaby in my sleepless ears.

The clock in front of the Sherry Netherland Hotel at Fifth Avenue and sixtieth Street said 4:35 when I began my first ride, a simple, familiar route through midtown and Central Park, very early on the first Sunday of October. I'd worked many years in midtown, had walked most of these blocks more times than I could count, yet they looked and felt different in the quiet dark. At lunch hour on a sunny summer day

Sixth Avenue's plazas, benches, steps, and fountain walls are lined with the office girls from Bensonhurst, Long Beach, and Elizabeth, smartly dressed in their Loehmann's finds and nursing bottles of water or eating salads and falafels purchased from the corner carts, trying not to get caught sneaking peeks at the boys who hang on the fringes, smoking and braying into their cell phones and pretending in turn to be here for something other than the girls. And in the daytime chaos of the cramped street there is the relentless, creeping army of traffic: trucks, stretch limos, and the countless indomitable yellow cabs, as common and inde-structible as pigeons, fighting for every inch and dreaming of taking a mile. I'm not afraid of that kind of traffic; truckers and taxi drivers are as focused and aggressive as assassins, but unlikely to target me. Instead, I reached Thirty-fourth Street and found the wide and rutted pavement was virtually mine from the looming façade of the Empire State Building to the squat industrial ugliness of Madison Square Garden. Maybe it's the fact that the late and much-lamented Penn Station once stood here and that the building is across the street from the General Post Office, an extraordinary structure in the Federalist style guarded by a regiment of Doric columns and enough marble stairs to reach heaven, but never has anything deserved less to be called a garden. This one always reminds me of the enormous industrial air-conditioning units found on the roofs of midtown office buildings, and I barely gave it a glance. Although cabs shot across the avenues with regularity, there was almost no one else out and around. On Thirty-fifth Street I peered into Han Bat, a well-known twenty-four-hour Korean restaurant whose oversized seafood pancakes, called *pa-jon*, were once among my favorites. It was deader than heaven on Saturday night: just a waiter and one very bored chef. They were doing a little better over at the brightly lit Gray's Papaya stand at Thirty-seventh and Eighth, where several nighthawks who obviously don't share my desire to live forever were wolfing down dogs while a pair of cabbies leaned against their cars drinking the stand's famously frothy concoctions of fruit-juice-and-God-knows-what.

In the world of New York street food, the drinks at Gray's Papaya are the culinary equivalent of alligators or coelacanths—living fossils, the remnants of a once flourishing world. What happened to Orange Julius?

They were the kings of New York's hot-dog-and-fruit-juice stands into the early sixties, as ubiquitous as the Chock full o'Nuts counters with their "heavenly" coffee and cream cheese sandwiches on raisin bread. I never drank an Orange Julius—it was one of those things Jewish mothers wouldn't let their children have, like Bungalow Bar ice cream or any luncheonette sandwich with mayonnaise made between Memorial Day and Labor Day—and I guess I miss them the way I miss the old Penn Station, which I never actually visited. But I would be cheered an hour later by the discovery of a new Tad's Steak House in an otherwise Disneyfied Times Square—their $4.99 dinners of broiled steaks (as thin as the sole of a shoe but a good deal tougher) served with garlic toast, baked potato, and salad were once a common New York delight. And a little later at Fifty-seventh and Sixth, I snickered at the new restaurant— a faux landmark clearly aimed at the tourist trade—which boasted of being a New York tradition since 1935. The building used to be an Automat, one of the Horn & Hardart restaurants where you fed nickels into the coin slots of small, individual glass display cases to buy pots of franks and beans or egg salad sandwiches and slices of pumpkin pie while an unseen army of women in hair nets and tan-and-white uniforms hustled on the other side of the glass to reload the cases. Later, when I was working in the neighborhood, it was a pretty good deli and the last place where I saw my friend, Elliot. He was a publicist and the kind of old hipster who began and ended each day with Lester Young, quoted Lord Buckley, and looked out for young writers. Just a few weeks before our lunch he had taken early retirement following the sale of the company he'd worked for and was starting a little PR shop with one of his cronies. Finally freed of a job he had loathed for twenty years, he was exuberant and ready for action. A lively, almost hyperkinetic man in his early sixties who if he was growing up today would likely be pegged ADD, he still played pickup hoops on Saturday mornings near his home in Brooklyn. He attacked his lunch with gusto while ranting about the hopelessness of the Knicks, railed against an article a mutual friend had just published in the *Village Voice*, and hocked me to come fishing with him in Eleuthera. Two weeks later he was in the hospital, diagnosed with a rare and particularly virulent form of lymphoma; three weeks after that he was dead. I remember how enraged and terrified Elliot was. It was all so fast, such a dirty trick, and he couldn't accept it.

Ghosts. There are ghosts in New York. Someday I'll be one of them—no matter how far I ride.

Is that really why I'm up at this hour? Because you only see ghosts in the dark? In the pre-dawn of Manhattan the doormen and night watchmen—hovering in front of their buildings, sitting on the loading docks, leaning against alley gates, wispy cigarette smoke curling from their mouths into an ink sky—could be spectral sentinels of another world. They certainly aren't like the smattering of other working people I saw: young Mexican women leaving the late-night shift at a loft shop in the garment district, construction crews jackhammering Times Square at Broadway and Forty-second Street, or the Con Edison workers rising up out of the sewer at Forty-fifth Street. Like me, they are trespassers from the day world. I think of the construction workers as undertakers, digging down beneath the temporary holes in the skyline where buildings, like people, have departed.

Biking across Times Square while the sky showed its first real signs of light, I saw the clock on the *New York Times* building: 6:16. Inside the lobby a security guard thumbed through the *Daily News*. What will the street be like when the paper moves its offices a few blocks downtown? They are sure to tear the building down—it's outdated and the land is worth a fortune (the rival *News* has already unloaded its extraordinary Deco office building on Forty-second Street, a busted-out hustler pawning the family jewels for another shot at the craps table). Architecturally, the *Times* building isn't nearly as striking, although the squat, tawny box with its iron trim work is perfect for the paper, deftly managing to suggest both modesty and self-importance. Oddly, I found myself thinking of Walt Whitman, perhaps because he was a New York newspaperman. Or perhaps because I saw an old, ratty homeless man nearby who looked a bit like him in the half-light. The bum was parked on the pavement, his back leaning against the Dumpster by the kitchen door of an Eighth Avenue Blarney Stone. He had a long, dirty beard and wore the kind of battered hat Whitman liked to be photographed in. He was talking to himself, which didn't surprise me. Then, as I rode closer, I saw that he was actually talking on a cell phone. *New York City—where even the bums have cell phones!* That clinched it—I really must be the last person in America without one. Well, let him get brain cancer if he wants. I tried picturing the scene in the store when he signed up for the plan. *That* must have been something. Of course, he could have found the phone— or stolen it. But here's an even better question: Who the hell is this guy talking to at quarter after six on a Sunday morning? A daughter? A wife? The king of the bums? The unfortunate person whose telephone number coincides with the first seven digits he punched in? And what if he really is Walt Whitman—then whom would he be calling? Me, I hope. I know he'd recognize himself in the bum's face, or in mine. But I'd like to know if he recognizes our skyline here in the half-light of an unknown dawn, if he still sees the proof of his own immortal soul in its shattered steel and glass profile.

I finished a neat hundred-block chunk of midtown by riding north on Central Park West and entering the park at Ninety-seventh Street. The wraiths of the dark had evaporated with the night, replaced by the steady flow of people out for a warm, sunny Sunday morning, as different as dreaming and waking.

Although closed to traffic on Sundays, the etiquette among the joggers, skaters, and bikers who infest Central Park like fleas on a lion is to move in the direction motor vehicles would take on the traffic loop, i.e., south on West Drive and north on East Drive. It is, to put it mildly, a unique route, with every tree, every rise, every dip, every vista as carefully conceived as a museum show, yet all somehow maintaining the illusion of spontaneity. The way the park has managed to maintain its coherence in the face of the phenomenal pressure exerted by the millions who not only use it but also feel it should serve their personal need is a not-so-small miracle. Ball fields, dog runs, stables, skating rinks, restaurants, amphitheaters, zoos, lakes—yet all is pastoral, unhurried, and seamless. I came across an old stone marker tucked in a glade off the West Drive dedicated to the members of a Masonic lodge killed in the First World War, and wondered at all the city organizations and interest groups that feel the need to leave their graffiti-like mark on the park. Frederick Law Olmstead, who built the park with Calvert Vaux, preferred his design for Prospect Park in Brooklyn, and it's hard to think of a better example of an artist's inability to judge the quality of his own work. Possibly Olmstead was just being a doting father, trying to make sure the world didn't overlook the shapely contours and youthful charms of his Brooklyn gamine, but he didn't fool anybody. In Olmstead's day Brooklyn was called the City of Churches, and today you need only to walk its streets or rumble through its heart on the subway to know it has an old and deep soul, deeper at least than any other place in this world that I've ever been. Olmstead must have known that he didn't do it justice—that Prospect Park is just a beautiful place and not the bright green reflecting pool of all the hopes that fuel Brooklyn's singular spirit. No one can say the same thing about Central Park. She is everything there is to say about imperial Manhattan: the queen on her throne, with the world and all its power come to pay court.

Perhaps that's what makes me uncomfortable. Or maybe I'm just a snob. Either way, I found myself immensely self-conscious among the crowd of weekend skaters, bikers, hikers, daytrippers, and drifters promenading around and around in a big circle on the world's grandest stage, several hundred middle-aged adults on overpriced kids' toys. Is that all I'm doing? No, it can't be. I won't be a landlubber—I'm desperate to see the watery part of this world! Of course, no one ships out of New York anymore, but we still have tales of Wall Street, can still ponder infinity and its opposite in the blank, viewless brick wall of an air shaft. I won't do this, I won't ride with them. I want to see the secret city. I broke off from the pack at Columbus Circle.

There's a coffee kiosk near Sixtieth Street where I propped my bicycle against a nearby tree and grabbed a cup. Maybe I was just overdue for coffee, but I felt much better sitting beneath the *Maine* Memorial monument than on the Park Drive. There isn't much action around Columbus Circle on a Sunday morning. Instead, I looked at the Memorial.

It is overhung by trees, trumped by the nearby statue of Christopher Columbus in the middle of his Circle, and dwarfed by the buildings rising on three sides. It was intended as a tribute to the sacrifices of a war the country was quick to fight, but became a symbol of a war it has been quick to forget. Unnoticed, it might make a good New York riddle: what's forty feet tall and practically invisible? I was looking at it hard for the first time, even though I worked around the corner for several years. That particular morning it was an impromptu altar, strewn with flowers, dotted with votive and *yartzheit* candles, and covered with photographs of the dead and missing, sketches, scrawled prayers, and naked pleas to man and God. The monument itself sports a dozen marble figures. It is crowned by a triumphant Columbia, ringed with a prow of the dead, and attended by a grieving widow and orphan. This last statue is particularly graceful and moving. It has none of the mythology of Columbia, none of the formality of the ship of the dead. Its sorrow is honest, and the piece is beautiful. I make a note to find out who carved it.

A little later, back on the Park Drive and heading home, I catch a glimpse of a much different statue. This one, below East Seventy-second Street near Willowdell Arch, is cast in bronze and its subject is a dog. I ride off the road and onto a pedestrian path to have a look. The animal is Balto, the sled dog credited with hauling vaccine to Nome during a diphtheria epidemic in the winter of 1925. ENDURANCE FIDELITY INTELLIGENCE are emblazoned on the pedestal, sounding like an ad for a brokerage firm. I later do a little research and learn that Balto, like many heroes, had an unhappy slide from celebrity. His team was sold to a circus and badly abused. In failing health, his plight came to light and his release purchased with two thousand dollars raised by schoolchildren. Following his death, Balto was stuffed and put on display in a Cleveland museum, perhaps an early foreshadowing of the Rock and Roll Hall of Fame. The other interesting fact I discover is that this is reputedly the only statue of a dog in New York—something I find hard to believe considering both the number of statues and dog lovers in the city.

Indeed, there are a slew of them (dog lovers, not statues) congregated just a few blocks north at the East Ninetieth Street entrance to the park. There, along the footpath, is a water fountain for dogs. The spigot is encased in a stone carving of a dog's muzzle, and the dogs slobber and drink enthusiastically from the bowl beneath, while their owners circle each other. It is one of two dog fountains in the park, erected with the help of the ASPCA. This is where I leave the park and end my maiden voyage. But just as I'm about to leave I notice one more monument.

Across the road from the fountain, embedded in a stone wall above a broad staircase leading up to the track around the reservoir, is a plaque with a shiny gold portrait in bas-relief. Its subject is John Purroy Mitchel. I'd never heard of him, although the tablet says that he was mayor from 1914 through 1917. A steady stream of joggers hustled past the memorial without giving Mitchel a glance. And most likely I wouldn't have had a second thought about him, either, except I ran into him again the next night on Broadway.

I made just one mistake: I fell asleep after my ride. By 1 a.m. I was wide awake and an hour later I was back on the bicycle, this time in Inwood, a little-known neighborhood at the island's narrow, northernmost tip.

Inwood doesn't feel much like the rest of Manhattan. A mostly white and Hispanic enclave north of Washington Heights and Harlem, it's a portion of the borough most people never see. I like it. With a generous sprinkling of parks, quiet tree-lined blocks, a mix of pre- and postwar apartment buildings and an absence of commercial space, it feels young for a Manhattan neighborhood, more like Fieldston and Riverdale in the northwest Bronx, or the part of Yonkers abutting Van Cortlandt Park at the city line. It's also tiny, no more than forty blocks, bounded by Dyckman Street on the south, the Harlem River to the east, and Inwood Hill Park on the west. Despite the noisy presence of the elevated subway on Broadway, the blocks between there and the park—Payson, Seaman, West Indian, Cooper, and East and West Park Terrace—are downright sleepy.

Inwood Hill Park itself was a surprise. I'd often seen it from above while driving the Henry Hudson Bridge, whose enormous blue steel arches tower several hundred dramatic feet above Spuyten Duyvil at the confluence of the Harlem Ship Canal and the Hudson River and connect the Bronx and Manhattan. Baker Field, Columbia University's sports and athletic facility, sits alongside the park and is also visible from the bridge, as is the curving black spit-curl of the salt marsh crowning the park. At ground-level, Inwood Hill has two faces, and they're easy to differentiate even in the dead of night. Along with the neighborhood park of well-maintained playgrounds and benches near Payson Avenue, there's an extensive back country of trails, woods, and steadily climbing bluffs cresting in spectacular and untarnished views of the Hudson River. You can get lost there—both literally and in time. Once the Weekquaeskeeks Indians lived here among the rough hills and the mounds of boulders, debris from the Wisconsin Ice Sheet. They made their canoes and foraged for oysters and clams in the rich waters of the Hudson until the day they had the misfortune to meet one Peter Minuit. Although I'd always envisioned the powwow at which the Weekquaeskeeks sold the Dutch governor the island of Manhattan for twenty-four dollars in beads and assorted gewgaws happening downtown where New Amsterdam was settled, legend says it was actually beneath a giant tulip tree that still stood in this park into the 1930s. Wherever that first great Manhattan scam was perpetrated, it was a lulu: the Weekquaeskeeks got screwed. But to judge by the couples who can be found lolling any warm, sunny day on blankets out on the wide meadows, the old men fishing the incoming tide, the strollers meandering along the blacktop paths, and the steady soundtrack of shouts and laughter from the playground swings, no one calling Inwood home today did.

I covered tiny Inwood in just over a half-hour, its quiet rows of apartment buildings tucked in for the night, but a surprising number of bedroom lights lit. If Inwood's inhabitants were sleepless, I certainly knew why, and I continued riding south for Fort George and Washington Heights. Bicycling these neighborhoods is a good deal more ambitious than tooling around insular Inwood. One of the things bicyclists love most about Manhattan is that much of it was leveled for development. But not up here. Fort George Hill proved a brutal ride, carved with hidden terraces and grindingly steep climbs, and no matter how I schemed I invariably wound up rounding a corner to face an unexpected incline, some as daunting as any in the city.

Washington Heights grew on the site of Fort Washington, which stood on what is now tidy little Bennett Park, sandwiched between 183rd and 185th streets. Oddly, the most prominent reminder of the key

Revolutionary War battle fought here are the tributes to Margaret Corbin in nearby Fort Tryon Park. Corbin, like many other women, followed her husband when he joined the Continental Army, washing and cooking for him. When he was killed manning a cannon during the unsuccessful battle to hold Fort Washington, she took his place and was herself seriously wounded. Corbin later became the first woman to receive a soldier's pension from the government, was buried at West Point and is much celebrated by the DAR. The entrance to Fort Tryon Park is named Margaret Corbin Plaza, and as I buzzed around the figure-eight road in the Cloisters, I noted in the streetlight that it is also named for her. Yet there is nothing left of Fort Washington, which was erected to take advantage of the commanding view of the Hudson.

The fort may be gone but the hills aren't and it was a relief to finally huff past the George Washington Bridge, its steel feet planted firmly in the Hudson, concrete shoulders rubbing up against the Palisades and the old Weekquaskeeks' cliffs. From here, Washington Heights is a less demanding ride. The neighborhood, once Irish and Jewish and now largely Dominican, has seen its borders melt into Manhattanville and Harlem. Over the last fifty years Washington Heights has survived white flight, the murder of Malcolm X at the Audubon Ballroom, and the crack epidemic. What it may not be able to beat is the seemingly endless growth of Columbia Presbyterian Medical Center, which has been gobbling the neighborhood block by block, knocking some down for medical facilities, turning the area's rental stock into staff housing. All that construction isn't doing anything for the roads, either. At West 168th Street I was barely quick enough to notice that a steel plate placed over an open ditch in the street was askew—not something to bother a car, but definitely enough to send me ass-over-teakettle. I swerved to avoid it, bounced instead into a deep pothole, and felt my front tire go soft and wobbly with a flat. I'd gotten off lucky, though: the wheel rim wasn't bent, and I knew from experience that the hole in the inner tube would look like a snakebite, two small puncture wounds easily repaired in twenty minutes with the aid of my cheap patch kit. Around the corner, where Broadway intertwines with St. Nicholas Avenue, I spotted a wedge-shaped sliver of green and gray park and headed there for repairs.

There are hundreds of these vest-pocket parks around the city, as common and modest as a newsstand and just as easy to miss. Some are blacktop playgrounds, others, like this, a spot of reclaimed green. A sprinkling of trees—several modest spindly black locusts but also an American elm, a London plane, and an old pin oak—stand like wispy green shafts of light ringed by the surrounding buildings. A curved ribbon of blacktop is the park's only pathway, its contours limned every twenty yards by a sweep of old iron benches with new wooden slats. Like the benches, the park looks recently renovated, and there is new decorative ironwork around the Broadway gate. Still, the park seems little used, most likely because the neighborhood is growing more and more remote. Across the street where an apartment house once stood, there is now only a huge hole and a sign announcing the coming of a cancer research center. When complete, the hospital will surround the park on all sides, even the south, where much of the refurbished Audubon Ballroom is now medical offices.

I took off the wheel, changed and pumped a new inner tube, and remounted the tire. To patch the old tube, which became my new spare, required giving the glue a while to get tacky before applying the patch. I leaned the bike against a bench and strolled to a historic marker near the park's Broadway gate. Most of the city's pocket parks are named for someone associated with the neighborhood, such as a popular or powerful city councilman, a war hero, an activist, famous composer, or religious leader. This one turns out to be named for John Purroy Mitchel. I don't find much information about him on this historic marker, either—most of it is about Gertrude Vanderbilt Whitney, who executed the World War I memorial at the northern end of the park, a statue of three falling soldiers propping each other up that is ringed with carved tablets featuring the names of deceased and otherwise forgotten soldiers from Fort Washington Heights and Inwood. Barely a mention in his own park—I feel a pang for this Mitchel. How anonymous can you get? I know that it is natural, that every major city in the world is decorated with statues and tributes to faded figures, the transient heroes, ancient power brokers, and champions of causes hard-won, dearly paid for, and swiftly forgotten. After all, how much can we hold on to? Still,

Mitchel was mayor, arguably the most important man in New York. It seems a particularly cold judgment of time that barely a lifetime later five thousand joggers a day can run past his Central Park memorial and none recognize his name. I feel even worse when I discover a concrete slab near the south foot of the park recalling Mitchel's death in 1918 at the age of thirty-nine as a member of the American Expeditionary Forces. A mayor *and* a war hero? Here, in our own awful moment, when the current mayor of New York is finding his personal and political redemption with a display of humanity and depth no one ever suspected, when he is being rightly celebrated for comforting a reeling city, I shudder at the thought that another mayor could have given his life at the cataclysmic moment of his era and it's not only meaningless to us—it's as if it never happened. Is that all the unspeakable becomes—something long ago that happened to someone else, as present but unseen as the *Maine* Memorial? And is that what these unbearable, unthinkable days we are living through are? The paragraph to be deleted in the revised, 2045 edition of a high school history textbook? Does John Purroy Mitchel have something to tell me about what is happening in New York right now? I decided to find out.

The next day I took my first trip to the New York City Municipal Archives on Chambers Street, just behind City Hall and catty-corner from the Manhattan Borough Hall. Nonessential traffic was being barred from lower Manhattan's municipal district and a line of police defined the perimeter of City Hall Park. Wooden barricades formed a dull blue gauntlet running from the Borough Hall subway entrance to the court houses on Centre Street and up past Federal Plaza, where bomb-sniffing dogs and armed and helmeted soldiers guarded doorways. An overwhelming, rank smell like that of a massive industrial incinerator hung a hard, invisible varnish on the now empty blue sky. There were still the thousands dressed for business, but the public benches were all deserted, and the row of food kiosks beside the U.S. Courthouse silent and shuttered. Surprisingly, the Archives were unguarded and apparently unaffected, and I was pleased to discover that a request slip and a few minutes' wait were all it took for me to be lodged at a table in the building's main research room, a stack of manila file folders in front of me—the lion's share of the Archives' correspondence generated by the Office of the Mayor of New York, 1914–1917.

The files convinced me that John Purroy Mitchel had been a one-of-a-kind amalgam of urban visionary and priggish dolt—a political naif and idiot savant of good government. Like Rudolph Giuliani, he rose to prominence as a crusading prosecutor, bringing successful corruption cases against both the Manhattan and Bronx borough presidents. And like Michael Bloomberg, he was a political outsider who saw the mayor's role as akin to that of the CEO of a company. Indeed, in Mitchel's case he staunchly believed it was the mayor's *sole* function in the life of the city: the memos and speeches in the record make no secret of his contempt for the obligatory gladhanding and horsetrading that are the bread-and-butter of most politicians. Known as "the Boy Mayor," Mitchel was elected at the age of thirty-five on an independent anti-Tammany ticket and remains the youngest mayor in city history. The grandson of the Irish journalist, patriot, prisoner, and politician John Mitchel (whom he never knew), he was an avid reformer and a role model for Fiorello La Guardia. Yet he lacked his student's flamboyantly common touch. Elegant and fiercely protective of his private life, Mitchel struck much of the electorate as aloof and high hat, and his honesty, zeal, and distaste for political guile didn't serve him well as mayor. Yet he was a progressive through and through who sought city ownership of the subways, championed vocational education, was an outspoken anti-isolationist years before the United States entered the World War, and devised the first zoning plan in the country to govern city development. He seemed to derive special pleasure from stepping on toes, regardless of whether they belonged to powerful government interests or blocks of voters: he steadfastly refused to make political promises, but took on many urgent tasks with scant political upside such as reining in the city budget, reforming a very corrupt and entrenched police department, and investigated Catholic, Protestant, and Jewish charities for their mismanagement of public funds.

But reading through the files I discovered that the greatest challenge of Mitchel's term was the devastating polio epidemic that terrorized New York City in the summer of 1916. At a time when the city had approximately two million fewer residents, nearly two thousand five hundred children died, most of them under the age of five. The mass panic Mitchel had to quell is difficult to appreciate: along with quarantines and restrictions—children were not allowed, for example, on streetcars or in movie theaters for fear of spreading disease—the epidemic badly fractured the city along ethnic and class lines. Because polio was inaccurately portrayed as a product of the slums, immigrants, and particularly Italians, were scapegoated. And on the other side of the equation, working-class parents resented the ease with which well-to-do families were able to remove their children from the city and the reach of the all-powerful city health inspectors who could condemn the children of the less fortunate to the substandard public pediatric wards, viewed with terror as a virtual death sentence. Along with the street-level panic, Mitchel's correspondence shows him under continual pressure from all sides, particularly the business community and Washington, the later very likely on the verge of imposing an economically disastrous quarantine of the entire city.

Elected in 1913 with an extraordinary plurality, Mitchel received less than half as many votes for reelection in 1917 and suffered a humiliating loss to Tammany hack John Hylan. At the conclusion of his term he joined the army aviation corps: as mayor, he had long advocated U.S. intervention in the European war (a stance that further eroded his support with the city's key blocks of German and Irish voters) and had enlisted while still in office. We'll never know whether Mitchel might have continued his public career after the war had he not fallen out of an open-cockpit plane during his pilot training in Louisiana, apparently because he didn't fasten his belt. According to several fliers on the ground, Mitchel's descent was a horror: he flailed his arms and legs throughout the entire three-thousand-foot fall, working and recalibrating his body position in an attempt to hit the ground feet first, which he did. He bounced several yards and was dead when the first man reached him. Aside from his plaque and park, there is a memorial at his alma mater, Columbia University. Mitchel Air Field in Long Island (which has subsequently given way to a mall), was named in his honor, a tribute perhaps akin to dedicating a munitions factory to a shooting victim. I also discovered that despite dying in the service of his country on the distant shores of Lake Pontchartrain, Mitchel is buried in the Bronx soil of Woodlawn Cemetery. So, I would later learn, is his savvy pupil La Guardia and four other New York mayors whose names evoke no recognition today. Sitting in the Archives, I suddenly conjured a fleeting picture of the dapper and stiff-necked Mitchel standing alone in the gray garden of headstones, watching my commuter train whiz past on a cloudy late afternoon.

There was another elusive fraction of thought—that Mitchel should remind me of someone else interred in Woodlawn. But whom? I knew that several of my idols were buried there. Duke Ellington, for starters. Miles Davis, too. But I was trying to remember someone else, someone who was not a musician. *Damnit! Who?* I looked out the Archives window at the police barricades on Chambers Street and the broad, white, blank north wall of City Hall.

Herman Melville.

I returned the Mitchel files to the librarian, left the Archives, and immediately headed west on Chambers Street for the river. Two squad cars and a group of policemen blocked the route at Broadway, obliging me to turn north until I reached Canal. There were more police, more barricades on the south side of that street, and I felt a growing queasiness not just at the omnipresent sharp stench of chemicals and smoldering debris but at my shortening distance from the river. At Hudson Street I turned north again and rapidly walked twenty-five blocks, finally turning to face the Hudson at Gansevoort Street. It was here, in a building by the watery highway to the ocean, that Herman Melville, the writer who plunged deeper into the mysterious depths of the American soul than any other artist, spent twenty years fading from the national consciousness as a four-dollars-a-day customs official.

If I'm to come clean, I should confess to a longstanding fascination with Melville, whom I've come to think of as the patron saint of scorned artists, having paid with what should have been the best years of his life for pursuing the unsettling visions that swam up enormous, malevolent, and bafflingly complete from the deepest, darkest depths of any man's soul. On my honeymoon years ago I dragged my wife two hours out of our way to visit the house near Pittsfield where he wrote some of his greatest works, only to have some self-important old crone refuse to let us in because her tour ran twenty minutes and the house was closing in fifteen. It was a beautiful, quiet Friday afternoon in August and there was no one else there. But the woman planted herself implacably in the doorway with a smug, proprietary expression on her face while I, impotently staring into the first-floor window, asked which nearby Berkshire peak was Greylock, the "Imperial Purple Majesty" to which *Pierre* is dedicated, and begged repeatedly and without luck for admission. I was outraged: no man should have to spend even a minute of his honeymoon with that kind of shameless, dried-up old *Moby-Dick* teaser.

I suspect my fascination is an attempt to reconcile our eras; I've never been interested in knowing anything about the private lives of the contemporary artists I admire. Miles Davis is a good example—I had an opportunity once to meet him at a party and passed. He moved me so much as an artist that I very nearly worshipped him, and that's the way I wanted him to stay: known only through his work. I could recognize my world in his, understand why his work touches me so much. But Melville is the opposite, a complete mystery. I can never seem to get close enough to read his face, and I'm puzzled how someone from a different and unfamiliar time can speak so perfectly to me. We live in a digital age, when all information is reduced to ones and zeros, while Melville boomed his yeas and nays with the cosmic certainty of the earthshaking thunder rolling down from the crown of Greylock. I don't understand how this man—who by all rights should read like an anachronism— makes his ancient thunder rumble in my soul.

Of course, I know why I want him so much today—I'm just not ready to admit it. I can't turn southward and look at that filthy hole in the ground, that blasphemous and disgusting open grave. *Herman, the twin piers are gone and the moorings cut, so many souls sailing into the obliteration of anonymity!* He would know what to say about our boat, drifting on the ocean of the city. And if it turns out that there is nothing to be said, I believe Melville would know best how to say Nothing. He understood anonymity, because unlike Mayor Mitchel, he didn't have to wait to die to find it.

A best-selling author at the beginning of his career and virtually unpublished later, Melville died a failure. His great perplexing master-piece was not what his public expected or wanted, and they would not follow him into the deep water. When he subsequently tried his hand on land with the difficult *Pierre*, which included an incestuous affair, it proved a scandal and a flop. No longer able to support his family through his writings, he sought an appointment with the American con-sulate in Italy, but had only enough juice to land a job as a customs inspector.

Melville's tenure at the New York customs house coincided with that institution's golden age as America's foremost patronage factory. The harbor was a very busy place, but the New York Republican party, under the steely leadership of Senator Roscoe Conkling, filled the hundreds of jobs at the customs house with men who understood their first duty was not to the Port of New York but to the party, for whom they served as foot soldiers come election time. Running it all for Conkling was New York customs director Chester Alan Arthur, a lawyer and Lincoln Republican turned political stooge who, through an almost unimagin-able mix of backroom politics and assassination, would one day find himself president of the United States. As head of the Port of New York, Arthur made more money than he would as president—it was the highest-paid government post in the country. Melville, of course, was earning twenty dollars a week and was not unmindful of how far he'd fallen in the world. He winced at his work address: he was from an old Albany family and actually related to the Gansevoorts; he was known to ask people in the street's taverns if they had any idea who the Gansevoorts were (the invariable and depressing answer, Melville dis-covered, was that they didn't). When he died in 1891, the news surprised many in the publishing world who could still recall his best-selling early South Sea romances, *Omoo* and *Typee*; they thought he'd been dead for years. The final official badge of anonymity was supplied by the *New York Times*, which carried his obituary under the headline "Henry Melville."

Standing here, I see him come out of the squat brick building that faces the harbor. Distraught and panicked people are running in either direction and the cry of sirens near and far is ceaseless. He crosses the wide expanse of West Street and stands beside the river just on the fringe of a crowd, and I finally watch with him as first one and then the other building crumbles. Some in the crowd are wailing, some are yelling, but no one notices him and I don't see him speak. A gray snow of ash is falling, sticking to his shoulders and the wide brim of his hat. It is still falling several hours later when, silent yet, he walks with his head down first east and then north toward his home. I trail him through the brownstone row houses of Chelsea and farther east to Twenty-sixth and Park where his house once stood and watch him disappear. Across the street is Madison Square Park where, on the day the buildings come down, there will be statues to his earthly bosses, Chester Alan Arthur and Roscoe Conkling.

There are three hundred thousand bodies buried in the four hundred Bronx acres of Woodlawn Cemetery. Some were wealthy, some were powerful, some were wise, and many were decent. But I believe it is safe to say that only one, Herman Melville, is more famous, more alive to us, than he was on the day he died. Why only him? What of all the others? In John Purroy Mitchel I recognize the fears and emotions and panics of my own time. If I put the flesh back on his bones, will he tell me that I'm wrong when, awakened in the dead of this night, I think no one has been here before and anonymity is all that awaits?

Listen: I have an act of faith to perform. I want to tell you my story about our cemeteries, the big one up in the Bronx and the other one that we're walking around in. It goes like this.

2

WOODLAWN

There are any number of ways to get to Woodlawn Cemetery. Of course, people generally have an aversion to the most common and prefer taking the old IRT Number 4 subway to the end of the line and then walking the two blocks to the big Jerome Avenue gate; no matter what you think of the subways it still seems less traumatic. I elected to pass under my own motor through the smaller, deeply shaded Webster Avenue gate of Woodlawn Cemetery—the one I used to see from my commuter train—on a mild and cloudless late-summer afternoon when the weather was so fine as to be invisible. But even on a sunny day there is something daunting about approaching the cemetery. Perhaps it is the old-fashioned heavy iron fence surrounding the four hundred rolling acres and the convoluted honeycomb of roads, or the way the short steep hills rise above this back entrance, throwing everthing into deep shade. Maybe it is the three hundred thousand graves. Yet once beyond that forbidding perimeter, I found myself surprisingly at ease.

A quiet and undeniable grace wraps the small hills and deep shaded glens, a bucolic rural air hangs over the long, silent, tree-lined streets and seemingly endless vista of slowly eroding stone markers. It is as empty and undisturbed as the most pastoral fantasies of heaven. As with Central Park, the relaxed sense of nature—as if this, and not the surrounding landscapes of concrete, is the true soul and state of the city—is far from accidental. Opened in 1863, Woodlawn was conceived before the advent of either the automobile or the urban park movement, and it was the greatest and grandest example of the then-fashionable rural style of cemeteries. That style differed dramatically from the other dominant cemetery plan, the necropolis—literally "city of the dead." In a necropolis, the emphasis is on monuments and headstones, and the result—rows and rows of tightly packed stone—is decidedly urban. The rural style, with its landscaped, open spaces, was meant to double as a public park, serving the recreational needs of the living as much as the final requirements of the dead. When America's first planned rural nonsectarian cemetery, Boston's Mount Auburn, opened in 1831, it was a sensation and a major tourist attraction. Families often came to the cemetery on Sunday for a picnic—an idea most of us would find aberrantly morbid today (indeed, in the 1950s the comedian Lenny Bruce used a picture of himself picnicking in a graveyard for the cover of an album entitled *The Sick Humor of Lenny Bruce*). Woodlawn was conceived along similar but bolder lines, and its natural geography made for an extraordinary spot. Built on high, rolling farmland with streams feeding west to the Hudson and east to the Bronx River, its southwestern corner faced Manhattan and housed the cannon redoubt built to guard George Washington's retreating army from General Heath in 1776. Today, when the city's generous parks beckon and highways can whisk you out of town, nobody hangs around a cemetery. Well, I thought, strolling alone on Woodlawn's Central Avenue, almost nobody.

The guard at the gatehouse had given me a map showing Woodlawn's major roads and listing several hundred specific grave sites of historic or architectural interest. I found a marking for Melville on it easily enough but Mitchel was off the map, and I was obliged to stop in the office and request the site number. The feelings I had been developing for the Mayor deepened when I eventually located his plot in Hillside 42. A Bronx native, Mitchel was born just south of Woodlawn and grew up at 2597 Webster Avenue, right near the Fordham Road station of what was then the New York and Harlem Railroad and is now my Metro-North line, and just a few blocks from where the cages and ersatz veldt of the Bronx Zoo would rise twenty years later. Mitchel might have forgotten to buckle his safety belt, but I believe he and his people had long memories: Hillside 42 overlooks Webster Avenue.

He is buried alone beneath a simple black marker; the mayor and his young wife were childless, and perhaps she remarried. All in all it is a modest and unremarkable grave site and a passerby unaware of the facts of Mitchel's life would not detect anything odd. But of course it struck me right away that the headstone identifies Mitchel only as a major in the aviation corps—and makes no mention of his having been the mayor of New York City. There is also a short, biblical-sounding inscription, less a benediction than a tart and not particularly good-natured invective:

> *May His angels lead thee into paradise which is thy home.*
> *For in Israel there is corruption.*

Did the reformer harbor a lingering bitterness toward the constituents who had turned him out of office? The inscription sounds like something one of those jeered-at Old Testament prophets might have said as he smugly awaited the vindication of the destruction of the temple. And did Mitchel and his family really believe death had freed him from a polluted world undeserving of his goodness? A minute ago I had admired the sense of poetry and modesty in the location of his grave site; now I wasn't so sure. What kind of asshole am I out here chasing, anyway? Maybe this guy doesn't have anything to show me. Why should I bother resurrecting him? Perhaps he deserves to be forgotten.

Such angry, godlike thoughts poured through my mind as I walked the quiet, shaded slopes of Ravine and Prospect avenues, searching for Melville. Of course, there's nothing like a stroll in a cemetery to bring on a feeling of cool superiority. After all, everyone alive *deserves* to be— an understandable and reasonable point of view that, unfortunately, also carries the suggestion that anyone *not* alive deserves that as well. Well, let's be fair: why couldn't Mitchel be a jerk? There are plenty of them alive right now, right?

In the quiet solitude of my walk everything seemed clear, felt closer, and I knew it was Woodlawn itself and not just the spectre of plain old vanilla death. People imagine cemeteries as invariably quiet—as quiet as the grave, isn't that what they say?—but that's not always true, especially in New York City. The seam between Queens and Brooklyn is buttoned together by cemeteries, and none of them are quiet: from Calvary near Newtown Creek and the congested mouth of the Midtown Tunnel deep into the heart of the boroughs where the Jackie Robinson Parkway runs roughshod over more than a dozen cemeteries, you can't get away from the steady sound of heavy traffic, of life rushing indifferently past. Then there's the Bronx's other big cemetery, St. Raymond's, an unsheltered and unlovely necropolis of granite and marble headstones cut through its heart by not one but two of Robert Moses' expressways, the Bruckner and the Cross-Bronx. Critics of that urban planner like to point out that Moses, the master builder who thought little of dicing and destabilizing New York neighborhoods in his quest to bulldoze a massive modern highway system through the area, couldn't be bothered to learn how to drive a car himself. That probably doesn't surprise the people who run St. Raymond's: Moses is buried in Woodlawn.

Like St. Raymond's or the city cemeteries on Long Island, Woodlawn wasn't spared the indignity of a girdle of highway. The Bronx River Parkway is a block to the east, the Major Deegan Expressway a block to the west. Yet they don't disturb the quiet of Woodlawn, a testament to the success of its original design as an urban oasis. Edward F. Bergman, the chairman of the Department of Geology and Geography at Herbert H. Lehman College in the Bronx and the author of a book on the history and architecture of Woodlawn, rates the cemetery one of the finest arboretums in the city, with nearly 3,400 shade trees including five of the 113 designated by the Parks Department as the city's most beautiful. Planned when the surrounding area was farmland but now ringed by apartments and highways, Woodlawn remains a peaceful island: walking in the sun-dappled shade of the tree-lined paths, the only sound to be heard was the shuffle of my own steps across the leaf-strewn earth.

An empty afternoon is tailor-made for Melville, and it didn't take me long to find the family plot. He is tucked inconspicuously in Catalpa, one of Woodlawn's older, more modest sections that sits, like an old New York tenement neighborhood, in the shadows of all that has come since. The grave itself is marked by a gray headstone that is larger than Mitchel's yet still simple: erected by Melville's widow, it features a quill and a blank scroll, heartbreakingly suggesting a life unwritten or a soul never expressed. While the area can't be called run-down—the entire cemetery is assiduously groomed—it is obvious that the Melville family plot receives special attention. Many of the others in this old area of the cemetery aren't so fortunate. One or two headstones are laying on the coarse grass, broken or heaved up out of the ground by roots, evidence that whole families die out or move on, and that even granite crumbles. It's obvious that Melville gets a lot of visitors. It is a Jewish tradition to place a rock on the headstone when visiting a graveside, and I had to comb through the weeds and scurf of several plots to find my own rather than give in to the temptation of simply appropriating one of the two dozen stones already atop Melville's marker. But what's really striking about the plot is the tree to the left of the Melville family headstones. By New York standards it is ancient and spectacular; by Woodlawn standards, it's only notable.

It is an old, squat, weather-beaten oak. The crown of the tree no longer exists, apparently decapitated a long time ago by lightning. It grows in some funny directions, but it grows, and I think not of what remains above ground, but of what might be below. I can picture Melville's skeleton and the soft pulpy traces of his coffin wrapped in the hairy embrace of its roots, and wonder if it isn't his nature and not our mother's which twisted this tree. "*I bequeath myself to the dirt to grow from the grass I love / If you want me again look for me under your boot-soles.*" That's not Melville, it's Whitman—canny, self-mythologizing Walt Whitman, who lived until 1892, long enough to see himself justly celebrated as America's great zen-rhythm poet of life and death. But if ever a man was a wrecked oak, it was Melville, who had preceded Whitman to his grave so unnoticed just the year before.

So I sat under his tree and waited to hear what Herman Melville might have to say to me about living in our unsettling days and dying anonymously. The leaves rustled gently and the occasional car whispered past on nearby Central Avenue. The day was warm and the sun finding its way through the branches felt good. I sat for a long time. If there was another answer beyond that, I couldn't hear it.

I finally rose and set off and found myself back on Central, gazing catty-corner across the intersection at a large and impressive granite monument that was the polar opposite of Melville's modest plot. Flanked by a pair of benches and fronted by a bronze statue of a seated and thoughtful-looking figure, the thirty-foot installation was executed in the style and scale of the public memorials often found in a park or in front of a government building. I was immediately hooked, impressed by the kind of ego and chutzpah it must take to assume people will want to come and meditate at your grave. Who the hell was this?

The newspaper publisher Joseph Pulitzer, it turned out. Publishers are hardly ever as ethical as they like to make out but in Pulitzer's day the breed was downright rough-and-tumble. Rupert Murdoch can only wish that he was powerful enough to start a war; Pulitzer's great rival, William

Randolph Hearst, famously did it. Together, he and Pulitzer took sensationalism and newspaper circulation wars to new levels, and the panting prose of yellow journalism was a significant portion of their legacies.

Never letting the truth stand in the way of making a fortune, Pulitzer, like so many in that era of robber barons, invested a sizable chunk of his booty in lobbying history for a flattering judgment. Along with endowing the Columbia University School of Journalism, he also set aside sixteen thousand five hundred dollars—a sizable sum in 1906—to establish the Pulitzer Prize. It was more effective than a WINGO promotion. Today some are aware of the magnate's less admirable contributions to the public dialogue, but their numbers pale in comparison with those who recognize the name Pulitzer as synonymous with journalistic excellence.

Obviously, Pulitzer didn't invent this little sleight-of-hand but his grave was the first intimation of the revelation Woodlawn was about to offer regarding just how fashionable the purchase of immortality had been in his day. Through a copse of pines behind the Pulitzer monument I saw that the crowded, crumbling headstones of Melville's working-class neighborhood gave way to long, spacious lawns and seemingly endless rows of grand boulevards flanked by aisle after aisle of big, ornate mausoleums. I walked down a gently sloping hill toward a large, carefully sculpted lagoon whose banks were lined with dozens of fantastically opulent marble vaults. Despite the countrified setting, it felt oddly akin to leaving one section of Manhattan for another, as if I had just crossed south on Ninety-sixth Street from Spanish Harlem to the Upper East Side. To hear that the cemetery covers four hundred acres is one thing, to walk it quite another. What looks like nothing from the window of a commuter is in fact a secret city.

When Woodlawn opened, New York City—which was then just Manhattan—had two major burial issues. First, most of the original churchyards downtown were either filled or too valuable as building property to remain grave sites; the occupants of some of Woodlawn's oldest graves were long dead before arriving in the Bronx, having been disinterred from Manhattan cemeteries. Second, the only major cemetery with room to grow was Green-Wood in Brooklyn, an extremely inconvenient location—especially for the wealthier residents of the tony new neighborhoods above Forty-second Street. For them, a burial in Green-Wood meant a grueling all-day funeral procession through the congested streets of lower Manhattan and then across the harbor by public ferry—a particularly rough ride that no well-bred woman of the time could be expected to endure. As a result, women were often excluded from the funerals of even their husbands and children. Woodlawn, just ten miles north of midtown and situated near the new Harlem Railroad (and eventually, although not yet, the Jerome Avenue subway), solved those problems. With private cars available from the railroad, funerals were immeasurably simpler and once again open to women, and Woodlawn quickly became the cemetery of choice for the "Four Hundred" of New York society. For aside from its location, Woodlawn's painstakingly planted Elysian fields came ready-made for the hubris of the Gilded Age.

Flush with the power and wealth of the new industrial era, New York's financiers, robber barons, manufacturers and merchants built townhouses on Fifth Avenue, mansions on Long Island, and pharaonic monuments to themselves at Woodlawn. Leading architects such as John Russell Pope, Hunt and Hunt, James Renwick, and McKim, Mead and White all designed mausoleums here that drew inspiration from classic Greek, Roman, and Egyptian tombs, while Robert Caterson, a Woodlawn-based monument builder, constructed a mausoleum for railroad baron Collis P. Huntington that rests on a single forty-two-ton slab of granite and is fronted by a reproduction of the main stairwell from the old Pennsylvania Station. Caterson's need for massive amounts of the best granite available knew no bounds: he eventually purchased ten thousand acres in the mountains in Burnett County, Texas—where the pink granite used to build that state's enormous capital building was found—and quarried his own stone.

Who hasn't worried about fading away? Who wouldn't use money to try and beat death, to spray-paint his tag on the passing subway car of history? But the way they did it at Woodlawn during the Gilded Age just isn't the way it is done anymore. To stand along the lakeside glen and look up at the gently rolling fields sprouted with seemingly endless stands of snowy marble, of towering statues, of concrete cupolas and carefully chiseled Celtic crosses, is to lose yourself in someone else's time. I know that enormous economic inequities are part and parcel of our own time, that an entrepreneur might make $500 million in a single stock option transaction, or an American CEO make ten thousand times the annual salary of his average employee. But I still can't picture Bill Gates getting planted in one of these marble monsters. Yet right in front of me stood not hundreds, but *thousands* of them.

Part of the explanation, I suspect, is that these monuments no longer accomplish their intended goal. Once, when people took their Sunday stroll in the cemetery, an elaborate, impressive vault was a constant and public reminder of power and importance, and consequently money well spent. But we have a serviceable number of urban parks and no shortage of cars for escaping the city now, and hell, forget picnicking—they won't even let me ride my bike in the cemetery. Times change. Still, there is something shocking about this landscape of polished stones. I never imagined opulence and self-aggrandizement of this scale as part of the American personality.

Gazing over the rail of an old stone bridge on the lagoon, my attention was drawn by what seemed the most massive of the vaults. Far across the wide sunny lawns, perched alone on the crown of a distant hill beside what was far and away the largest weeping birch I'd ever seen, stood a scale version of—could it be?—the Parthenon. Approaching, I saw it was ringed by a road which, for all intents and purposes, acted as a barrier beyond which no other monuments encroached. Oddly, there was no family name or inscription of any kind on the mausoleum, and I later learned this was intended as a deterrent to grave robbing. It seems that in the New York of the 1890s it was not uncommon for corpses to be stolen and ransomed back to wealthy families. But no one in his right mind could build a tomb this ostentatious and obvious and then expect anonymity, and I suspect there is another explanation. Perhaps the man for whom it was constructed believed he needed no introduction. I wasn't surprised when the mansion on the hill proved the tomb of mega–robber baron Jay Gould.

What did surprise me was the nearby ring of wannabes. Lining the far boundary of Gould's circular drive under a bower of mature hard-woods were fully realized miniature cathedrals and Greek temples as well as numerous other impressive mausoleums regally decorated with sphinxes, gargoyles, stained-glass windows, winged angels, and statues of children. But this time it wasn't just the unrestrained opulence that struck me—it was the fact that *I didn't recognize a single name carved on any of these grand eloquent memorials.*

How could this be? This wasn't the Dipylon Gate in Athens or some relic of antiquity—this was a major, modern, active cemetery, as much a part of the history and day-to-day life of the city I had spent my entire life in as Wall Street. I felt embarrassed—much as I had when I'd been riding in Central Park and come across James Purroy Mitchel's plaque—but I also felt a shiver of recognition and sympathy at history's cold judgment. For all their planning and ego, anonymity had found the rich and powerful as surely as it found their servants and office clerks. If it took another thirty or fifty years, that was no more than a blink to the universal eye. Who were these men so powerful in the life of New York and America yet so quickly forgotten? I decided to pick one at random and find out.

I picked Austin Corbin.

Perhaps the name simply caught my eye because it reminded me of Margaret Corbin, the Revolutionary War heroine whom I'd only just learned of during my recent ride through upper Manhattan. It's unlikely they were related. But it's not impossible that you would know who Austin Corbin was because, really, if you live in New York you should. Yet I certainly didn't until I started digging through the files at the public library the following day.

Armed only with just the barest facts of Corbin's life—the birth and death dates on his tomb—I could see no road to follow other than to start with his obituary. And if the newspapers of the day had no idea who Herman Melville was, they were at no loss when it came to Austin Corbin: in 1896, the day after he was thrown from a carriage in a freak accident on his twenty-five-thousand-acre New Hampshire estate, the *New York Times* ran a page-one obituary with an eight-deck headline that didn't bother to say who Corbin was or what he had accomplished until paragraph sixteen on the inside jump. The reason for this omission was obvious: everyone knew who Austin Corbin was.

Dubbed the "King of Long Island," Corbin was a successful banker and real estate speculator following the Civil War. When a doctor prescribed sea air as a cure for his sickly son, the family decided to summer in the wilds of south Brooklyn. Ever keen, Corbin quickly recognized the appeal an exclusive resort just ten miles from Manhattan would have and subsequently developed Coney Island's Manhattan Beach section. Within a few years Corbin and his investors owned nearly ten miles of Long Island beach front property and they erected massive resort hotels as far east as Babylon. Since the biggest problem was getting people to his resorts, Corbin started his own train line, and by 1880 he had cobbled a hodgepodge of small, financially strapped regional lines into the focused and extremely successful Long Island Railroad. No one with the exception of Robert Moses had a more profound effect on the opening of Long Island.

Yet I could find little evidence of him in modern histories: there were just two quick mentions of Corbin in Edwin G. Burrows and Mike Wallace's massive and authoritative *Gotham*—i.e., that Corbin had wooed the money crowd by becoming an unapologetically anti-Semitic hotelier, and that his massive Manhattan Beach Hotel had been a haven for the well-heeled racing crowd of the day including August Belmont, Leonard Jerome, and William K. Vanderbilt—and nothing at all in Kenneth T. Jackson's *Encyclopedia of New York City*. But I considered it a lucky stroke that Corbin's career had grown beyond banking to include hotels and railroads: though it's never caught my fancy, few subjects excite amateur history buffs as much as trains, and I went looking for the most authoritative telling of the Long Island Railroad's story I could find. It turned out to be Long Island historian Vincent F. Seyfried's seven-volume *History of the Long Island Rail Road*. Seyfried's books would prove a treasure trove of information regarding Corbin. Unearthing them would prove surprisingly difficult.

Although the volumes were published locally in the seventies, I could locate just one complete set in the card catalogs of New York area public and private libraries, and that was in the special local history collection at the main Queens branch of the New York City Public Library in Jamaica. I'm not crazy about special collections—there are always limited hours and access, extra rules, and onerous conditions—and instead headed for the small public library in the Bayside section of Queens with an eye toward seeing if their incomplete set included coverage of Corbin's era. When I arrived, I found the library in the process of a major reconstruction: much of the collection, including Seyfried's books, was boxed up in storage. History can be as buried as its subjects. I reluctantly headed for Jamaica.

I was rewarded. In his portrait of Corbin, Seyfried provided many of the features only hinted at in the obituary: the hard-nosed banker who would force all the small, destitute Long Island railroads into his pocket; the industrial patriarch/dictator who lived high but insisted on temperance from his employees; the canny speculator who saw a future gold coast in the swamps of Brooklyn and packed a town meeting with paid "residents" to acquire the land for next to nothing; the snobbish and insecure architect of an elite playground for the wealthy and properly born; a real estate mogul who rightly recognized that his railroad would turn the thin, sandy soil of Long Island into suburban gold; a man who—as befitting a self-crowned pasha—acquired grand estates including one with herds of elk and buffalo described as the largest private preserve in the Western Hemisphere. In short, an empire builder and a shaper of our New York.

Yet the most intriguing discovery was that Corbin's unforeseen demise may have had a greater impact on New York than anything he accomplished in life.

Having run his tracks all the way to Montauk, Corbin embarked on his grandest scheme: already the owner of most of Southampton, he and an associate managed to screw the Montaukett Indians out of ten thousand acres on the Long Island fork and were well on their way to convincing Congress to appropriate funds for dredging a deep water bay. Corbin's pitch was a beauty—since New York Harbor was badly congested, he proposed freighters and luxury liners dock at Montauk, unload directly onto his trains, and save several days. Of course, it would have been a phenomenal boon to Corbin's business—*his* ships would have been the primary beneficiaries of the proposed Liverpool-to-Montauk routes, *his* railroad would have become the express route into Manhattan—and he personally lobbied the White House for dredging funds, entertaining Melville's former boss, President Arthur, at his Babylon estate. Had Corbin lived to see his scheme come to fruition—and I believe, based on what he accomplished in life, that the impracticality and expense of what he was asking the government to do would have proven only a temporary stone in his path—such a turn of events would have completely recast the future of Long Island's east end. It isn't hard to imagine what the region might look like today if Corbin had lived and Montauk became a major port of entry and shipping. Elizabeth, New Jersey comes to mind.

I wouldn't know these facts for some days. But standing in front of Corbin's tomb, I rediscovered how overwhelmingly unknowable the city we call home is. It occurred to me that Woodlawn might be second only to the public library as a repository of New York history, and I suddenly imagined the rows and rows of stone as the basement stacks of some incredible archive—only instead of countless shelves of yellowing books on forgotten subjects I was standing amidst the numberless graves of forgotten people, each a story told and filed away in the earth and lost. I thought I might stop my drifting if I sat down and read those books.

But that wasn't all. That city of stone made me feel that the terrorizing face of anonymity and oblivion stalking the city was not a stranger or a once-in-a-lifetime catastrophe but a natural state of affairs. And as unsettling a notion as that should be, I somehow found it comforting. Hadn't Walt Whitman spoken of New York City as the lasting physical proof of our immortal soul? The people might be gone but their cemetery still bore physical testament to the fact of their lives. And so did their city. They weren't in the ground with their rotting remains, they were in the streets.

From somewhere far behind me I could faintly hear the Number 16 bus accelerating west on 233rd Street toward Jerome Avenue, with its gray cloud of exhaust rising steadily in the hot air as it revved up and took off at a light. I looked around at the city of headstones. If I can hear the bus and picture it on the street, why can't I see the stones and picture these people on the street? They laid those streets and walked them and rode them and their traces have settled back down onto them as surely as the filmy soot from the bus. That *is* what survives, at least for a little longer and hopefully long enough for us to see. It's the best proof we have that our lives are larger than the people we know. Herman Melville's work was rediscovered approximately thirty-five years after his death—he's more alive to the world than he was when he was walking around New York. So why does John Purroy Mitchel have to be dead to us now? He's not only still out there, he seems like a man for our moment. Adrift and disconnected, I longed for a communion of the disconnected.

In the days after learning about Corbin, I would return again and again to Woodlawn, seized by the impulse not only to resurrect the formerly famous and forgotten, to simultaneously embrace and fight anonymity by admitting that someday I, too, would bequeath myself to the dirt, but also to declare that I was part of the continuum of the city, a briefly passing and lucky traveler who saw in the bricks and steel proof of all that had come before and hopefully after, and would add to the clay and not let it be meaningless. But who among the disconnected and lost to raise?

I met everyone by happenstance, but Henry Bergh was a mistake. Not a *mistake* mistake, because Henry Bergh is buried in Woodlawn, but still a mistake. Yet the Berghs led me to the Fowlers who, weirdly enough, led me back to Walt Whitman. Naturally, that was a good thing, even if Whitman is buried in Camden, New Jersey. Here's what I mean.

One of my first calls was to the Bronx County Historical Society. They maintain a modest office and archive in half of a drab mock Tudor in the middle of a row of identical houses on Bainbridge Avenue. The building is just a few blocks south of Woodlawn and faces the old reservoir oval and playground between Gun Hill Road and the Mosholu Parkway. The people at the Society are very helpful, and they do some nice things like publishing a small journal on Bronx history (truthfully, it's more like a newsletter) and making Lloyd Ultan, the official Bronx historian, available on Friday mornings to answer queries by telephone. But their archives aren't really set up for the public, and if you want to research anything in the files you have to call and make an appointment, which I did. A few days later I again found myself seated before a pile of manila folders, albeit a much smaller stack than I had recovered for John Purroy Mitchel.

There wasn't much in them in the way of essays, overviews, encyclopedia entries, or any of the other easily digestible goodies that a casual reader like myself tends to think of as history. Rather, there was only a handful of newspaper clippings about the neighborhood and the cemetery, a photocopy of a handwritten "History of Woodlawn" that seemed to be a spoken preamble to a cemetery tour, and the 1969 transcript of the childhood recollections of James Havender, a Jerome Avenue attorney who'd grown up in Woodlawn during the 1890s. But together they provided a glimpse into the evolution of the neighborhood, which very clearly owed its existence and identity to the cemetery. Prior to that, the area was virtually all farmland, although the coming of the Croton Aqueduct—which Havender says everyone in the neighborhood only called "the pipeline"—during the 1840s also brought the Irish sandhogs who would comprise the bulk of the area's residents. To this day, Woodlawn's main street, Katonah Avenue, is the site of the Tunnel Workers Union headquarters, and the area remains a magnet for Irish immigrants. But more important for the community was the huge new cemetery, along whose northern border a thriving row of related businesses took hold: taverns, inns, florists, stonecutters, and, of course, undertakers. Between the sandhogs and the cemetery, Woodlawn was the only community in New York able to brag that it specialized in running businesses into the ground.

The drive to start the cemetery was spearheaded by the Reverend Absalem Peters and incorporated in 1863. The original Woodlawn comprised 313 acres purchased from the Bassing family. Some of the land had been farmed and some was still wooded, which gave Woodlawn's planners a good deal of latitude in fashioning its features. The cemetery officially opened for business on January 14, 1865, with Mrs. Phoebe Underhill breaking ground as the first interment and the cemetery reached its current size of four hundred acres just a few years later with the purchase of a neighboring farm. Woodlawn then sat back and waited for the City to come to it.

Judging from the long list of notable burials in the file, the City came en masse. I recognized contributors to the world of New York arts like Juilliard, Damrosch, and Hammerstein; retail names Macy, Kress, Woolworth, Strauss, Constable, and Penney; everyday brand names including Armour, Borden, Colgate, Gulden, Shaeffer, and both Wittnauer and Bulova; national figures like Admiral David Farragut and Chief Justice Charles Evans Hughes; suffrage leaders Carrie Chapman Catt and Elizabeth Cady Stanton; journalists Grantland Rice, Nellie Bly, Damon Runyon and lawman-turned-sportswriter Bat Masterson; and, along with Pulitzer, publishers Richard K. Fox, who put out the once extraordinarily popular *Police Gazette*, and Generoso Pope, publisher of the Italian newspaper *Il Progresso Italo-Americano* and father of the publisher of the *National Enquirer*.

But most tantalizing was how few of the "notables" rang even the faintest bell. The feeling I'd had standing in front of Austin Corbin's tomb had been neither wrong nor isolated: if I was looking for a payoff on the idea that history has a short attention span, the Woodlawn file was the jackpot.

Here, for example, are just a few of the hundreds of Woodlawn denizens deemed significant enough to be included in various guides to New York cemeteries or on the Bronx Historic Society's list of "Well-Known Persons Interred in Woodlawn":

- George Ripley. He was a leading transcendentalist, utopianist, literary critic, and close friend of Horace Greeley.
- Serge Rubenstein. A financier and Park Avenue playboy whose gruesome 1950s murder was tabloid fodder for months and remains unsolved.
- Major Edward Howard Armstrong. The inventor of FM radio.
- Benjamin Franklin Butler. One of Woodlawn's oldest inhabitants—he actually died before Woodlawn opened and was reinterred from a Manhattan graveyard—Butler helped settle the border between New

York and New Jersey, and is one of the few people to serve in the cabinets of two separate presidents, having been Attorney General for both Jackson and Van Buren.

- Ruth Nichols. A pioneering pilot and rival of Amelia Earhart who simultaneously held the woman's altitude, speed, and distance records. The first woman to receive a pilot's license in New York and one of the first to fly for a living, she was still learning to pilot supersonic jets when she was fifty-eight and lobbying to get into the space program. She was also a suicide.
- Michael Pupin. The physicist and inventor's work made X rays possible and several of his patents greatly improved telephone technology.
- Henry Bergh. Founder of the ASPCA.

Now, Bergh caught my eye when I read that among his first crusades was ensuring livery creatures and other animals ready access to water. Obviously New York no longer relies on draft horses to pull its fire pumpers and beer wagons but some of those fountains remain to this day, the 125-year-old physical traces of Bergh's work and spirit. I flashed on the dog spigot across from Mitchel's gold bas-relief in Central Park. It is one of two fountains that Bergh and the ASPCA installed in the park.

Perhaps because it was easy to find a physical tie, to find some literal, concrete proof of his crusade, I immediately annointed Bergh one of my resurrected. But the more I learned about him over subsequent weeks, the more I became convinced that, nice as the physical traces were, Bergh's real resonance wasn't corporeal at all.

I like animals and I've almost always had a dog, but I have wondered if some New Yorkers love their animals because it's a good deal simpler than loving another human. That doesn't mean I doubt the zeal and honesty of those agitating for the compassionate treatment of animals—which is why I was surprised when I couldn't find anything significant written on Bergh during the last sixty years. Indeed, the best and most recent source I found was a 1942 biography by Zulma Steele, *Angel in Top Hat.*

It is not an exaggeration to say that Henry Bergh deserves all the credit for the founding of the modern humane movement in America. In 1867, Bergh convinced the New York state legislature to enact the country's first anti-cruelty laws, which also granted all the enforcement powers to his new SPCA. Bergh personally took to the streets of Manhattan every day to monitor teamsters, butchers, coachmen, dairymen, stable owners, and stockyard workers. He had the power to issue tickets and make arrests, and he did both liberally. While he found it impossible to outlaw such pursuits of the wealthy as foxhunting, he shut down dog and cockfighting (no mean feat considering its devotees reportedly included President Lincoln) and stopped an effort to establish bullfighting in America. He was, frankly, relentless to the point of obnoxiousness. Stiffnecked and insufferably self-righteous, Bergh sought the spotlight for his cause constantly and was apparently even ready to offer himself up as a figure of ridicule if it might benefit the Society. His work cultivated many admirers and supporters, yet he was a cold fish who seems to have had few friends.

But what interested me most about Henry Bergh was that he had a surprising secret. The secret was that he didn't particularly care for animals.

A failed playwright and a mid-level envoy to Tsarist Russia during the Civil War, Bergh desperately hungered for respect and authority. Still, it would be wrong to suggest that his exhaustive years-long crusade for the rights of animals was undertaken only to service his own ego. It would, however, be right to say that all the hectoring and lecturing and moral thunder Bergh dispensed from every dawn until well after every dusk really wasn't for the benefit of the animals. Bergh didn't care all that much about their suffering per se—he was completely incensed at the notion that *man* was capable of barbaric and offhand cruelty and he wasn't so much interested in eradicating the practice as the practitioners. I leave it to you to decide whether that made him a deeper man, but I think it worth noting that while the childless Bergh also started the Society for the Prevention of Cruelty to Children, he did it as an afterthought to the SPCA and did not devote anywhere near as much energy to it.

All this I would learn over a period of weeks, largely from old magazine and newspaper pieces from the nineteenth century and via the Steele book, which was undeniably the best single source I found. Indeed, it's unfortunate that *Angel in Top Hat* is out of print because it's a lot of fun to read, and it was with a sense of real regret that I turned the book's final page as Steele followed Bergh's 1887 funeral cortege down the steps of St. Mark's Church and out into the street and on to his final resting place.

In Brooklyn's Green-Wood Cemetery.

How could she make a mistake like that? I'd read enough of the old magazine profiles of Bergh to recognize where at least some of the material in Steele's book came from and knew she'd been scrupulous in transferring information from other sources. I'd seen Bergh's name on a couple of Woodlawn lists, and I even had a copy of the plot number from the cemetery office—Highland 7238 and 7239. I hustled back to Woodlawn.

The Bergh family plot is on a flat, sunny sweep about fifty yards west of John Purroy Mitchel's grave. The grass is wide and course, and there are ten Berghs including two Henrys all resting under modest matching black headstones. Unfortunately, neither of these Henrys died in 1887. They were, in fact, related to my Henry and one of them—the one that died in 1924 at the age of seventy-five—was his nephew. A reluctant assistant to his eccentric uncle as a youth, this latter Henry Bergh may not have shared his namesake's zealotry, but he subsequently found enough of an affinity to continue the family's involvement, serving as the SPCA secretary.

I wasn't sure what to do. I found a gray stone bench on Lawn Avenue and plopped down to ponder the problem. A few plots south, just in front of the massive art intallation that marks the tomb of lawyer and reformer Samuel Untermyer, a work crew was raking the first leaves of autumn, pushing the piles onto canvas drop cloths and dumping them into the back of a pickup truck. I approached the crew foreman, a thin man with salt-and-pepper hair who was wearing a blue Woodlawn work jacket, to see if he knew anything about the Berghs. He seemed to know a good deal about the cemetery but nothing about them, and when I mentioned the erroneous listing he shrugged.

"Oh, they write all kinds of stuff about Woodlawn that isn't true," he said. "I remember a piece that said we'd buried a member of a motorcycle gang on his bike. Of course, the most famous myth is about the Lindbergh kidnapping—that there was a rendezvous at Herman Melville's grave with the kidnapper." At this I perked up but he quickly scowled. "That never happened. But a fellow who coached the swimmers at Fordham had offered to pay fifty thousand dollars to get the baby back, and he supposedly spoke with someone claiming to be the kidnapper over by the Jerome Avenue gate. It's a shame to have so much misinformation, especially since there are some real mysteries here."

I gave him a quizzical look as an invitation to continue.

"There's a fair number of unmarked graves here. I always wonder what that's about—whether there's some sort of deep scandal or if people are just private."

"Or just too cheap to put up a stone?" I suggested.

"That, too, I suppose. There's a real interesting one somewhere over in the next section. A fellow named Fowler. Orson Fowler. He was one of those fortune-tellers who read the bumps on your head." The man nodded, then leaned a little closer and gave me a conspiratorial look. "Apparently the unmarked grave is because he was a bit of a perv."

I spent a fruitless afternoon in Hillside searching for the exact location of Orson Fowler's unmarked grave and, after my experience with Henry Bergh, truly felt I was chasing ghosts. Yet I would find their worlds.

The Fowlers were a unique and impressive family: Orson's sister, Almira, was one of the first American women to earn a medical degree while his sister-in-law, Lydia, was the first female professor of medicine at an American university. But the family's notoriety was earned by Orson and his brother, Lorenzo, who, along with their brother-in-law Samuel Wells, were America's leading phrenologists.

We ridicule the idea of a physical correlation between the shape of the skull and personality and intelligence today, but the field enjoyed a great deal of traction as a science of the mind in the nineteenth century. Among the Fowlers' thousands of clients were John Brown, Clara Barton, Oliver Wendell Holmes, Horace Mann, Mathew Brady, and Allan Pinkerton, and the brothers also provided screening and employment tests for many of Manhattan's leading businesses in order to determine whether a perspective employee had the proper faculties and propensities to succeed in a particular position. The Fowlers applied the same principle to a robust business determining marital compatability. But their reputation and financial bread-and-butter were earned on the traveling lecture circuit where their presentations on phrenology and twenty-five-cent examinations were extraordinarily popular.

That the Fowlers positioned themselves as practitioners and popularizers of phrenology was greeted with not a little chagrin by some of the school's original theorists, physicians and scientists who, in their search for a theory to explain mind and personality, weren't all that different from those who would explore psychiatry and neurology a little later.

The Fowlers, however, were not Viennese doctors but Yankee intellectuals, and they had a belief in the democratic dissemination of knowledge and moral enlightenment—they were, in every way, progressive reformers—with a healthy appetite for business as well. At the Cabinet of Fowlers & Wells on Broadway, the brothers and their associates conducted readings and gave consultations; promoted a variety of scientific and health causes including mesmerism, hydropathy, vegetarianism, and animal magnetism; and exhibited a collection of skulls and busts—a veritable hall of fame—that was second only to Barnum's Museum as a New York tourist attraction.

The real moneymaker, however, was Fowlers & Wells's publishing company. It produced dozens of scientific magazines including *The Phrenological Journal, Water-Cure Journal*, and the *Illustrated Hydropathic Review*. The company also produced a popular series of how-to books including *How to Behave, How to Talk, How to Write*, and *How to Do Business*. Orson, a noted lecturer, was the firm's most prolific author. While the majority of his books were on the application of phrenology in such areas as matrimony, parenting, love, the cultivation of memory, and the ethical and humane rehabilitation of prisoners, his interests were wide-ranging and he believed his intellect and creativity capable of handling any subject. With no formal training as an architect, Fowler in 1848 authored *A Home For All*, a bestseller that advocated octagonal houses and started an architectural craze. His rationale was straightforward: the circle is the shape which circumscribes the greatest area; since the octagon approximates the shape of a circle it is therefore superior to the rectangle as a basic building block. Tens of thousands of octagonal homes were built on Fowler's plans throughout the mid-century. None were as grand or ambitious as Orson's own sixty-room octagonal house overlooking the Hudson River in Fishkill, New York. Built on the cheap with local gravel, the house was a modern marvel that included indoor plumbing, forced hot-air heating, and a range of gymnasiums, studies, and meditation parlors. Plans were also drawn for an octagonal-shaped agrarian commune in Kansas.

Orson was the star of Fowlers & Wells's publishing list. But only one title from the Fowlers & Wells list is read today, and it isn't on phrenology, octagonal houses, the duty of temperance, or a paen to the pleasures of a bran-free diet. It is a collection of poems entitled *Leaves of Grass*.

Walt Whitman, an insatiable reader of books on human improvement and himself the author of a temperance novel, was a devotee of the Fowlers. He not only read, but also peddled many of their books to supplement his income as a writer for the *Brooklyn Eagle*. Whitman agreed with the Fowlers that physiology was destiny—he believed the body to offer clues and manifestations of the mind and spirit and made use of the jargon of phrenology in his poems, writing that the "perfect head, and bowels and bones" were "the easy gate" through which the soul comes and appears to sight. And like the Fowlers he was what was then known as a strict anti-lacing man who always wore his collar open so as not to restrict the body or spirit.

Whitman was a canny self-promoter and vain—he was proud of his physique and included a daguerreotype portrait as a frontispiece to *Leaves of Grass*—and liberally promoted the results of his phrenological reading by the Fowlers, publishing it several times. (It apparently got successively more flattering with each publication.) Just how he came to finagle it is unknown, but in 1855, Whitman convinced the Fowlers to publish an updated version of a slim volume of poems he had just set and printed privately himself. Expanded by twenty poems, the second edition of *Leaves of Grass* contained the debut of what was then named "Sun-Down Poem" and subsequently republished in the three later versions of the collection as "Crossing Brooklyn Ferry."

I can't say whether it was Woodlawn or the days we were living in, but I'd found myself drawn back to the poem that fall. Written almost thirty years before the Brooklyn Bridge would connect the two cities and give further impetus to the creation of greater New York, Whitman described his daily ferry ride between Brooklyn and Manhattan, glimpsing the rush of time in the harbor's currents and experiencing a transcendent vision in which he saw himself as one traveler in a timeless brotherhood with the countless New Yorkers who would follow, the physical city—like the physical human body—proof of the existence of their spirit.

I wondered over the coming days at how Whitman and the Fowlers might have met, and what they made of each other. Late in life, Orson would bring scandal and opprobrium upon his family when he expanded his teachings to include frank sexual instruction to young women. If phrenology was in spirit and intention the psychiatry of its day, perhaps Fowler may be described as its Wilhelm Reich. For his part, a struggling writer, promoter and self-mythologizer like Whitman would have seized the opportunity to associate with a bigger-than-life figure such as Fowler. No one knows much for certain about their association, and I found myself wondering how it was formed.

But before I could sit down to write, I had one more bicycle ride to take. I'd discovered the existence of a Corbin Place out by Brooklyn's Sheepshead Bay area, and I started by crossing Brooklyn Bridge early on a sunny morning, the wooden slats thumping steadily under the bike's tires. Below me the sun reflected in the water like spokes of light.

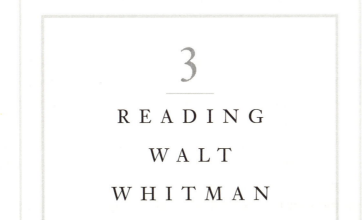

3

READING
WALT
WHITMAN

Anyone looking beyond the normal flow of traffic that passed before Clinton Hall at the corner of Broadway and Beeckman Street on one sunny July morning in 1855 could have seen a robust man in his early thirties—tall, tan, red-bearded—leaning amiably on one leg and gazing intently into the front window of the renowned Phrenological Cabinet of Fowlers & Wells. One ink-stained hand held a five-cent notepad and a slim book with a green felt cover while the other, hidden in his pocket, fingered the change from breakfast and the Fulton Ferry. Beneath an old, brown jacket he wore a clean white linen shirt open wide at the collar, and his pants, showing the same evidence of the printer's trade as his hands, ended in frayed cuffs resting comfortably upon a pair of old shoes. On his head was a battered hat once fine enough to be favored by any dandy—and even that morning it was still angled confidently—the worn-soft brim like a frame placed just so around his face. From the scuffed shoes to the old hat, he seemed less a man than a walking daguerreotype, an image made by an artist for the passing world to view.

All this might be seen in a glance; less apparent was the game he had contrived to play while looking in the window. He was fond of games—especially the little private games that only he partook of—yet those who knew Walt Whitman, his exasperated former publisher at the *Brooklyn Eagle* and his new coworkers at *The Brooklyn Weekly Freeman* (whose patience he was already testing), wouldn't be surprised to discover he was daydreaming. Not daydreaming, exactly—more like amusing himself. He imagined his own reflection in the shop window was not a reflection at all but one of the dozens of other faces looking out from among the rows and rows of casts, busts, death masks, and skulls in the incomparable and famous collection of Fowlers & Wells. He looked at Jefferson, the impressive brow curved with the strength of memory and language, and Jackson with his long forehead of Individuality, Combativeness, and Secretiveness. Van Buren was there, too, and a death mask of the scoundrel Burr. Flanking them were senators, governors, judges, a who's who of American public life: when the Fowlers were based in Washington, few important men declined the honor of sitting for one of their unique and exact casts. Standing before the shop, lost in his own world, the printer was unaware of what any passerby might plainly see: his stained hands tracing his face, absentmindedly measuring its contours against the impressive features before him. On a lower shelf, the heads of thirty-two Indian chiefs, an eskimo, three notorious murderers, and a bear. These, too, he measures himself against, but he especially concentrates on the spiritualists, the philosophers, and the men of letters. He recognized the familiar face of the recently deceased Poe—a wastrel but the first to recognize the literary applications of phrenology!—and smiled. Poe's head seemed so . . . small, so unimpressive; his sunken eyes two black flags of self-debasement. Yet it was the head of the Frenchman, Lafayette, all but alone in the sea of Americans, that held him rapt.

"You see something in the Marquis?"

Startled out of his meditation, Whitman turned to look into a face as impressive and engulfing as any in the window: a regal mane of pure white hair falling on wide, square shoulders; a tapered, matching beard riding the collar. The nose was long, firm, and true, the eyes alive and deep. An animated face, it seemed suitable for a gambler, the erect and powerful bearing more suggestive of a frontiersman than a Manhattanite.

"I knew the Marquis de Lafayette—and I know you, Professor Fowler," said the printer, proffering his hand. "Whitman, editor of *The Brooklyn Weekly Freeman*. I've heard you lecture many times and I trust that you have read at least some of what I've written in your praise. We are in great agreement on many subjects and I am among your most ardent supporters. Since you are to speak this evening at Plymouth Church in the Heights I wondered if you might allot me a few minutes of your time this morning—in the interest of providing my readers a better appreciation for your insightful and important work."

"Gladly. I am, of course, fully versed in your view of my books and lectures, Mr. Whitman, and grateful for any opportunity to make your acquaintance. But I had no idea you would be so old as to have been a contemporary of Lafayette—my ideas are not usually welcomed by my elders. And looking at you now I don't wonder if I was right." A smile played gently around his lips. "Come now. How could you know him?"

If Whitman caught the tone of gentle mocking, he made no sign.

"Are you aware that the Marquis came to Brooklyn on his final tour?" the newspaperman asked. "And that he laid the stone for what was then to be the Apprentice's Library on the corner of Henry and Cranberry? It was the Fourth of July, 1825. I was just six years old, yet it is as vivid to me now as if it were this very morning. He was such a great hero to us. Many of the old veterans greeted him at the ferry landing, and children climbed the elms in hopes of being the first to spot his coach. And what a coach! A magnificent old yellow carriage drawn by four of the most powerful horses you would ever hope to see. Such an outpouring of affection from the people lining the streets! I can tell you, there was no fanfare, no speeches, no claptrap. Just an air of simplicity, naturalness, and freedom from ostentation. Americans came simply to greet and honor the old French gentleman and soldier who was our first and truest friend. Of course, we could have no such turnout today—so free of politics and pretensions. Oh, but you can't imagine how exciting it was, Professor Fowler! And especially for me. Do you know, he picked me up, held me on his knee, and kissed me on the cheek! To be held up in front of that crowd by the Marquis de Lafayette was like being annointed by a god. A great heroic god of democracy!"

"Well, Mr. Whitman!" said the phrenologist with a smile. "It isn't every man who can claim to have been annointed by a god!"

"Oh, but every man should! I am no more modest than immodest and I have no desire to stand above or apart from my countrymen and women."

"Yes," said Fowler, his look of playfulness now gone. "Yes. Do come inside with me, Mr. Whitman."

It was far from Whitman's first visit to Fowlers & Wells. In fact, it was one of his favorite stops in Manhattan and he knew its exhibits and specimen walls intimately. His interest, however, hardly made him unique: the Phrenological Cabinet of Fowlers & Wells was one of the great attractions of New York, and Whitman made it a rule to never come on a Saturday afternoon when the noisy crowds spilled out onto the Broadway sidewalk, littering the street with oyster shells and the cobs and burnt husks of roasted corn purchased from street vendors. Mornings like this, though—warm, sunny, quiet weekdays when the rest of the world was occupied with the business of making a living—were his time. Then, when he was all alone save for a handful of out-of-towners, Whitman could wander through the hall for hours, reading the books and magazines the firm published and studying the colorful Symbolical Head charts that graced the walls, memorizing the locations of the dozens of organs of personality. Sometimes he would watch the phrenologists in the rear examination hall conduct readings while taking notes in his ever-present book. Other times he would listen to whatever lecture was to be heard, perhaps on physiology, temperance, diet, the reform of women's clothing, hydropathic cures, or the application of phrenology for selecting a mate. But he never failed to return to the specimen wall. With the afternoon sunlight streaming through the front windows, he would find a chair and park himself like a great, loafing calico cat, to drift and drowse, his eyes dreamily caressing the great collection of famous heads. Even that morning, with the famous phrenologist himself taking his elbow and guiding him through the door, Whitman could barely manage to keep his eyes from gazing up at the wall of fame, with its hundreds of heads.

"I have conducted thousands of examinations, Mr. Whitman, many of them quite fascinating. Unbelievable, really, some of them. Yet like you I can never pass this wall without pondering its mysteries. What riddles of genius could modern phrenology unravel if given the chance to examine the great minds of the classical world? What dark times might mankind been spared? Look," he said, reaching up for one bust, "here is Socrates."

Fowler held the plaster head, cradling the bottom as lovingly as a greengrocer might weigh a prize cabbage. "You know, there is a legend that Socrates was visited by a phrenologist. Of course, many of the master's students were skeptics and cynics, much as students are today. So to make sport, they insisted on blindfolding the doctor and presenting their teacher as just another in a group of slaves and beggars. When the phrenologist placed his fingers on Socrates, he declared without hesitation that this was the head of a great lecher and glutton given to monumental bouts of debauchery. As you can imagine, a gleeful chorus of laughter and howls of derision greeted this diagnosis—until the philosopher silenced them with the admonition that the reading was completely accurate in every way, adding that it was only through great and cease-less effort that he was able to supress his true self." He smiled at Whitman, putting the bust back on the shelf. "I don't really like selling these classical heads. Our only models, of course, are the statues that survive from the period and we must not suppose too much about their veracity. Who knows what licenses the stonecutters took, what flatteries they may have engaged in? Why, it's even too much to hope the subject's cranium was ever measured! There just wasn't today's dedication to sci-entific precision. But . . ." he waved a hand dismissively in the direction of the milling tourists viewing a nearby exhibit on the new sciences of mesmerism and animal magnetism. "The copies of the ancients are among our most popular sale items."

The two men continued toward the back of Fowlers & Wells, past a mural depicting a variety of hydropathic cures for women and a table dis-playing literature from the new and very smart Glen Haven Water Cure, whose weekly prices included direct conveyance from Manhattan to a fine hotel and clinic on Skaneateles Lake. "Of course," continued Fowler, "like all legends there's more than a touch of truth in the Socrates story. What he called his 'true self' we now think of as the raw, unimproved man. Certainly what we know about human sentience today in compari-son to then—it would be like pitting a steamship against a birch-bark ca-noe. Plato thought intellect a function of the liver; Aristotle, the heart. Still, each man's mistake doesn't negate his real insights, and modern American phrenology only gives scientific confirmation to precisely the idea suggested by Socrates in the story: the improvability of man."

At this, Whitman nodded vigorously. "Perhaps this is the best place for us to start our interview, Professor. Your emphasis on phrenological sci-ence as a tool for such improvement is the greatest contribution the Fowlers have made, and it is certainly an aspect which excites me endlessly. The practical phrenology of the Fowlers is so different, so *American*, when compared with the theoretical European science which bore it."

Orson smiled. "I'm a practical man, Mr. Whitman, and what good is science without practical application? I had my introduction to the sci-ence of phrenology at Amherst, but didn't understand its uses until I took to the road. It was actually something of a lark, you know. I had planned on seminary school but a classmate I despised went to Brattleboro to lecture on the 'Battles of the Revolution'—one of those rehashed of collegiate lectures that students are wont to try their luck with out in the small towns. He failed miserably and that fired me with a passion to try *my* hand at lecturing on phrenology. Well, sir, I printed up my handbill and advertisements and studied our charts; I hired a printer and got out a thousand copies along with my handbill; I ordered a bust and thirty-two-dollars' worth of works on phrenology. And lo and behold, when I opened my lecture and threw out my card there was no shortage of takers. It was twelve-and-a-half cents for a chart and reading per man, six-and-a-quarter for each woman and child—and I cleared forty dollars! I headed straightaway for Saratoga, sending word for my brother, Lorenzo, to meet me. We spent the next two years traveling about the country, from Cape Cod to Hannibal, Missouri, examining every kind of head from senators to mining camp gin-sots. What I learned is that the phrenological organs, like any other, may be excited, exercised, and improved. Yes, we have our propensities; yes, we have our predilections—but man is not static. Were a man to be shown weak in one of the phrenological organs—say, Amativeness, he need not remain in that state, he need not be sentenced to a life without love! He may exercise and grow the organ. And this is why I know that phrenology is the great key to the improvement of mankind. Let me show you something."

Set off by a wooden rail, the rear third of Fowlers & Wells evinced quite a different air from its front and looked more like the offices of a successful barrister or broker than the proprietors of a collection of curios. Here, the Fowlers and their associates did the real work of the firm. Three carved mahogany partners' desks (for Orson and Lorenzo Fowler and their brother-in-law, Samuel Wells) dominated the space, and against one wall a long, heavy side table held nearly two dozen stacks of the company's publications and several hundred copies of *A Home For All*. It was this table which most excited the printer, and it was with a sense of real disappointment that he followed the phrenologist past it to a row of wooden filing cabinets in the rear of the work pen.

"Do you know what's in here?" Fowler asked, resting an arm on the top of the cabinet. "These are the records of phrenological tests conducted at the behest of hundreds of employers. As a newspaperman you're no doubt aware of the number of advertisements appearing almost daily that specify a recommendation from Fowlers & Wells as a condition for hiring. Privacy precludes me from enumerating the firms maintaining accounts here, not just for new employees, but for advancement and consultation as well, and I can assure you that the list includes dozens of the biggest and, I might add, some of the most conservative firms in New York. These staid men recognize a truth that somehow eludes my most clever critics: how foolhardy it is not to apply our scientific knowledge. Why hire a man as a carpenter or mechanic if he has a small organ of Constructiveness? What kind of attorney would a man make without Eventuality to recall his cases and the myriad details of law? A teacher without strong Philoprogenitiveness? Would you trust your life to a ferryman with an underdeveloped organ of Aquativeness? And what of your own business, sir? Would you wish to hire a reporter not endowed with large Individuality or Language? I know I should not like to read his broadsheet!

"You see, it is no more difficult for us to chart the course of a career than it is for a mariner to navigate the course of his ship. For we read the compass of the mind by which we may direct with unerring certainty the steps from childhood to youth, from youth to manhood. With the help of phrenology, man may yet steer his ship through the longest nights and deepest ocean of this world."

"Yes!" Whitman exclaimed. "I've been many of these things—a carpenter, a teacher, a newspaperman—and I know the truth in your words, especially when it comes to the education of children. I have read and reviewed your superb book on intellectual improvement and juvenile instruction. You've got it right—dead right! There is more intelligence and compassion in your philosophy of education than in all the schools in America, I fear! Leisurely self-discovery, that is the program for children, just as it is for any who would call himself an adult! For what the child sees, the child becomes. What is it you have said? 'Self-made or never made?' We need to loaf and invite the soul, to see the world in a spear of summer grass."

"Well said, sir, well said!" Fowler's years on the circuit had honed his

ear to when and how a man sought praise, and he had perfected the art
of delivering it as a diagnosis. He did not now miss the moment. "I begin
to understand you are a complete man of your profession! Your hands
and clothes are proudly stained with the ink of the press, your mind is
filled with stories, and your soul is alive with words!"

The phrenologist's words could not have been more greedily
devoured had they been an enormous beefsteak and Whitman a famine
victim. "All that and more, Professor! You cannot possibly know. It is all
of a piece to me, and I mean all. And I do it gladly and make no distinction—whether printing, binding, writing, or riding the country to
deliver the news. Why, I even maintain an account here as an agent, selling your books in Brooklyn. Like you, Professor, I make no apology for
practicality, and I go where the country and its people are." The printer
paused just long enough to carefully assess the effect his words were having on the phrenologist. Detecting nothing loathe, he plunged on.
"There is much we have in common. I've heard your lecture,
'Phrenology versus Intemperance.' Do you know I've also published a
temperance tract—a novel? And I've written this. I have only recently set
the type myself and printed it with Rome Brothers in Brooklyn, and it is
just published." He held out a slim book with a green felt cover and
embossed gold lettering. "I hope you'll take this copy."

Fowler flipped the slim volume open and his look turned appreciative. "You are familiar with our work on the phrenology of the poet?"

"Of course."

"And your own reading found you well rounded?"

Whitman paused, almost imperceptibly. "I have no doubt it would."

"Would?"

"Professor. I am a poet and a printer, but I am only with this slim volume a publisher. I have an aged mother and an ill brother yet and must
often postpone my pleasures . . ."

"Pleasures? *Pleasures?* Have we not been speaking of necessities? Of
duty to self and society?"

"I agree in my soul that we have. Sadly, my thoughts are deeper than
my pockets."

"Then we must pay back the gift of your work in kind. Of course, I devote most of my energies these days to lecturing and writing. But my brother, Lorenzo, remains the world's foremost practical phrenologist. Come, Mr. Whitman. Let me thumb your book while Lorenzo places his expert fingers upon you."

As soon as he sat down Whitman was surprised to discover that, despite having attended numerous examinations, he was uncomfortable, very nearly queasy with doubt. It was, in truth, partly the fault of the chair, a rather large and oddly proportioned straight-back affair which forced him to sit bolt upright, his spine rigid. The chair was mounted on a small platform designed to assure the patient's head would be no lower than the phrenologist's chest. There was certainly nothing unsettling about Lorenzo, who now stood smiling and humming alongside the chair, absentmindedly twining a cloth tape measure between his fingers as if anticipating a game of cat's cradle. If anything, Lorenzo seemed even more relaxed and genial; a domesticated, short-haired version of his older brother. Lorenzo's secretary, though—that was another story. Not that there was anything overtly threatening in her practiced, professional manner. Quite the contrary. Seated at a small, marble-topped table, a writing tablet before her, she seemed to be striving for nothing so much as invisibility. Whitman had simply forgotten that, aside from marking his chart, Lorenzo would be dictating his analysis. Well, what was wrong with that? After all, he prided himself on holding back nothing. And though he loved to deprecate himself as a rank exhibitionist to the other writers in the evenings at Pfaff's, those who really knew him understood that behind the loafing, the daydreaming, the endless self-obsession, was a man whose willingness to be a public embarrassment— yes, to even be pilloried as a pervert if it came to that—was an indicator of a gargantuan will and its attendant aspirations. But . . . but. To let another hand hold the pen—that was quite another thing. It took all of Whitman's self-control to suppress a shudder.

"I'm pleased to see you have included your portrait in your book," Orson said. He had seated himself casually upon a nearby rail in order to both observe the exam and peruse the book of poems, from which he now looked up. "I note that you are an anti-lacing man and favor an open collar on all days—good! The spirit needs to be unencumbered! Oh, my friend, so few artists understand the relationship between physiognomy and art as you do."

Whitman nodded, feeling the base of his neck rub the straight back of the chair but glad to have his mind off the impending exam. "Men are just beginning to appreciate that the soul is always under the beautiful laws of physiology—isn't that what you are really proving to the world, Professor?"

As he spoke, Whitman could feel Lorenzo's fingers holding the tape measure to his skull just above the ears, measuring the circumference of his cranium.

"Nineteen," he said to the secretary. "The head is held firmly." Then, speaking to Whitman: "You were blessed by nature with a good constitution and power to live to a good old age. You are undoubtedly descended from a long-lived family."

Whitman could feel his skin blush warm with pride. "I have the perfect mother. A Van Velsor—among the earliest Duch settlers to Long Island—and she gave me a Hollandisk firmness, an ability to endure."

"Perhaps she gave you more," interjected Orson. "Poetry is inherited. The poetic temperament, the first great condition of the poetic talent, is transmitted. We need only examine the parentage of Goethe, of Schiller, of Burns—especially their splendid mothers—to see that great poets are born."

Lorenzo removed the tape and placed his hands on the sides of Whitman's head. Gradually, he moved his left hand onto the forehead and with the other, grabbed the back of his neck. With the balls of his fingers, he manipulated the scalp gently, wandering slowly around first the base, and then the sides and top of the skull. Though still leery, Whitman found the movements soothing, and oddly electric.

"You were not prematurely developed," said Lorenzo. "But you can last long if you are careful to obey the laws of health, of life, and of mental and physical development. You have a large-sized brain giving you much mentality as a whole." At this last remark, Lorenzo could feel Whitman relax markedly under his touch.

"You need not concern yourself with our Mr. Whitman failing to obey the laws of health," said Orson, who had been stealing glances at his brother's ministrations as he flipped through the thin volume in his hand. He read aloud:

> *"Was it doubted that those who corrupt their own bodies conceal themselves?*
> *And if those who defile the living are as bad as they who defile the dead?*
> *And if the body does not do fully as much as the soul?*
> *And if the body were not the soul, what is the soul?*

Oh, this is marvelous, marvelous! Lorenzo, here is a poet who speaks in the plain language of our time, offering verses shorn of the old conventions, old myths, old tricks. Yet there is the sublime beauty of the truth and an appreciation of the window our science opens and the light it throws on man!"

Lorenzo, feeling his patient continue to relax and expand under his hands, concentrated on his task. "I'm going to read the individual organs now, sir. As you no doubt know, we assess each organ from underdeveloped to overdeveloped, on a scale of 1 to 7. It is as much a tool, a guide for your daily living and exercise, as an evaluation. I trust and pray you will not feel dejected over any assessment wherein the organ is rated underdeveloped. It is as much a prescription for exercise and cultivation as an evaluation of your current strengths. Nor, I hope, will you feel any undue pride over a highly developed organ."

Whitman nodded, a slight motion of assent, but at these words his nervousness had returned. Lorenzo now placed his hands at the basilar portion of the skull, and his fingers probed gently along its edges, measuring and feeling its contours.

"Adhesiveness," Lorenzo announced, "6." His fingers slid purposefully through the long, red hair, seeking specific spots. "Amativeness, 6. Ideality, 5. Sublimity, 4. Acquisitiveness, 4. Alimentiveness, 6. Secretiveness, 3. Calculation, 6. Self-esteem, 6 to 7. Individuality, 6. Mental apparatus, 4. Observing and knowing faculties, 3. Hope, 4. Marvelousness, 3.

Veneration, 4. Intuition of human nature, 4. Destructiveness, 5 to 6. Benevolence, 6 to 7. Philoprogenitiveness, 4. Vital temperament, 5. Mirthfulness, 5. Intellectual faculties, 5. Language, 5. Strength of system, 6. Size of brain, 6."

Lorenzo stepped away from Whitman and crossed to the table where the secretary was seated and picked up the results.

"From the raw data, Mr. Whitman, I find that you are are well calculated to enjoy social life. Few men have all the social feelings as strong as you have."

"Yes, sir!" exclaimed Whitman. "I recognize and greet my brothers wherever I go!"

"Your love and regard for woman as such are strong and you are for elevating and ameliorating the female character. You were inclined to marry at an early age, for you could not well bear to be deprived of your domestic privileges and enjoyments."

This piece of analysis caused Whitman to turn uneasily in the chair— a reaction not lost on Lorenzo.

"Ah!" He spoke with some delicacy. "Not yet married?"

Sheepish, Whitman shook his head. "But it is certainly true that I am for elevating the female character."

"We need not worry about Mr. Whitman on this score," interjected Orson. "I have just concluded reading a section of verse on the furtive sexual passions of a woman which even I—*I*, whose frank sexual guidance to women is the great scandal of the scientific world—would think twice before reading in public! Only a brave man and a great poet could conjure your bathers, Mr. Whitman. Oh, this portends well for your future, poet! For surely you know that no man can ever become extra great, or even good, without the aid of powerful sexuality. Every intellectual genius on record evinces every sign of powerful manhood, while the ideas of the poorly sexed are tame, insipid, emasculated, and utterly fail to waken enthusiasm." He saw that his words had erased the doubts caused by his brother's remarks about marriage, and motioned for Lorenzo, who was now eyeing him skeptically, to continue.

"You are one of the most friendly men in the world and your happiness is greatly depending on your social relations. You are familiar and open in your intercourse with others, but you do not by so doing lose your dignity. You are a sincere friend and a feeling, obliging neighbor. You can easily pass from one thing to another and you prefer short comprehensive speeches to long yarns about nothing. You have much energy when you are aroused, but you are not easily moved at trifles. You would if obliged to, fight bravely for friends, woman, moral character, children, and honor. You choose to fight with tongue and pen rather than with your fist. You are not quarrelsome, but you mind your own business and like to see others do the same."

At this, Whitman flushed with pleasure. "True! All true, sir! You read me so well!"

Lorenzo, who had given a variant of this speech well over twenty thousand times, smiled at the familiar reaction to the flattering homilies. "You are cautious and look well to the future, to consequences and obstructions and are generally pretty sure you are right before you 'go ahead.' Your courage is probably more moral than physical . . ."

" '*Walt Whitman,*' " Orson read aloud from the little green book, " '*a kosmos of Manhattan the son* . . .' "

"Your appetite is most *too* strong naturally and your food relishes well. You are pretty well calculated to resist disease and to soon recover if you are attacked by it."

" '*Turbulent, fleshy, sensual, eating, drinking and breeding* . . .' "

"You are no hypocrite but are plain spoken and are what you appear to be at all times."

" '*No sentimentalist, no stander above men and women or apart from them* . . .' "

"You are in fact most *too* open at times and have not always enough restraint in speech."

" '*No more modest than immodest* . . .' "

"You are more careful about what you do than you are about what you say."

At this, Whitman, who had been nodding his head vigorously to each of Lorenzo's pronouncements, paused. The phrenologist did not notice.

"You are independent, not wishing to be a slave yourself or to enslave others. You have your own opinions and think for yourself." Once again,

Whitman was bobbing his head—like a listener at a recital who has refound the melody after a wrong note. "You wish to work on your own hook, and are inclined to take the lead. You are very firm in general and not easily driven from your position. Your sense of justice, of right and wrong, is strong and you can see much that is unjust and inhuman in the present condition of society . . ."

" '*By God!*' read Orson. " '*I will accept nothing which all cannot have their counterpart of on the same terms.*' "

"You are but little inclined to the spiritual or devotional and have but little regard for creeds or ceremonies . . ."

" '*I believe in the flesh and the appetites / Seeing, hearing, feeling, are miracles, and each part and tag of me is a miracle . . .*' "

"You are very sympathetic and easily moved by suffering, and take much interest in those movements that are of a reformatory and philanthropic character . . ."

" '*Through me forbidden voices / Voices of sexes and lusts, voices veil'd and I remove the veil / Voices indecent by me clarified and transfigur'd . . .*' "

Lorenzo shot his brother a sharp look, and then continued. "You have both reason and perception, and hence can reason well. You have a strong desire to see everything and your knowledge is practical and available . . ."

" '*Now I will do nothing but listen / To accrue what I hear into this song, to let sounds contribute toward it . . .*' "

"In summation, sir, you are a great reader and have a good memory of facts and events much better than their time. You can compare, illustrate, discriminate, and criticize with much ability. You have a good command of language, especially if excited." Lorenzo paused, as if waiting an extra beat to increase the finale's crescendo. "By practice, Mr. Whitman, you might make a good accountant."

"I beg you. My brother insists on acting the perfect idiot. Believe me—*believe me*—his crude barb was aimed at me. It hasn't a thing to do with you or your abilities."

They were alongside the privy which occupied much of the small alley behind Clinton Hall. Whitman, his face beet-red with humiliation, the muscles of his neck twitching in spasms of anger, was only just beginning to regain his composure and Orson, standing beside him, feared the newspaperman might yet explode. He had seen the effect of Lorenzo's spiteful words the moment they were pronounced. *Oh, what is wrong with him! This is how Lorenzo would punish me? By poisoning a reporter's pen against us?*

"An accountant . . ." It was spat from between clenched teeth.

"Please." Fowler touched Whitman's hand with a folded handkerchief, encouraging him to take it. The poet just shook his head.

"An accountant. An ac-*count*-ant!"

This was the moment Orson had been waiting for. He could hear the shock and anger being supplanted by a defensive cynicism and knew he would have to speak now to retain the newspaperman's good will.

"I don't know how to put this, Mr. Whitman. I'd like to speak with you frankly and confidentially and then you may make of it what you will. May we speak privately—as fellow gentlemen and writers?"

Whitman nodded warily. His shirt, which had been rakishly open at the collar, was now completely undone save for one button, and its left tail hung raggedly out of his trousers. His hair, which he normally obsessed over, could not have looked any wilder had he just completed an electromagnetic treatment. Still, Whitman's eyes were focused and searching, and Fowler was immediately seized with the realization that, whatever he needed to say to right the situation, he should not underestimate this man.

"As gentlemen and writers."

"You said earlier that you had heard me speak, that you are familiar with my book on raising children. And I trust you know that unlike Lorenzo I prefer writing over practical phrenology. I'm a strong writer, and that's led me to tackle many subjects. Physiology. Memory. Diet. Parenting. Matrimony. Penal reform. Education. Housing.

"But Fowlers & Wells is a house divided against itself. My writings have, I believe, always been frank—but now they have become dangerously frank. Or so my brother fears. He frets that my philosophy will destroy Fowlers & Wells. You know that we advocate phrenology as an aid to successful matrimony, a system for composing well-matched pairs. And now my studies have led me to the most dangerous ground yet. I exalt nature's laws, Mr. Whitman, and I can tell we have that in common. I hope I am not speaking indelicately and I trust it won't shock a visionary artist such as yourself, but I must confess baldly that I have come to believe a wrong love is the trunk cause of human degeneracies and miseries." He paused, studying the effect of his words, looking for a sign that his words either shocked or dismayed Whitman. And there was something—something fleeting—but it passed so quickly that Fowler could only just mark it and its immediate burial. "And naturally, a right love is its cure. For women as well as men. I could not help but feel in your words a similar belief. But Lorenzo fears that the step I now wish to take—to speak candidly about the pleasures and healing powers of the marriage bed, for who better than I to instruct men and especially women?—would be the ruin of Fowlers & Wells. I believe his words to you come from this, from his desire to discourage me from my way and to drive away a kindred soul. For that is what he knows you to be, Mr. Whitman. And, shocking as it is to consider, I shouldn't be surprised if some of the scores on your reading are artificially low."

Fowler searched the face in front of him to see if his words had hit home. They had. But he saw more—he saw also the deeper light of a superior chess player who divines an opportunity for his next half-dozen moves and likes where they will land him.

Whitman held up his hand, as if to stop a teamster's cart. "Say no more of these matters, professor. I know what it is to be dismissed, even ridiculed. And yet, like you, nothing can dissuade me from my words, or move me off my path. Do you know that even with this troubling state of affairs, I still envy you? Fowlers & Wells is a great and prestigious publisher and distributor of books and magazines. Imagine what that means to a poor poet and printer who dreams of the enormous audience you take for granted! Why, regardless of the subject your own books never fail to garner an astounding number of printings. And I can only guess, Professor, at how many homes have been improved by your firm's handbooks—I can attest that a day doesn't go by without seeing someone reading either *How to Talk* or *How to Behave* or *How to Do Business*.

Naturally, my own shelf includes many of your books as well as some of Fowlers & Wells's most thought-provoking titles—Smee's *Electro-Biology* and Trall's *New Hydropathic Cook-Book* are among my personal favorites. But I'm particularly taken with D. H. Jacques, whose *Hints Toward Physical Perfection* so wisely speaks of love as "nature's grand cosmetic." And the periodicals! *The Phrenological Journal, Life Illustrated, Water-Cure Journal*—why, you've an empire at your fingertips! Or should I say you've built an empire at the fingertips of the nation!"

Fowler smiled, less at the joke than the masterful way the newsman had led him to the offer they both knew he would now make.

"Why, Mr. Whitman—I have the most wonderful idea! Why don't you let Fowlers & Wells distribute your poems? Of course, we advertise all our titles in *Life Illustrated*, so there will be that as well to awaken the public to . . . I'm sorry. What is it entitled?"

"Leaves of Grass."

"Oh, that's splendid! It's a shame you didn't put that on the cover!"

"But I certainly shall next time, professor! For I've written several dozen new poems already. And perhaps I shall include something from this as well." Reaching a hand into the rear pocket of his trousers, Whitman produced a slim envelope. "I received this yesterday."

Opening the letter, Fowler scanned the short, neatly composed note. "'I am not blind to the worth of the wonderful gift of "Leaves of Grass." I find it the most extraordinary piece of wit and wisdom that America has yet contributed . . . I find incomparable things said incomparably well, as they must be . . . I greet you at the beginning of a great career . . .' It's from Ralph Waldo Emerson! This is gold!"

The poet, who had only just noticed that his shirt was hanging out of his pants, rearranged himself while Fowler reread the letter. Combing his fingers through his hair, he allowed himself a slight smile. "I have already shown it to my friend Charles Dana at the *Tribune*," he said. "Since he himself has prepared a favorable review for next week."

Fowler nodded appreciatively. "If only scientists would operate in the same spirit of brotherhood as newspapermen!"

"Oh, but you've got that wrong, professor! Good Lord! I can't be the only writer to undergo an exam here! If I know a thing about my ink-stained brethren, it's that their organs of Benevolence and Self-esteem are underdeveloped, and their Destructiveness overly large. There's no doubt the book will be attacked—and not just for what it says, but because it says it in a strong, unequivocal voice devoid of all the usual European frippery. Writers are a jealous and confounding race of men— eager to receive praise and slow to give it—and one as generous and generously advanced as Emerson an exception."

"Well we should certainly assign it for review in *Life Illustrated*—it will appear in the very first issue advertising Fowlers & Wells as its distributor. Naturally, since the poet's views are so in tune with the professional philosophy of the periodical's publisher—yours truly—I think our readers deserve a review unstinting in its praise. Can you recommend a writer who might be favorably disposed to the job?"

A boy's grin—the one normally reserved for stealing apples—broke across Whitman's face. "I do know of two very positive anonymous reviews that are about to appear in *The Brooklyn Weekly Freeman*," he said. "But the author is a modest man. Could he enjoy such anonymity in *Life Illustrated*?"

"I like you, sir. I like you. But I'm certain that won't be necessary. Among our regular contributors I'm sure we'll find no shortage of men who can divine the philosophic connection between your words and our science."

At this, Whitman's smile sagged. "No doubt you're right," he said. "But *Life Illustrated* is such a well-read magazine, and known among writers as a generous employer. Missing such an opportunity is a disappointment."

"Oh! But there are any number of opportunities for a sharp-eyed observer such as yourself! Why should you be limited to book reviews? I should rather see you contributing to our reports on the life of the city and its leaders in the arts and sciences. Covering the concerts at Castle Gardens or just ruminating on an afternoon's stroll up Broadway." Once again, Fowler saw that he had hit his mark: Whitman's eyes had taken on a decidedly dreamy, faraway look. He allowed the writer a few seconds of his reverie before closing the deal.

"So it's agreed, sir? Fowlers & Wells is to distribute your existent volume of poetry and publish a second, expanded edition. In return you will do all you can to promote and present it—and, I hope, any other Fowlers & Wells work which may impress you—and keep it before the public. Naturally, we will do our part through regular advertisements. And, of course, we welcome your contributions to any of our periodicals and agree to pay you our top rate. Is that satisfactory?"

Whitman smiled broadly and stuck out his hand. "Professor, you make a man's organ of Acquisitiveness positively throb with delight!"

Later that afternoon, after an interview for *The Brooklyn Weekly Freeman* had been logged in the pages of Whitman's nickel notepad, the two men agreed to travel together to Fowler's Brooklyn lecture. It was a scant block down Broadway and a ten-minute stroll east along Fulton Street to the ferry, but few rambles, even along the shore of his beloved Long Island, moved Whitman more. It wasn't the grandeur of Broadway that excited him—although no country cousin stepping off the train at Chambers Street for the first time could be less immune to the spectacle of that boulevard, be it Barnum's Museum or the opulence of Stewart's, the massive six-story dry-goods store with its four hundred employees, or the finely attired crowds dining on French fare at Taylor's. Rather, it was the mix of high and low. It wasn't *just* that the city was the pinnacle, but that it was the low point as well, and home to all persons and possibilities in between. He loved the wide, formal expanses of Broadway—but his heart really quickened whenever he turned the corner into an unfamiliar side street. Those residential byways, where endless rows of lidless barrels and decayed tea-chests brimming with coal ashes lined every curb, and pigs roamed the vacant lots scavaging amid piles of old clothes, broken carts, and refuse, were to his mind easily Broadway's equal, and he invariably found himself a good deal more eager to spy on the lives of its inhabitants, to listen to the argument between a husband and wife coming from an open upstairs window or the kitchen clatter of a basement oyster house. But the greatest thrill was to reach Water Street and gain the first narrow hints of the harbor, and so it was today.

It was an odd sensation; the buildings were low compared with those on Broadway, yet the streets were dark and close and somehow the rows of brick town houses, interspersed with older, wooden structures housing ship's chandlers, gave him the sensation of emerging from a shadowy tunnel into the bright, late-day sunshine of the open expanse that was the New York waterfront. Reaching the Fulton Ferry landing on the other side of South Street, Whitman's gaze was, as always, momentarily tangled in the endless riggings and captured by the countless flapping pennants of the mast-hemmed harbor. His eyes lured skyward, he picked out one of the hundreds of circling gulls scavenging the docks and waterfront, and diligently followed its flight as it wheeled farther and farther from shore. When the bird was suitably removed from land, he let his eyes drop to the water beneath it, focusing upon the first ship he saw. It was a secret indulgence he gave himself whenever he crossed on the ferry—a combination of talisman, superstition and child's game—and the object was to find the personal connection between himself and the boat. Commercial schooners, luxury liners, hay barges, freight-car lighters, ice boats, tugs—it didn't matter, his mind could always make a simple jump from either the ship's business or name to some bit of personal history, acquaintance, or interest. He knew he could always do so; that was what made it an indulgence. Today, despite the scores of vessels flying exotic flags and plying every imaginable cargo, his gull's ship proved a long, flat, common barge, the kind one saw every day transporting coal or timber or dead horses. This one was mounded with piles of earth, large stones, and gnarled roots; it was coming from upper Manhattan, where the City's topography was constantly being massaged and leveled for the ever-advancing grid of streets. Whitman smiled: he could make his connection with ease. He knew the earth and debris were bound for the enormous salt marshes of Jamaica Bay on Long Island's south shore, knew that area well. He loved to go rambling along its banks, seeking out the isolated shacks of its oystermen and walking barefoot in the cold water. He thought of himself walking that very bargeload of transplanted dirt on some future wandering, and of the changes the fill would bring to the waterfront and of the farms and islands that would rise from the shallow depths. And he felt a pang of longing for a warm summer afternoon just like today, when he'd spent hours watching a young oysterman dipping and scraping his rake along the quiet bay's bottom, endlessly hauling oysters up into his short, flat trawler. The teenager's face had been to the water, but his muscular brown back was turned to the sun and the poet.

With five lines operating between the cities of Manhattan and Brooklyn, the Union Ferry Company made over one thousand crossings every day. Fulton was by far the busiest line, and at this hour, with the sun beginning to descend beyond the Battery and the rush of commuters heading toward Brooklyn, Whitman was not surprised to see the awaiting crowd overflowing the ferryhouse while one of the newer ferries, the *Montauk*, pulled alongside the slip. In the bow, a crush of Manhattan-bound travelers surged toward the gate, impatient for the first opportunity to disembark, and on shore the outbound crowd of merchants, shopkeepers, and travelers eager to get home waited for the chance to displace them. A line of more than a dozen carriages, carts and wagons also waited to board. Amidst the jostling and pushing of the two crowds shouldering past each other—one arriving, one departing— Whitman spied a teamster sitting atop his cart. The brim of his cap was pulled low against the sinking sun over Manhattan, and he was smoking and waiting for the ferryman's sign to disembark. In the wagon behind him—a simple single-horse rig with two large wooden wheels—more than three dozen sheep and calves were stacked like firewood. Bound for the slaughterhouses on the West Side, the animals were already all but dead from the hot, day-long journey from the Long Island farmlands, and they shifted and groaned heavily, their long necks hanging over the wagon sides like wilted sunflowers, their open, panting mouths leaking long strings of thick saliva onto each other and the wagon sides.

"Disgusting," said Fowler, who had been following Whitman's gaze as they boarded. "If we believe in a millennium, we must, inevitably, give up our belief in animal food."

Whitman nodded. "But you'll forgive me if I haven't the passion of your friends for hard mattresses and stale bread."

Fowler guffawed as they took up a spot beside the ferry's rail. "Nor I. Sylvester Graham was a very popular lecturer at Clinton Hall but an impossible man. Impossible. What was it your friend Emerson said of him? 'The poet of bran bread and pumpkins'? No, I'm not one to celebrate the glories of farinacea. I'm frugivorous."

Whitman raised an eyebrow. "Is that really satisfying?"

"Oh, quite! The country around my house in Dutchess is fantastically fertile and the strawberries we grow this time of year are as sweet as any confection—I make a meal of them three times a day! Soon there will be apples as well! I never leave home without preparing something to take with me. Here, look." Fowler placed the large leather valise he had been toting at his feet and sprang its brass hasp. Reaching in, he produced a quart mason jar. "I mix strawberries, raspberries, chunks of brown bread, and a bit of milk," he said. "It's really lovely—won't you join me?"

Whitman looked at the warm, gooey suspension inside the jar—a mass of floating red and purple pulp, flecks of disintegrated bran, and pinkish-white liquid—and barely managed a wan smile. "Thanks, no," he said. "I'm not partial to strawberries."

"A shame!" Fowler flipped the wire latch holding the glass cap in place, raised the rim of the jar to his lips and, winking at his companion, drank deeply. It was too much for Whitman to watch, and he found himself gazing instead over the rail into the foul sewage slick ringing the first thirty yards of the Manhattan shore. When he looked back up, Fowler was wiping his mouth with the back of a large hand and beaming. "Not a strawberry man, eh? Well, perhaps you'll come up and visit us later in the season when the pears come in. There's nothing so nice as a warm bowl of stewed pears with molasses on a cold morning in the country! Unless it's hominy boiled with apples and honey. Delightful!"

Whitman smiled weakly. The teamster's cart which had occasioned Fowler's unappetizing demonstration was gone, replaced by a funeral procession bound for Brooklyn's Green-Wood Cemetery. In the lead was a brand-new ornate black hearse hitched to a pair of stately, well-groomed horses. The vehicle's four polished corners were defined by decorative Doric columns topped by lanterns, while a carving of birds in flight with a draping of curtains carried in their beaks framed a thick pane of window glass. Through it, a flower-covered coffin could be seen. Following the hearse were two expensive carriages, then three more open carts. The hearse and the carriages were each driven by a black-suited liveryman, the carts by their owners. Each was filled with somberly dressed men.

"A rich man's procession," Fowler said with unconcealed disdain for the fine hearse. "See what comes of indulgence and gluttony?"

"How well we live and honor our nature is important. But I've yet to meet the man who wasn't born to die," Whitman said. He couldn't resist adding slyly: "frugivorous or no."

"Of course," Fowler said, reddening. "Of course. But sickness and premature death are sinful. And all this pomp, this illusion of continuing wealth. I'm sure you've strolled through Green-Wood. Some of these new merchants entomb themselves like pharaohs! It's shameful and obscene!"

Whitman shrugged. "Last week in the *Freeman* we reported two deaths by drowning, six from consumption, one from abortion, and thirty-two assorted others of which twenty-two were children. Half of the children born in our country this year will not live to be twenty-one. As much as the present time is vaunted over the past, and despite your good works, in no age of the world have so many other influences been at work, averse to health and to a noble physical development, as are working in this age! I don't object to the fine hearse or big tomb of a wealthy man. What does it mean to me? Perhaps it is even good: death is inevitable and as meaningful to life as birth. But if it's hard to welcome death, perhaps it may be shorn of many of its frightful and ghastly features. Among the ancients, art did that. In the temple of the Greeks, Death and his brother Sleep were depicted as beautiful youths reposing in the arms of Night. Such were the soothing influences and the perception of beauty in all the works of Nature that art gave to the last fearful thrill in those olden days. Was it not better so? Or is it better to have before us the idea of our dissolution, typified by the spectral horror upon the pale horse, by a grinning skeleton or a mouldering skull? I know perfectly well my own egotism, and it is no different than the egotism of every other man, rich or poor. Still, the bitter hug of mortality doesn't alarm me. You love your home in the country, love its trees and grass. But you and I must be sweet manure for the grass others will love and ponder."

Fowler, struck by the amount of thought behind his companion's outburst, remained quiet. After a moment, he sought to shift the subject. "It is a sad thing, I suppose, that the women don't accompany the processions out to Brooklyn, even for their sons and husbands. I imagine that is the ferry?"

Whitman nodded.

"A shame!" Fowler shook his head ruefully. "A room without a woman is an empty one, and this ferry the poorer for their fears of being treated roughly! Now this, I'm sure, you'll agree is a scandal! That a woman should fear to come and go on a public conveyance! I see some do, but I can tell from their dress and manner that there is no option, and I notice none among us who isn't escorted by a husband or brother or some other acquaintance or guardian. Oh, the absence of womankind makes the day for all its sunshine that much darker! I'm sure you'll agree, Mr. Whitman—I deduce that you are a poet of the body as well as the soul and delight in the physical company of our sisters." He leaned forward, conspiratorial. "Of course suffrage is all fine and good—I am for the advancement of women in this world and my own sister is a physician—but there is a greater liberation that must take place as well. I'm speaking of course of the liberation of female passion. How can some say it doesn't exist when it is as obvious a fact as the sunshine? But love must be fed, or starve to death. It must be talked up, written up, and become an absorbing topic of human investigation. And of course, we have our role to play as men, eh?" Whitman saw that Fowler, always animated, now seemed quite agitated. "Each sex requires the tutelage of the other. This is what my brother doesn't understand. But I do! By God, I do!"

Fowler scanned the crowd on deck, his eyes pausing each time they detected the rare female among the commuters, looking her up and down, assessing each with an eye Whitman doubted was purely scientific. He also noted that the paucity of females was having a deflating effect on Fowler, who was taking on the taciturn look of a diner who has just been informed the kitchen is out of his favorite dish.

"It must be very gratifying that your lectures on phrenology and physiology have achieved such resonance with women," Whitman said with a charitable eye toward cheering him up.

"Oh, indeed!" Fowler said brightening. "Indeed. I hope you won't think me vain if I allow myself to believe it isn't just our message of improvability that attracts them. I like to think it's something more, that somehow they recognize a sympathetic spirit, a kindred animal—"

"Walt!"

The voice came from the stern of the deck where several of the ferry crew were removing the carriage ramp and locking the passenger gate in preparation for shoving off. One of the ferrymen was walking toward them, smiling and waving. He was wearing heavy gloves for handling rope and chain, and his sunburned arms were coated with gray and black streaks of dirt and grease, as were his trousers. Beyond that, he was young and tall and strong, and it was clear that being in the open air was altogether agreeable to him: his brown hair was streaked gold and red, and his eyes had taken on a permanent squint in deference to the sun and its glare on the water, giving his face a permanently bemused, playful look. Reaching them, he put a long, tan, greasy arm around Whitman's shoulder, hugging him genially. "I almost lost my job because of you," he said.

"What?" Whitman, who had appeared somewhat flustered at his friend's approach, now seemed shaken. "How can that be?"

The ferryman grinned. "I was up half the night reading your poems. When I awoke my head was still on the book you gave me—guess I had my nose buried in your grass, eh?—and it was ten minutes before my shift. Ran all the way from Pierrepont to the Fulton slip, but that bastard Tyler was up in the wheelhouse and he blew the whistle soon as he saw me tearing down the hill. I still thought I could make it, even with the ferry pulling away. And of course the rest of the crew is waving and yelling, Henry and Horgan and them all egging me on, screaming that I can make it. So I leapt—and just got the tips of the toes of my front foot on but couldn't grab the rail. Right in I go! Christ, I thought I'd broken my ankle and you should have seen those guys doubled over, and all the passengers laughing, too. 'Course, some joker threw me a line that wasn't attached to nothing. I had to climb out and wait on the slip until they come back." He shook his head and laughed.

Taking his gloves off, he extended a hand to Fowler. "Bill James," he said.

"Professor Orson Fowler."

"Really? The bumpologist? I'll be damned. I don't know how he does it, but Walt manages to meet more people than I do opening and closing these ferry gates all day! Christ, I can vouch that he knows damnnear every ferryman on the line and half the carriage drivers on Broadway!" With that, he casually rested his other hand, which held the gloves, on the poet's shoulder. And although it was clear that James hadn't given it a thought, Fowler saw that his proximity and touch were having a definite effect on Whitman, who was blushing a deep crimson and looking down, and remembered how something earlier had flashed briefly when he spoke of wrong love.

"Hey, Walt—I sure like your poems. I don't know that I'm the person you should ask because, truth to tell, I don't go in much for reading anything but *Rake*." At this, he winked at Fowler and jabbed Whitman with an elbow. " 'Course, some of the things he seemed to be saying in some of them poems made me wonder if old Walt here ain't been sneakin' peeks at *Rake* hisself! It's not much like the poetry I remember from school, that's for sure. Nothing at all, really. You don't think they're going to sound like poems when you first start to read them—they ain't flowery and such, more like listening to Walt talk—but somehow they do. They really do."

Whitman felt the words as hotly as the hand resting on his neck. Flushed with pleasure, he looked up. The expression of disgust he saw on Fowler's face immediately robbed him of the feeling.

"Can't be standing about," said James as they felt the ferry slip its mooring and push off for Brooklyn. "I'll have to be ready to open the Brooklyn side and I've already been chewed out for my morning swim, thank you kindly, Mr. Whitman." He slapped his friend's head playfully with the gloves. "Pleasure to make your acquaintance, Professor. If it's too crowded on board, have Walt take you up to the pilothouse. The boys always love to see him!"

"Not as much as he them, I wager," said Fowler. But the ferryman had already turned and gone, and it was hard to say if he had even heard the remark. Whitman, however, hadn't missed it or its meaning.

"Bill's a fine young fellow," Whitman quickly said. "And did you hear what he said about my little book? I gave copies to several other men I know as well—a coachman, a printer's devil, a teacher, a farmer—curious as to what they'd see in it. Of course, I crave their kind words. Bill is the first to say something, and I won't pretend it doesn't fill me with a good feeling—for the success of both my work and Fowlers & Wells as its publisher." At this, Fowler just grunted, and Whitman realized it would take more to regain his standing. "Yes, Bill's a fine fellow," he continued. "Unpretentious. Hardworking. A welcoming friend. A complete man." The poet paused a beat for effect. "Just the kind I hope my sons will become."

"Sons?" Fowler shot him a look of raised eyebrows.

"Yes. Didn't I tell you? I have two. No daughters. So far."

"Didn't you tell Lorenzo that you have yet to marry?"

Whitman smiled slightly and offered a casual shrug. "Professor, fatherhood and husbandry are not now and never have been mutually exclusive conditions."

Fowler would have disapproved if he wasn't fairly certain it was a lie. He considered probing the point, asking after their ages and circumstances, but then decided he didn't wish to know. If he was going to have a relationship with Whitman, then this would certainly be preferable to the other. And there was still his newspaper coverage of the evening's lecture to consider. Fowler let it go and flashed a tired smile. "You are certainly a surprising man," he said. "Not at all what I imagined when I saw you dreaming in front of the office window this morning in your ink-stained trousers."

The other raised his eyebrows quizzically.

"Most come to Fowlers & Wells to be entertained," he replied. "To gawk at the oddities on display—no different to them than viewing General Tom Thumb. We give them what they want, and they give us their money. Many others come looking for knowledge, for wisdom, for improvement. That's our true work, so of course we welcome them. But

that's not why you come to Fowlers & Wells, is it? Oh, you find our language useful—I hear it in your poems. And you do recognize that we are
progressive. But it's more—what was it you called yourself in your little
book? 'A kosmos?' Perhaps it is so, perhaps you are so complete. Yet in
my most candid moments even I blush at the hubris of a man who would
dub himself 'professor.' And though it's a rare occasion, I certainly recognize another man inventing himself with an eye toward posterity." He
gazed steadily at Whitman, who had been leaning over the rail and looking into the water while Fowler spoke, and saw that he did not flinch. "Is
that all?"

It was a long moment before Whitman answered, and in that time he
felt the ferry move beneath his feet, the wind tug gently at his clothes
and hair, and the anonymous but steady presence of the other passengers. "Do you mean to ask 'am I vain, greedy, shallow?'" he asked, keeping his eyes on the water. "'Have I lied?' 'Am I a man of lust and guile?'
The wolf, the snake, the hog—none of these are wanting in me,
Professor, as they are not wanting in any man. Do I play a part? I do.
Each man does, and he makes it as great or as small as he likes—or *both*
great and small." He could see his shadow being cast on the small caps
and waves, saw that the sharp, sundown light of the late afternoon was
piercing the water and that its refraction created a halo of fine spokes
around the shadow of his head. The illusion made him shiver. "But your
question, I believe, was 'is that all?' No. Not for me. But perhaps sometime after you've read my poems you'll tell me what you think of them
and what, if anything, I've heard in your words."

Fowler nodded, and joined Whitman in leaning over the rail. They
were silent for a few moments, during which Whitman's eyes never left
the surface of the water. "It's flood tide," said the poet. "Where do you
suppose the waters ebb at this hour? The China Sea? The Mediter-
ranean?"

Fowler grunted. "Is that what makes a poet? Where another man may
look in the harbor's waters and think—what? of work? a woman? dinner?
of nothing?—you see two Chinamen leaning over a ferry rail on the
other side of the world, pondering the reflection of the rising sun on
their way to work?"

"Perhaps I don't have to look that far," Whitman said, pointing south across the harbor to an identical ferry bound for Manhattan. It was the *Paumanok*, after the old Indian name for Long Island. At the front of the carriage deck where the *Montauk* carried its funeral procession, the *Paumanok* held two long brewery wagons. And like its twin, it carried a full load of passengers. At the corresponding spot along the rail where they stood, a boy entering his teens leaned, his head bent toward the ship's churning wake.

"Shore to shore and shore to shore and shore to shore," said Whitman. "Do you imagine you are the only bumpologist among us? How would you chart the personality of our cities, Professor? Can you lay your hands on the granite storehouses or the docks, upon the foundry chimneys burning high and glaringly into the night with their flickers falling over the tops of the houses and down into the clefts of the streets and by them read the everlasting soul they evidence? I can. I am the phrenologist of this harbor. Its clouds, its sundown, its schooners and sloops, steamboat pipes and spars, are the head and body through which the immortal soul of the endless hundreds and hundreds that cross and will cross are made visible. That boy—that young blade with the dew still upon him—knows not that we look upon him, or that we feel the same abrupt questions astir in our own late-night walks or laying abed or gazing over the ferry rail. But his questioning—and the questioning of his grandson, and his grandson's grandson when they cross this harbor—are as real to me as my own. They are like today's tide and the sundown, no different yesterday or tomorrow whether I witness them or no. But I witness the body of the harbor."

4

THE
ANIMAL TSAR

A stinging snow hardened to pinpricks of ice and nailed home by the gusts off the East River ricocheted like tiny glass pebbles against the paving stones and echoed along the quay of Water Street's empty shipyards. On such a night the surest way for a man to stay warm was to drink, and the white knot of sailors in front of the inn at the corner of Ferry Street were good and warm. Huddled around their own hazy glow, they took no notice of the street: not the nearly empty horse trolley rolling past, nor the small gang of hard young toughs wearing the red-striped pants of the Dead Rabbits. They didn't even see the two boys climbing noisily up from the rocks below the wharves, straining and struggling with a pair of heavy, filthy jute sacks.

Winded and arm-weary, the boys dropped their bags at the edge of the street, standing tall to stretch their backs. Each leaned on a long, thick, filthy wooden stick topped with a small coil of rope hung like a tiny noose. The smaller boy, catching his breath in great, wheezing gulps of icy night air, cast a nervous eye down Water Street and then looked at the other boy.

"We should have been done and back an hour ago," he said. "I wager Burns is hopping by now."

"You'll wager he's hopping? I'll wager he's hopping from wager to wager. What's that ugly bastard going to do—start without us?"

The smaller boy grabbed his sack by its cinched end and slung it across his slim shoulders, grimacing as it landed awkwardly on his back. "Well, I just don't want Burns thinking that stinking Tommy or any boy from Mulberry Bend might do as well."

They carried the bags across Water Street and up the two blocks to Peck Slip, the footing made just as treacherous by the hail as it had been below the wharves, and entered a saloon named Sportsmen's Hall.

The air in the low-ceilinged Hall was stale with sweat and smoke and alcohol, but deliciously warm. Mostly men, but also a few women, sat around heavy oak tables beneath framed prints of hunting hounds, race-horses, and bare-knuckle prizefighters, drinking and laughing loudly. The boys hobbled unsteadily toward the bar, their sacks bending them nearly to the waist and listing oddly in every direction. In the gaslight of the saloon, the bags moved of their own accord, as if each contained dozens of tiny infants, their hands pushing outward for escape. Each boy wrapped his arms around his back, supporting his bag from the bottom. It seemed the sacks would fly off if given a chance. A huge, muscular bartender with a dark, generous mustache and face shiny with sweat waved them forward.

" 'Bout time," he said.

The taller boy twitched and winced, feeling something sharp as a needle dig into his neck. "He'll be happy," he said.

"I hope so—the boys are gettin' itchy." The bartender smiled. "But with a full house at two dollars a head, I can't imagine he'll complain too long." He cocked a thumb over his shoulder toward a narrow doorway behind the bar. "You know where it is."

It was dark and narrow in the passage, the ceiling even lower than in the barroom. But the proximity of the walls made it easier to balance the sacks, which rubbed against either wall as the boys pitched forward, bouncing from side to side with each awkward recalibration. From the short staircase at the other end they could hear the din, an echo of laughter and shouting, and they smelled the room before they saw it—an unpleasantly pungent mixture, as if the saloon were in the putrid heart of the West Side poultry market.

And then they were in it. A small warehouse—a former chandlery—it had been refitted as an arena. Tightly packed rows of wooden benches rose from the dirt floor on concentric platforms until the backs of the highest seats touched the room's lime-and-stone walls—room enough for four hundred. Sportsmen's Hall was alive with the sounds of drinking and shouting men, for there were no women back here, and pulsed with an animated vigor. There was an air of expectation and excitement as hot as the breath of an animal and as enveloping as the cloud of tobacco smoke which drifted above the room's plain, iron four-lamp gas chandelier and up and out through its only window, a partially open, ice-encrusted skylight.

The semicircular ring was centered on the raw dirt floor directly beneath the skylight. The four-foot-high walls were wooden and the insides lined with dull sheets of zinc. Around the perimeter, men leaned over its edges, laughing and shouting just to be heard. Indeed, it was so loud the boys couldn't hear Kit Burns until he was practically in their faces, his gray muttonchops hanging like an old hound's ears, his soft gray pock-marked face split by a sloppy grin.

"Well! I see our little wranglers reach trail's end at long last! Where the hell have you been? This place is about to riot!"

The boys looked down. "They don't like to come out in the cold," said the smaller one.

"Well, we'll make it hot enough for them, won't we, eh?" A smile lit Burns's face as the gaslight danced in his eyes. "What's the count?"

"Seventy-five."

"Me, too," said the other. "And some pretty damn big ones, too, Mr. Burns."

"Excellent! Let's have us a look, shall we?"

They slung their sacks to the floor, the taller boy immediately un-cinching the rope binding the neck of his. In the glare of the gaslights, countless small cuts were evident from the boy's fingertips to above his wrists and the heat of the room made several of them ooze blood, but he took no notice. Instead, he plunged his right hand into the sack and quickly jerked it out, his prize held aloft.

"How's this, Mr. Burns?"

It was the men surrounding the pit and crowding the benches behind Burns who provided the answer, erupting in a roar. Above his head, the boy swung a dazed, twisting, ten-inch wharf rat by its thick tail.

"No wonder you lads've been gone so long," said Burns. "I'll bet you had to go all the way above Union Square to find a cute little field mouse like this!" He laughed loudly at his own joke, clapping the boy on a shoulder. "Nice work. Let's make it seven-cents apiece instead of five." The two boys grinned at each other. "Just put those sacks over by the pit and go see Jimmy upstairs at the bar for your money."

"Wait a minute," said the taller boy as his brother headed for the stairs. "Don't you want to see the rat bait?"

"Why don't we get our money first?"

"Oh, come on, where's Jimmy going? He'll be at the bar whenever we get there. Don't you want to see Billy Fagan's bitch? Cousin Johnny says she's the best ratter ever—he saw her kill a hundred in less than fifteen minutes over in Secaucus. I bet we can squeeze in right by the ring."

The younger boy made no reply, rubbing the backs of his sore hands against the sides of his trousers, but followed. He took a good look at the crowd: there were sailors, printer's devils, a couple of Burns's tougher buddies from his days in the gangs, and more than a few swells from up-town. Squeezing between the crowd, the boys indeed edged their way right up against the four-foot pit wall and soon stood alongside two tall, well-groomed men in crisp black overcoats and matching stove-pipe hats who looked like Wall Streeters. One smiled at the boys.

"Well, fellows, care to make a wager?"

"Sure," said the older boy. "If I can take Fagan's."

The banker laughed. "A man who knows what he wants. How long did it take you boys to catch all those rats?"

"All evening. It's a lot easier in the summer. I once filled two sacks in thirty minutes at the dead horse pier." He warmed to the subject with the pride of a professional, as if he were a carpenter questioned about the proper pitch for a roof. "Plus, Mr. Burns wants them big, so most house rats won't do. Down by the wharves is best."

"How do you keep them from biting?"

"Can't. Oh, we catch most with these sticks—see the little noose? Right through there. But sometimes you can't just shake them out into the bag, or one jumps up as you're putting in another. And don't ever put your face over the bag, neither. I wish someone had told me that."

The man nodded appreciatively. "I gather since you're still here that this isn't just business for you. Are you a sporting man?"

The boy's eyes lit up. "Sure. Excepting Kit won't let me bet on the rat-ters. He says I have to wait until next year when I'm twelve. And I'm get-ting my own dog. My uncle and cousins are sportsmen, too—they fight gamecocks at the Weehawken Ferry pit. But I like dogs—if a gamecock loses, all you've got is soup. There's a breeder with good fighting dogs up-country by the Bloomingdale lunatic asylum, and he says he'll sell me a pup if I muck the kennels. Plus he knows all about training them." The boy brought the back of a hand to his mouth, absentmindedly salving one of the deeper cuts.

"Yes," agreed the man, "dogs are best. Although it's not always better than a rooster when they lose. You've got to be strong enough to put them down. The best fighting dog I ever saw, a black-and-tan named Mardi, is buried not twenty feet from where she fell." He cast his eyes toward a corner of the room and pointed to where a group of drunken teamsters were arguing furiously. "Right over there. It was a brave end to a great night."

"I've heard about Mardi," said the boy. "Do you think Kit still has the bear chained up somewhere?"

"I doubt it. Otherwise I think he'd fight him."

"Did you see that?"

"Unbelievable. I wouldn't have dreamed a man could fight a bear and win. Took him three rounds."

"How much did he win?"

He shook his head. "As I recall he fought for drinks. A sailor."

"I liked to have seen that. I wish they still had bear-baits like a hundred years ago. I bet that was—"

A shout went up from the crowd and a short man with goatee and mustache who was dressed in a gray, button-down wool shirt, suspenders, dirt-caked trousers and an old, battered union cap swung a leg over the pit wall. In his arms he cradled a brown-and-white fox terrier, which he immediately thrust aloft for the crowd to see. Entering the pit behind him was Kit Burns.

The boy studied the dog closely. It wasn't Fagan's Venus, but Dick Hill's Nellie—literally the underdog, and an animal he'd never seen before. She twisted fitfully in Hill's arms, a knot of excited muscle, and sprang free even as he bent to place her on the pit's earthen floor. Compact, the dog wasn't more than fifteen inches high, but her muzzle pointed up, sniffing the foul, heavy air in excited anticipation as she bounded around the ring.

The throng of bettors pressed forward as one, leaning over the pit walls for a closer look and crushing the boys in the process. Still, neither even considered conceding his ringside view and watched raptly as Burns bent and snatched the dog back from the floor.

"Whoa, Nellie!" he barked, laughing along with the men at his own joke. "Let's see what yer made of!" Holding the dog up to his face, Burns bared his own teeth and snarled fiercely, as if about to grab the bitch's muzzle between his jaws. She twisted frantically in his arms in a desperate bid to get away but quickly subsided, pinning her ears back and exposing her throat in a show of submission. Burns roared with laughter and tossed her playfully onto his shoulder. "Well, she's smart enough to know who's top dog!" he cried. "Let's see what kind of a ratter we've got here, eh, gentlemen? I like her—I like her enough to bet her over Venus! Who wants a piece of that?"

Hands and shouts went up from the ring of benches. Placing Nellie back on the floor, Burns climbed heavily over the wall and waded into the crowd. At the other end of the pit, two men hung one of the cinched rat bags from a meat hook mounted on a swinging rope and eased it over the barrier. The dog, at first frozen by the motion of the bag, was suddenly in a fever of excitement—bounding across the pit in a single leap, jumping up at the bottom of the bag, yapping loudly, and turning tight, excited circles around it.

"Oh, it's a ratter all right, boys!" shouted Burns. "Any other fools want to make me rich?" The bag was now twisting violently in the air, in danger of leaving its hoist as the dog leaped and nipped at the increasingly terrified rats, frantic to escape the danger they could only sense.

The last bet covered, Burns shoved both hands above his head. One held a fistful of bills, the other a stopwatch. Crouching behind the wall, Dick Hill held Nellie at bay. At the opposite end of the pit, one of the men who had hoisted the sack onto the hook held a Jewish butcher's long, razor-sharp knife near the bottom of the bag. Mesmerized, the crowd leaned closer, a congregation awaiting a fiery sermon. Burns, a seasoned showman, held them a moment longer. Then he cocked his thumb dramatically over the stopwatch before grinning and nodding. The man with the knife slit the bottom of the sack.

Like a broken hive the angry contents spilled into the pit and the room erupted into excited shouts through which somehow the desperate whining of Nellie could be heard. The boys leaned in just as Dick Hill released the terrier.

She was across the ring so quickly they couldn't see her get there, head dipped, shoulders up. Shaking her head furiously, she tossed her first rat, a large gray, through the air and against the zinc-lined pit wall. Before it had time to slip to the floor, its neck broken, a second thudded against the opposite wall. Swarming around the dog in a terrified riot of hair and teeth, the rats lunged and leaped desperately at her legs, chest, belly, and neck. A pair of rats, one long and brown, the other streaked with blood, hung desperately from either side of Nellie's muzzle, digging in with teeth and claws. Shaking one loose and banging the other against the pit wall, she yelped and spun in the air as an enormous old brown rat sank its long front teeth into her underbelly. Flipping on her back, the dog grabbed her tormentor in her paws and bit it angrily, breaking its spine. Her gyrations upset the pack, and the rats moved as one with a loud, pitiful chatter to hug the pit's farthest wall before Nellie regained her feet. With the swagger of a lioness she chased them around the pit, picking at the pack's edges and shaking each catch with such furious force that she frequently sent a rat flying beyond the pit and into the crowd. There, each unlucky animal's skull was quickly ground under a boot heel for good measure, the vermin's corpse then flung high in the air by its still-warm tail to land wherever it might.

"She's tough and fast, eh?" the banker said, nudging the boy. "Is that the kind of dog you had in your mind?" But he was so spellbound by the bloody spectacle of the relentless terrier fiercely ripping after the fleeing pack that he only vaguely heard the question. And it was only when he looked up into the man's face in an effort to figure out what he had said that he saw the skylight high above the pit swing up and open.

A shiver of winter air and hail blew down into Sportsmen's Hall and four heavy coils of rope slowly unfurled out of the night wind, their ends swinging herky-jerky just a few feet off the pit floor. All eyes, until then held by the dog and rats, now turned upward beyond the hanging gas lamps to the open skylight. Policemen in heavy winter overcoats clambered over the window ledge and down the ropes. Standing on the roof above them was a tall, gaunt man in an elegant black overcoat and top hat, peering over the edge and down into the pit. In one hand he held a cane, in the other a lantern. Its light illuminated his face—a long, thin, serious face with humorless eyes, drooping mustache, and bushy, ice-encrusted muttonchops.

"Scatter boys, scatter!" cried Kit Burns. "I'll be hanged and blasted if it ain't that goddamn milksop Henry Bergh!"

In one motion, Dick Hill was over the wall and into the pit in a mad scramble to extricate his Nellie from the rats. It was no good, though: indifferent to the hubbub, the dog remained in fevered pursuit of her prey, dashing madly around the ring. Worse, Bergh saw what Hill was up to. "Sergeant," he called down from the roof, pointing his cane toward Hill, "grab all the dogs first."

One after the other, four policemen swung free of the ropes. The dog, at last distracted, was lifted handily by the sergeant. Then, as if contemplating for the very first time that they had landed in an enclosed area with fifty terrified rats, each officer began stamping madly at the squeaking, desperate rodents, their heavy boots making an even quicker job of it than Nellie. A sailor, standing on a bench on a riser above the pit, pointed to a squat policeman kicking a half-dozen rats he had cornered in a crease of the pit wall. "I shoulda bet on that mutt!" he yelled. "Burns, you bastard! Take my bet!"

The joke did nothing to cheer the outraged men, several of whom began throwing bottles at the police. Most, however, focused their rage at the man on the roof. "Coward! Woman! High-hat bastard!" But if he heard, he showed no reaction. Rather, he tugged on one of the ropes until it attracted the sergeant's attention.

Bergh pointed down at the other policemen, busily crushing the last of the rats. "Was that really necessary?" he shouted. "After you've arrested Burns and the dog owners, make sure the contents of the remaining bag are disposed of in a more humane manner, if you please, sergeant."

The older boy looked on in near shock. "Well m'boy," said the gentleman, "no Venus tonight. There used to be grand fights and rattings here every week in the good old times, but no more. The better days have given way to Bergh's days."

"How can he do this?" asked the boy. He twisted his hands into a frustrated knot, worrying the scabs dotting its top. "Ain't New York got enough rats? If Mr. Bergh is looking for rats he can have to take care of, he can come to my house—we've got more than he could shake that cane of his at. God! Protecting rats! What an idiot!"

The smaller boy at his side burst into tears. "An idiot?" he asked as two policemen grabbed Kit Burns by either arm and led him out through the narrow hallway. "An idiot? I'll tell you who's an idiot—you're an idiot! And I'm an idiot for listening to you! I told you we should have got our money first!"

Why did Uncle always have to keep the office so damn cold?

He knew he was being unkind but he couldn't help himself. It just wasn't fair. His bed had been as deep and cozy as a feathered nest, so perfect for drowsing away a snowy Saturday morning. Worse, while he dressed and fought his way into his boots, Edwin, his older brother, made an unbearably ostentatious show of languidly stretching and sighing. "Hug a horse for me, Henry," he heard Edwin say into his pillow as he was closing the door. Bastard. Well, next year he'd be at Columbia College, too, and beyond the age of being forcibly impressed by mother and father into Uncle's army. The thought briefly lifted his spirits. But it hadn't lasted beyond the front door. Each laborious step through the nearly knee-deep snow seemed to tax his strength and sap his optimism. The stinging ice storm of the prior night had given way to a steady, silent fall of heavy wet flakes, but not before encasing the streets in a hard, slippery undercoat upon which the still-falling snow lay like a treacherous white field. The going was extremely slow: it took the better part of an hour to trek the six blocks from his house on Fifth Avenue to the Society's brownstone at the corner of Fourth and Twenty-second, and by then he wanted nothing more than to turn around and go home.

That was really why he had cursed his uncle's parsimony. He knew why the office was cold, knew that every shovel of coal was treated dearly. Uncle Henry loved his crusade but hated soliciting funds. "I have stood in the street on dark nights while rain fell in torrents," he would intone in a voice more appropriate to delivering a stump speech than speaking to his teenage nephew, and his narrow, sad face would burn with its usual heat of self-drama. "I have entered horrible slaughterhouses, and fought my way into dog-fighting establishments at the head of a platoon of police. But this was as naught to the difficulty of raising funds for my society." When his uncle spoke like that—and he almost always did—Henry wasn't sure whether to worship or laugh. Most people tended to do the latter, his father included. Oh, they spoke admiringly of all Uncle had accomplished with the Society. And certainly no one doubted for an instant that he *was* the Society, that he alone had willed it into existence, made people pay attention—important people—and kept it going these years.

Nor would they deny his triumphs. No one could recall, for example, the last sighting of those horrific, overloaded butcher carts once so common to the streets of New York; they had been Uncle's first targets back in 1867, just two weeks after the legislature in Albany passed the anti-cruelty laws he had written, granting enforcement powers to his newly chartered SPCA. When he arrested three incredulous teamsters that first afternoon and Justice Kelly of the Court of Special Sessions fined them each ten dollars and a day in city prison, it made the front page of the *Tribune*. That was really the beginning of the Society.

It was also the beginning of Uncle's torrid and ceaseless affair with the press, who loved him almost as much as they loved to mock him. Of course, they weren't the only ones: as his uncle's namesake, Henry could well attest to that. Too well. There never seemed a shortage of wits among his schoolmates, ever ready with a smart remark or a dramatic reading of the tabloids' coverage of Uncle's latest escapade. But the worst was when they hit on calling Uncle "Henry the Horse Lover," because he knew it was just a matter of days before the sobriquet was transferred to him. God, he'd hated that. Hated it so much he had tried to fight three of them. Henry would never forget the humiliation of being held down in the street, of having horseshit in his eyes, hair, and mouth—and that hated name in his ears.

Of course, they weren't interested in the fact that Henry didn't even like horses. But, and this was truly odd, he suspected his uncle didn't, either. He knew beyond doubt that Uncle didn't like dogs. Still, it was strange that he couldn't ever recall seeing him place a hand on the nose of a horse out of pleasure or kindness, since he had done so much for draft horses. Henry found his eyes drawn to the office display case featuring some of the more dramatic check reins and bits the Society's agents had seized from coachmen. The painful devices were crudely ingenious metal prods placed in the mouth and designed to jerk the animal's head back and keep it held high. "It wasn't so long ago," Uncle would lecture the

wealthy owners of hansom cabs in hopes of discouraging such showman-
ship among their grooms, "that Dame Fashion in London conceived a
fancy for high-stepping horses. Do you know how this caprice was grat-
ified? The eyes of the animals were cauterized with a red-hot iron, so
that fearing to stumble, the creatures would lift their legs up high." Such
heavy-handed horror stories and revolting parallels were typical of Uncle, and one of his propensities which most embarrassed Henry. Still,
there was one item in the display case that he couldn't look at without
shuddering. It was a burr bit, a leather pad studded with thirty sharp steel
needles. When placed in a horse's mouth, the constant pricking would
make the animal shake its head and dance in agony—although passersby
saw only a prancing, high-spirited horse. Last October alone, the Society
had seized one hundred and fifty of them.

Those were far from the only exhibits of booty in the Society's war on
cruelty. Not counting the new horse-ambulance and lift and stretcher on
display in the lobby and the stuffed black Newfoundland facing the
vestibule, the office was a virtual testament to man's unending genius for
inflicting pain on any creature unfortunate enough to share the planet
with him. There were effigies of bloody fighting cocks, their talons torn
and necks ripped, and horrific photographs of dead pit bulls. There were
hooves of trick ponies burned off in circus fires, and deformed horse
tongues floating in formaldehyde. A long table along the far wall of the
office held a collection of thirty-seven stones, some weighing over two
pounds, which had congealed in the stomach of a single horse—testimony to the shady practice of weighting hay with plaster of Paris and
chalk. There was even a board with a collection of homemade slingshots
confiscated from boys who'd been caught shooting at birds. Henry
smirked to think that no abuse was too small to escape the withering stare
of his uncle's flagrant morality, and wondered if the city's unfortunate
urchins were being made to pay for his failure to dissuade New York's
more powerful citizens from the sport of pigeon shooting. He sighed,
knowing how Uncle Henry would answer such criticism—he'd heard it
so many times: "The child that serves its apprenticeship to inhumanity
by tearing the wings off a fly will later insult the poor, beat his inferiors,
and show but the same cruelty, intensified by age, which characterized

his early training. All things have a beginning. The harmless glass of wine may become the precursor of the drunkard's doom; the stealing of a robin's eggs from its nest may attain its climax on the scaffold." Oh, his uncle could be such a bore!

That fact, like his crusade, came as something of a surprise to the family. Unlike father, Uncle Henry had shown no interest in succeeding grandfather Christian at the family's thirty-six-lot Corlears Hook shipyard. Instead, he had been something of a young dandy and dreamer, given to long trips to Europe during which he wrote plays of either the soupiest sort—proven beyond doubt by the fact that even Henry's mother, an unfailingly sweet and generous woman, couldn't resist rolling her eyes at the mere mention of *Love's Alternative*, a five-act abomination in blank verse set in a ruined castle on the Rhine—or the meagerest drawing room satires with such unwitty titles as *Human Chattels* and *Married Off*. All that had changed during the war, with Uncle's commission from President Lincoln to head the legation to St. Petersburg. Henry Bergh's abysmal plays might lampoon the propensity of New York matrons for marrying their daughters off to the sons of bankrupt European aristocrats, but he found no serfs who laughed at the nobility in Russia. Indeed, he quickly discovered that the gold braid of the diplomatic corps worn by his liverymen meant any peasant who didn't get out of the way of his carriage was entitled only to be run over. Not that he did such a thing—quite the contrary. But he found the power of his office inspiring. There came a day when he saw a Russian cart man beating a starving, exhausted horse because it would no longer move. And although he had never shown any interest in animals before, he took it as his duty to use the power of his office to end such beastly behavior. It required just a word from his footman for the terrified peasant to immediately climb down from the cart, unhitch the horse, and pull the load himself. The next day Bergh had his driver ride around the city in search of similar abuses, which were easy to encounter and just as easy to extinguish with a quick command from the carriage. It was Uncle's transforming moment. But the younger Henry knew his uncle well enough to suspect some hard-to-describe but consistent thread between the mushy young playwright and the dour, hectoring New York tsar of animal rights.

He was reading the framed copy of Uncle's 1866 speech at Clinton Hall calling for the formation of the Society, when he heard him come in. Uncle's tall, gaunt figure blocked the doorway, making it impossible to see if it was still snowing. The gold-headed cane was already stowed in the umbrella rack with his silk stovepipe hanging above it, and when he noticed his nephew, he was in the process of taking off the black frock coat he always wore.

"Why are you wearing your hat?" he demanded.

Henry had forgotten. "I'm sorry, Uncle," he said, removing it swiftly. "It's just so cold in here."

"This is my office. I would remove *my* hat were I calling on you."

"Yes, sir," he sulked. Henry noticed that the shoulders of the coat his uncle had removed were filthy, almost as if it had been used to wipe up some slimy, bloody mess. "What happened?"

Bergh's already down-turned mouth headed still another notch south, belying the shrug he gave. "After we took Mr. Kit Burns to appear before Judge Dowling at the Tombs night court, I made my usual 6 a.m. tour of the meatpackers and markets. I particularly wanted to see what kinds of loads they were putting on the milk carts at the Jersey ferries, for in this weather I won't allow the horses to pull a full weight. Then I drove to Forty-second Street, where the live hogs are unloaded, to make sure they were properly penned instead of left in the railcars to suffocate and trample each other. Finally, I stopped to check the butchers in Washington Market, which is where I got my 'epaulets,' " he said, indicating his coat.

His nephew winced at the realization that his uncle had been pelted with offal. "They are barbaric," he said with real indignation. "How can you put up with it?"

"They are barbaric," his uncle agreed. "But the Hebrew butchers are even worse, so I suppose I am thankful it's Saturday. Three-fourths of the butchers of the city are Hebrews, and I simply dread watching them execute their office since their religion obliges them to bleed to death the animals they slaughter. Of course, I'm not suggesting they should be proscribed from practicing their religious dictates, but the manner in which they accomplish that duty is nothing short of brutal and shocking torture. They usually hook a chain around the hind leg of a bullock, jerk up the struggling beast, head downward, and slit his throat. Their religion hardly requires them to suspend an animal, dislocate its hip and lacerate the flesh. And I must admit our own hog butchers are no better. They hoist their unfortunate victims on chains as well, dipping them bodily in boiling cauldrons. It has been nearly a hundred years since Benjamin Franklin advocated electricity as a humane method of slaughter, and still we bludgeon and torture these animals with more clumsiness and barbarity than you would think possible, let alone efficient."

"And how did it go with Kit Burns?"

At this, his uncle actually smiled. "Splendid!" he said. "Do you remember the last time Burns came before Judge Dowling? The charges were dismissed for lack of evidence. Lack of evidence? Surfeit of friends more likely! Well, this time a word or two from Mayor Hoffman seemed to have impressed the judge. Oh, Henry! You should have seen the look tonight on Burns's face when Dowling said no bail! Well, the man can see all the rats he wants in the Tombs while awaiting his date with the Court of General Sessions."

"I wish you had let me come, Uncle." It was the kind of Society action that Henry found exciting, but it wasn't actually true this time. On a dare from a couple of schoolmates he had been to Sportsmen's Hall a few weeks earlier, and he had feared someone would remember him.

Bergh frowned. "The raid itself was a bit of a botch," he said. "Those oafish police managed to crush more rats than the dogs, both of whom slipped away with their handlers. Can you believe it? Two hundred men in the Hall and the only one they managed to arrest was Burns. Then—and this is simply beyond the comprehension of any civilized human being—as I was standing outside by the paddy wagon, this vile, ragged little ruffian with unspeakable filth beneath his fingernails ran up and bit my hand! Bit it! Like a rabid dog!" Bergh shook his head. "I tell you: the two-legged wild beast is no more needed in the world than the four-legged."

"All the same," said his nephew, "I wish I had been there."

"Don't worry—you won't lack for excitement today."

Henry doubted that. "What are we doing?"

"We are paying a visit at the cowsheds by the Second Avenue salt marsh."

"All the way out there? Won't the roads be impassable in this storm?"

"Ah—that's just it, don't you see? They won't be expecting us. I've rented an extra team for the carriage, so we'll get there, all right."

The boy winced, thinking of the long, cold ride and what was likely to be waiting for them at the sheds. For once he had been hoping they would just catch up on the week's correspondence, a task he usually found extraordinarily dull. "Aren't you tired, Uncle?" he asked hopefully. "You've been up all night and probably without a bite of food. You've got to think of your health." But it was no good. His uncle had already taken a clean topcoat from the hall closet and was grabbing his hat and cane.

"What are you waiting for, boy?" He rapped his cane against the bare floor impatiently. "Come on!"

The snow was still falling, although without the insistence it had shown during Henry's early morning march to the office. He couldn't remember a winter with more snow than this, and here it was only December. Henry hoped the New Year would bring a change and 1871 wouldn't be quite so white. If it hadn't been for the presence of Uncle's carriage, he couldn't have said where the curb ended and the street began.

It was odd to see Uncle's carriage parked in front of the office. An indefatigable walker, he preferred to make his daily rounds on foot and easily traversed ten miles of Manhattan streets on any given day. That habit, coupled with the fame his crusade had garnered in the papers, had made him quite a favorite with the cartoonists, especially Thomas Nast. They never tired of recasting his long, thin frame and drooping, sad-eyed countenance as a horse-faced Don Quixote, and had made him a famous figure about town. Indeed, one columnist had recently listed Uncle second only to Horace Greeley among the most frequently recognized New Yorkers. That assessment had pleased Uncle, and Henry didn't doubt its accuracy. He couldn't remember ever trailing Uncle down the street without someone calling his name—either to doff a hat and offer a word of encouragement, or to shout a vulgar insult. The carriage, really, had been for poor Aunt Matilda, whose worsening paralysis had finally forced her commitment to a sanitarium above Albany late last summer and left Uncle Henry alone in the big Fifth Avenue house. Henry hadn't seen his aunt since then, and he hadn't seen her carriage in well over a year. Ever penurious, Uncle hadn't bothered retaining the liveryman, and Henry was relieved to see this morning's driver wasn't a hired man but Tommy Childs, one of the Society's best enforcement agents. Maybe the cow barns wouldn't be so bad after all.

Heading across town, Uncle Henry shifted impatiently on the leather bench, his heavy-lidded eyes scanning the white city beyond the cab window while his nephew checked him carefully, curious as to what might catch his attention. Down Third Avenue they could see a crew of boys younger than Henry shoveling the snow from the New York and Harlem Railroad Company's tracks. A wagon with several hogsheads of cinders followed, and whenever the boys cleared a few feet of track, a man on the wagon would rain several shovels of black ash onto the cobblestones. Henry heard his uncle snort in derision.

"In the daylight they throw cinder," Bergh said disdainfully. "It wouldn't surprise you to hear that I saw a company crew tossing sugar last night on the Fourth Avenue line." He sighed. "I guess this means another unanswered letter."

Henry knew "sugar" was slang for rock salt, which had been outlawed in New York as a road deicer at Uncle's insistence because of the damage it caused to horses' hooves and fetlocks. He also knew his uncle was speaking of writing another letter to William H. Vanderbilt, the president of the New York and Harlem, a long-standing exercise in futility. He was forever writing letters to Vanderbilt about some abuse by the company—lame horses, overcrowded coaches, callous drivers—but rarely received a response, let alone satisfaction. He had much better luck simply hauling the drivers off the trolleys and arresting them for cruelty than lobbying the company's president, and it particularly bothered him since he considered Vanderbilt's father, the Commodore, a friend. Of course, nothing had really come of Uncle's letters to the Commodore, either.

That was one of the more frustrating and troubling aspects of Uncle's crusade: to the extent that it worked, it only seemed to work in the streets. That is, he'd had no trouble getting the courts to recognize cruelty when practiced by teamsters or cockfighters, but railroad magnates and foxhunters—that was something else. Uncle knew it, too, and it wasn't for want of trying. He'd even tried to speak their language, delivering speeches to meatpackers and railmen outlining how shipping underfed and under-watered sheep, swine, or cattle in overcrowded boxcars killed too many animals to make it economical. They just didn't care. The railroads were insured, and the meatpackers and butchers took the animals dead or alive. And such "gentlemanly sports" as pigeon shooting and foxhunting were just as abominable in Uncle's eyes as the meanest dog pit. But he couldn't sway its enthusiasts, and judges were slow enough to reprimand the likes of Kit Burns, let alone the directors of clubs to which they themselves belonged.

With few strollers out in the snow, Henry was surprised when they turned up Second Avenue and spotted a modest but boisterous crowd in front of a cider shop. Bergh, attentive as a hound, momentarily froze at the sight. He quickly opened the carriage window, lifted his cane out, and rapped furiously on the roof.

"Childs!" he shouted. "Can you see the front window?"

"No, Mr. Bergh. Shall I pull over?"

"Yes, do."

Puzzled, Henry lifted an eyebrow to his uncle, who only frowned.

"I've been here before," Bergh said, opening the door as soon as the carriage pulled alongside the curb. "Come along."

The boy jumped out on the street side, his boots landing softly in the snow. Emerging from behind the carriage, he saw the mill's fat, apron-clad owner standing near the door of the wood-frame shop, offering small cups of hot cider from a large tin tray to the crowd. It was clear, however, that the free samples weren't the only attraction. Nearly everyone was huddled tight around the mill's front window, and there was a great commotion and excitement in the air. The mill proprietor was laughing, apparently sharing a joke with two men on the fringe of the crowd when he sensed the approaching figures. He turned, smiled, and held out the tray. Young Henry, his feet numb with cold and his back stiff from the frigid carriage, reached gratefully for a cup. He had just about set his hand on the rim of the fullest one he could discern when the tip of his uncle's cane tapped none too lightly on his fingertips.

"Henry."

Oh, damn. He looked up at his uncle, expecting the dead-stern gaze of admonishment which accompanied the unavoidable dressing-down each minor transgression produced. But to his surprise, he wasn't even looking at him. His uncle's eyes were locked, rather, on the man with the tray. And the man was no longer smiling.

"Mr. Bergh!"

"Ah, good," his uncle said. "I see you haven't forgotten me." He paused for a moment and when he again spoke his voice was every bit as sharp as the look he had fixed on the proprietor. "I trust you also remember what I told you."

The fat man, quite visibly agitated now, made a choking sound in his throat but failed to reply.

"Nothing to say, sir?" said Bergh. "Then let's have a look."

A narrow path to the front of the shop had opened when several in the crowd turned from the window during this exchange and Bergh, his cane pointed outward, strode through the opening like an oversized anteater following its nose. The celebratory atmosphere had evaporated, fading like Bergh's crunching footfalls in the muffled silence of the snow.

At the window, Bergh stood stock-still, his only discernible motion a brief sagging within his frock coat as his bony shoulders fell and then rose again. But from behind the crowd it was impossible for his nephew to see anything other than the black outline of his uncle's back, and he shouldered his way past the other onlookers in order to find out what was going on.

Inside the window was a goodly-sized cider mill. Its bottom was a large piece of rough-hewn granite, out of which a bowl had been hollowed and an angled sluice cut for the juice to run off into a five-gallon wooden bucket. A second piece of stone, the grinder, was mounted on a thick pole through the middle of the bowl. Alongside the stones was the treadmill that drove it, and driving the treadmill was a St. Bernard, tightly harnessed in such a way that she couldn't jump off or stop moving. The exhausted dog was panting and whining, her mouth oozing a thick string of saliva in the habit of the breed. The harness was obviously choking her neck, and where it came up between her legs and chest, it pushed aside the fur and rubbed the skin raw. Standing behind the dog was a small Negro boy, whom Henry guessed to be about ten years old, feeding apples into the grinder and picking mashed pieces out of the screen about the sluice.

"Mr. Walker," Bergh thundered at the mill operator, "unharness that dog this instant!"

"And just who might you be?" asked one onlooker standing to Bergh's side. He was a tall, rough-looking fellow, poorly dressed for the weather and carrying a shovel on his shoulder.

Bergh barely flicked his eyes at the man. Instead, he flipped the lapel of his overcoat, revealing a badge pinned to the underside. "The law," he said.

"The law?" snorted the heckler. "The *law?* Don't the law protect people? Hell, you're just that crazy fellow who wants every turtle to travel by yacht in its own stateroom."

At this the crowd erupted in howls, and Henry felt the heat of embarrassment rise in his neck and ears. Two years earlier, Uncle had created a sensation when he boarded *Active*, a just-arrived schooner tied at a pier in the East River, arresting the captain and his entire crew for transporting one hundred sea turtles stored on their backs in the hold, ropes run through holes punched in their flippers. When the Manhattan Attorney wouldn't prosecute the case, Uncle did it himself—and lost. The captain claimed the turtles didn't feel any pain, and the judge ruled the animal cruelty laws weren't written to extend protection to turtles. Worse, the *Herald* devoted six columns to its coverage of the trial, including a stinging satire—apparently missed by no one in New York—in which Uncle presided over a Union Square rally of animals demanding their rights. Uncle's reaction had perplexed Henry. He knew the barbs hit home: Aunt Matilda had once confided it wasn't unusual for Uncle Henry to come in late from his rounds and lock himself in his office for "a good little cry" (indeed, he hadn't failed to wonder whether the constant ridicule engendered by Uncle's crusade had contributed to his aunt's illness). But he noted also that Uncle was not displeased by his notoriety, and was quick to say he would endure any humiliation if it only alerted the public to the SPCA's mission. After his thrashing in the *Herald*, Uncle even went so far as to suggest that he had undertaken his turtle gambit with just such an end in mind, recounting that a book publisher friend had counseled him that the next best thing to merited applause was downright virulent abuse. "The only fatal thing," Uncle had intoned, "would be for the press to say nothing at all." It was the one time Henry had ever heard his father shout and berate Uncle, who nevertheless seemed unfazed. Henry had no doubt he would stand his ground now.

"A cruel man often excuses himself for showering blows on a dumb animal with the plea that the animal does not feel pain," Bergh said, pointing at the dog in the window. "So why does he strike him or mistreat him? By his action, he gives the lie to his words. Whenever you see a man abusing any animal, you will almost always find that the man is in the wrong and the animal is in the right."

"Oh, come on," replied the man with the shovel. "Has it really been so long since you and yours had to work for a living?" At this the crowd murmured appreciatively and the mill operator seemed to stand a little taller.

"It doesn't matter what some ignorant foreigner thinks is right or wrong," Bergh answered flatly. "I say it's wrong and so does the law. And if it is not agreeable to you, then you are free to return to whatever filthy, diseased bog you sprang from. I'm certain back home you were free to take up a shillelagh against any unfortunate horse or dog, but not here. Childs! Unharness that dog. Mr. Walker—lock up your shop, you are under arrest for violating the animal cruelty laws."

"But Mr. Bergh," cried the cider man. "How should I feed my family?"

"Anyway you like, sir—that's your right and no concern of mine. But the pursuit of a living doesn't entitle you to abuse an animal, for then it will be my concern."

Bergh insisted on walking the three blocks to the nearest police station—it was unclear to Henry whether he objected to tethering the dog to the carriage or allowing Walker to ride up top with Childs—but he handed Henry the leashed dog and bade Childs follow them with the coach.

All told, the investigation and arrest consumed the better part of two hours, and it was nearly noon before they resumed the journey up Second Avenue to the salt marshes. It was rare that Henry found himself above Thirty-second Street, and he was surprised at the extent of construction. He had heard the shantytown by Forty-second Street at Dutch Hill was gone, but he had not expected to see so many new four-story tenements on Second, their absence of privies signaling that the greatest of all luxuries, indoor plumbing, was now a reality for the masses. Nor had he anticipated the new brick and brownstone row houses on the cross streets, all watched over by fancy but still unconnected street lamps. Even his uncle, who came up this way with some frequency, had to remark on the changes, particularly the demolition of the Beeckman's old house on Fifty-first, and the Astors' estate in the Eighties. The snow, which had never completely stopped, rose and fell throughout the ride, and white drifts covered the new city, creating an unfamiliar and unreal landscape. It wasn't until they had almost reached the marshes that this new, half-real, half-imagined city seemed to recede, replaced by the old raw patchwork of farmland, empty and overgrown lots, and fenced-in junkyards piled variably with broken wagons, building material, and scavenged machinery. If they couldn't see it in the snow, they could certainly feel the end of town as the wagon, leaving the wide, newly paved avenue, rumbled and lurched over the frozen ruts of the old country road.

A dilapidated carriage house, a half-empty stable, and several old squatters' cottages with refuse-strewn side lots announced the salt marshes. A tannery and rendering plant, giving out an awful smell, stood near an old and still-active garbage dump, and on the far side of the dump stood a wood-frame warehouse. There were several large metal tanks by the warehouse, and from its chimney issued a steady plume of smoke pushing up like gray hands against the cold, snowy sky. The smoke was acrid and it had an oddly irritating smell; still, it left a not unpleasant taste in the back of Henry's throat, like burnt sugar or sweet corn.

"What am I smelling, Uncle?" he asked.

"Money," said Bergh. "Money and misery. This is the distillery of Frank Walls, a very enterprising man. He also owns the tannery and the rendering plant and the dump and the carting company that fills it. His specialty is picking up from the markets and restaurants. He mixes much of the refuse with the swill from this distillery, packs it in hogsheads, and sells it to farmers and dairymen as slops for livestock. It's quite a big business. In theory, it's not a bad idea. There are still quite a few vitamins in alcohol swill, and mixed with grain—which it usually isn't—it would provide an adequately nutritious diet for an animal. Provided, of course, that the flesh in the market and restaurant refuse isn't diseased or putrid, which it often is. Don't look so aghast, Henry. You've been to the markets with me. You've witnessed how rotting, diseased flesh gets dressed and sent to the dinner table—what do you imagine the rejects these animals feed upon is like?"

It wasn't the notion of the swill that horrified Henry—he knew about swill milk, had once heard his father and brother discussing an article in the *Tribune* crediting the thin and often tainted milk from swill barns with driving up the city's infant mortality rate and calling for its banning— what startled him was the suggestion that he himself might have inadvertently drunk the vile liquid in a restaurant.

Coming beside the distillery, Henry could see dozens of large, old swill barrels caked with a greasy grime and waiting to be filled. The swill was fed from the distillery out to the barrels in a long spigot-operated pipe system not unlike the kinds used by the railroad to water its engines. Henry was puzzled, however, by the presence of a second pipe which wrapped around the building at a descending angle before disappearing into the ground. "Why is there a second swill pipe?" he asked.

Bergh gave his nephew a tight smile. "I said Mr. Walls is an enterprising man, did I not? Aside from picking up at the restaurants, he supplies them. Whiskey, naturally. And milk. The second pipe goes to his own dairy barn. If you can call it that."

The carriage had come around to the far side of the distillery, tucked behind the mounded hill of the dump. There was, indeed, a dairy barn there, although not of the kind Henry had envisioned. Instead, it was a variant on the dugouts used in some of the colder regions of New England, where barns were built into the side of a hill and the sloping ground carved out to create a two-tiered system of stalls. Here, one set of stalls had been jerry-built upon the foundation of an older building which had apparently burned down, and a ramp built into the old foundation to create a lower set of stalls. The flat-roofed building was low-slung, and there was no door to speak of. Rather, a portal wide enough to drive a wagon through led to both floors. Just outside that opening was a snow-covered cart, and as they drew closer, Henry could see the name of a well-known Washington Market butcher on its side. The stiff and frozen carcasses of two milk cows formed a mound under the still-falling snow.

"You there!" Bergh had thrust his head and shoulders through the carriage window and was waving the gold head of his cane at a stable boy shoveling snow off the roof. "Where's the supervisor?" The boy glanced briefly at the carriage and simply shook his shovel up and down, indicating the barn. Then, speaking to Childs, Bergh said, "Block the entrance with the carriage."

The agent maneuvered the coach to occupy the center of the portal with Bergh's door opening into the barn. Applying the brake, Childs jumped down and swung the carriage door open for Bergh, who, silk hat in hand, quickly alighted. Henry slid across the bench after him.

Despite the cold eddying winds around the doorway, the odors of the barn wrapped Henry in a bear hug. The sensation was akin to trying to breathe on an unbearably muggy summer night, of fighting through something that wasn't air but some heavier, wetter, less hospitable ether, and its fetid odor made him gasp. If his uncle or Childs heard his labored breathing, they responded no more than they did to the vile air itself. Both men, Bergh in the lead, were already following the swill pipe, bounding down the ramp to the barn's lower level. Henry held his breath and hurried to catch up.

Even before the U-turn in the ramp he could see the cows through the gaps in the wooden beams. There were four rows of animals tethered in shoulder-to-shoulder, their backs sloped, stomachs sagging, heavy heads set in place above low, rusted troughs. Looking at their haunches, Henry could see several suffering from stump tail, a sure sign of malnutrition; three of the first four cows sported large, festering sores on their udders and legs. Except for the aisle between rows of cows, the barn's dirt floor was thick with manure, and it seemed to coat the walls and beams as well.

A boy at the end of one row was dragging a bucket across the dirty floor between two cows, milk sloshing up and over its sides. Because the animals were so close together, he had to shove the haunches of one with his shoulders in order to make enough room to kneel in the filth between them while milking.

"Boy!" Bergh shouted as he came down the aisle. But the boy continued his preparations for milking and gave no sign of hearing. "I said *boy*! Look at me when I speak to you!" Still he made no move and it wasn't until Bergh stood practically on top of him that the boy, without taking his hands from the task of milking, briefly turned his face just enough to let Bergh know he was aware of his presence.

"Who is your boss?" demanded Bergh. "Where is he?"

The boy shrugged. "Up top. Time to swill."

Bergh brought the tip of his cane, which he had been careful not to place on the floor, down to the boy's face and held it a few inches from his nose. "Your manners are every bit as abominable as your appearance," he said. Turning gingerly to avoid as much manure as possible, Bergh did not see or feel it when the boy turned a teat in his direction, squirting the back of his trousers.

Bergh, Childs, and Henry were already halfway back up the ramp when a low rumbling noise brought them up short. The sound seemed to Henry to somehow simultaneously come at him and emanate from the building itself, and he had no idea what it was until he saw Childs looking at the metal pipes.

They heard the swill splash into the trough and saw the steam first, like a cloud of dust announcing the approach of a distant army. Beneath it, the scalding mash of spent grain roiled—a hot, angry sea, pushing and splashing against the sides of the trough as it ran quickly to the far end of the barn and doubled back on itself like a wave upon a beach. The hungry cows, unable to wait, dipped their noses to the troughs and stuck long, thick pink tongues into the steaming slop. It was clear to Henry from their incessant lowing that the liquid's temperature was scalding and blistering their mouths. Still, they seemed unable to stop eating.

"Hey!" The voice came from above them. "Who the hell let you in here? This is private property and I'll thank you to leave before I—"

"Are you Walls?"

"Walls?" The man was now standing ten feet from them. He held a large, heavy wrench in one hand and was every bit as dirty as the boy milking the cows. "Yeah, I'm Walls. Did my dinner jacket give me away? Who I am is none of your business, mister." He swung the wrench meaningfully. "But I aim to find out who you are and what you think you're doing here. Or did you just get lost on the way to Delmonico's?"

Bergh flipped the collar of his coat to expose the badge.

"Coppers?" the man asked with sudden confusion.

"SPCA."

The man rolled his eyes. "Are you the cow cops now, too? Christ, mister. What are you wasting my time for? I been working in milk barns all my life and I seen them a lot worse than this. It's business. As long as they give milk we try and keep them alive, and as long as they're alive we milk them. And that's about all there is to it and that's about all they're smart enough to do except shit—but I think even you can see that. Don't misunderstand my meaning. I hate to see a horse beaten, and you won't get no argument from me even on the harmless stuff like when you stopped those Spaniards from bringing their bullfight to New York. But this? We're just a milk barn, not criminals."

Now it was Bergh's turn to look weary. "There is not a corporation nor individual that practices cruelty to the lower animals but utters a similar sentiment when rebuked by us," he said. "But look around you. Look at this misery and filth—not to mention the sickness you cause with the vile, poisonous liquid that can be the only product of this unwholesome environment. You belong in Sing Sing, and I will have you there and this stable demolished if you keep on in your infamous traffic. If I were president of the Board of Health, I would not leave a single swill-milk establishment standing in the city."

"Well, you ain't and I'll thank you to leave," said the dairyman. "Or would you rather I call my 'milkmaids'?"

The threat had no apparent effect on Bergh, but it terrified Henry.

He often considered what Uncle did an embarrassment, but not dangerous. That morning he had woken filled with loathing for what the day might bring, but he certainly hadn't imagined being beaten in some distant corner of the salt marshes.

"I'm going to come back," Bergh said. "There are too many animals in here and I expect you will rectify that. As you will the temperature of that slop and the lack of ventilation causing this horrendous stench. I won't even begin to speak to you about the filth covering everything including you and the men who milk these cows. And I expect to see salve on the sores."

The man gave a dismissive wave. "Get out," he said, turning away.

"You can elect to believe me or not," Bergh said to his back. "But next time I won't be alone, and I promise that if I am not satisfied you and everyone here will leave in handcuffs."

On the way out, Henry caught sight of a series of stalls set off from the others. Peeking in one, he saw a boy milking a cow suspended in a sling tied to the rafters. It was clear that the cow could no longer stand on its own and that it was far sicker than any Henry had seen on the floor.

Glad for the safety of the carriage, Henry nonetheless couldn't bring himself to close the window even as Childs turned them back toward the city. Instead, he leaned his head against the frame, letting the cold wind and snow hit him full in the face, hopeful his uncle wouldn't see him surreptitiously sucking gulps of clean, snowy air. But Bergh was preoccupied with his own thoughts, churning over the events at the dairy.

"My most vicious and lifeless enemy," he muttered.

"Who, Uncle?" Henry turned from the window.

"Human apathy. It is morality's lifeless enemy. That is always the same, Henry. The laws I enforce are a matter purely of conscience. There are no perplexing side issues. Not economics nor habit nor politics, no matter what that manure-encrusted criminal and his ilk would like us to believe."

Henry never knew how to respond when his uncle spoke like this. He thought he understood him, but even seeing what they had just seen, he could not fathom his uncle's crusade. It was plain enough that it wasn't the abuses against the animals which revolted Uncle so much as the men who committed them. And yet he never thought of his uncle as a compassionate man. Quite the contrary: he often wondered if Uncle even *liked* people. He tried hard to recall a tender moment between Uncle Henry and Aunt Matilda, yet all he could remember were mannered, courtly scenes through which Uncle moved like a stiff and polite actor ever aware of the audience at his elbow. He was much more himself here and now, fulminating in the back of a carriage rolling through a frozen world.

"I know it's hard not to be upset by such scenes and impudence," his uncle said, misreading Henry's silence. "But we'll arrest that blackguard."

"Did you see the cows in the slings? The ones that were too ill to stand? My God. To think that people drink this . . . And children! It makes no sense."

Bergh shrugged. "You saw the butcher's wagon. The cows are worth as much to Wall dead."

"It's frightful, Uncle. But what's to be done? People need milk and meat." A thought occurred to Henry. "Uncle—is there a reason you've never become a vegetarian?"

"I suppose that is the best way to be. But regardless of what people may think, I am a realist. Everything on my table has always been humanely slaughtered by my butcher and thoroughly cooked until it is devoid of any trace of blood." He paused long enough to allow himself a sly smile. "I'm surprised by the question, Henry. Vegetarianism? Isn't that a bit pedestrian for someone with my queer notions? We'd be better served by hippophagy."

"How is that, Uncle?"

"Horses. If people will eat flesh, let them eat that of the horse and mule, which is known to be quite as nutritious and palatable as that of the ox. On the Continent, the *boucherie de cheval* is quite common, nay fashionable. In Germany, it causes no remark, nor has it caused any for a hundred years."

Henry was aghast. "You're joking, of course."

"Certainly not. Think about it for a minute, Henry. You've been with me in the stockyards when cattle cars are unloaded. You know what seventy hours on a train packed as tightly as possible with cattle—eighteen or twenty in a thirty-foot car—means. It means the carcass of at least one or two gored and trampled bullocks in each car. Just last summer at the Morris and Essex depot, I opened one car whose extraordinary stench was the result of twenty-one sheep, twenty lambs and thirteen calves all lying dead. I have seen cattle, unwatered for fifty hours, literally mad with thirst, others covered with sores from disease and wounds from the Chicago loaders' spike-poles. And just prior to their arrival in New York the livestock is fed a heavily salted feed to make them drink an enormous amount of water and increase their weight. No matter that a steer thus fed may drink enough water to burst its stomach—or that an animal too tired to move will be 'revived' by an unloader breaking the joints in the animal's tail to make it 'frisky.'

"Now, compare that inhumane treatment with the care lavished on a beer horse or engine company horse. They are, of course, the fattest, sleekest creatures in the city—as well cared for as most human beings. So why not eat them? It is far more humane than mutilating and torturing these herds, and a good deal healthier for humans. I even once thought of giving a grand public dinner and serving a fine dish of horseflesh, cooked in every known manner, at a nominal price of six or ten cents."

"It sounds a bit extreme, Uncle. What about fish?"

Bergh snorted. "The Fulton Fish Market is no better than the cattle yards. Many of the fish are penned in the harbor alongside the market where two large sewers from Fulton and Beeckman streets discharge into it day and night. As if that weren't enough, the Union Ferry Company empties its WCs—enormously popular with the neighborhood vagrants—right there as well."

The long ride grew comfortable as the carriage reached the paved roads, and it was only when he felt his uncle shaking him awake that Henry realized he had fallen asleep. They were back in town. It was late into the afternoon and Henry was relieved at the thought that his Saturday duties were coming to an end. But his heart sank when he realized that they were already well south of the Society office and nearly to Houston Street.

"Where are we going?"

"To have a look at the carriages on the Third Avenue line. I want to see what young master Vanderbilt is putting on the streets today."

They could see the uptown horse trolley approaching Spring Street. Built to seat twenty-two, the cars normally carried twice that. But with the snow, the trolley literally overflowed with passengers, at least sixty by Henry's estimate and maybe more. Men were everywhere, seated in the windows, their legs dangling over the streets, up front with the driver, and hanging from the back. An additional fifteen men and boys were seated on the roof. Worse, Henry saw just two horses pulling this gargantuan load—a contravening of the Society's foul-weather guidelines.

Bergh, silk top hat in hand, was out of the carriage and into the street even before Childs had halted the teams. Henry trotted a few paces behind. He could tell from his uncle's determined stride that there would be a confrontation, and the boy found himself hanging back, watching to see what would happen. Planting himself in the middle of the avenue, Bergh put on his hat, tucked his cane under an arm, and drew himself up straight. When the trolley was within fifteen yards, Bergh raised an arm.

"Stop! Unload!"

"You must be a madman!" yelled the driver. "Get the hell out of my way, or I'll run you down!"

Bergh flipped the lapel of his coat just long enough to reveal the badge. "I said unload. Now climb down off there!"

"I'll climb down, all right." The driver applied the brake, reached for a thin birch whip, grabbed hold of a rail to his left, and slid smoothly down to the street. "Stop my coach, will you? We'll see about that!"

As the angry driver came toward Bergh, Henry saw Childs rush past and automatically fell in step with him. The driver, seeing Bergh reinforced, dropped his whip hand to his side.

"Unharness your team and hitch them to that lamppost," Bergh told the driver. "Henry—we're going to unload this trolley, so please go help the ladies off." Then Bergh turned to the crowd on the trolley and spoke loudly: "Ladies and gentleman, this car is overloaded and being taken out of service. I realize the weather is not good, and that—I'm afraid—is the point. The Third Avenue Company is bound by the animal cruelty laws of the state of New York to provide extra teams in such weather. To expect two horses to pull such a load through the snow is indecent. Now I realize this is an inconvenience, but I beseech you: If we are a civilized and Christian people, let us show it now and walk."

"What? Walk? The hell I will!" shouted a man seated near the front of the car, even as others around him were rising. "I've paid my fare and if I have to come out of here, you'll be goddamned sorry!"

"Some kind of big man you are!" replied a woman behind Henry. "Why, if you were any kind of man you wouldn't even be sitting leave alone complaining! I'd like to see *you* drag that carriage uptown, you big, stupid mule!" The crowd on the trolley roared in appreciation, and Henry turned around to see a pretty young woman in a long, luxurious fur overcoat standing on the sidewalk, a small dog in her arms. She smiled and nodded toward them, and Uncle removed his top hat and bowed in return. "Mr. Bergh isn't asking us for very much," she added. "Just a little decency."

Henry helped the women off the carriage while Bergh sent Childs down the avenue where the next trolley was just coming into view. Childs stopped the coach, pointing up the block at the empty trolley, and unhitched the team. A few moments later Childs continued downtown in anticipation of the next car.

"Henry! I've a job for you! It won't be long before the starters at the trolley garage hear about our little blockade and reroute their cars up Fourth Avenue. I want you to meet them at Grand Street as they come onto the Bowery and make them discharge. Here, take this." Bergh reached up under his lapel, unpinning the badge. "If you have any trouble, find a policeman and identify yourself as a Society agent."

Henry thrust the badge into his coat pocket, and the cold metal burned in his hand during the entire ten-minute run through the slush to Grand Street. Reaching the corner, he found it quiet and used the time to catch his breath, brush the caked ice from the hem of his overcoat, and pin the badge to the underside of his lapel. The evening sky was darkening, and it was snowing again. He pulled his collar up, stamped his feet to try to warm his toes, and stood as tall as he could. It felt like the trolley would never come, but at last Henry saw it turn up the block, two horses straining and slipping. He was surprised to discover that the closer it came, the more confident he felt. Indeed, he felt an odd serenity as he stepped alone into the dark street.

"Halt!" He flipped the lapel. "SPCA—unload!"

The driver, briefed on the detour at the start of the line, offered no resistance. Instead, he climbed down to help Henry unhitch the team. But when he saw how young he was and heard the catcalls from the frustrated riders, he couldn't resist giving him the needle. "You ain't much to be stopping traffic, are you, son?" he said. "Sure you're up to it?"

"Me, sir?" Henry smiled as he took the horses' reins and led them away from the trolley. "I'd say you're the one who's sunk. You've got to be careful in these winter storms. You never know when you're going to run into a Bergh."

The next morning was sunny and mild and Henry—who slept heavily and awoke happy—couldn't get dressed and out of the house fast enough. He had stopped three more trolleys before Childs finally came around with the carriage to tell him Vanderbilt had capitulated and added double teams to the Third Avenue cars. Uncle had stayed behind to make sure all of the halted trolleys returned to the barn without passengers, and Henry and Childs did the same at the Bowery before driving the carriage back uptown.

It was Sunday, the cook's day off, and he thought to go out and pick up fresh bread and cakes for his parents' breakfast. In truth, he couldn't wait to see the morning papers. Reaching the news hawker at Fourteenth Street, he wasn't disappointed. "A Triumph for Mr. Bergh," was the headline in the *Tribune*, while the *Mail* dubbed Uncle "The Good Genius of the Storm." Not surprisingly, the *Star* blasted him, their exaggerated story headlined "Bergh on a Bender—Five Thousand People Go Without Their Dinners to Oblige Him—Interference Unnecessary." But even that didn't bother him. Henry stood on the corner and read the accounts twice, particularly pleased to see his part mentioned in each, and wondering what his classmates would say on Monday. Then he folded them under his arm and headed uptown, intending to drop the badge off at Uncle's office.

But he was unable to control his feet: it was a day made for walking, and the sunshine felt glorious. The city was perfect—the streets clear enough for horse or pedestrian to traverse, yet the snow still fresh and white—and Henry felt an irresistible compulsion to nod and say hello to everyone he passed. He walked for well over an hour, not caring where, just so long as he was moving, moving, moving—moving and breathing deeply and feeling the blood in his veins. At length, however, thoughts of his parents and the rest of his day overtook him and he began a circuitous route back to the office. Passing a large group gathered near a corner, he gave it no thought at first; then he was seized by an odd sense of familiarity. Stepping back, Henry looked up to read the sign above the shop. A palpable buzz of outrage, like an electric shock, seized him when he realized what the crowd was gawking at. He was back at the cider mill.

Anger and indignation welling up in his neck and ears, Henry ran a hand through his hair, straightened his coat, and felt for the badge still pinned to the underside of his lapel. Plunging into the back of the crowd, he shoved his way forward. "Step aside, please," he said loudly, drawing surprised and angry looks as he roughly forced a path. "SPCA."

Henry saw Walker and his tray of samples in the doorway. The large stone grinder in the window still churned in its granite bowl, a thin brown stream of juice trickling steadily down the sluice. On the treadmill, harnessed in place of the dog, was the Negro boy.

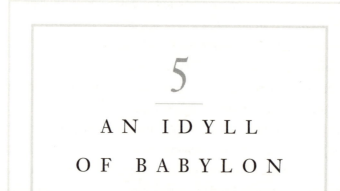

5

AN IDYLL
OF BABYLON

The window of his top-floor suite in his Manhattan Beach Hotel provided Austin Corbin with a commanding view of his Marine Railway as its tracks turned east through the farms and villages of the Brooklyn flatlands and then south across the Sheepshead Bay bridge. Corbin wasn't in the habit of idling or admiring his holdings, but he took a great deal of pride in his trains. He often popped up unannounced on the run from Greenpoint or Bay Ridge to keep the conductors on their toes and check receipts, or to make sure the coaches were clean or even just to berate some young loafer for propping a foot on his benches. The slobs! Why should a nickel fare entitle them to mistreat his property? Their own mothers would cuff their ears if they ever dared be so ill-mannered at home—at least he trusted they would! But no, there wasn't a whiff of nostalgia in Corbin's makeup, and it gave him scant satisfaction to simply sit and watch his trains come and go. He was, rather, the kind of man who took it as a matter of course that he would accomplish what he set out to and, once he had, couldn't be bothered to look back. The challenge was in the getting, the skill in the plotting. Nothing else was interesting.

He was surprised to discover he felt anxious. Entertaining presidents was old hat by now: Grant had dedicated the hotel five years earlier in 1877, Hayes the nearby newer Oriental just two years back. But nothing had been riding on those visits. He needed Chester Alan Arthur, although he doubted the president had any inkling that the trip involved more than the weekend of fishing he had been promised. Fishing—who could afford to waste such time? Not Corbin, but he was grateful for his own foresight in cultivating the president back when Arthur was a genial Republican Party hack and the collector of customs for the Port of New York. Of course, a man in that position was always useful in his own right, but Good Lord! Who would have ever imagined Arthur would wind up in the White House! Perhaps, Corbin thought, the newspapers are right and I really am lucky. No, that was wrong. He had planned carefully and done what was smart and that was enough to put him in the position to succeed now. Earlier this morning he had sent his private railcar to meet Arthur at the Brooklyn Ferry and was now scanning the tracks for the white-flagged engine announcing its return.

Corbin turned an appraising eye to the hotel's train station. The uniformed Manhattan Beach Hotel band stood at attention, and a growing crowd of hotel guests was gathering in anticipation of the president's arrival. Yes, it all looked right, as he at all times insisted it should. Staying on top of it all was a tremendous job—between the Oriental Hotel and the Manhattan Beach there were nearly seven hundred rooms—but keeping track of details was his strength. Like enormous wooden castles the hotels rose, their mansard roofs and ornamental towers facing out over the Atlantic: the last outpost of privilege between New York and London. The hotels boasted every conceivable luxury, from rosewood furniture to private dining rooms, with the Manhattan Beach Hotel alone employing over two hundred waiters. There was a mile-long bicycle track with seats for ten thousand, a zoo with elk from Corbin's own private herd, nightly concerts, and magnificent displays by the world-famous Pain's Fireworks; Corbin's personal favorites were the pyrotechnic tableaus that re-created historic events, and even he had gaped like a tourist at the spectacles of "Togo's Victory in the Sea of Japan" and "The Last Days of Pompeii."

It was still quiet at the beach this time of year—the season wouldn't begin in earnest for two more weeks and only a few of the five thousand benches and chairs on the lawns and verandah were occupied—but he was pleased to note nature's cooperation: there were already lilies in the koi ponds and the peonies were in bloom along the borders of the wooden walkways leading from the hotel across the deep green lawn of the broad esplanade and on to the beach. The sand, a soft fine white which Corbin had brought in from the east end of Long Island, was carefully raked and spotless. A lone Adirondack chair was planted in the sand, a fluttering bathrobe and thick Turkish towel laid over the chair back. It was only May—what kind of lunatic would wade let alone swim in a frigid ocean? He squinted out toward the water and spied what could either be a piece of driftwood or a lone head bobbing in the chopping surf a good hundred yards from shore. Corbin hoped it was the former: there was a strong undertow and he often worried about drownings and their impact on the hotel. He looked again, using a pair of powerful opera glasses he kept in the suite desk. He should have known. It was Conkling.

Roscoe Conkling wasn't Austin Corbin's kind of man and he had no idea what savvy men like Collis Huntington and Jay Gould saw in him. Impetuous, unpredictable, insufferably vain and given to fits of rage, he was a disaster in the offing, a bomb waiting to be triggered. Naturally, he was respectful and appropriate toward Corbin, but just look what he'd done to his own career! Until last year Conkling had been the senior U.S. Senator from New York—the undisputed boss of the state's massive Republican machine and probably the most powerful man in the Senate. Yet his pride had made a complete and utter botch of it and all had evaporated. How could someone so egregiously miscalculate their strengths and position? Imagine quitting a perch like that! And over what? Picking postmen and customs inspectors? Corbin shook his head. He certainly appreciated the importance of influence and territory, but he would never allow a prima donna like Conkling to be an officer in one of his companies, never. Yet Gould had sworn with great seriousness that Conkling was the best lawyer in New York and Corbin had hired him, hoping at least to build a back channel to Gould. But he still didn't like Conkling. Worse, he worried for the weekend's business: Conkling had made Arthur but Corbin suspected he no longer had his old protégé under his thumb. Why wasn't he in Washington, pulling the strings the way he did before resigning from the Senate? He looked once again through the opera glasses at the distant figure pounding steadily at the surging waves and sighed. He hated games with wild cards.

Corbin's fears disappeared when he spied the train turning the bend at Coney Island Avenue. He didn't bother with his private elevator and went quickly down the four flights of stairs. Surprisingly nimble for a big man of fifty-five, Corbin made a point of walking faster than any of his employees. He emerged onto the esplanade and signaled Sousa to begin playing "The Manhattan Beach Hotel March" just as the engine and its two cars pulled into the station.

Short as it was, it was a striking train. The president was riding in Corbin's new private car, which, to help promote the hotel, was also dubbed the "Manhattan." As lavish as its namesake, the platforms were girded with silver gates and railings and the coach's interior done in Mexican mahogany with brass trimmings, Wilton carpets, and Indian silk curtains; the washroom fixtures were silver plate. The second car, though also unique, was far less lavish. A twenty-year-old coach converted into a work car with the addition of a caboose cupola, it was generally used as a photographer's train, since the railroad was both the primary publisher of Long Island tour guides and its leading real estate agent. Where Corbin's car had deep plush parlor chairs, this one was divided in half, with the rear portion given to a darkroom and the fore a work area featuring tables and commuter benches. As the train pulled up to the hotel, several men came out onto the forward platform of the rear car, and one jumped down before it even came to a stop. Corbin guessed correctly that he was one of the U.S. marshals who always accompanied Arthur as a result of President Garfield's assassination, still so fresh in the country's mind. But, wondered Corbin with a wicked amusement, where was the danger? Arthur was no reformer. Indeed, it was inconceivable that any civil servant owing his job to the spoils system could view this president as anything short of a guardian angel—no matter how deranged. Aside from the marshal, Corbin recognized two of his own Pinkertons and assumed the rest were reporters. One seemed to be waving at him. Looking hard, Corbin recognized Stanley McKenna of the *Herald*. He didn't particularly like McKenna. It hardly mattered, though; Corbin was on close terms with James Gordon Bennett, the paper's publisher—he had just purchased Bennett's Fifth Avenue home. Moreover, the *Herald* had always turned a blind eye to the excesses of the Conkling machine. He barely gave a brief, wan wave back to McKenna and continued marching toward Arthur's car. McKenna wouldn't make any mischief. He couldn't.

The slight wasn't lost on McKenna. "That's it—don't pay me no mind," he muttered. "Ya big, bald idjit." But though the snub was real, his conviction was not: he knew Corbin to be anything but an idiot. Worse, McKenna was embarrassed to realize he was keeping his voice low to avoid being overheard by the Pinkertons. Still, when the band switched from "The Manhattan Beach Hotel March" to "My Country 'Tis of Thee" in preparation for the president's disembarkation, he couldn't help groaning loudly.

"What's the matter, McKenna? Not a patriot?" It was Swenson of the *Brooklyn Eagle*.

"You're asking the wrong man, Johnny—I didn't pick the tune and I'll wager a sack of your best Brooklyn potatoes that Sousa didn't, either. Why not 'The Battle Hymn of the Republic,' or even one of Sousa's own patriotic marches? You know why? Because it's really 'God Save the King'. That's who Corbin *wishes* he was hosting. He's a hopeless Anglophile, impressed by titles and snooty accents."

"You're grasping, McKenna."

"Am I? Corbin spends half his time in London sucking up to the bankers and the Duke of Argyll, and the papers over there say he's angling to be made an Honorary Knight Commander. Face it, Johnny— he's a snob. The swaggering King of Long Island would rather be a stable boy on bended knees at the court of St. James."

Swenson shrugged. "Who cares? Europe is done and we're just getting started. Besides, every industrialist with an ugly daughter dreams of marrying her off to some bankrupt aristocrat. I don't care about that stuff—I'm not covering the society beat, and thank God for that. Here's the man I'm after."

President Arthur, tall, thick, and as carefully groomed as a prize bull at a country fair, was being led from Corbin's coach. A crowd of several hundred guests from both the Manhattan and the Oriental had gathered behind the band in the mid-morning sun, and at first sight of the president the men began to cheer and the women applaud. Arthur grasped a gleaming silver rail with one hand and waved his hat with the other. McKenna, reading more than a hint of the dandy in the elegant trim of the president's mustache and muttonchops and the deep, rich velvet of his collar, scowled. "Now who in hell is interested in what Chet Arthur has to say?" he asked. "For God's sake man, he's the living proof that America is indeed the greatest country in the world: *anyone* can be president."

"For shame, Stanley—you don't sound very much like a *Herald* man. Why, he's one of our own, isn't he? Aren't you pleased to have a New Yorker in the White House? Don't you think your readers are flush with pride at having him home? Why, just look at this crowd!"

"You look at it! Nothing but fat leeches—and Arthur's just the kind of slow-swimming bottom-feeder they love to grab onto. It would be high comedy if it weren't so dreadful! An assassin's bullet turns a party hack barely suitable for a Brooklyn judgeship into the president. He has to be the luckiest man alive!" McKenna paused, then slyly added, "Provided you believe it was luck."

Swenson gave him a steady, disapproving gaze. "I had no idea they started drinking so early at the *Herald*." Swenson leaned closer. "Are you insane?" he hissed. McKenna scowled and watched Corbin bound up the steps of his coach and grasp Arthur firmly by the hand and shoulder. Big men, they looked for an instant as if they were about to wrestle.

"Mr. President!" Corbin said breathlessly. "I'm honored to welcome you to Manhattan Beach, honored! I hope you're hungry from your trip—we've prepared a little lunch. Nothing fancy, just something to break up the day and provide a chance for you to relax and freshen up before we continue on to Babylon. I trust your ride went well?"

"Never better, Austin!" Arthur grinned, flashing a mouthful of unusually large teeth, yellow as old piano keys. "And I can't tell you how jealous I am of your coach—it's a damn sight nicer than the White House, that's for certain. Now I'm obliged to ask Congress why the president of the Long Island Railroad has a finer railcar than the president of the United States. I daresay, Austin, it's damn unpatriotic of you!"

Arthur laughed heartily and everyone joined in. Corbin began to lead him down from the train platform, but Arthur hung back, looking over his shoulder. "Austin," he said, "have you met my boy, Chester Alan, Jr.?"

He was hardly a boy—in fact, he looked to be in his early twenties. Standing over six feet tall, he was as big as his father but a good deal slimmer. He was also quite good-looking. And whatever spark of vanity existed in the elder man's style had been fanned into a bonfire in the son, a flaming Beau Brummel. He wore hand-stitched Italian calf boots, a silk collar and cuffs, a rich maroon necktie, and a double-breasted cream-colored suit that Corbin recognized as the work of a Saville Row tailor whose exorbitant prices even he wouldn't pay. Young Arthur offered a limp hand to his host. "Hullo," he said.

"Hullo," McKenna mimicked flatly, just loud enough for Swenson to hear. He was pleased when the *Eagle* reporter snorted to cover a laugh.

The morning was going splendidly, Corbin thought, even better than he had planned, and the band struck up a march as he took the president by the elbow and set off across the lawn toward the hotel. It was quite a parade: close on their heels came Arthur's son, two marshals, two Pinkertons, a White House secretary, two presidential valets, five reporters and the railroad's photographer, with Sousa's band and the hotel guests trailing along behind the president's entourage.

"Look at that surf!" Arthur cried as they crossed the esplanade. "I can't believe I let you talk me into trout fishing when the ocean is at your front door! We used to love boating on the Sound—Junior is a born yachtsman—or even just roughing it and fishing from the beach. There's really nothing quite so engrossing as surf fishing, you know. Best way for a man to lose himself."

"Have you ever been out to Montauk?" Corbin asked.

"I only took a thirty-five-pound striped bass there! Now there's a fisherman's paradise! Arthur Benson used to give me the loan of his cottage back in the old customs house days."

"Really?" In fact, Corbin already knew about Arthur's Montauk trips and was steering the conversation. Benson, the owner of the Brooklyn gas company as well as great chunks of Brooklyn and Long Island real estate, was one of Corbin's partners. "Arthur has just agreed to sell the railroad a right-of-way for a line out to Montauk."

"Oh, that will be splendid! Do you know where I'm going next month? Restigouche. I'm a member," he added proudly. The fishing lodge, built and owned by a group of America's wealthiest industrialists, was located on the river between Quebec and New Brunswick and was the most exclusive anglers' club in the world. Corbin had once tried unsuccessfully to wrangle an invitation when the Prince of Wales was to be a club guest. "Of course, the salmon fishing is spectacular and the company first-rate. But even with the private train line it's a hell of a trip. Can't possibly find the time more than once a year. Now if I could get out to Montauk on a whim—what a treat that would be! How long do you reckon a trip out there by train will take?"

Corbin laughed. "Mr. President, we haven't even finished surveying the route yet!"

"Well, just suppose it's straight with nothing irregular or unusual. There's no place flatter than Long Island and I can't imagine there's anything out there you'll have to knock down. Come on, guess."

Corbin was delighted at how animated Arthur was by the subject. "Well, I'm not an engineer, Mr. President, but if we employed one of our faster engines—say that Rogers Locomotive that brought you to the hotel—I'd wager the trip from Greenpoint to Montauk could be made in under two and a half hours."

"No!"

"I admit it's purely conjecture, but you'd be surprised how fast we can run our engines."

"You must show me!"

Corbin laughed. Things were going well. Very well.

Then they saw Conkling.

Dressed in swimsuit and robe, he was stamping up the wooden walkway from the beach, obviously intent on intercepting them before they reached the hotel verandah. Up close, the unclinched robe proved a rich blue silk; it hung on Conkling's muscular shoulders and fluttered angrily behind him as he came, twisting haplessly like a set of broken wings. The suit was still wet and it clung to Conkling's thick torso and oversized thighs. Although the boardwalk was rough and covered with long splinters, he was barefoot and, judging by his pace, unfazed. Arthur stopped the second he recognized Conkling, bringing the entire parade to a halt. It was an incongruous sight: the presidential entourage, the uniformed band, and the richly dressed hotel guests, all waiting on the esplanade for one half-dressed man. Corbin cast a quick glance at the president but couldn't read his expression.

"President Chet!" Somehow Conkling's raspy voice made the glib greeting sound even more offensive than it was. Yet Corbin could read no indication of its true intention in those dark eyes. Drops of seawater were still collecting and trickling through the kinks of Conkling's hair, catching in the rakish forehead curl that was his trademark, clinging to the pointed gray beard. He looked like Poseidon crossed with Pluto.

"Roscoe." It was exhaled more than spoken, and the one word carried as much meaning as a finely wrought speech. McKenna, standing just a few feet away, was reminded of certain very old couples he'd known, couples who'd lived their entire lives together—not always happily and not always productively—but always seeming nonetheless to die within a month of each other. When the two men shook hands, McKenna watched closely, noting the way the president grasped Conkling's bicep in his left hand and gave it a squeeze, and the way the senator's free arm hung iron-stiff at his side, his hand clenched in a fist. It was a bizarre tableau: the president and his entourage paying fealty to the muscular, nearly naked creature from the sea. He saw both men smile and look hard into the other's eyes for a long minute, measuring—measuring what? he wondered. He wasn't surprised when Arthur proved the first to look away, offering a sheepish smile to Corbin. But McKenna was surprised to discover that it mattered to him, that he was disappointed it wasn't Conkling who blinked.

McKenna had been around Republican politics long enough to remember Arthur back in the early days when he was an earnest attorney in sympathy with the radical antislavery Republicans and not just a creature of the party. He'd liked him then. He seemed, if nothing else, competent and decent, characteristics in short supply around the New York party. But he'd never really known what to make of his extraordinary later success. Did Arthur lose his way or find it when he'd met Conkling? That was the question. And there was no doubt Conkling had made him: Grant would have consulted no one else before selecting a collector of customs. Arthur had proven the most faithful of stalwarts, vetting every appointment down to the lowest customs clerk through the senator's office, making sure they were filled by men who could be counted on to do Conkling and the party's bidding. But could he ever have envisioned his own rise? McKenna didn't think so; he doubted Arthur had either the imagination or the hubris. His selection by Garfield as vice president—the first and only elected office Arthur ever stood for—had been intended to heal a rift with the New York faction and was a complete surprise to everyone at the convention, including Arthur and the man it was meant to mollify, Conkling. But could it be true what they said? That Conkling, who seemed ever to prefer cultivating enemies to friends and was not beyond placing his

vendettas ahead of the party, had urged his protégé to refuse the proffered prize and see their own party defeated? Perhaps only a man of
Roscoe Conkling's pride and ambition could refuse to answer the door
when opportunity knocked, preferring to wait for the more satisfying
moment when he could wrest his prize from fortune's bloodied hands.
Certainly Chester Alan Arthur—whom they had called the "Gentleman Boss" back in his custom-house days—was not that kind of
a man.

"You're looking wonderful as always, Roscoe. Is this your secret, cold
dips in the sea?"

"I have no secrets, Chet. You know that."

"Ah, yes, I'd forgotten." Arthur gave a tired smile. "I'm glad you're
joining us this weekend."

"If that's all right with you, Mr. President."

"I wouldn't hear of anything else. You haven't by any chance taken up
fishing, have you, Roscoe?"

Conkling scrunched his brow into a sour face, the movement forcing
another drop of water to run from his curl. "I don't have that kind of free
time."

"No? I should think you'd have nothing but free time."

The testy exchange sent a paroxysm of panic through Corbin.
"Gentlemen! Let's get out of the sun and into lunch! Mr. President,
everyone is waiting to meet you. I'm sure the senator will rejoin us as
soon as he is dressed."

Arthur nodded. "All right. Roscoe, we'll hold a seat for you."

This remark more than anything else seemed to discomfit Conkling,
but only momentarily, and McKenna had to wonder if he was surprised
by the kindness in Arthur's voice or the notion that he could possibly be
sitting anywhere but the president's table. Conkling gave a curt wave
and split off from Arthur and Corbin as they reached the mob on the
verandah, heading briskly for the hotel lobby and the stairs toward his
suite. McKenna followed. "Senator!" he called. Conkling didn't turn
around. "Senator!" Still no response, and the reporter broke into a trot
across the red floral carpet, only barely reaching Conkling before he
started up the stairs. "Lord Roscoe!"

"McKenna, even a dog can sense when it's not wanted."

"Yes, but a dog isn't paid to take your kicks. Is this the first time you've seen the president since he took office?"

"What's this about, McKenna? Shouldn't you be keeping your eyes on the president? You never know when something is going to happen. I even heard a rumor that the last one was shot."

"I trust you know a great deal more about that than I do." McKenna couldn't believe he'd said it. Conkling's face turned bright red, and for an instant McKenna feared for his safety. As much as he loved controversy and snubbed his nose at conventions, Conkling could not tolerate being maligned, especially in print. McKenna recalled a Washington newspaperman once preparing a story on an alleged affair between Conkling and the wife of a congressional colleague. Conkling had visited the editor, demanding to see the story before it ran. He sat down at the editor's desk and read the piece through without comment, pronouncing it in the end to be factually accurate. He then looked the editor in the eye and solemnly pledged to kill him when it ran. Which, of course, it never did.

"Although I've seen the president several times since he took office, I don't speak much anymore to His Accidency. And I certainly don't advise him."

"What do you think of his presidency thus far?"

"That's why you're making me stand in this frigid lobby in a wet bathing suit? Fine, McKenna—here's a quote for you: I have but one annoyance with the administration of President Arthur, and that is, that, in contrast with it, the administration of Hayes becomes respectable, if not heroic."

It was a bombshell quote. Conkling hated Hayes. They had fought throughout his entire term over civil service reform—Hayes had even managed to oust Arthur as customs collector.

"Why are you telling me this?"

"Write it down. Go ahead," Conkling laughed. "You and I both know we will never read that statement in the *Herald*."

He was right. Bennett would fire any editor who let it through. For the first time McKenna realized why the *Times* and *Tribune* didn't have reporters on the train and the *World*—owned by Jay Gould and represented by Conkling—had two. He was here because they knew the *Herald* wouldn't play tough. They were laughing at him, at the way he imagined himself uncovering and writing something he wasn't supposed to know about or say.

"Why don't you go get something to eat and let me change?"

"Lunch is closed to the press."

"I'm sure Austin is going to treat you jackals better than you deserve and set you up in another dining room." Conkling grinned—malicious yet playful. "He doesn't know dogs prefer table scraps." It was true enough, and even McKenna had to chuckle. "Go on," he said, starting up the stairs. "If you're a good boy, I'll pass along anything interesting I hear. Although that seems extremely unlikely with this crowd."

Corbin was relieved to discover that Arthur, despite a distaste for the ceremonial, greeted all the guests waiting in the private second-floor dining room with great warmth and even good humor. It was apparent that he already knew or had met many of them before and, despite having spent almost no time on the stump, moved with the air and confidence of a seasoned politician. Indeed, he had an ingenious way of positioning himself on the receiving line which assured he would be looking at the next person as soon as he let go of someone's hand, a tactic that made monopolizing the president impossible. For his part, Corbin did his best to keep everyone moving. But as the president neared the end of the receiving line, he suddenly bellowed impatiently.

"Mr. Corbin! There are limits to my civility!" Corbin could feel the blood draining from his face as all eyes turned his direction. "I'm a realist, sir, and I've had to do some distasteful things in my career but this is too much! Do you actually expect me to shake hands and dine with so odious a creature as this? Why, this man is—is—why, he is a *Democrat*!" Arthur was standing whisker to whisker with August Belmont, the city's leading sportsman. Both men, ramrod straight, stared evenly into each other's eyes. The waiters ceased filling water glasses; the ruffling of dresses hushed. And then the men broke into simultaneous grins and shook heartily.

"Are the racetracks open already, August?"

"They're open when I say they're open—you know that, Chet! Much like you and the treasury!"

"The post office—I keep telling you, the real money is in the postal service. You see, you make the case against yourself with such ignorant prattle, and this is why the public won't put a Democrat in the White House. It would be a complete waste," he said, adding in a hushed but devilish tone: "Like a eunuch in a brothel."

The chamber orchestra was taking its place on the podium, tuning up for lunch, and the noise level had once again risen high enough to allow Arthur to lean in toward Belmont for a private word. "I wonder if you could do me a real favor," he said hopefully, placing a hand on Belmont's shoulder and turning him toward a corner. "I've got Junior with me and I think you know how mad he is for racehorses." In fact, the president's son was a regular around Saratoga; Belmont knew the boy, who had a reputation as a soft mark. "Not that I've ever encouraged him at it— quite the contrary. But he's reached the age where it doesn't matter what I think or say, and it's a dead certainty whatever money I send his way now and in the future will end up financing this passion. I can't do much to guide him, August; the only thing I know about racing is that you own the finest stable in New York."

"No, Mr. President. I own the finest stable in the country."

"Just so. I mean no offense, but you can tell it's not my world. I know I'm asking a great deal, but could you ever see your way to taking him under your wing and helping him get set up? Teach him—at the very least—how his passion can pay for itself instead of wasting whatever I can leave him. Help him to hire the right people. I think you'll find him an attentive student when the subjects are horses and money. Of course, I'd expect no favors—I insist you take a profit. But I'd be in your debt. And very grateful."

Belmont could hardly believe his good fortune. Arthur might be a weak president, but he was the president nonetheless. "I can't think of a thing in this world that would please me more, Chet."

"Thank you. I have every faith that this is the start of many good things." He clapped Belmont on the back. "Come. Before they find more guests for me to meet, I want to see what our host has for lunch. And up his sleeve."

The dining room was arranged with the president's table in the center. Corbin had planned to seat his wife and daughters with Arthur and his son but now saw no tactful way to separate Belmont from the president, especially when they were joined by Belmont's good friend, Leonard Jerome. Although they didn't generally socialize, Corbin had grudgingly discovered that he liked Jerome, a surprise considering how different they were. Corbin was first and at all moments a banker, and he owed his success to careful planning, to an almost superhuman ability to keep track of a myriad of minute details. Jerome was a reckless gambler. He had made and lost fortunes as a stock speculator and thoroughly enjoyed his reputation as a daredevil. No one could ever tell if Jerome was up or down, or how much he was dependent upon the help of his good friend Belmont at any particular moment. But most surprising was the family's social success. His freewheeling style did not impress Mrs. Astor and they had been largely shunned by New York's Four Hundred. Yet his daughters had married extremely well in England, earning Corbin's envy. Jerome's eldest daughter, Jennie, said to have been named for Jerome's former mistress, the singer Jenny Lind, had married Lord Randolph Churchill, the son of the seventh Duke of Marlborough. Corbin's own daughters could do with a little of the Jerome girls' luck, and he was loath to do anything to alienate Jerome lest he someday provide a valuable overseas introduction. The president's table was rounded out by Nannette Cassatt, the pretty daughter of one of Corbin's partners; young Chet had only been introduced to her, but seemed intent on keeping her by his side. Oh, his daughters would *hate* him.

Whether by design or natural inclination, Belmont and Jerome immediately began describing their new track, the Coney Island Jockey Club. "Are you going to be joining us this summer?" Jerome asked the president's son.

"I—I just don't know." He was embarrassed to appear so unambitious, and smiled sheepishly at Miss Cassatt, blushing up to his ears.

"Well, I know you're a serious horseman and you must come here and join our club," said Belmont. "We race from now until it's time for Saratoga, and New York is the best place to learn the business. Have you started assembling a stable?"

Chet Jr. sat up taller. "Only just. But I think I've gotten my mistakes out of the way."

Corbin laughed. "Son, anyone who says he's finished making mistakes isn't worth being in business with." Belmont and Jerome nodded appreciatively, the president watching the proceedings closely but without comment. "The idea isn't to avoid mistakes at all costs—just to learn from them."

"If you're up here this summer, Leonard and I would be only too glad to help you," said Belmont. "The Coney Island Club is a new club—it should have some new blood." He paused, looked quickly at Nannette, and smiled at Chet. "And I trust you'll find the evenings in New York far more entertaining than those in Washington."

"Oh, there's no arguing with that," said the president and everyone laughed. The waiters had distributed bowls of terrapin in consommé, and Arthur leaned over the bowl, inhaling appreciatively. He noticed the heavy china was decorated with both the presidential seal and a painting of the Manhattan Beach and Oriental hotels. "Austin, I hope this wasn't minted solely for today's lunch?"

"Sorry, no. But it's only been used once before, when Hayes dedicated the Oriental."

Arthur smiled broadly. "Well there's an irony for you! That man lived in mortal fear that Roscoe and I were going to eat off his plate, and for all we know that's exactly what I'm doing!" The men laughed loudly.

The banter carried them through a rich lobster Newburg, Belmont dominating the table with the retelling of how the dish had been created at Delmonico's at the behest of a regular, Benjamin Wenburg, and renamed when Wenburg was banned from the restaurant for brawling in the bar. Belmont himself had been particularly close to Lorenzo

Delmonico and a much-treasured patron—not surprising since he was reputed to have spent upwards of twenty thousand dollars a month there on wine alone. Corbin was also a regular, but he usually dined downtown at the Citadel, the Delmonico branch favored by bankers and railroad men, while Belmont took most of his meals uptown at the Madison Square restaurant. "I have to say, Austin, were Lorenzo still alive, even he'd admit you've got one of the best kitchens in the country. I dread the weight you'll put on me this summer! I can't imagine anyone being able to resist such excellent fare."

"Really?" said Arthur. "Well, you're about to dine with him." Conkling was standing in the dining-room doorway, surveying the room. As soon as he saw their table, he strode quickly over. "Good lord, Roscoe!" said the president. "Where did you get that outfit?"

More than a dandy, Conkling had been a peacock among pigeons in the Senate, where his love of eccentric and colorful clothes was discussed nearly as much as his legendary romantic dalliances and the ever-churning wake of carnage produced by his brutal political tactics. But he had outdone himself this time: Conkling was wearing mint-green trousers under a black cutaway coat, with a paired purple velvet tie and waistcoat set. His sandy-blond hair was carefully arranged so that his famous curl sat in the middle of his forehead. He gave no reply to Arthur save a grunt and a tight smile, seating himself in the empty chair between Jerome and the suddenly blushing Miss Cassatt. Everyone at the table was aware that there had been a time, and not so long ago, when Arthur never would have presumed to speak in such mocking tones to Conkling. Or at least that was what Conkling assumed they were thinking. "I trust I haven't missed anything," he said, looking from face to face without a trace of humor.

"Horses," Arthur said derisively, glad of the chance to mask his hand in his son's sudden good fortune. He gave Conkling a warm smile. "Roscoe, it was a complete surprise to run into you on the beach. It's wonderful to see you. Are you vacationing at the hotel?"

"Vacationing?" Conkling looked at Corbin, who had turned a deep red. *The idiot! He didn't tell him?* "I'm the attorney for the railroads, for the Manhattan Beach and the Long Island."

"Ah," said Arthur, beginning to discern the true contours of his weekend. "Austin, you've got a hell of an attorney and the toughest man in the country. If I'd been aware that Roscoe was joining us, I'd have left Washington a good deal sooner. It's awfully dull there without him, you know."

Corbin, seeing Arthur glad of having Conkling on hand, knew he had committed an uncharacteristic mistake. He had assumed Arthur and Conkling were in constant contact if not outright cahoots—that everything he said to Conkling made its way to Arthur—and he had assumed too much. Whatever had happened between Arthur and Conkling, Corbin saw it was time to stop speculating, to be himself and take the lead. As the waiters lay plates of Arthur's favorite dish, mutton chops, in front of each diner—Conkling waved his away, asking instead for a plate of boiled fish and raw vegetables—Corbin saw his opening. "Mr. President, you'll have to tell me what you think of these chops," he said. "They are from one of our farms."

"Your farm? It's wonderful. And the potatoes Delmonico as well."

"Not my farm personally, but yes, land just east of here that the railroad owns and leases. We've been doing quite a nice business. The land is excellent for crops as well as grazing, and the plan is to expand the program as the railroad moves east. We've hired an agriculturist from Cornell to run tests out on the east end where it's very sandy, to see what might grow. Of course, there's already a good deal of grazing out there. In most of the towns everyone just turns their livestock and horses loose to roam the land for the summer—I saw sheep grazing out on the Heather Hills just last week—and they're simply rounded up at the end of the season." He made a sour face. "Picturesque, but not very efficient."

"Is that your plan for Long Island? To sell and lease farms all the way to the tip?" Jerome asked.

"We're not turning all of it into farms, no. We're going to keep building luxury hotels on the south shore, and further out we're starting to build beachfront bungalows near Shinnecock. Only about eight or ten of them right now."

"When you say 'bungalows,'" said Arthur, "I take it to mean the kind of vacation home Arthur Benson erected at Montauk?"

"Precisely. That's special country. We're going to be very careful about keeping it that way. And just as you were speaking earlier about the difficulty of reaching Restigouche, I know that once it becomes widely known how efficient the railroad is, families won't want to travel all the way to the Adirondacks when they have Long Island so much nearer at hand."

Belmont shook his head. "Give up the Adirondacks? I can't imagine it. And as much as I love the shore, I'll never give up Saratoga."

"Agreed. Believe me, August, I have an estate up in New Hampshire that I wouldn't surrender for the world. But it's just a matter of time before the railroad brings people out to Long Island and they discover how unique it is. I think it can one day rival Newport."

The absurd claim produced an embarrassed silence. Arthur, teasing the last bits of meat from the chops, assiduously kept his eyes on the plate while conjuring a picture of Mrs. Vanderbilt selling her Newport estate in order to spend the summers in a Sag Harbor fishing shack. Well, he had no doubt James Renwick could design a very *nice* fishing shack, and that made him chuckle. Arthur's reaction was not unnoticed by Corbin, and it made the railroad man angry. "Tell me, Mr. President," he said when a few moments had elapsed and the waiters were clearing the dinner plates and replacing them with servings of Victoria pudding and truffle ice cream and glasses of champagne, "what do you think of my hotel?"

"Oh, you know it's quite magnificent, Austin. Really incomparable."

"Thank you. The secret is to set a standard suitable to the top clientele, and I take it as a supreme compliment that our guests have no idea the number of people required to provide services and maintain standards. It's over one thousand. For security alone we have forty men in uniform and several dozen Pinkertons in plainclothes. That's essential, of course, otherwise we'd be inundated with Coney Island's usual assortment of hustlers, pickpockets, cardsharps and thieves. Ten years ago, when I first came to Coney Island with my wife and children, the east end was a desert waste and the west end a human waste. There was only one decent hotel. But I was astounded by the beach and the fact that it

is just an hour from Manhattan. You know, New York is quite unique this
way among the great cities of the world: they have no such access to the
sea in either London or Paris. That started me thinking about what this
area could be with a hotel for the best crowd. So one day I went explor-
ing out on the wilds of the east end. It was called Sedge Bank then and I
can assure you, you would not recognize it. The land we are currently
seated upon was a tidal swamp and I remember having to take off my
boots and stockings to wade through a creek. But beyond the creek I discovered miles of sand and dunes and I could picture what it should be. It
took about two years, but I bought all of the property east of Coney
Island—about six hundred acres. No one else wanted it." That was only
partially true. With the help of the Gravesend town surveyor, Corbin
had tracked down the owners and purchased about two hundred acres
outright; he had acquired the rest by bribing the town supervisor into
ramming through a voice vote on transferring all of the town's common
holdings to a Corbin-controlled corporation for virtually nothing. The
night the unscheduled vote was taken, Corbin packed the town meeting
with two hundred goons—each of whom voted "yea" in consideration of
five dollars and round-trip train fare. All told, Corbin had spent about
fifteen thousand dollars to acquire a two-and-a-half-mile-long oceanfront property in the shadow of the country's greatest city. "Of course,
they all said I was mad to propose a luxury hotel on a godforsaken spit
of swamp." Arthur squirmed, and a satisfied Corbin gave the president
his best smile. "How's the pudding?"

"Marvelous. I never would have imagined it such a natural pairing
with this ice cream."

"Funny, isn't it? Some things just go together yet you never think of
it until they're on the same plate. It's been that way with me and the railroads, you know. I got into that quite by accident. As a banker I understood the value of the land the minute I climbed back out of that creek
and saw the beaches, and of course my own privations in Coney Island
that summer convinced me of the need for a first-rate hotel." He knitted
his brow momentarily. "But it wasn't until later, when things had already
begun to take shape, that I saw the hotel required its own rail station.

When the existing lines weren't interested, I was forced to take matters into my own hands. It turns out to be a good business, or should be if you know what you're doing. Fortunately, most don't."

"You're talking about the different Long Island rail companies," said Conkling.

"Yes. Although the population of the island has steadily increased, the roads were in financial ruin when I bought them two years ago. Part of the reason was that they hadn't always built the right branches and that was an invitation to rivals. The hardest part was making the deals for those lines at prices that made sense. But of course, when you're offering cash to people who are broke, it's really not *that* difficult to get a good deal." He smiled smugly. "This year the Long Island Railroad will make five hundred thousand dollars."

As the railroad's attorney, Conkling knew the financial turnaround was real and that Corbin's figure was only slightly exaggerated. But the others were clearly impressed, and none more than Arthur.

"Of course, we're only just getting started," said Corbin. "Now it's time to put the pudding with the ice cream. Last fall I went to England and raised $5 million for a new syndicate, the Long Island Improvement Company, in order to purchase land and develop resorts, hotels, cottages, farms, and even villages. I purchased Blythebourne, my estate in Babylon, with an eye toward building another hotel. And if everyone is finished with lunch, I'd like to get out there and show it to you."

Arthur quickly poured himself the last of the champagne, which he'd been eyeing. He was pleased when Belmont offered to bring Chet Jr. out later in his own private railcar following the afternoon races—Belmont owned the horse farm adjoining Corbin's Babylon estate—and was delighted to see how confident the boy looked squiring Miss Cassatt. Conkling, watching the party break in two, nodded politely to Jerome and Belmont, and then took Miss Cassatt's hand to his lips and affected an exaggerated bow. It wasn't so much the bow which caused her to blush a deep red as his intense and meaningful look.

Outside on the hotel verandah, Corbin's wife and daughters were waiting, and he immediately steered the president toward them. He knew he had to make it up after shunting them aside at lunch, and was grateful to have the opportunity presented by the ride out to Babylon. But before he could make a proper introduction, he felt a firm hand at his elbow.

"Mr. Corbin, do you think we might get a moment with the president?" It was McKenna.

"Oh, there'll be plenty of time for that when we get to Babylon."

"Well, sir, I do have an evening deadline that I won't make unless I can wire my story from the hotel station before we leave."

"Not true, McKenna. I've installed a telephone at Blythebourne and we can connect to the line in Mr. Bennett's office. I'm sure they'll find someone to take down your copy." McKenna had never phoned a story and the idea excited him. Still, he wasn't happy about being kept at arm's distance.

"What are you doing this weekend, Mr. President?" he asked.

Arthur smiled benignly. "After that lunch, my only plans are to nap."

"It's purely a social weekend," Corbin interjected. "The president is here to relax, to enjoy his home state. There's nothing nefarious afoot, McKenna. What is it that makes a newspaperman so untrusting? Do you know what you remind me of? When my girls were little, they were briefly captivated by ridiculous stories in magazines involving mediums. Whenever the girls found something on the street—a key, an old button, a ratty windblown scarf—they'd take it home, douse the lights and conduct a séance to contact the owner. Of course, the button always came from the coat of an industrialist abducted by anarchists, the scarf had been ripped from the throat of a girl forced into servitude and shame by the financial misfortunes of her family, and the key to a young man who'd been brutally murdered. Funny how the key never belonged to a careless or drunken porter. And so it is with you gentlemen. You'd always rather dream up some romance than accept the obvious. You're like a pack of little girls."

"*Daddy!*" The story had been his daughters' final mortification.

Corbin gave a sigh of exasperation. "McKenna, please. If I don't introduce my wife and daughters to President Arthur this instant, I won't have a home to go to."

Corbin turned the party back across the lawns for the train. Arthur proved a good sport, teasing the girls that they must be bored with meeting so many presidents. Relieved, Corbin actually smiled at McKenna. "See? The president is here to fish and relax, nothing more. He wanted to see the hotels, and who doesn't?"

"Well, I understand that not everyone can." It was something McKenna had been hoping to raise with Corbin. "I hear you've revived the distinction of past Saratoga seasons regarding Jews."

"It's a question that has to be handled with gloves. Personally, I am opposed to Jews and it stands this way: we must have a good place for society to patronize. We cannot do so and have Jews. They are a detestable and vulgar people." McKenna was taking notes as they walked. "Granted, there are some well-behaved people among them, but as a rule they make themselves offensive to the kind of people who principally patronize our road and hotel, and I am satisfied we should be better off without them than with their custom."

"But how can any call himself cultured or democratic and discriminate against a particular religious group?"

"It is not the Jewish religion I object to, it is the offensiveness which they possess as a sect or nationality. The Jews simply have no place in first-class society. They are a pretentious class who expect three times as much for their money as other people. Worse, they are driving away the class of people who are beginning to make Coney Island the most fashionable and magnificent watering place in the world. We simply cannot bring the highest social element to Manhattan Beach if the Jews persist in coming. They won't associate with Jews and that's all there is about it."

"So this is what your clients insist upon? And what of your own experiences? Do you speak for your class or yourself?"

"Personally, I never knew but one 'white' Jew in my life. The rest I found were not safe people to deal with in business. They are contemptible as a class. But please heed my distinction: I would not oppose any man because of his creed."

They had arrived at the train and McKenna noticed that the rest of the party was listening. "Mr. President, what do you think of Mr. Corbin's policy?"

Arthur shrugged casually. "We'd all object to any policy or persons preventing the Hebrews, or any one else for that matter, from practicing their religion. Certainly that freedom is one of the greatest features of our democracy. As is the freedom of association. But it's a moot point in polite society since no man with a shred of self-respect insinuates himself where he is unwelcome, does he?"

McKenna, suspecting this last remark was doing double duty as a barb, felt the heat of debasement rising in his neck as Arthur and the Corbins boarded the front car. "Pretty weak beer, McKenna." It was Conkling. He strutted up the platform stairs behind the others, then turned and leaned over the silver rail. "A weekend with the president of the United States and the best you can come up with is a sob story about a Brooklyn hotel that won't cater to Jews? God, were you ever any good? You couldn't find lice in a Coney Island whorehouse."

"So what are we doing here?"

"Fishing."

"Yes, I know," he said without enthusiasm. "The president is going fishing."

"Who said anything about the president?" Conkling winked quickly and vanished into Corbin's private car.

Fifteen minutes later the train was heading for Babylon. McKenna sat on a bench in the photography coach looking out at the passing farms of East Jamaica and trying to figure out what Conkling was pointing him toward. Whatever it was, he was positive Corbin would not want it in the newspapers. So if Conkling was Corbin's lawyer, what sort of mischief was he up to?

Thirty feet to McKenna's east, Conkling sat in a plush armchair, smiling benignly at the vapid chitchat between Arthur and the Corbin girls and asking himself the same question. Alerting McKenna was a stupid thing to do. When was he going to learn to control himself? He knew he never would. It was the secret of both his success and his failure, the precise reason he had been able to rally his colleagues in the Senate and why they had so eagerly licked his boots even when it was plain he had nothing to give them. It wasn't his intelligence but his recklessness, his bottomless anger, which gave the deadly edge to his personality and made him a man to be feared. A runaway train, Kate had called him during one of their spectacular fights, meaning it as an insult. But she could never fool him: his unfailing ability to overwhelm was what she craved. It pleased him endlessly that the most impressive woman in Washington was his mistress—Kate Chase Sprague's husband was the senior senator from Rhode Island, and her father had been the chief justice of the U.S. Supreme Court—and her intelligence, savvy, and extraordinary beauty were unmatched in the capital. He loved her for those reasons, too, but there was another: they both knew his power had seduced her and that his reflection in her eyes completed passion's circuit.

Conkling gave an unseeing glance at the window. There wasn't much out there that interested him. Farms, salt marshes, small villages, unbroken patches of scrub pine and oak, all went rolling slowly, far too slowly, by the window. Yes, he'd pick a runaway train over this one any day.

Corbin, however, was relishing the ride, pointing out some of the railroad's land holdings to Arthur. Through a web of partnerships, Corbin and the railroad had acquired much of Long Island's south shore, and he singled out a few of the more picturesque bays and bluffs and described what would be there in five years' time. The entire rail line, too, hummed and shook with activity. There were uniformed flagmen at every grade-crossing to prevent collisions with wagons and livestock, and each to a man removed his cap at the sight of the flags flying from Corbin's private coach.

"I can see that his men have great respect for your father," Arthur said to the girls.

"I'm tough but just," Corbin said matter-of-factly. "I insist every man in my employ adhere to the strictest moral tone. That means avoiding both liquor and tobacco. We employ the Pinkertons as spotters, they check all the saloons near the rail stations to see that no man is drinking before or after a shift."

Back in the photo car, the obligatory tip of the cap greeting the train at each crossing had not gone unnoticed. "Pretty impressive," said Swenson, nodding his head toward the window as he dealt a hand of poker to McKenna and two other reporters.

"Oh, yeah," said McKenna. "I'm surprised Corbin didn't have to station a Pinkerton behind each flagman to knock his hat off." At this, one of the two Pinkertons playing cards with the U.S. marshals at the other table gave him a hard look and appeared to be on the verge of getting up and coming over.

"Are you insane?" Swenson hissed. "I'd like to walk off the train at Babylon!"

McKenna returned the Pinkerton's stare. "I'm sure Corbin would be delighted to hear his goons beat up a carload of reporters. We're guests, not employees."

"Still, there's no need to make trouble," said one of the writers for the *World*.

"Who's making trouble?" McKenna took out his tobacco and began to roll a cigarette.

"This is a photo car," said the Pinkerton. "You can't smoke in here with all these chemicals."

"Oh, leave it alone," one of the marshals replied. "No one is making pictures. Besides, I could use a smoke myself." He stood up and walked to the door near the platform, lit a cigar and tossed his match out the door. "Hey, what's that?" He pointed to a half-dozen old wheelless box-cars placed around a side spur. Several of the car doors were open and a mother with young children could be seen in one, an old Negro man in another. Smoke from a stovepipe drifted from a third.

"Corbin Heights," McKenna said.

"How's that?"

"They're the homes of railroad day laborers, if you can call them homes. Gandy dancers. Track layers, grade builders, road clearers. Mostly Italians and niggers, although the niggers don't take to it too much. I hear the railroad uses a lot of Indians out on the east end. Sometimes there are forty of them living in a car, their wives sharing one stove."

"And a goddamn lot of trouble they are," said the other Pinkerton. "Fighting. Stealing crops and fowl from farms. Two Guineas from the sand train were shot dead last week cutting timber on private property."

"What the hell were they stealing timber for?" asked the marshal.

"Ah, they're always trying to build their own shacks, especially the married ones. They think they can take what they want and do what they want whenever they want instead of saving up an honest wage. I don't know too much about Italy, but it must be a hell of a place."

"An honest wage?" McKenna asked. "The railroad pays those men a dollar a day. They don't pay the flagmen or the ticket agents much more, but at least they're not tied to the railroad at the end of the day. Usually these shacks and boxcars are far from towns, out where the railroad is extending new track, and the only provisions they can get their hands on come from a shanty store. The selection is small and the prices triple what they'd pay in town. Worse, it's all done on credit and the railroad paymaster settles the accounts before paying the men. Which makes you wonder who owns the shanty stores. How about it, Mister Pinkerton? Are you getting rich selling bologna at caviar prices?"

"I wish. But I'm not smart enough to do that. I have to make my money the Pinkerton way."

"How's that?"

"Shutting up loudmouths."

McKenna snorted. "You guys kill me."

"Now you're talking, mister."

"Whoa!" said Swenson. "Gentlemen! This is turning dark and unsociable! I recommend we stop right here and enjoy some refreshments." He reached into his jacket pocket and produced a flask of whiskey, which he held up in general offering.

"Now that's the smartest thing I've heard yet," said the marshal with the cigar, and his partner stood as well. Neither of the Pinkertons moved, however, and Swenson walked toward them after the marshals had taken swigs.

"Gentlemen? Care to join us?"

"Thanks, no."

"No?"

"Don't take it personally, Johnny," said McKenna. "Those guys won't drink on duty."

"See? Who says government work is all bad?" cracked the second marshal as he helped himself to another pull on the bottle.

"I'm sure Lucretia Garfield will raise a glass of her own to your high standards," said McKenna.

For a long moment the only sound was the wheels of the car clicking steadily on the tracks. Finally, the first marshal said, "I guess this Pinkerton knew what he was talking about. You are horseshit."

"Yep, that's me. Old Horseshit McKenna. Come on, Johnny, what do you say? Are we playing cards or not?"

At six-thirty the next morning, Corbin looked up from the desk in his study to see the first strong rays of sunlight shine across the gleaming wet grounds of Blythebourne. He was certainly not a sentimental man and it was one of his first rules of business to avoid the indulgence of contentment, but there was no denying the warm feeling of satisfaction this view always produced. The mansion, the groves, the gently rolling lawns, the mill, and the three ponds—they had a self-assured elegance which Corbin had only accented with herds of deer, antelope, and elk, as well as a pair of tame buffaloes. It was pleasant to imagine himself actually in the English countryside, the squire of an old and historic fief. He saw the sunrise here often, he did not need much sleep. What he needed was the uninterrupted silence of late nights in which he could complete the plans and paperwork required to knit the patchwork of railroads, hotels, land companies, shippers, construction firms, suppliers, and investment partnerships under his control into a single quilt covering Long Island. He was surprised to discover he was not the only one up so early this morning.

Across the lawn amidst the thigh-high grasses and cattails ringing the millpond, Corbin could see the chest and shoulders of President Arthur. Later Corbin would be cynical, wondering how a man could squander so much industry on recreation. But his first reaction was admiration and wonder at the unexpected grace of his movements. Arthur was always courtly and careful regarding his grooming, yet there was something nonetheless bulky and ungainly in his presentation. In the water, however, with his favorite custom-made split-bamboo fly rod in his hands, he moved as easily and naturally against the pond as its swans. There was a rhythm, a lilt, an accomplishment and confidence in his motions that bespoke an intense focus and precision not readily evident in the man's walk and conversation. Or in his work, for that matter. For a fleeting instant Corbin saw and understood it. But then just as quickly he dismissed it for its waste, and the illumination was gone.

Fifteen minutes later Corbin had Mr. Burnap in his office. Corbin's employees were accustomed to being summoned at all hours, none more so than the manager of the Manhattan Beach Hotel. A small, spare, punctilious man in his fifties who always wore an inconspicuous dark suit, Burnap showed no sign of having gone to bed only two hours ago. Corbin had sent him out to Blythebourne in advance of the president's party to prepare the partners' dinner and see to Arthur's needs.

"Were you aware that the president is out alone in the millpond?"

"I was aware that he meant to get an early start on fishing this morning, sir. Following dinner the president took a late-night walk about the grounds with his son and Mr. Belmont and Mr. Jerome, and then entertained those gentlemen and several of the railroad's partners at an impromptu midnight supper in his suite. Miss Cassatt was with them as well."

"Yes, I know. I heard them." Corbin's office was directly below Arthur's rooms.

"I stayed on call until supper was cleared and his guests had departed. That was at about two-thirty. I then went to the kitchen and prepared sandwiches for the president and his party to take fishing. I was told that his son and a marshal would be accompanying him."

"Mm. I suspect the president's son wore himself out last night. I heard footsteps in the hall and doors opening and closing in Miss Cassatt's suite this morning."

"Begging your pardon, sir. I was coming up from the kitchen at that hour and I did not see young Mr. Arthur."

"No?"

Burnap shook his head. "No, sir. Just Senator Conkling."

Corbin had long ago perfected the ability to conceal his emotions, and his face betrayed nothing. Yet Burnap had spent enough time around Corbin to divine his moods from the smallest sign, and knew from the way he quickly picked a stack of shipping manifests up off the desk and repeatedly rifled a thumb over their edges like a deck of cards that he was angry. Indeed, he was furious. *Why was everyone so stupid?* Conkling's reputation preceded him, but what was wrong with this girl? What made a man like that so attractive to a woman as to make her risk the chance of a match with the president's son? It made no sense. How could someone risk an arrangement like that? If men behaved like women, we'd still be living in caves.

"Obviously he's out there alone. I don't know where his marshals are and I don't care. If anything should happen to the president while he's my guest, the railroad will be ruined. I don't want you to disturb him, but take a Pinkerton and watch. He can fish for another hour, but then bring him back. We've got to take the train out to Shinnecock. Do it now."

"Yes, sir."

"And please." Burnap was already halfway out the door. "No more surprises."

The water in the millpond was cold. Of course, it would have to be for trout. Arthur, anticipating a creel filled with fat brookies and browns, welcomed the instant shock of numbness the cold water transmitted through his waders. He never felt so alive as when he was fishing, and he frequently yearned for its sudden sensation of total immersion.

In fact, the fishing was good, better than he'd expected. The trout were on the small side and disappointingly lean, having only just begun to gorge themselves on the first real insect hatches of summer. Still, he was pleased to discover the fish were wild rather than stocked, something he was able to tell from the vigor with which they fought. He'd never have expected that, not with Corbin's ridiculous pension for zoos. He'd half-expected to find a stagnant lily pond filled with Japanese carp. Arthur had decided he didn't like his host. Washington was full of men like Corbin. Pompous, self-serious, avaricious men who had perfected the art of presenting their own needs as synonymous with those of the nation. They were boring. All of them. Arthur deftly played out his line in a delicate arc over his head and laid the fly exactly where he wanted it, just beyond a small rock at the mouth of the stream that fed the pond.

The fly drifted for just a moment before being sucked under in a tiny whirlpool. Arthur felt the tug of another fish and forgot about Corbin. A brookie, a good one. He placed it in the creel with the three others he'd already taken and looked forward to having them prepared, sharing the breakfast he'd caught with Chet.

Chet. His afternoon with Belmont and Jerome had done the boy a world of good, as had that nice-looking Cassatt girl. Upon his return from the track he'd been brimming with a rare confidence. Maybe this was finally the start of something good for him. Arthur felt more than a little affection in recalling how he couldn't get his son out of bed this morning. Why is it young people sleep so damn much? Well, hopefully it's because they still have a lot to dream.

Checking the fly, he heard a rustle in the cattails behind him and froze, an unavoidable frisson of fear suddenly making the cold water unbearable. It sounded like a deer, he prayed it was a deer. Garfield's shooting had left Arthur in constant terror of assassins—*he'd* been popular; who voted for *me?*—and he fought the fear by denying its existence and slipping the marshals whenever he could. Now, his heart hammering, he wished to God he hadn't. Perhaps there would be no gunshots to hear, maybe they were going to drown him. He swiveled his head slowly, feeling the painfully taut muscles in his neck, and summoned all of his courage to cast a watery and cautious eye to his rear.

"Roscoe! How can you sneak up on a body so? I think I've pissed my waders!"

Conkling gave him an unfriendly smile. "How can you tell?"

The president was literally jumping out of the pond and, if he heard him, gave no sign. "Damn! Really—you gave me a terrible fright." He unclinched the waders and, without asking, placed a hand on Conkling's shoulder for balance while removing them. "God Almighty!" He was still shaking when he picked up a light hunting jacket lying in the grass and took a cigar and a silver lighter from one of its pockets. After a half-dozen puffs, Arthur had regained his composure and Conkling raised a quizzical eyebrow. "Can't help it," said Arthur.

"It's funny, isn't it? Garfield's death should have been the moment of our liberation. And just look at us."

"I suppose I should stop ducking the marshals. Then I wouldn't have to fret like this."

"No reason to fret anyhow. There's a Pinkerton watching you. I passed him and that glorified bellhop from the hotel on my way out. They were sitting on a tree stump with a pair of binoculars. No one save me is going to sneak up on you, and I haven't carried a pistol since I stopped going on the Senate floor." He gave his trademark poker smile, the one that challenged the listener to decide whether he was serious or not.

"Are you ready to come back to Washington?"

"For what?"

"For Ward Hunt's seat on the Supreme Court, of course. You know the Senate has approved you. It's just sitting there waiting for you."

"Never. No. Go to hell."

"Oh, Lord's sake, Roscoe."

"No. *No.* At least Grant had the decency to offer me Chase's seat as chief justice. I turned him down, too, you know. Or have you forgotten?"

"I haven't forgotten anything."

"On the contrary. You've forgotten everything. You owe me the presidency, you dull-witted ox!"

"I owe you the vice presidency. For the office of president, I am indebted to the Almighty."

Conkling rolled his eyes. "Still the preacher's son, are you, Chet? Where was the Almighty when you were a junior partner in a not-very-good law firm? It was my hand that lifted you up and put you in the customs house, my hand that pushed you into the back room at that convention, my hand that put you in the White House! And I never heard you call anyone else's name before, either!"

"Now who's forgetting? You didn't even want me to accept the nomination!"

"And a damn sight better shape we'd be in if you hadn't!"

"Better shape? Roscoe—*I'm the president!*"

"Incredible, but true. But the president of what? The system is in ruins, the party is in ruins. And you turned your back on me."

"Every editor in the country predicted my first move would be to put the customs house back under the control of the party and auction off the postal routes. Well, I shut them up. How could I do anything else? Lord, Roscoe, what a world! Who would have imagined I'd have less power as president than I did back at the customs house? I don't think there's a single congressional race in the country I can affect. God, what I wouldn't give to have it like the old days again." He smiled. "Remember Auburn? Now that was power."

In his days at the customs house, Arthur had been Conkling's field commander, marshaling over a thousand politically appointed employees as the New York Republican Party's foot soldiers. There often seemed no limit to what that government-funded army could accomplish and the congressional elections of '72 were a textbook case. That year the Republicans were given no chance of winning the seat from the Finger Lakes, yet Conkling and Arthur had dispatched nearly two hundred customs workers from New York by train just three days before the election, and their thuggish presence—turning out the vote, watching the polls, culling and contesting the rolls—had delivered the party the seat. They had been unstoppable, and after that no one questioned Conkling's control over the state. Of course, such clear-cut evidence of naked power would eventually lead Hayes and Garfield to cloak their own interests in the mantle of public reform and move against them. That was the game and, despite the fact that both of those enemies were no longer around to torment them, they had effectively destroyed their world. Spoils wasn't dead, but civil service reform had taken hold for good, robbing Conkling and his rivals of their primary power base.

"I'm still not ready to take to my wheelchair and wrap the comforter of 'the good old days' around my shoulders," Conkling said.

Arthur worked his cigar for a long moment, staring at the smoke and worrying the tip. When he did speak, his voice had a different, softer quality, as if the smoke had mellowed his every crack and crevice. "There's something else."

Conkling looked at him evenly, waiting.

"I was having a lot of back pain and some other things I won't humiliate myself by describing. Turns out it's my kidneys—Bright's disease. The doctor says that if I run for reelection, I won't finish the term." He paused, waiting in vain for Conkling to say something sympathetic. "That doesn't mean I'm not going to run," he added somewhat angrily, "just that picking my vice president is particularly important."

"It's going to come out."

"No. I haven't told anyone, even Chet, and I'm not going to."

"It's all academic in any event. Blaine is going to beat you for the nomination. No matter how moral you pretend to be as president, he'll never let them forget who you are."

Arthur sighed. "Yes. Well, maybe." He took a long puff on the cigar. "I've been giving that some thought, too. The White House isn't my biggest concern, Roscoe. It's Chet. I can leave him well fixed, but not inexhaustibly so. I've asked Belmont to look out for him and I think he will." He looked directly into Conkling's eyes. "Tell me, Roscoe: have you done the math yet on the '84 election? I'm still the favorite son here, but if I don't run and Blaine is the Republican candidate, can he win the general election without New York?"

Arthur could see the light of understanding dawning as the furrow in Conkling's brow relaxed. "You treacherous old bastard! Work behind the scenes with Belmont and the Democrats to ensure Blaine loses New York? You son of a bitch. You did learn something after all."

The president waved his cigar dismissively. "I'm only a father thinking of his son."

Conkling nodded appreciatively. "Sure. It's good, Chet. Quite excellent."

Arthur knew this was major praise and he was not going to miss his advantage. "Now I want you to tell me what I'm doing here, Roscoe."

"It's pretty straightforward. Corbin is going to run the railroad out to Montauk. He's got a scheme to make it a major U.S. port of entry. He and his partners in London will sell it as a quicker alternative to the traditional London–New York routes—I don't have to tell you that traffic at New York harbor often means a two-day wait for docking. This way, passengers disembark from Corbin's boat at Montauk, get on Corbin's train, and are in New York in a few hours. Plus there are huge shipping advantages. He and Benson have the waterfront sewn up for warehouses."

"Isn't that Indian land?"

"Not anymore—it's Corbin's now. And he's going to present a bid on the overseas mail route that is four dollars a mile less than the government is presently paying."

"What does he want?"

"Fort Pond Bay, the harbor at Montauk, is too shallow for oceangoing vessels. He wants the government to dredge it."

Arthur snorted. "No."

"No? Goddamn it, Chet! Your whole career I've done nothing but say yes to you, and since you've become president you've done nothing but say no to me! Enough! I don't care if you are dying! We're *all* dying! Is it all right if we accomplish something first?"

"The party wants to make spending by the congressional Democrats an issue and attack them in the districts in '84. I'm going to condemn the River and Harbors Bill as pork and veto it—and that's even without Corbin's project in it."

"I can't argue with that strategy. But why don't we at least get one of the New York representatives to introduce funding for a modest feasibility study by the army engineers? By the time they finish, you'll be out of office."

"All right, I'll do that. But it's for you. Your man is not my cup of tea."

"He's no fool. And quite useful."

"Useful? I don't have to tell you what it's like getting the railroads to pay taxes. Corbin, Vanderbilt, Gould, Huntington, Stanford, and that whole gang just want to keep their money and let everyone else do their heavy lifting. Huge land grants, easements, they want it all. Look around you: everywhere Corbin runs his road, he owns the land. I can't pretend he's an altruist or a patriot. Hell, as far as I can tell he'd rather not be an American! I know this is going to sound strange, but I never thought I'd be president. And now that I am, I can't ignore the higher duties and trusts of the office."

"Very moving. Do you know what was out here prior to Corbin? A handful of busted railroads and more lamb chops than even you could eat. You call his project pork, I call it the lifeblood of the country. So he wants to be rich—so what? Not everyone has your refined sensibilities. Of course, that's why you'll go down in history as such a great and effective president. I simply take the world and its men as I find them. I don't corrupt them, and they don't corrupt me. The business of government is simple: to maintain law and order and protect property rights. Period. And I'll take it one step further: not only is Corbin right to want the country's support, you're wrong to refuse it. Think about it. People like to pretend that freedom is in the breeze and that economic abundance simply bursts forth from the richness of the land. But someone has to make it. Civil service reform is the worst thing that every happened to this country. You want your Auburn army back? You want the chance to get in power and do a little good? Who is going to pay for the Republican Party? Grateful niggers? Why do you think I'm doing this instead of wasting my time on the Supreme Court? Corbin and the corporations are the only future we have. The only people who will pay for government are the ones who understand that nothing in life is free and that you get what you pay for."

"Or what someone is willing to sell you."

"Spare me. We're all for sale. All of us. I've bought and sold you a dozen times, Mr. President. That's how it works. That's the only way it works. The rest is just bedtime stories for children. God! Chet Arthur—president! What a monumental waste!"

It was an argument Arthur knew he would never win, and he was grateful to see Burnap and the Pinkerton heading up the trail toward them. But just as they were coming in hearing range, the Pinkerton said something to Burnap and dashed off the trail into the waist-high grass. Burnap, though clearly disconcerted by what the Pinkerton had said, put on his best face.

"Mr. President! Senator Conkling! Mr. Corbin wishes me to remind you that the train to Shinnecock will be leaving shortly. There's a special fishing spot for you by the inlet, Mr. President, and we've scheduled our arrival to coincide with the last hour of the rising tide."

"That's very thoughtful, but I haven't brought any saltwater gear."

"Mr. Corbin sent a man to Hiram Leonard's in Central Valley yesterday to acquire a nine-foot bamboo salmon rod built to the specifications you keep on file. We've brought you several reels as well." Leonard, one of the country's leading rod-and-gunsmiths, counted the president among his best customers. Indeed, Arthur had cut the ribbon at the new Central Valley shop in '81, accepting the first rod off the line as a gift. Burnap had made Arthur happier than a six-year-old in an ice cream parlor, and it was easy to steer the president back to the house on a different path.

If possible, the Pinkerton fifty yards behind them was even happier than the president. While Burnap led the others away, the detective stood stock still, leaning forward and pressing a revolver to the back of the head of a man lying face down in the grass.

"Well, well, well. If it ain't my old pal Horseshit McKenna. And believe me, mister—you are horseshit now."

McKenna was shaking so violently the grass around him rustled. "I'm unarmed," he managed to croak.

"Now how could I know that? I can't chance that when Mr. Corbin wants me to guard the president." He leaned all of his weight forward, pushing the nose of the revolver deep into the reporter's vertebrae and causing him to groan.

"Getting ready to kill the president, Mr. Horseshit? Gonna be the next Guiteau? Gonna be famous? Well, don't worry—you'll be famous all right."

"I swear to God, I was just trying to hear what they were saying! That's my job!"

"And this is mine."

"Do you think you'll have it long when James Gordon Bennett asks Corbin why he killed his unarmed reporter? You'll be charged with murder."

"I don't think so. I had to act fast in an emergency."

"An emergency? They'll never believe that—they all know you've been standing here a while. For God's sake, don't kill me!"

There was a long, interminable moment in which the Pinkerton continued to lean on the gun, twisting the barrel, using it like an awl to dig at the knob of nerves in McKenna's neck. When he finally relaxed and stepped back, McKenna was numb and unable to lift his head; the back of his neck, an angry red, burned as fiercely as if he'd been hanged. But he let out a long breath, knowing he had dodged the bullet. "Thank you," he said, his voice breaking in a sob.

"Don't mention it, pal." The Pinkerton unleashed a vicious kick to McKenna's ribs.

The first thing McKenna did when he got off the train at the Shinnecock spur was throw up. He wasn't sure whether to blame it on the pain, the motion of the railcar, or killing the rest of Swenson's whiskey. The pain—he would learn the next day that he had three cracked ribs—was there whenever he inhaled, but the ceaseless jostling of the train had been nearly unbearable. Suffering through pain was not in his nature. McKenna was neither brave nor noble and consoled himself with the knowledge that very few men were. Still, once the cold terror of having a gun held to his head had dissipated, it was replaced with a rare rage. He had been around newspapers too long to have any illusions, knew the people he wrote about viewed him with annoyance rather than fear. He was just a pest—he didn't merit physical harm. Besides, he'd only heard bits and pieces of Conkling and Arthur's conversation regarding the dredging of Fort Pond Bay and wasn't sure what it all meant. He had, however, heard enough to know Arthur wouldn't give his approval if McKenna wrote anything. He wasn't sure what to do. Personally, he had nothing against Corbin. Still, he thought with no small amount of pleasure, the railroad might have to let a few Pinkertons go if they didn't get their prize.

Wiping his chin with the back of a hand, McKenna looked up to see everyone trailing after Corbin and the president. They were walking the several hundred yards to the inlet, and the president was clutching a new fishing pole. It was a good-sized party including the president's son, Corbin's wife and daughters, the Cassatt girl, Conkling, Burnap, and the reporters, marshals, and Pinkertons. Several fishing boats and a fifty-foot yacht were moored to a new dock. At the mouth of the inlet a long stone jetty stuck out into the ocean like a gray, bony finger. The party stopped from time to time so Corbin could describe plans for a particular piece of property or point out the three cottages already under construction. It was all very leisurely and McKenna caught up as the party reached the dock. He saw crews on the yacht and one of the fishing boats.

"Oh!" exclaimed Arthur. "This really is a spectacular spot, Austin. How much south shore property did you say you own?"

"We've acquired about ten miles of the oceanfront between Montauk and Manhattan Beach."

"Amazing. Roscoe is right—you are quite brilliant." Corbin flushed with pleasure, and Conkling gave Arthur a slight nod of appreciation at this bit of embroidering. But Arthur's attention had already shifted, and his face was suddenly very animated. "Do you smell that, man? Give the ocean breeze a good sniff and tell me what it is you smell."

Everyone dutifully craned their necks, poked their noses, and adopted the appropriately quizzical look. "It smells like basil," said Hannah Corbin.

"Yes, very good my dear, it does!" Arthur said. "But it's not basil it's something else." They looked expectantly at Arthur, who grinned cattily. "Those gentlemen can tell you," he said, pointing to the crew on the fishing boat, who were just unloading two large buckets of live bait onto the dock, one holding eels and the other menhaden. "Well, gentlemen, what do we smell?"

"Blues," said the oldest of the crew. He was the color of sun-bleached driftwood and McKenna took him to be the captain.

"Precisely! Bluefish! Is that my bait you're unloading?"

"Yep. I mean, yes, Mr. President."

"Wonderful! Let's get to it, shall we?"

The press crew already knew they were barred from accompanying the president while he fished, an arrangement made with the express promise of interviews during the return trip to Manhattan. Indeed, only Corbin and Conkling would be accompanying Arthur; the rest of the guests were slated for a cruise on Corbin's yacht, and the reporters were now delighted to discover Burnap had counted them while making provisions. The rear deck was stacked with blocks of ice upon which sat four bushels of freshly harvested oysters and clams and about a dozen bottles of champagne; nearby, a chef was already tending steaks on a portable grill, and the rich, fatty smell of sizzling meat came drifting deliciously on the air.

"Basil, huh?" The voice in McKenna's ear was Swenson's. "I'm beginning to think the leader of our great nation isn't a particularly bright man." He clapped McKenna jovially on the shoulder, then glanced at him. "You don't look so good."

"No. I'm not getting on that boat."

"It's not a boat, Stanley, it's a yacht. The vessel those gentlemen over there employ for fishing is a boat. Anything you can get a glass of champagne on is a yacht."

"Yeah, fine. Count me out."

"Have it your way. But I wouldn't try any more funny stuff. I heard your friend tell the marshals he took a knife away from you."

McKenna rolled his eyes. "I'm done. I'm just afraid I'll be sick again out on the ocean, that's all."

"Well, watch yourself. Now excuse me, I have to go eat your steak. I wonder if your editors are aware of how frequently I have to cover for you out here in the field."

McKenna grinned, his first of the day. He watched Swenson and the others board and shove off, then peered all the way down the jetty to where Arthur, Corbin, and Conkling already sat on folding camp chairs. They were waiting for the tubs of Arthur's bait, which the marshals and the Pinkertons were still slowly carrying, water sloshing occasionally over the sides. The president, watching their progress, kept standing up and then fitfully sitting down, and McKenna could see he was impatient to get started. It was Corbin rather than Conkling who was pulling him back into his seat, seeming to try and engage him in conversation. McKenna had a pretty good idea what Corbin wanted to talk about. He could still taste the metallic residue of vomit, and felt inside his jacket for his tobacco. It was there, a little crushed but fine, although not his matches. He walked over to the fishing boat, where the captain was leaning against the gunwales and smoking a pipe while his three men scrubbed the boat. It already looked clean enough to McKenna. Having himself grown up on Long Island, not far from Huntington station, he was well aware of the intense maintenance fishing boats required and it was the primary reason he'd never wanted one. "Excuse me," he said. "Can I trouble you for a match?"

The captain managed to light up McKenna without otherwise acknowledging or seeming to even look at him.

"Much obliged." He puffed quickly to strengthen the draw. "Say Captain, how deep is Fort Pond Bay?"

The man shrugged. "Gotta know where, gotta know when."

"Well, is it deep enough for oceangoing vessels?"

"What kind?"

"You know, freighters, big liners."

"Are you crazy?"

"Why? What's it like?"

"Shallow and rocky. Very rocky."

"Could it be dredged?"

The captain thought for a minute. "I suppose. If you had all the money in the world."

"My uncle's got that."

The captain smoked his pipe for a moment. "No, wait," he said. "Even if you can dredge it'll be no good."

"What's the matter?"

"You'd have to build a breakwater to enable any steamers bottled up in there to ride out the northeasters. That's first of all, and I guess if money is no object you can do it, but it ain't cheap. But you got another problem. A steamer entering the bay is obliged to cross Block Island Sound. That means going west of Block Island in good weather and east in foul. That water is also shallow and loaded with rocks. I don't know about shipping lanes through there. Then there's the fog. It's as bad as Sandy Hook over in New Jersey and they can't bring ocean vessels in there because of it. You wouldn't save no time over New York harbor sitting out here for days at a clip waiting for the fog to break. Nope, I don't see how you can do it."

"So it's impossible?"

The captain shook his head. "Nothing's impossible, I suppose, if you want it bad enough. Just don't make any sense."

"Thanks." McKenna politely smoked a few minutes more with the captain before ambling back to the train. His side hurt something awful and he needed to rest. He tried Corbin's car, with its plush chairs, but it was locked and he had to settle for lying gingerly on a wooden bench in the photo car. He fell asleep immediately. It was several hours later when he awoke with a sharp, persistent pain in his side and the realization that everyone was back and the train moving.

"Hey, look. It's alive." It was Swenson. He was drinking from a bottle of champagne and was half in the bag. McKenna waved back weakly. "You missed a great party, Stanley. You know, Arthur's kid is okay. I like him. Gonna be at Sheepshead this summer."

"But did you get your interview with his father?"

"Oh, yeah. Went great. Just great."

"What did he talk about?"

Swenson pointed a wobbly finger toward the two bait tubs, which were now sitting on a table in the center of the car. "Them."

McKenna, slowly sitting up, craned his sore neck and peered over the sides. Both tubs were now filled with large bluefish, their thick, muscular bodies already frozen in curved rigor mortis and covered with a thick, clear slime. Each appeared to be about two feet long and there must have been twenty in each bucket. "Oh, Jesus," he said, the morning's nausea returning. "Just wait," said Swenson. "Burnap and the conductor are gonna fillet 'em in a minute."

Sure enough, Burnap and a second man, both wearing rubber aprons, entered the car and wasted no time in cleaning and butchering the president's fish. Both men knew what they were doing: they used short, sharp knives to separate each side of meat from the fishes' skeletal frames in two long strokes, leaving each a ghastly parody of head, tail, and entrails. Everything was going smoothly until the train accelerated sharply. Then the wet pile of bloody fish frames slid off the table and skidded across the floor.

"What the hell is going on?" McKenna yelled to Swenson over the rumbling of the cars.

"I heard the president bet Corbin five dollars we couldn't get back to Greenpoint in two hours."

"Two hours? Christ, we'd have to go sixty miles an hour!"

"Well, better hang on then!"

McKenna laid back down on his good side, babying his sore ribs. But every bounce, every twist of track, was like a fresh kick.

"Hey!" yelled Swenson. "What about you? Did you ever talk with Arthur?"

McKenna shook his head.

"What are you going to file?

He thought about what he knew and also of what Conkling had said regarding Bennett never printing anything to antagonize Corbin or Arthur. He shrugged. "'President Enjoys Gracious Homecoming at Corbin's Lavish Long Island Estate'?"

Swenson grinned and passed McKenna the champagne bottle. "'Atta boy! Flat on your back but still spinning shit! You're a pro, Stanley." He belched. "A real pro."

McKenna took a swig of champagne. It was warm and sticky sweet and not to his taste at all. He gave the bottle back to Swenson and closed his eyes, but the pain and motion and thick, fetid smell of fish innards made him dizzy. Yet when he opened his eyes, all he could see was the wealth of Long Island, now reduced to a bloody mound of entrails, shaking its way across the floor like rich gooey pudding caught in an earthquake.

6

GRAFFITI

Corbin Place proved to be a short quiet street of apartment buildings bending toward the ocean from Emmons Avenue. It is the de facto border between the divergent worlds of Brighton Beach and Manhattan Beach and about as far south as you can bicycle in Brooklyn. Austin Corbin's enormous and elaborate hotels, the Oriental and the Manhattan Beach, are long gone, torn down and sold for scrap nearly ninety years ago. Much of the oceanfront he carved has also changed, although a descendant of the Oriental's beach and boardwalk survives as a public park, and immaculate, tree-lined Oriental Boulevard is still Manhattan Beach's main thoroughfare.

The neighborhood provides a kind of mindless bicycling when the ocean winds aren't too stiff: the old spit of beach is still flat and breezy, and the straightforward checkerboard of streets is subdivided into neat green plots, each studded with a split-level ranch home and making the neighborhood feel more suburban than any other part of Brooklyn. But to ride west across Corbin Place into Brighton Beach is to enter another world: a messy tangle of narrow, deeply gashed, and garbage-strewn back roads with names like Brighton Fourteenth Street, where impoverished Russian immigrants are crammed into small, mean, dilapidated houses. Though just a block from the ocean, the main drag of Brighton Beach Avenue is dark and grimy, and the elevated subway line blocks the sun from shining on the battered fruit and vegetable bins, the cheesy discount clothing stores and rambunctious Russian night clubs. The most popular items at the newsstands are the prepaid overseas phone cards, and it's been a long time since any New Yorker thought of Austin Corbin when speaking of Brighton or Manhattan Beach. It's the Russians who are synonymous with Brighton now, while Westend Avenue, which runs parallel to Corbin Place, is home to several good-sized synagogues and a kosher catering hall. I can't help but wonder how many Jews must live on Corbin Place. Who says you can't find justice in this world?

Biking a few blocks north to Sheepshead Bay I came upon another relic of Corbin's era in Jerome Avenue, the former site of Leonard Jerome's Coney Island Jockey Club track, which closed in 1910. It's not much of a street, just five blocks of private houses and nondescript apartment buildings, and nothing like the major artery that Jerome Avenue in the Bronx is. That lengthy thoroughfare, which Leonard Jerome originally financed and built, originates in the south Bronx near Yankee Stadium in High Bridge and runs north through Mount Eden and Fordham until it ends just shy of the Yonkers city line at the northwest corner of Woodlawn Cemetery. It is the major commercial strip for the west Bronx and, like Brighton Beach Avenue, most of its stores sit in the shadow of an elevated subway line, in this case the IRT Number 4, erected in 1917. Leonard Jerome was dead by then and, like Sheepshead Bay, his Jerome Park racetrack in the Bronx disappeared long ago, in this case giving way to the city reservoir that still sits across Goulden Avenue from Herbert Lehman College and the Bronx High School of Science. Jerome's grandson, Winston Churchill, was very much alive the year the Number 4 crowned Jerome Avenue, having just helped engineer a military disaster at Gallipoli. Closer to home, Leonard's grandnephew, William Travers Jerome, had made a name for himself as the Manhattan district attorney, and in 1917 he was paddling against the political tide, trying to shore up the city's anti-Tammany movement under the increasingly unpopular reform mayor, John Purroy Mitchel.

Even in the farthest reaches of Brooklyn I could feel the compass of Woodlawn pulling me back. Like a satisfied tourist whose fond memories of a recent package tour to Rome now cause him to stop and read all the newspaper stories with Italian datelines he once ignored, my antennae have become tuned to any vibrations emanating from that well-fertilized patch of Bronx earth. I've been keeping tabs on the new celebrity interments, which include the seventy-seven-year-old "Queen of Salsa" Celia Cruz, after a long cancer battle, the jazz vibraphonist Lionel Hampton, who died of old age at ninety-four, and the rapper Christopher Rios. Known as Big Pun, Rios weighed seven hundred pounds and was just twenty-seven when he died of (surprise!) a coronary. Pun was the first Latino hip-hop artist of any real commercial significance and a source of local pride along the strip of Westchester Avenue that runs through his tough Bronx neighborhood of Morrisania. A petition drive to rename Rogers Place near 163rd Street as Big Pun Place garnered three thousand signatures, even after a posthumous documentary on Pun—short for "Punisher"—featured footage of him cracking his wife across the face with the butt of a gun. The bill died in the city council—not as a result of his onscreen misogyny but over objections to rap music.

Honoring someone's memory with a renamed neighborhood street is a surprisingly popular idea in New York. According to one estimate, two-thirds of all the bills that come before the city council deal with this, and in the Bronx the honorees run the gamut from dentist-turned-local-historian Dr. Theodore Kazimiroff to police shooting victim Amadou Diallo. On the first anniversary of the attack on the World Trade Center, the city announced eighty-eight streets were being renamed for firemen and police officers killed in the disaster. Most are in Queens and Staten Island. In the Bronx, Stickball Boulevard, a section of what had previously been Newman Avenue in Castle Hill, was renamed yet again, this time as Steve Mercado Stickball Boulevard. Mercado, a fireman who grew up in the neighborhood, was president of a local stickball league, a game originally played in the streets by kids with broomsticks and red rubber Spaldings, but generally limited now to men of a certain age in organized leagues and tournaments on ball fields or streets temporarily closed to traffic. Mercado picked the game up from his father, taught it to his kids, and played competitively, traveling to a tournament in San Diego the week before he was killed. Personally, I didn't play much stickball and I only know about Mercado because of his memorial wall.

Despite being a recent phenomenon, there are many memorial walls in the Bronx and they stand not just as sentinels against forgetting, but as the most moving applications of public graffiti art. Like the mausoleums of Woodlawn, the Bronx's memorial walls are different and they are the same. Usually painted by neighborhood artists, almost all feature a billboard-sized portrait taken from a photograph, a message of remembrance or faith, and the bookends of birth and death dates. Too frequently, the symbols are those of a narrowly circumscribed and barely begun life: sneakers, a basketball, the Mercedes-Benz the deceased told everyone he'd someday own. Sometimes those remembered are pictured with loved ones, but usually they are alone. More often than not it is a kid, arms folded in a pose of exaggerated confidence, haunted eyes brimming with bravura, searching for a future that won't come.

Woodlawn has made me curious about this impulse to rename city streets, to scrawl a signature across the map like a tagger in a subway yard. Wasn't that what Corbin and his crowd were up to when they erected their pharaonic tombs in Woodlawn? What, for that matter, do we imagine Donald Trump is up to putting his name on any building he can get hold of? We're all pleading with history, begging not to be forgotten, pretending and flattering ourselves that the judgment is ours to make. I mean no disrespect: Steve Mercado died trying to help us—if renaming Stickball Avenue reminds us of that and comforts his family, I can't think of a better use for a street corner. If Big Pun's wife and neighbors celebrate him as a superstar instead of the Big Punisher, I understand. Yet its ultimate meaning beyond their circle and the comfort it affords them is as negligible as Corbin's elaborate mausoleum and as lasting as any other piece of graffiti. Still, I find it a comfort to believe the city I love endures timelessly and carries me with it, our fading graffiti marks somehow ingrained and vibrant as the day we made them, resonant in the repetition of millions and there for any who would take the time to uncover and read them. How better to defy death?

Big Pun didn't get his street but he got his memorial wall, painted— like Steve Mercado's—by TATS Cru, a tribe of Hunts Point graffiti artists who trace their roots back to the days when they were called vandals. Then TATS stood for Tough And Talented. Later it meant Train Art Theater and now its Top Artistic Talent. The Cru is a going concern: hired not just by local businessmen to do neighborhood walls and signs but also by international brands like Coca-Cola and Bacardi Rum seeking a little *sabor local*. Their offices are on Garrison Avenue behind a barricaded courtyard that looks more like a prison yard than the community center it also doubles as. Hunts Point is the capitol of the midnight autoparts business, and the TATS Cru's neighbors are mostly chop shops and small garages. On my bicycling map I draw a line from Stickball Avenue through Garrison to Rogers Place.

The neighborhood of Castle Hill is a mishmash of industrial and residential buildings hard by the Bruckner Expressway—block after block of sun-stroked, treeless streets, most in desperate need of resurfacing. It's

not the worst neighborhood in the Bronx, but it's a long time since anyone called it picturesque, and the looming, noisy Bruckner just kills any
sense of community. The only vestige of green from the area's earliest
farmland is Pugsley's Creek Park, which backs up into Stickball Avenue.

The memorial to Steve Mercado, located on an athletic field across
the street from the Bronx offices of the New York City Board of Education, can be seen from the street through a chain-link fence. Painted on
the back of a field house sitting off to the side of a track, it is unique in
that it doesn't feature a portrait of the deceased. Instead, the mural is an
urban pastoral of a stickball game, played not on a city street but in a hot
summer field of shimmering greens and baked browns, the faceless play-
ers floating like a mirage. A playground is represented off to one side of
the painting, but it is like no actual park in the city: mountains rather
than apartment buildings rise in the background, suggesting that the
game is being played someplace else—the country, perhaps, or maybe
heaven. In the foreground a coiled batter unleashes a drive. Along the
side is a poem by Mercado about the game he learned from his father and
taught to his children.

I bicycle up the Bruckner walkway and over the Bronx River into
Hunts Point. Longfellow Avenue leads up a hill to Garrison, a tough-
looking street of low-lying wooden garages wedged into the shadow of
the expressway. Like a spreading greenery announcing the approach of
an oasis, the walls along Garrison begin to sprout art the closer I get to
the TATS Cru headquarters at Manida Street. Soda ads, a mural for a
muffler shop, and then an enormous painting of a neighborhood scene,
heavily stylized and hard to decipher while riding by in the lengthening
shadows of an autumn afternoon. The courtyard walls in front of the
TATS Cru office are a riot of jungle greens and blazing yellow, an artifi-
cial rain forest, but the office itself is shuttered behind a blackened steel
curtain. Perhaps the Cru still does its best work at night.

Rolling up Longwood to Dawson Street, I spy Big Pun's memorial
wall at the side of Star Auto Sound on the corner of 163rd and Rogers.
Unlike the Mercado mural, this one is traditional: Pun—half a block of
him—portrayed from the shoulders up (no doubt the most flattering way
to paint a seven-hundred-pound man), a Puerto Rican flag worn as a ban-

danna across his head, eyes turned toward the heavens. The mural also depicts the buildings on the block and, city council not withstanding, a fanciful green municipal street sign: Big Pun Avenue.

If Pun's friends and family have a vision for the Bronx of the future, my next stop is an attempt to find a piece of its past. Since becoming aware of the *Maine* Memorial during my ride around Central Park, I've identified it as a piece of Woodlawn graffiti. Its creator, the sculptor Attilio Piccirilli, is buried there. The large Piccirilli family plot, located just south of 233rd Street in the northwest quadrant of the cemetery, is quite individual. For one thing, there are no headstones. Instead, Piccirilli and his parents, five brothers, and many of their wives and children, lie beneath the grass that surrounds a bronze statue, *Fortitude*. The statue has the same figures of mourning that, done in marble, captured my attention at the base of the *Maine* Memorial. That work itself is a copy: the original was part of the San Simeon collection of William Randolph Hearst, whose newspaper sponsored the *Maine* Memorial. One suspects the work was also a moneymaker for the Piccirillis: I've discovered at least one other copy of it at another Woodlawn grave site.

Despite creating both the *Maine* Memorial and the Fireman's Memorial on Riverside Drive, Attilio Piccirilli never truly achieved the kind of career as an artist that he longed for. At a time when many of the most famous and celebrated sculptors didn't carve their own statues, the Piccirillis, who were from a long line of stonecutters in Carrara, Italy, developed a lucrative business in New York, transferring the work of others from clay models into stone. Most famously, the six Piccirilli brothers carved the massive statue of a seated Abraham Lincoln created by Daniel Chester French for the Lincoln Memorial, as well as several of French's best-known New York pieces including *Manhattan* and *Brooklyn*, for the Manhattan Bridge, *Four Continents* for the U.S. Customs House at Bowling Green, and several of French's commissions for the Metropolitan Museum of Art. Some of the Piccirillis' other carvings included Edward Clark Potter's *Patience* and *Fortitude*, the pair of stone lions also known as Lady Astor and Lord Lennox that sit in front of the main branch of the New York Public Library. They also executed John A. Q. Ward's pediment for the New York Stock Exchange and several of the figures on the

Washington Arch in Washington Square Park, including pieces by Frederick MacMonnies, Alexander Stirling Calder, Herman Atlins MacNiel, and Philip Martiny. The Piccirillis, who also sold funereal pieces and did a land-office business in architectural decorations for clients like McKim, Mead and White, operated an enormous studio on 142nd Street in the Mott Haven section of the Bronx.

The notion of a ride encompassing the work of the TATS Cru and the Piccirillis is irresistible. Though their work is separated by a half-century in which figurative sculpting has been laid to rest and spray paint elevated, it only takes a few minutes to bicycle from Westchester Avenue and 163rd Street to St. Ann's Street and 142nd.

At its apex, the Piccirilli studio employed as many as a hundred stonecutters. The main floors served as a combination warehouse, shipping and receiving department, and work area, with several enormous custom-built elevators used for transferring huge blocks of stone to and from the brothers' studios on the second floor. Along with the main buildings, which photographs show to have looked like any of the small factories that still dot the south Bronx, the Piccirillis owned the adjacent house where several of the brothers and their parents lived. The family had a reputation for unpretentious hospitality: the Piccirillis entertained clients, visitors, and friends in the house's large basement kitchen, where they prepared and ate lunch together every day. School trips to the studio were popular, with those tours as a rule including sandwiches for the children and homemade wine for the teachers. Aside from the massive marble Lincoln, carved piecemeal at 142nd Street, the studio carved many, many public monuments and played host to three living presidents in Theodore Roosevelt, William Howard Taft, and Woodrow Wilson. John D. Rockefeller also came for lunch to discuss a pair of bas-reliefs Attilio was carving for Rockefeller Center. The opera legend Enrico Caruso, a close friend of Attilio's, was a frequent guest, and Woodlawn's own Fiorello La Guardia—who was the attorney for the Piccirillis before launching his political career—was also extremely close to Attilio; he affectionately and respectfully called him "Uncle Picc." The two maintained a standing Sunday dinner date for over twenty years, and the sculptor appears to have been a moral compass for the politician, despite the fact that their fortunes were moving in opposite directions. La Guardia, the reformer, was evolving into a catalyst on the changing political scene; Piccirilli, though financially successful, was on the verge of becoming a casualty of changing times and tastes, his beloved classic school of figurative sculpting soon to be as anachronistic as the horse and buggy. Yet La Guardia clearly revered the sculptor as a father figure who embodied all the Old World verities.

The Piccirilli studio and house are gone now, and a new building owned by the Jehovah's Witnesses stands on part of the site. Naturally, there's a movement afoot to rename the street Piccirilli Place, spearheaded by a local teacher and history buff named Bill Carroll. As I ride by, I try to imagine what the street might have looked like seventy years ago, but it is indistinguishable from the rest of Mott Haven, a battered block of poor brick tenements and junk-rich lots clutched against the exhaust-perfumed neck of the Major Deegan and the Bruckner expressways. At the corner of Third Avenue I pass a tall red cluster of public housing projects and note that it is named for John Purroy Mitchel. I decide on a whim to bicycle up to Woodlawn via the Grand Concourse—a great formal boulevard to rival any in the city and my favorite Bronx ride. With nothing left to show that the Piccirillis were ever part of 142nd Street, I want to search out two of Attilio's pieces in the cemetery.

Despite the size of the family plot, there is one Piccirilli buried alone, lying about a half mile from the rest of the family. In the great green heart of Woodlawn, tucked in a slight depression amid a cool and shaded district of mausoleums and family plots that are well-to-do but modest when measured against Woodlawn's Gilded Age standards, is the grave of Attilio's nephew, Nathan Q. F. Piccirilli, a U.S. Navy ensign. He was killed at the age of twenty-six in the battle of Ormac Bay in the Philippines, and his grave is marked by a copy of one of Attilio's most powerful pieces, *The Outcast*. The original, which stood in a church in Greenwich Village for many years before a fire caused it to be moved, has been lost. Whatever the initial conception, it is more than appropriate as a memorial. The larger-than-life form is that of a young man, folded upon himself in grief. In a nod to his youth, the figure is not wholly emerged from the stone. Yet he has a man's hands: big, strong, and filled with emotion. It's a bit more subtle than the TATS Cru, but the message is the same: death came too early and it was not welcome.

The other piece I've come to see is a headstone. The plot it marks, off Fern Avenue just south of the cemetery's northwest corner, is a little difficult to locate. Like much of Woodlawn, this section, which is called Lotus, was filled some time ago; judging by the dates on the stones, there haven't been more than a few burials here in the last four decades. Everything is fastidiously groomed, yet the old, enormous trees cast the kind of deep shadows found in remote pine forests. That pall, combined with the sense that visitors are rare to these long-filled sections, can make them gloomy despite the careful upkeep and the fact that they remain some of the cemetery's more elegant sections. By comparison, there are very few trees in the outer sections of Woodlawn, especially those along 233rd Street and in the southwest corners along Bainbridge Avenue and 211th Street. These sun-baked sections of unevenly rolling meadows, with row after row after row of small, same-sized headstones, are the cheap seats—the Woodlawn equivalent of the bleachers at Yankee Stadium. But the plot I'm searching for in Lotus is obscured by cool shadows and hidden in a stone thicket of markers. The only thing on my side is that this one has a unique cast-metal bas-relief mounted on the stone. Unfortunately, as I eventually find out, the metal has discolored until its dull green is all but invisible in the dark grove. But it's worth the hunt.

The headstone, erected in 1921, marks the graves of Thea and Fioretta La Guardia—the twenty-six-year-old wife and eleven-month-old daughter of Attilio's great friend, Fiorello. The baby died before her first birthday, and her mother, stricken with tuberculosis, followed seven months later. For La Guardia, whose pugnacious public persona would prove as much a part of his legend as his accomplishments as mayor, the one-two punch of losing a child and a wife almost broke him. He went through a terrible stretch—drinking, picking ill-conceived political fights, and seemingly losing the driving ambition and sense of engagement that would later define his mayoralty and help make it a high point in city history. The headstone depicts Thea, whom Piccirilli knew well, with her arms outstretched to guide the unsure steps of a toddling child. She is welcoming the infant, aiding it, mothering it. They are together in death.

La Guardia himself is buried in Woodlawn, although not next to Thea and Fioretta. He eventually remarried (to his secretary, Marie Fischer) and adopted two children, one of whom, Jean, was his first wife's niece. Jean, who died of diabetes in 1962 at the age of thirty-four, is buried alongside La Guardia and Marie in the cemetery's Oakwood section. Fiorello died in 1947, a year after leaving office and two years after the passing of his friend, Attilio.

Oakwood, like Lotus, is only sparsely studded with mausoleums but still manages to offer some of Woodlawn's tonier grave sites. La Guardia's protégé, Vito Marcantonio, who succeeded him as the U.S. congressman from Yorkville and East Harlem, is also here. Marcantonio managed to do his reform-minded mentor one better by becoming a left-wing firebrand and was variously elected to Congress on the Republican, Democratic, and American Labor Party lines. Those shifting endorsements not withstanding Marcantonio was a socialist at heart, and way out in front on civil rights, labor, and welfare issues. He also took a strong pro-Soviet line during World War II, arguing in the war's earliest days that it was a creation of the "Wall Street–Downing Street axis" and that the American people should opt for isolation—a stance he reversed the day after Germany invaded the Soviet Union. Still, he was a consummate local politician and remained an effective advocate for his constituents, available every weekend without fail in his New York office, and so beloved in the district that it ultimately required a three-party coalition to produce a candidate to defeat him. That love was hardly universal, however: during the early days of the cold war he was a favorite whipping boy of the *New York Times*, whose editorial pages characterized him as a left-wing demagogue and an embarrassment to the city. Worse, when he died in 1954, the Catholic Church—staunchly anti-red under Cardinal Spellman— would not allow a mass to be said for him or bury him in sacred ground. Instead, he lies just a few plots from La Guardia. His headstone, which simply reads "Congressman, Defender of Human Rights," echoes La Guardia's unadorned epitaph of "Statesman, Humanitarian," which, like that of John Purroy Mitchel, chooses not to mention the fact that he was mayor.

That Marcantonio and La Guardia remain close in death is not uncommon—Woodlawn is rife with similar cases, although none as cheeky as Joe Sultzer and Charles Dale Marks. Known as the vaudeville team of Smith and Dale, the duo worked together from the 1890s through the 1950s, were frequent guests on *The Ed Sullivan Show*, and are reputed to be the inspiration for the dyspeptic geriatric duo in the saccharine Neil Simon play *The Sunshine Boys*. They are buried side-by-side in Woodlawn's Rhododendron section and their shared stone, which faces the cemetery's Park Avenue, is inscribed "Booked solid."

By contrast, a game of one-upmanship is being played into the next world at a pair of grave sites just up the road from Smith and Dale. Facing each other across the spoke-shaped convergence of five paths are the graves of two jazz giants, Edward Kennedy "Duke" Ellington and Miles Davis. As with other areas of the arts, Woodlawn boasts more than a few notables from the jazz world, including cornetist and composer W. C. Handy, New Orleans trumpeter Joe "King" Oliver, tenor saxophone great Coleman Hawkins, Ellington trumpeter Charles "Cootie" Williams, singer and club-owner Ada "Bricktop" Smith, and now, Lionel Hampton. Woodlawn legend has it that Ellington, who died in 1974, had the best-attended interment in the cemetery's history: despite a steady rain, hundreds of mourners stood on the rise of plots overlooking his resting place, a long low black cloud of umbrellas cloaking the hill. Almost universally regarded as jazz's greatest composer—an understatement of his stature and contribution to American art and, in my opinion, a slur—Ellington was nothing if not unfailingly elegant and courtly, with a graceful public persona that actually did suggest royalty and all its entitlements. That may explain how Ellington came to be the only person in Woodlawn with two headstones. Yet the grave site, at the corner of Heather and Knollwood, doesn't look grandiose at all. It is clean and spare if no less elegant than its tenant, the two headstones placed beneath a grove of trees.

Where the Ellington memorial clearly keeps faith with the life Duke led, the grave of trumpeter and bandleader Miles Davis, situated just across Heather Avenue where Fir comes in, is more problematic. Unlike Ellington, Davis had no interest in courting the public. On the contrary, it was Davis—perhaps even more than James Dean or Marlon Brando— who made having a bad attitude so fashionable during the fifties. At a time when any African-American artist with commercial or creative aspirations had to pay extremely careful attention to how he was perceived, Davis very pointedly would not, insisting instead that he be judged solely on his work which, for much of his forty-five-year career, was the apex of the art form. One might reasonably expect Davis to be buried in a simple grave whose design echoes his public ethos: here I am—take it or leave it.

Instead, Davis is interred in a sarcophagus mounted on a low pedestal that stands behind a large slab of polished black stone upon which two measures of music and the perplexing inscription "Sir Miles Davis" are carved. To my knowledge it is an honorific Davis never used while alive and seemed to know very little about, mentioning it just in passing in his autobiography. The title was bestowed in 1988 in Spain by the Knights of the Grand Cross in and for the Sovereign Military Hospitaller Order of St. John of Jerusalem of Rhodes and of Malta—a successor to the nine-hundred-year-old order of the Knights of Malta. Now, although the only titled Maltese that any American will possibly be aware of is Baron Miguel Secluna, the professional knockdown artist who once took regular poundings at the hands of Bruno Sammartino, the original Knights of Malta was a true order of knights—and the same order upon which Dashiell Hammett contrived a tale of a legendary, jewel-encrusted falcon. Constituted by the Church during the Crusades, they were chased from base to base in southern Europe by the Moors before finally holding Malta in a bloody sixteenth-century siege, although the order ultimately petered out during the mid-nineteenth century. As its name implies, the group that inducted Davis is actually a service organization, and it currently claims eleven thousand knights and dames. I don't think it insults the order's good works to suggest that employing it to put "sir" on your tombstone is a little like inscribing "president" over your grave because you were head of the Rotary Club.

So what to make of this? Did Miles Davis really care what everybody thought after all? It's possible, but I prefer to subscribe to another theory:

Davis, who had more than a bit of the devil in him, could have done it to break Ellington's chops, to lampoon and one-up the Duke. I'm not aware of any bad blood between the two and whenever Davis mentions Ellington in his autobiography he invariably attaches the highest accolade in his lexicon, which is to say he repeatedly and unswervingly calls Duke "a bad motherfucker." But Woodlawn is a big place—four hundred acres of graves. The odds that Davis just *happened* to wind up right across the road from Ellington are about the same as Davis coming back to life and hosting a fund-raiser for Trent Lott.

Until I'd begun my Woodlawn rambles, I hadn't considered the possibility that the relationships between the dead can be as complex and loaded as those of the living. It's doubtful even Ellington, the master composer and orchestrator, considered that his grave might serve as a counterpoint in another musician's requiem. It is, perhaps, a reminder of how little control we actually have over how we are remembered. If, in fact, we are remembered at all.

Of course, people also make plans which they come to rue. It's not unheard of for lifelong friends like Smith and Dale to want to spend eternity together, yet as sometimes happens things come between even the best of friends and later events can place those decisions in an odd light. So it is with two men buried in Woodlawn's Spring Lake section, Ephraim Squire and Frank Leslie, who formed two-thirds of the Gilded Age's oddest love triangle. The woman who came between them was once Ephraim Squire's wife—and later actually *became* Frank Leslie.

Though drawn from vastly different worlds—Squire was originally a civil engineer from upstate New York and Leslie a glove-maker's son from England—their paths crossed in publishing. Squire was a brilliant man of wide-ranging interests and had successful careers as a writer, newspaper editor, archeologist (his paper on Native American burial mounds was the first scholarly study published by the Smithsonian), diplomat, secretary of a Honduran railway, and publisher of a New York–based Spanish-language newspaper. Meanwhile, Leslie spurned his father's glove business for a career as an engraver, a trade in which he proved quite ingenious: his system drastically cut the time required to create finished plates and made Leslie a leading publisher. He owned dozens of magazines and periodicals, and his flagship titles, *Frank Leslie's Illustrated Weekly* and *Frank Leslie's Illustrated Newspaper*, were trendsetters and enormous moneymakers. In 1861, he hired Squire as editor of the *Illustrated Newspaper*, and the two men quickly became close friends—so close that they purchased a joint plot in the lovely new Woodlawn Cemetery in the farmland north of the city. And when Leslie's marriage ran aground, Squire invited his boss to come live with him and his wife.

Mistake. Big mistake.

Miriam Squire was extremely bright, extremely beautiful, and extremely ambitious. More to the point, she was the kind of woman only a complete sap would put on an intimate footing with his best friend—especially if that friend was one of the richest, most powerful men in Manhattan.

Before long, rumors were rife around New York regarding what *really* went on behind closed doors at the Squire house. But if Ephraim heard them, he paid no mind and the trio embarked together for a European vacation. There Leslie had Squire arrested and locked in an English debtors' prison, enjoying the continent and Mrs. Squire for several weeks before bailing his pal out. Returning to New York, Miriam divorced Squire and married Leslie, and a few weeks later Squire was carted off to Sanford Hall, an insane asylum, where he spent the remaining fourteen years of his life. As one periodical of the time not published by Frank Leslie put it: "He was cast into a madhouse, and his successor sat down to enjoy life and love at the hearth he had polluted." Hey, what are friends for?

Miriam soon proved her worth as an editor and businesswoman, and legally changed her name to Frank Leslie following her husband's death in order to keep rights to it for the publications. An astute publisher, she saved the barely solvent company by making a meal out of the Garfield assassination in 1881 with special editions and extras that posted astronomical sales and put her company back in the black. In later life she used her position as the grand dame of publishers' row to push for women's rights, briefly married Oscar Wilde's thirty-nine-year-old brother, William, when she was sixty, and returned from a trip to Europe claiming descent from a baron whose family emigrated to her native Louisiana, insisting from then on that she be addressed as the Baroness de Bazus. In

1914, when she joined Squire and Leslie in Woodlawn, she left her entire estate of $2 million to suffragette Carrie Chapman Catt. As fate would have it, Catt, who put the money to excellent use in orchestrating the movement that led to the ratification of the Nineteenth Amendment, is buried in Woodlawn with her close friend and companion, the suffrage and temperance leader Mary Garrett Hay. So is Catt's mentor, Elizabeth Cady Stanton, who is buried alongside her husband, the abolitionist Henry Brewster Stanton.

But sometimes couples aren't buried together, regardless of what their memorials say. Ellen Runyon, wife of the famed Broadway scribe Damon Runyon, is the only one in the Woodlawn plot that bears the unadorned inscription "Runyon." Damon, who died fifteen years later in 1946 from throat cancer, was cremated and his ashes scattered over Broadway from a plane piloted by his friend, World War I ace Eddie Rickenbacker. Legend has it that Rickenbacker flew over Woodlawn and dipped a wing, but that seems doubtful as Runyon was no family man. A notable night owl and womanizer, he took little interest in his children, leaving them to the care of the alcoholic Ellen. He left her for a nightclub dancer he'd reportedly been supporting since she was a young girl in Mexico.

Like the Runyons, department store tycoon Isador Straus and his wife, Ida, are separated in death if not in Woodlawn memorial. Unlike them, however, the Strauses were inseparable in life—which is why they died together. Passengers on the *Titanic*, Ida famously refused a seat in a lifeboat to remain onboard with her husband and, according to the account of Archibald Gracie, the pair sat side-by-side in deck chairs, holding hands as the liner sank. Gracie, whose Upper East Side family estate, Gracie Mansion, is now the official residence of the mayor of New York, fared better than the Strauses, but only marginally: he, too, stayed onboard to the end, and a life vest lifted him back to the surface after the ship was sucked under. Eventually hauled onto an inflatable life boat and picked up by the *Carpathian*, Gracie returned to New York but never fully recovered from the injuries or trauma he sustained that evening, dying before year's end. It's unclear how many other *Titanic* survivors are interred in Woodlawn, but there are at least four casualties if you include Gracie. Isador Straus's body was the ninety-sixth recovered; Ida was never found. He was initially buried in Brooklyn, then moved to Woodlawn some years later when the Straus family mausoleum was constructed by his three sons, all buried here. Designed by architect James Gamble Rogers, whose work helped define the campuses of Yale, Columbia, and Northwestern universities, it is one of the most graceful and moving memorials in Woodlawn. Built on long, low lines with brown slabs and small, wrought-iron garden gates, it combines two then-stylish trends in funereal architecture, Egyptology and Deco. It looks more like a compound than a crypt, as if Rogers had imagined a dacha inspired by the strong, clean stone lines of Rockefeller Center. Mounted between the gates on a low wall is a cast of an Egyptian funeral barge, marking the spot where Isador is now buried. On a stone is inscribed an epitaph from *Song of Solomon:* "Many waters cannot quench our love—neither can the floods drown it."

Even in a cemetery as large as Woodlawn, the legend of the Strauses is uniquely touching. Yet the eternal Woodlawn companions who most intrigue me have nothing to do with romance. Just up from the Strauses at the start of the formally named Myosotis Avenue (*myosotis:* the genus of herbaceous plants more commonly known as forget-me-nots) sits the equally formal Garvan mausoleum. A classic Greek temple as executed by John Russell Pope, its portico rests upon a quartet of Ionic columns and an entryway features a frieze of mourners by sculptor Edward Sanford, Jr., who also worked on the enormous statues adorning the Bronx County Courthouse that depict the history of the rule of law. Sanford was an apt choice to decorate the final resting place of Francis Patrick Garvan since, among other things, Garvan was an assistant district attorney in Manhattan, an assistant attorney general in Washington, D.C., and the dean of Fordham Law School in the Bronx. His wife, Mabel, is with him, but it's the presence of Garvan's great friend Finley Peter Dunne—also, oddly enough, interred in the Garvan family mausoleum—that piques my curiosity.

Although he still has scattered admirers, especially among American historians and the handful of journalists with the inclination to date their profession further back than the break-in at the Watergate Hotel, Dunne, who was both a superb observer of American society and politics and one of the most successful and influential columnists in newspaper history, is now largely unread. But in the 1890s, as the editorial page editor of Chicago's *Evening Post*, Dunne created the character Martin Dooley, an Irish bartender, and anonymously used his thickly brogued voice through over seven hundred weekly columns. At first Dunne focused on local Chicago politics, but he soon found that the comic figure of Dooley, holding forth to his customer, Mr. Hennessy, gave him just the right mask and platform for commenting on national affairs. Dunne had a deep grasp of politics and human nature and a phenomenal talent for crafting malapropisms and misquotes in Dooley's voice that somehow dug a deeper meaning. "*Onaisy* is th' head that wears a crown," Dooley sagaciously intoned, crediting the line not to Shakespeare but to his own Chicago crony, Hogan. "They'se other heads that're *onaisy*, too; but ye don't hear iv thim." Among some of Mr. Dooley's more pungent observations (offered here without the brogue): "I'm strong for any revolution that isn't going to happen in my day"; "No matter whether the Constitution follows the flag or not, the Supreme Court follows the election return"; "All you've got to do is believe what you hear, and if you do that enough, after a while you'll hear what you believe"; "The reason you have no money is because you don't love it for itself alone. Money won't ever surrender to such a flirt"; and "The presidency is the highest office in the gift of the people. The vice presidency is the next highest and the lowest. It isn't a crime exactly. You can't be sent to jail for it, but it's a kind of disgrace." He also coined at least one transcendent law for living: "Trust everybody—but cut the cards."

Dunne, who died in 1936 of throat cancer, really reached his apex of popularity and influence around the turn of the century. Mr. Dooley was carried in papers from coast to coast, and in Washington the column was regularly read in cabinet meetings. There it created the uneasy sensation that Mr. Dooley was looking over shoulders not accustomed to being closely scrutinized or held up to ridicule. When Dunne was outted as Dooley, it made him a national celebrity and the highest paid newspaperman in the country. Perhaps his most famous and influential column was a book review of Theodore Roosevelt's *The Rough Riders*. Mr. Dooley cut the book—a self-serving, nearly egomaniacal telling of the Spanish-American War—down to size when he marveled at its author's adventures and superhuman prowess and suggested a more apt title would have been *Alone in Cuba*. A chastened Roosevelt, who was then the governor of New York, was savvy enough to woo Dunne, writing that "I regret to state my family and intimate friends are delighted with your review of my book." He later told Dunne of meeting a young woman on a train who earnestly identified *Alone in Cuba* as her favorite book. Such was the power of Mr. Dooley, and such was the charm of Roosevelt that Dunne never really raised his claws in his direction again.

Indeed, while Dunne was an independent thinker and principled man, success didn't serve his work well. Part of the problem was the extraordinary success of Mr. Dooley. Dunne moved to New York where he wrote on politics and national affairs and edited such publications as *Collier's* and *The American Magazine*, often with great wit and insight. Yet when he wrote seriously as himself and with just as critical an eye on the subjects he'd skewered as Dooley, Dunne found nowhere near the same audience. And as often happens with successful journalists, he didn't prove wholly capable of dealing with his own celebrity. Dunne, as his relationship with Roosevelt indicated, could be seduced. He never completely stopped taking shots at his targets, but he lost sight of the fact that the honest political satirist's raison d'être is savaging whoever has the biggest collection of guns. Instead, Dunne very much enjoyed being an insider, liked the finer things in life and sought the company of men he considered to be his intellectual and professional equals—which is to say he reached a point where he was just as apt to be golfing with the president as criticizing him. He also spent a good deal more time drinking and playing tennis at the exclusive men's clubs he adored than he did writing.

Ironically, it may have been an act of love which put the final nail in Dunne's professional career: in 1927, his close friend, the oil millionaire Payne Whitney, collapsed after a rigorous afternoon on the clay courts and was laid to rest in Woodlawn. Concerned about Dunne's future, he'd left him five hundred thousand dollars—an enormous sum of money at the time—and the hard-drinking Dunne never again worried about living beyond his means. But he found it tougher than ever to write, and couldn't even complete his own memoirs. Yet in his eldest son, Phillip, a successful Hollywood screenwriter and activist, Dunne left a worthy intellectual and spiritual heir. While the younger Dunne's screen credits included the adaptation for the John Ford classic *How Green Was My Valley*, he also had his father's passion for politics: Phillip—who wrote speeches for Adlai Stevenson and managed the ill-fated congressional race of Helen Gaha-gan Douglas, smeared as a red and defeated by opponent Richard Nixon's infamous whisper campaign of 1950—was one of the few in Hollywood to speak out long and steadily against the House Un-American Committee. Very likely it was a matter of public principle for Phillip. But I wonder if he wasn't trying to right his father's wrong. In 1919, at the height of an-other red scare, the normally fearless Finley Peter Dunne had been con-spicuously silent during one of the country's darker moments. Known as the Palmer Raids, the government—in the name of national security—without warrants rounded up thousands of immigrants, held them with-out charge or access to counsel, and deported hundreds. According to one biographer, Dunne justified his silence in a conversation with a friend by saying that no one could stand up to the overwhelming tide of postwar jingoism, yet he seemed all the same to say it with the shame of knowing that he was not rising to the moment. He also had personal reasons not to speak out. The Palmer Raids were masterminded in large measure by his close friend Francis Garvan—a man who named one of his own sons Fin-ley Peter and ultimately paid for Dunne's funeral at St. Patrick's Cathedral and welcomed him into his family's mausoleum.

Whatever ambiguous feelings we might entertain regarding both the shortcomings and humanity of thoughtful, principled men like Dunne whose weakened wills sometimes fail them, how should we feel about strong-willed, principled men who see themselves as infallible? We are living through challenging and upsetting days, days that have caught us by surprise and seem so unique. But in our grief and anger and fear we flatter ourselves: our deaths are not unique. Nor are our days made any less upsetting by the emergence of people and policies whose moral cer-titude precludes admitting that such prescriptions for securing freedom as secret trials, military tribunals, the suspension of due process, profil-ing of immigrants, and open-ended incarcerations are tantamount to de-stroying it, and that while those actions can't actually protect us, they will leave us with a well-deserved sense of shame. I didn't have to raise Francis Patrick Garvan from among Woodlawn's dead and forgotten. Our response to this New York autumn has.

The son of a newly wealthy Connecticut paper mill owner, Garvan made his reputation as an assistant district attorney in Manhattan, prosecuting Harry Thaw in the sensational Stanford White murder case. An advocate of preparedness and a hawkish patriot, he went to Washington in 1917 as a dollar-a-year man. His first position was as an assistant to alien property clerk A. Mitchell Palmer, a post created when President Woodrow Wilson had all German property and assets in the United States seized. Palmer was a former congressman from Pennsylvania whose presidential aspirations were well known, and the no-nonsense Garvan did most of the heavy lifting at the alien property office, devising policy and running the day-to-day business. When Palmer was promoted to attorney general, he continued to rely on Garvan, who both replaced him as alien property clerk and became an assistant attorney general overseeing the Bureau of Investigation.

Where Palmer had the cautious mien of a politician, Garvan demonstrated the convictions of a nationalist in wartime: he had no doubts about what he was going to do and he did it. Like many others, Garvan believed that Germany's industrialists and corporations were hand-in-glove if not synonymous with the enemy's military, that they had long pursued a business course intended to weaken the economies and war efforts of the Allies. As alien property clerk he took an aggressive stance against Germany's powerful chemical cartel, whose enormous strength and strict proprietary practices kept the American chemical industry on a tight leash. Garvan seized all American chemical patents registered to German corporations.

If that action was part of fighting a war, Garvan's next was both that and the subsequent dividing of its spoils: he formed the Chemical Foundation to manage and administer the patents, naming himself president. The foundation's holdings were theoretically available to any American corporation interested in licensing them, and the fees it earned were poured back into the industry in the form of grants and scholarships, many personally supplemented by the Garvans. Yet there was no denying that the foundation, which had been put together by Garvan and a Du

Pont attorney, benefited that company far more than any other. Largely on the strength of the German patents, Du Pont was transformed within a decade from a munitions manufacturer to a global chemical giant, and the Du Ponts became one of the wealthiest families in America.

After the war, Garvan was attacked by the Harding administration as a corporate lackey who had sold his country's interests short by not auctioning the German patents to the highest bidder. Brought to trial, Garvan proved perfectly capable of defending himself, and successfully argued his own case in front of the Supreme Court. He didn't acquit himself anywhere near as well in his role as the assistant attorney general who helped devise the Palmer Raids.

Though undertaken in 1919 and 1920, the raids had their roots in the ultranationalist mood that had attended our entrance into World War I. That mood troubled Dunne, but Garvan wholeheartedly embraced legislation like the federal Espionage Act, which included provisions making it virtually illegal to oppose the war or question United States military policy. To help enforce this, the American Protective League was formed as a patriotic citizen's brigade investigating and reporting to the Department of Justice on un-American activities—with the result that United States attorneys brought close to two thousand prosecutions for disloyal utterances. Conscientious objectors and figures opposing the draft, including leading socialist Eugene V. Debs, were imprisoned. When *The Masses*, a left-wing journal whose contributors included writers Upton Sinclair, Sherwood Anderson, Carl Sandburg, and political cartoonist Art Young, resisted government pressure to tone down its opposition to the war, the U.S. Postal Service refused to handle it and Young was tried twice under the Espionage Act—both trials ending in hung juries—for a cartoon suggesting American capitalists favored war as a way to increase profits. The government also kept a close eye on resident aliens: due in no small part to the efforts of a Garvan protégé, young J. Edgar Hoover at the General Intelligence Division, about six thousand three hundred aliens were arrested during the war and two thousand three hundred were placed under military internment.

After the war, domestic intelligence shifted from German sympathizers and critics of the war to radicals and anarchists. Fears stoked by the

Bolshevik Revolution and a series of inept but nonetheless frightening terror bombings—including one aimed at the Morgan Bank on Wall Street that killed a clerk and numerous customers but no bankers, a mail bomb sent to the Georgia home of a U.S. senator that blew the hands off his maid, and an attempt to bomb Attorney General Palmer's home that only succeeded in leaving a shredded anarchist on the front lawn—led to a public outcry. In the Senate, a unanimous resolution all but forced Palmer to start legal proceedings against anyone preaching anarchy. Everyone, it seemed, from the cabinet to the editorial page of the *New York Times*, was demanding strong action against what was portrayed as a pervasive movement of foreign-born agitators. It was a view that Palmer, with a liberal, pro-labor voting record as a congressman and a cautious eye on the White House, had been slower than many to embrace. But his reservations evaporated after the attempt on his own home, and he now declared that the "very liberal" provisions of the Bill of Rights were expendable, adding that during an emergency there were "no limits" on the power of the government. Considering the results, the similarities between the stance of that government and ours is dismaying. A plan of mass arrests and deportations was put together at Justice, largely by the trio of Hoover, William Flynn—the former head of the Secret Service who was now in charge of the Bureau of Investigation—and their boss, Francis Garvan.

In late 1919, seven hundred people were arrested in New York and over two hundred and fifty immigrants, including the well-known radical Emma Goldman, were deported. Newspapers praised the actions and called for more "Soviet Arks." The Justice Department obliged in January 1920, with a new, wider round of communist, labor, and immigrant sweeps in thirty-three cities that netted ten thousand. The majority of the arrests were made without warrants, as thousands who just happened to be immigrants were denied bail and access to counsel, held without charge and sometimes given the third degree—all in the name of national security. Many of them would have been deported if Assistant Secretary of Labor Louis F. Post, who opposed the raids, hadn't refused to sign the deportation orders. Called to explain his actions before an enraged Congress, Post was not intimidated and his subsequent testimony actually succeeded in bringing an end to the red scare and the excesses at Justice.

In subsequent months, a group of distinguished lawyers and law professors, including future Supreme Court Justice Felix Frankfurter, would release a report on the raids roundly denouncing the Justice Department actions, while several other attorneys opposed to the raids formed what would become the American Civil Liberties Union. Today the Palmer Raids, with their suspension of our "very liberal" rights and the subsequent wrongful imprisonment of thousands, loom larger in our history than the feeble attacks which inspired them, and we recall the period—when we recall it at all—with a deserved sense of shame. Palmer, at first reluctant to act but linked to the raids forever, was ruined politically. Others weren't so easily chastened or quick to fall on their swords. The first response from Flynn and Hoover was to dig through the General Intelligence Division's files to see if any of their critics had radical pedigrees. For his part, Garvan appears to have never expressed any subsequent reservations or doubts. Indeed, when he died in 1937, Hoover was one of his pallbearers and Garvan's friend, Notre Dame President John Cardinal O'Hara, eulogized him as a patriot who'd fought a lifelong battle against reds and other enemies of the country.

I happen to find myself standing in front of the Garvan family mausoleum, monitoring it for vibrations the morning after Edward R. Becker, Chief Justice of the Third U.S. Circuit Court of Appeals in Philadelphia, ruled that our current attorney general has the power to hold secret deportation hearings as a tool in fighting terrorism. Suggesting that even innocuous pieces of evidence could provide valuable clues to terrorists, Justice Becker said he was "unable to conclude that openness plays a positive role in special-interest deportation hearings at a time when our nation is faced with threats." I wish I could tell you I felt something from that grand pile of cold white marble, or that I heard anyone rolling over. But the dead, alas, are dead. We're alive now and it's our turn to deal with these issues and the legacies we've been left and perhaps, I hope, the memory of regret that sacrificing democracy in the name of national security invariably brings. I wish those towers were still there and I want my sons to be safe. But I've also heard it suggested that when a person doesn't know which road to take, they have to pick the harder one. Finley Peter Dunne didn't do that.

Widowhood took Anna Altobelli by surprise. In her twenty-eight years she had never imagined she could wind up alone, and remained steadfast and stubborn in her faith right up to the moment Vincent died of the influenza. Yet somehow she had seemed to know what to do these past six months. Vincent had never discussed money with her, and she was relieved to discover he had been able to put something aside—just enough to get by with the help of the state's new widow's pension. Her three children always needed something, and while she was grateful for the way her neighbors on Vandam Street came by with outgrown clothes and shoes, it made her uncomfortable. She did not like taking such kindness for granted—and that itself was an unexpected discovery. But that wasn't the biggest surprise. Her own father had died just after the family arrived in New York and her mother, in the tradition of the old country, had worn black every day for the rest of her life. Yet Anna already wore only a black scarf. It had nothing to do with Vincent; they had loved each other and she missed his gentle personality, although there were moments when she blamed it for his quick death and was disposed to discourage signs of his nature in their children. These were the feelings she chose to wrap around herself rather than her mother's widow's weeds, and it had much to do with why she had brought Christina to Brooklyn this morning.

The area had changed a great deal in the ten years since Anna's sister, Julietta, had moved here. It was called Pigtown back then, and Anna would have preferred to live in Manhattan's dankest alley. But the subway had changed everything. Blocks of six-story apartments sprang up around Prospect Park like a range of clay and sandstone mountains, and it was hard to look at the enormous new baseball park and crisscrossing trolley lines and remember the hot, hard-baked fields, and the flies and filth of the old rough shacks, stinking chicken coops, and ramshackle pigpens. When Julietta and her husband took an apartment with its own bath in one of Mr. Ebbets's buildings, she urged her sister and Vincent to move nearby. Anna had resisted then—she did not like the way her brother-in-law treated Julietta and feared she would not be able to hold her tongue—but things were different. She would need a job soon. Now, with an apartment about to open in her building, Julietta was once again urging her to move, pledging to watch Christina all day and keep an eye on the boys after school. It made sense—Julietta had five children and Anna's own boys, Michael and John, adored their cousins. There would always be something here for them to do, someone to watch out for them.

Whatever reservations she harbored—about the neighborhood, about her brother-in-law, about leaving the apartment she and Vincent had called home—Anna could feel them evaporating in the warm morning sun. She liked Prospect Park, and never more than today. The maples and elms in their green early summer fullness overhung the entrance at Empire Boulevard, the leaves twisting indolently in the warm wind. Christina had been here often enough to know their destination, a large playground alongside Ocean Avenue, and Anna could barely contain the three-year-old.

Julietta, sitting with three other women on a pair of benches near the playground, waved. Christina ran straight to her, thrusting chubby arms around her aunt's neck.

"Why, look who's here! Is that Christina?" asked Mrs. Cohen, a playground regular. "You can't be Christina—you're too big!"

"Am so! I'm not a baby like Matthew! He can't even *talk*."

It was all so inviting, so comfortable; Anna knew she would agree later when Julietta invariably prodded her to move. That was the way it was with her sister—she always got her way. Anna immediately felt a sharp flush of guilt at the thought, remembering how often she had called Julietta a witch when they were children. Instead she leaned in between her daughter and her sister, giving Julietta a kiss and leaving a hand on her shoulder.

"Good morning, Mrs. Cohen. How are you today?"

"How am I? Tired, but I guess a mother doesn't need sleep. What a racket there was in the downstairs apartment last night! I'm not sure if it's colic, but you wouldn't believe the *geshreying!* Well, at least it drowned out the nightly opera from next door. That one's had more sailors in her than the old tavern by the Gowanus Canal!" At this Anna and Julietta looked at each other, while Mrs. Cohen clapped a hand over her mouth and blushed to the roots of her hair. "Oh my God! I can't believe I said that! And in front of the little one! I'm so sorry!" But the sisters were now laughing, as were the women on the next bench, and Mrs. Cohen waved her hands in defeat and turned to the women on the next bench. "Have you met Mrs. Pastore's sister? No? This is Mrs. Altobelli and Christina. Mrs. Altobelli, this is Mrs. Hamill and Mrs. Feldman. They have very nice sons who I'm sure your boys would just love." Julietta shot Mrs. Cohen a look of warning. "Okay, okay." She made a motion of zipping her lips. "I'll say no more. What do I know?"

Too much, thought Anna, who sensed in the tilted heads and sympathetic smiles of the two other women that they, too, had heard all about Anna's widowhood and Julietta's campaign to bring her to Brooklyn. Yet she doubted her sister had said anything too personal—Anna had always admired her ability to be both outgoing and guarded. Julietta made friends easily, yet Anna was the only one she ever truly confided in. They had shared a sense of propriety even as girls that was now second nature. There was nothing standoffish in it, although it was the kind of behavior people tended to view as dignified only in someone with money. For a widow from the Village or the wife of a street sweeper, it could only be seen as false pride.

The morning found a rhythm as easy as a playground swing. The park buzzed with the sounds of children running and yelling, and Christina was content to simply play with Matthew and several other small children in the sandbox. Anna was happy and dreamy in the sun. It had been a cold, rainy spring and she welcomed the unusually warm weather when it finally arrived. The distant sounds of Ocean Avenue traffic mingled with the voices of the children as the women chatted, and Anna watched Julietta steadily mend pair after pair of socks, the darning pin dropping into her hand like a wooden egg each time she finished. Mrs. Hamill was working crewel on a small tablecloth for a Manhattan department store. Still, Anna's eye was never off Christina for long, and when she saw her put a sandy hand in her mouth she was quick to berate the child. "Christa!" The little girl looked up but kept the hand in her mouth. "What's the matter with you? That's dirty! Pooh!"

"Oh, but that's why it's so good," said Mrs. Cohen.

Anna frowned. "I know. But can you imagine all the cats that must live in the park?" She turned back to the little girl. "Christina, right now! I mean it!" She rose and walked toward the sandbox, where Christina was now hiding her hand behind her back. "You know better than that! Come, let's get some water." She took the little girl by the hand and led her to a drinking fountain where a fat boy clutching a ball in one hand and leaning on the push-button spigot with the other was sucking up water. Anna watched disapprovingly as he put his lips right onto the metal fountain. Why did they always do that? The boy, aware of them, was slow to relinquish his place. He finally drifted away with feigned indifference, water dripping from his chin onto his shirt, and Anna lifted Christina over the fountain bowl, washing her hands and making her rinse her mouth.

In the early afternoon an ice vendor stopped his small wooden cart just beyond the playground gate and the children swarmed around. Anna bought two cups doused with cherry syrup, and Christina, her lips and chin painted red, soon fell asleep, a sticky hand on her mother's neck. Anna, knowing she would soon need to meet Michael and John, nudged Julietta with her knee. "Tell me about this apartment."

"It's on the floor below me," she said without looking up from her darning. "Two bedrooms and an eat-in kitchen. A nice, big living room. Private bath, of course."

Of course! On Vandam they shared a toilet with four other families and the nearest public bathhouse was on Houston Street. She'd been silly to hold out for so long. "Do you think it's too late for me to talk to the building manager?"

Julietta, closing the last gap in the toe-hole of a child's dark blue sock, pulled her needle through in a finishing knot and bit the thread. "I told him you'd take it last week," she said without looking up. "It's yours at the start of August—you just have to sign the lease. And you get the first month rent-free."

Anna shook her head and laughed. "You're always so sure you know what I'm going to do!" Julietta shrugged noncommittally. "No? No?" Anna playfully grabbed her sister's elbow. "How do you know all the time?"

Julietta scrunched her face and raised two quivering hands toward her sister. "I cast the spell and ask the crystal ball!"

Anna blushed. "You're going to be wrong one of these days. And then I'll never let you forget it."

"Oh no, no, no! Don'a say dat!" Julietta was wagging a finger and talking like Mrs. Spabari, the old woman from Verona who had been their neighbor growing up. Anna and Julietta had mimicked her endlessly at home and on the streets, using her voice to lampoon all the old ways. "Den I have to geeva you da Evil-a Eye."

Anna crossed her forearms and held them up like a crucifix to ward off evil. "Back witch! Back demon spirit! Give me back my sister!"

The other women smiled unsteadily, aware that they were hearing an old private joke, but unsure what it was exactly and whether there wasn't something vulgar in it. But the sisters offered no further clues beyond briefly holding hands before Julietta, taking stock of the still-sleeping Christina's cherry-smeared face, rose to wet a handkerchief at the fountain. "You should be going," she said.

Anna gently flexed a numb leg trying not to wake Christina. "It's Wednesday—the boys have Confraternity until five."

The fresh water from the fountain felt good between Julietta's fingers. She hadn't realized how hot the day was and couldn't resist rubbing the cool damp cloth against her temples and down her neck. Standing still, hoping for a breeze against her wet skin, she was gazing aimlessly around the playground when she noticed a boy bent over and leaning unsteadily against the iron railing beyond the swings. It was Mrs. Cohen's son, Max, who'd apparently had too much sun. She took the wet kerchief to him and was surprised to see that he had just been sick, the remnants of his lunch in a splatter across his shoes and the ground. The boy still clutched his stomach, a long thin line of saliva trailing from his chin to his shirt, and he started to cry as soon as he saw Julietta. "Come on, sweet boy," she said, picking him up and wiping his chin and mouth. "Let's get you to your mama."

Mrs. Cohen was up and waiting, arms outstretched. "What happened?" she asked.

"I'm sick," Max moaned.

"What did you eat?" The boy made no reply. "No more ices for you. Who knows where they come from or where they've been? You feel hot, too."

"My head hurts." His small wet face twisted in pain and he started to cry. "I have to be sick again."

"Poor boy!" Julietta said. Max's cries had woken Christina, who looked unhappily around. "Looks like your mama should get you home, too."

"My downstairs neighbor's boy had the same thing," said Mrs. Feldman. "The doctor came and told her it was a stomach bug. But the poor thing really was sick—diarrhea, vomiting, dizzy, headaches. She even had the doctor back again last night when he started complaining his legs were sore."

"What did the doctor say?" Julietta asked.

Mrs. Feldman shrugged. "That it's a bug. He should get up and walk around when he can. The stiffness will go away in a couple of days."

Anna nodded and sighed. "Well, I hope you feel better," she said to Max and Mrs. Cohen. "I know a couple of older boys who are going to want to play ball with you when they move into the neighborhood in a few weeks." Then, to Christina: "Come on, it's time for us to get that sticky juice off your face and go home."

"Sorry," Julietta said, making a face and holding up the dirty handkerchief, "but I think she'd better not use this."

The subway was hot and dark, and Anna could feel Christina tossing uncomfortably against her all the way back to Houston Street. The little girl never liked the ride under the best of circumstances, and she was particularly irritable and unhappy today, burying her head in Anna's skirt and covering her ears whenever another train rumbled noisily past. At home, Anna put dinner on the stove and waited for the boys. When they arrived—dirty and sweaty and late from stopping to play—she made them clean up and finish their work from religious instruction before dinner. Christina, worn out from the day, hardly ate and was asleep as soon as Anna put her down.

On Saturday, Michael and John spent the morning playing tag in the hallways with Little Willie, the son of Big Willie the iceman, who lived in the basement apartment. Little Willie's mother was a seamstress and spent Saturdays attaching collars and cuffs to shirts at a factory off Broadway, and the Altobelli boys were used to including him in whatever they did. That morning, when Willie threw up in the hallway, Anna recognized the same symptoms from Max Cohen's stomach bug and brought the boy into their apartment to lay down. He spent much of the rest of the day running down the hall to the toilet, and his attacks were frequent and painful enough for Anna to station John out on the landing, where he encouraged other tenants to use the toilet on the next floor. By the time his mother came home that evening, Willie had a fever of 103 and a headache. On Monday, Willie was still ill and complaining of aching arms and shoulders, and a doctor was summoned. As Anna had predicted, a stomach virus was the diagnosis, and she wasn't surprised when Michael woke Monday morning complaining of a headache and stomach pains. She watched him carefully during the day and was encouraged to see his bug was a good deal less severe than Willie's. On Wednesday Michael was still tired and weak, and Anna continued to keep him home from school. Still, she felt his case was mild enough to leave him home alone and take Christina for their weekly visit with Julietta, trusting Michael could get any assistance in an emergency from Willie's mother; poor Little Willie was still at home and showed hardly any improvement.

If possible, the day was warmer than it had been the previous Wednesday, and Anna looked forward to spending the morning in the park. But when they passed through the entrance at Empire Boulevard and turned up the path, she saw just a handful of children and no women she recognized. They stayed only to get Christina a drink from the fountain before walking the six blocks to Julietta's Maple Avenue apartment. The lobby, with a pink stone floor and white wall tiles, was dark and cool enough to revive Christina for the three-flight walk up to Julietta's apartment, and they could hear Matthew whining incoherently about something through the door, as well as Julietta's muffled response. When Anna rang, it was a long moment before she saw an eye in the peephole and heard the bolt slide. She was struck by how tired and pale Julietta looked—stray hairs popped from the twisted plait she wore up, and clung limply to her sweaty neck. "Oh, God," she said, letting them in. "Is it really Wednesday?" Then, turning to Christina, she said, "Honey, don't play with Matthew—I don't think he's feeling well."

Anna shrugged. "I wouldn't worry about her. Michael is already home with this stomach illness, so if she's going to get it, she'll get it at home."

Julietta shook her head. "Dolly has it, too. But I don't think it's really just a stomach bug. Three of the children from her class are in Kingston Avenue Hospital. One of them can't walk at all." She glanced down furtively at Christina and then leaned close enough to her sister to whisper in her ear. "Max Cohen is dead."

———————

Twenty months into his term as commissioner of the New York City Department of Health, Haven Emerson could say two things about the mayor with certainty. The first was that Emerson didn't like him. And the second was that the first was of no consequence: John Purroy Mitchel truly, forever, and for all time didn't give a good goddamn what he or anyone else liked or didn't like.

The Emersons had long enjoyed a well-deserved reputation around New York as public health reformers, but they also had a hard-won appreciation for the real limits imposed by politics. Haven had never encountered anyone in city government quite like this mayor. Indeed, he'd barely known him when Mitchel proffered Emerson the commissioner's post. Since then, he'd found him almost unbearable—remarkable since he and Mitchel agreed in principle and practice on nearly every aspect of the public health mission. In some ways, Haven was in awe of Mitchel—his intellect was truly intimidating. Yet it was hardly a counterbalance to the rest of the man's makeup. Mitchel was more than self-righteous and rude: he was a political naif whose near-maniacal disdain for cronyism delighted opponents and caused friends to turn their back. Frustrating didn't begin to describe it: the city finally had a progressive reform mayor with the brains and stomach to reinvent New York for a new century, and Emerson, who'd dreamed of such a man his entire adult life, couldn't stand him.

At 3 a.m., Haven had come out of a meeting at the Brooklyn Health Department and immediately telephoned Teddy Rousseau, the mayor's private secretary, to insist on the first available appointment with Mitchel. The hawk-eyed guardian of his boss's time, Teddy hadn't questioned Emerson—every commissioner knew wasting the mayor's time with fatuous meetings was suicidal—and simply said to meet him at City Hall at seven. Haven, with little time to go home, had dismissed his police driver with instructions to meet him at City Hall at eight and strolled the Heights collecting his thoughts. God, what if Mitchel exploded and blamed the department? Crossing the Brooklyn Bridge, he still wasn't sure what to tell the mayor, and his mind was as uneasy and jumbled as the East River flowing far beneath his feet.

True to his word, Teddy was waiting at the top of the City Hall steps.

He was a small man and his ever-toussled fluff of brown hair gave him a young and deceptively cherubic look, yet his fierce devotion to the mayor was legend. If people around City Hall viewed Emerson as a high-born dilettante, they approached Rousseau with a healthy mix of admiration and apprehension. To the extent that anyone actually had Mitchel's ear, it clearly was Rousseau, who served his prickly and unpredictable boss heart and soul. "Is he in already?" Emerson asked, his voice echoing hard against the marble walls of the empty formal lobby. The secretary grimaced and gave an exaggerated roll of his eyes. "He spent the night."

"Really? I thought he was the featured speaker at a big dinner in Brooklyn."

"Didn't go," Teddy said with a staccato shake of his head. Except for the two policemen at the desk near the door, the building was deserted and the sound of their own brisk footfalls all that greeted Emerson and the secretary. Because of Mitchel, Teddy had to develop the habit of walking fast and watching him try to keep up with the mayor was one of the great amusements of City Hall. Tall, young, athletic, and a devoted dancer, Mitchel moved not just extraordinarily quickly, but with a unique energy and grace. And two steps behind him—mouth open, shaggy hair bouncing—came Teddy, always seeming to require three times as many steps just to keep stride. Now, without the impossible yardstick of the mayor at his side, there was no comedy in Teddy's walk, just determination. "He had an emergency meeting with the city's counsel, a couple of the district attorneys, and Police Commissioner Woods. About the wiretaps."

So the wiretaps were real. Emerson had heard about them a week earlier from his chief health inspector, a man with excellent police department contacts, but hadn't believed it. Oh, this was what worried him about Mitchel! He'd ascended to City Hall as a crusading hero—the special prosecutor who'd sent the corrupt borough presidents of both Manhattan and the Bronx to Sing Sing—but his style of brawling horrified Emerson. The man always picked the right fight and the wrong weapon. No one could disagree with this particular cause—ensuring public funds dispensed to private charities were properly applied—and he knew some of the city's privately run orphanages and pest houses were downright medieval; even he couldn't believe some of the conditions at the city asylum on Randall's Island. But eavesdropping on priests! A wiretap on an auditor from the city's Department of Finance—a defrocked Protestant minister by the name of Potter—had apparently captured conversations with a Catholic priest in which the two men had worked out a little something for themselves while otherwise gilding the audit of a Church charity. What a mess! Although they were alone in the building, Teddy leaned in close and lowered his voice. "I hear Cardinal Farley went *berserk*. Threatened him with excommunication. Well, at least intimated it. God, wouldn't *that* be something! People probably think he wouldn't care because he doesn't attend church, but believe me, he'd care. Plenty."

Emerson felt a bit embarrassed to discover how relieved he was that it wasn't his department or his fight. He was more than happy to let Charities Commissioner Kingsbury be out front on this one. Besides, Emerson knew he would have more than enough trouble to contend with this summer.

"Mr. Mayor." Teddy's call and stage knock was intended to give Mitchel a moment to straighten up, but Emerson—who was feeling the effects of not going to bed—couldn't see any sign that Mitchel needed it. Alone in the large office, the mayor was sitting on the front edge of his desk facing them, hands gripping the edge, feet swinging quickly. Mitchel's black leather shoes were expensive and freshly polished, and he wore a dark gray suit and tie and a new linen shirt with stiff collar and cuffs. His blue-black hair, parted in the middle, glistened with the expensive French pomade he favored, and his lips were taut and bloodless. He had just been shaved; Emerson could smell the tart odor of witch hazel. Even at rest, Mitchel's body was long and powerful, and the swing of his legs and the tilt of his head were enough to suggest a preternatural energy. The commissioner couldn't look at him without thinking of a Pennsylvania oil well he'd once seen blow its cap and explode. But nothing was so unsettling as Mitchel's eyes. They were dark—nearly black—and intense. Yet they were oddly unfocused and frequently betrayed their owner's preoccupation. It was strange: even with the mayor staring straight at him, Emerson often felt Mitchel's mind was somewhere else. Yet he'd never once caught the mayor not listening, and his ability to absorb and retain information was a well-worn topic around City Hall.

"Haven." They were shaking hands, and it seemed to Emerson that

Mitchel hadn't moved—that he had simply been sitting one minute and standing in front of him the next. Or perhaps Emerson was just tired.

"Good morning, Mr. Mayor. Thank you for seeing me on such short notice."

Mitchel shrugged, a pointed finger directing Emerson to a small, round table with four chairs by the window. "Teddy, can you find us some coffee?" The secretary closed the door behind him and Mitchel took the chair opposite Emerson. As in walking, he spoke quickly and never gave one extra moment to a conversation. "What's the problem?"

"I've just come from a meeting in Brooklyn. Our top man there . . .

"Billings."

"Yes. They've been tracking an outbreak in south Brooklyn."

"Of?"

Emerson exhaled heavily. He wanted to slow the conversation and, steeling himself, looked directly into those eyes. "Well, at first we thought it was a gastrointestinal flu. The symptoms are fever, nausea, stomach pains with the usual attending side effects, and a weakness in the joints and limbs. Most of the cases were in an Italian neighborhood and we suspected food poisoning. Of course, we checked all the stores and carts for contamination but found nothing. Two days ago, Billings received a telephone call from a doctor at the Kingston Avenue Hospital urging him to come by." He paused for a minute. "John, their children's ward is at double capacity. Nearly four dozen of those kids can't even walk, and they've had eight deaths in the last three days. Billings called every hospital, every ward and police precinct in Brooklyn and as far as we can ascertain thirty-five children between the ages of six months and nine years have died in the last week. We haven't even checked any other boroughs yet. The doctors at Kingston think it's poliomyelitis—infantile paralysis. I'm certain they're right."

"How localized is it? You said south Brooklyn."

Emerson shook his head. "Originally. Not anymore. The Kingston ward has children from all around Brooklyn."

"So the rest of the city . . . ?"

"We'll find out. But in any event it would just be a matter of time."

Mitchel nodded, absentmindedly touching up his hair with a palm. "When was the last polio epidemic?"

"Nine years ago."

"And?"

"And not much. There are theories—it's probably a bug that enters through the mouth and nose and adheres to mucous membrances—but no one is sure. All we really know is that it comes and goes with the heat. If this is a polio epidemic, we're not going to be able to do much more than ride it out and wait for September."

"Oh, come on. You're telling me there's nothing we can do?"

"Well, there's some evidence the disease is carried by other animals, particularly flies and cats. Obviously the city is a good deal cleaner than it was just a few years ago, but I suspect it started in the immigrant neighborhoods because they're not as careful. Perhaps a concerted effort to educate and improve on sanitation could slow the spread of any epidemic."

Mitchel nodded. "That's a start. Get your inspectors out. You'll have whatever you need from the sanitation department. And if you don't, then just come see me. When are you going to know where things stand in the other boroughs?"

"By the end of the day."

"I want to know when you do. Is anyone else aware of this?"

"Nothing in the papers. But thirty-five pediatric deaths—someone's going to figure it out."

"They shouldn't have to. After you've heard from the other boroughs, I'll send a speech writer over and he'll help you with a statement for the papers. But if you don't find a significant number of cases outside of Brooklyn, there's no reason to report it as anything other than an isolated outbreak."

Emerson thought it a dubious strategy. "Polio can be highly contagious," he said.

Mitchel gave a slight shrug. "Then people should have all the information we can give them. Anything else I should know?"

"In the 1907 epidemic, there was a mortality rate of approximately 4 percent. This looks far more virulent. Based on the number of tentatively diagnosed cases in Brooklyn, we could be looking at a mortality rate of 20 percent."

"Then we better hope we can contain it. I want prominently marked quarantines wherever there are diagnosed cases. I also want treatment and prevention guidelines included in your statement tonight. Make it clear that wherever there is a diagnosed case and treatment guidelines can't be adhered to, the city will remove the patient to a hospital for proper treatment. If you're right and this is a particularly bad epidemic, the tone we set will be of paramount importance. Otherwise there'll be hysteria."

"I agree. But if you're asking whether I think we can contain the outbreak, I'd have to say probably not."

Mitchel scowled. "Can't you say anything good?"

"As a matter of fact, Mr. Mayor, I can. Thank God school ends in two days."

Horrifying as it was, the news of Max Cohen's death had been nearly incomprehensible and Anna hadn't felt the full cold thrust of terror's metal spike until the newspapers spoke the disease's true and terrible name. *Polio!* On her hands and knees, a hard-bristle brush in her reddened hands, a steaming bucket of scalding water and lye-spiked disinfectant at her elbow, she spent hour after hour scrubbing the floors and walls of her apartment, washing the windows, meticulously wiping down the furniture and buffing the doorknobs until her hands felt as if they were on fire. She no longer let Christina go to the toilet out on the landing alone, insisted on accompanying her and scrubbing the bowl inside and out first, and made the boys take disinfectant and rags. Yet Anna still found it impossible to even say the word aloud. Michael had recovered quickly, but she still blamed herself for his illness and couldn't stop obsessing over how much worse it might have been—she should have been more careful that day in the park! She should have separated the boys from Little Willie as soon as she saw him get sick—a mother should *know!*—and lived in perpetual dread that her next mistake would not be so slight. Even Vincent's death had not shocked her this way, had not made her fearful of the world outside her door. Everything had changed.

Her neighbors, for instance. Mrs. Van Eyck, normally so friendly and always giving Michael and John clothes her son Billy outgrew, passed wordlessly by in the hallway yesterday. As if she weren't there! And old Mr. Levine had used the most vulgar language to chase her boys and two of their friends off the stoop when they were just playing ball. And all she could do was thank God that Michael was well enough to be up and around! But of course all her neighbors knew that he had been sick—no secrets in a tenement—and now they avoided the Altobellis. Worse still, everyone knew that Little Willie had taken ill in their apartment. That poor family! The boy's condition had not improved, and Big Willie had been forced to change his ice route to another neighborhood when no one would let him in their apartment. And at home on Vandam Street, the boy's lingering illness seemed to seep from under the door of their apartment and hang over the building like an ominous summer rain cloud. Yesterday Anna noticed that the three old crones from the neighborhood who dressed in black and normally dealt with the summer heat by carrying their folding chairs down to the river near Spring Street had set up in the shade of the building across the street. The buzzards were waiting for Little Willie to die—as if it were a show! It was enough to send Anna defiantly downstairs to the iceman's apartment to see how the boy was doing. But she had only knocked once, and not very loudly, and was relieved when no one answered. Still, she made it a point to give the old women a dirty look whenever she came in and out of the building.

The doctors in the newspaper said flies carry the disease and all windows need screens—she had read that screens were even one of the conditions the Department of Health inspectors were insisting on for anyone treating a case of polio at home. The day before, Anna had dragged Christina to every hardware and general store in the neighborhood and scoured the stalls and pushcarts along both Canal and Houston, all to no avail. There wasn't a window screen left in lower Manhattan. This morning, in frustration, she'd asked a policeman and he'd said that landlords had to supply them to anyone who asked. Immediately cheered, she took Christina straight to the leasing agent's office down on West Broadway to see Mr. Greene, who managed their building and many others. She had always liked him—he was a nice man who invariably asked after her children and had urged her to call him Norman—and knew he would give her screens. But the office, normally staffed by several clerks and buzzing with tenants paying their rent or seeking repairs at that hour, was locked and dark.

All Anna could think about during the long walk back to Vandam Street was finding Norman Greene. She checked a telephone book in a Sixth Avenue drugstore and found him listed near Gramercy Park. At first she thought to call, but then decided it would be harder for him to refuse her in person, blushing as she realized what she was doing. But she had to have those screens—really, she should have had them last night. The apartment was sweltering with the windows closed, but she worried about flies landing on the baby while she slept. She'd hung more than a dozen limp sheets of flypaper over Christina's crib.

In the afternoon Anna dropped the boys at the green edge of Washington Square Park with strict instructions not to wander. She didn't worry about leaving them—school was out for the summer and the park's playgrounds, fountain, and paths were overrun with children. Still, something was amiss—she couldn't quite say what—and she was wondering what it could be when, climbing onto the Sixth Avenue trolley for the ride uptown to Gramercy Park, she spotted an empty seat and sat down gratefully, pulling Christina up onto her lap. The man to her right immediately rose and moved to the other side of the car. Only then did Anna realize she hadn't seen more than two or three adults in the park. She wrapped a protective arm around Christina and scowled at the man, who wouldn't look at them. No one was looking at them. Indeed, they all had their heads buried in the newspaper, or stared intently at the floor or out the window—anywhere else. And when the trolley reached the Twelfth Street stop and none of the passengers pulled the cord, the driver sailed past two dark-haired boys waiting at the corner.

"Oh, for shame!" Anna said, loud enough for the driver to hear her. Yet barely a newspaper rustled, and Anna was resigned to having her remark fall on deaf ears until she noticed the plump middle-aged woman across the aisle smiling sweetly at Christina.

"What a perfect little doll you are!" she said with an exaggerated point of a finger. "And you have the most beautiful blond curls. Yes, you do!" The woman looked at Anna. "Did she get that blond hair from her father?"

Anna smiled and shook her head. "It's hard to believe looking at me now, but my hair was the same color at her age. My sister's, too." She stroked her daughter's hair affectionately and the girl, always a little leery of strange adults, snuggled deeper into her bosom. "Maybe she'll be luckier than we were."

"Well, it's easy to see that she's a darling. I hope you are careful about where you take her and who she plays with."

"We're on our way to see the landlord's leasing agent. To pick up our window screens."

The woman nodded her approval. Then she leaned forward. "I don't say it to be nosy—I just worry when I see a beautiful girl like yours. I have a neighbor who's a doctor, you know, and he said that blond children are the most susceptible to paralysis. It's a statistical fact. Why, the doctor says he knows of no cases of Negroes contracting polio—they're virtually immune!" She shook her head. "Incredible, isn't it? These outbreaks always start in the worst neighborhoods, but who gets hurt? We've gone too far in letting just anyone come here. These people will never really be true Americans—they're not like you and me. They can't appreciate the responsibilities a free democracy entails." The woman reached her hand across the aisle and gave Christina's knee a playful waggle. "We've got to protect little dolls like this."

Anna could see the Twenty-first Street stop ahead. She scooped the child up and reached a shaking hand for the brake cord. "*Avanti*, Christa," she said moving toward the exit.

"Obviously I didn't mean her," the woman said to a nicely dressed man as they watched Anna pull Christina toward Gramercy Park. "I suppose if you're not raised in polite company you can't recognize it." The man nodded.

Norman Greene's apartment was in a large new building opposite the northeast corner of a lovely gated park. A uniformed man with gloves guarded a matching pair of glass front doors with gleaming silver bars depicting the rays of twin rising suns. It was, Anna thought, the most splendid building in the city. The doorman smiled at them.

"Can I help you, ma'am?"

"Yes, please. I'm here to see Mr. Norman Greene."

"Is he expecting you?"

"Well, no." She suddenly felt uncertain. "Is that a problem? He knows me."

"I'm not sure the Greenes are still here. They're leaving today." He nodded meaningfully toward Christina. "Taking their son out of the city to friends in the country. You know what I mean."

Anna nodded and without thinking ran her fingers through the child's hair. "Are you sure they've left?" she finally asked.

The doorman held up a finger and ducked just inside the doors. Anna could see him take up the earpiece to an intercom—oh, this was a splendid building!—and press a button. In a moment he was talking with someone, and he leaned back out the door, holding onto the earpiece cord.

"I'm sorry, ma'am. What's your name?"

"Anna. Anna Altobelli from 127 Vandam."

The conversation didn't last much longer.

"Mrs. Greene said you'll have to go to the office and speak with someone else. Mr. Greene has taken a leave."

"Oh, but I've *been* to the office! They're closed! Look, mister, I've got to have screens for my apartment, don't you understand?"

The doorman eyed Christina. "Sure. I got boys. Bunch of plug-uglies. Not like this one." He smiled, took a step closer, and looked over his shoulder into the lobby. "I know why you're here—Greene's a good guy and a soft touch. His missus, though—" he held out a hand and wobbled it. "Poor bastard." He eyed Anna for a moment, then nodded toward the side of the building. "They've got a hired car to take 'em upstate and they been loadin' suitcases and whatnot out the back service entrance on Twenty-second Street for the last hour or so. Maybe if you was to just happen by he'd see ya and you could get your screens." He held up both hands. "But I don't know nothin' about this, understand?"

She saw the car as soon as they turned the corner and waited until Mr. Greene came out of the alley alongside the building with a box. A small, thin boy with dark hair who looked to be about six years old tagged along behind him. Anna hoped his mother was still upstairs.

"Mr. Greene?"

He didn't recognize her at first, but then he saw Christina. "Anna? What are you doing in this neighborhood?"

"Oh. Well, it's such a nice day I was just—that is, we, Christina and I, were—" It was no use. "We came to see you."

"Me? Whatever for?"

"I'm so sorry, Mr. Greene, but I've just got to have screens for my apartment. Even with flypaper everywhere, I can't leave the windows open for long and you know how hot it's been these last few weeks. My middle one, Michael, he almost got sick already."

Greene gave her a funny look. "What do you mean, 'almost sick'?"

Anna felt her stomach drop but smiled weakly. "Oh, you know how boys are. They're out in the street with their friends, going in and out of other apartments. Too much sun, too much dirt, too much running around. And who knows what garbage they eat? Then they come home and say their stomach hurts and they don't want the dinner you've spent all afternoon cooking for them. He's fine. Really. Really, Mr. Greene." She looked straight at him for the first time. "The office is locked up. Can't you help me? Please?"

The boy had wandered over and was looking at Christina with good-natured interest. "Get in the car, Morton," Greene said sharply. Then, looking again at Anna, he shook his head. "They're not going to open again until this is over. They don't want to have to buy screens for fourteen hundred and fifty apartments. I'm sorry, Anna."

"But what am I going to do? I've been to every store I can think of— there aren't any screens anywhere!" Anna's lower lip wobbled and she could feel herself losing control. "Oh, Mr. Greene, what should I do?"

He put a hand on her shoulder. "Don't cry. Come on, I'll give you some screens." He turned to the boy in the car. "Stay put. I'll be right back."

Greene walked Anna and Christina back to the front of the building.

"Jimmy, this is Mrs. Altobelli," he said to the doorman, who was doing his best to show no interest in Anna until Greene gave him two dollars. "After Mrs. Greene and I leave for the country, I want you to go upstairs and bring her four of the screens from our windows. Tie them together so she can get them downtown, okay?"

"Oh, Mr. Greene, no!" Anna said. "Won't Mrs. Greene be upset?"

"She'll never know. I'll have someone from the office install new ones before we come back. But do me a favor—take Christina into the park or for something to eat for another hour and come back after we've gone."

"Whatever you want, of course! And thank you! Oh, you're such a wonderful man!"

He smiled, embarrassed, and started to back away. "Yes, well, I don't want to leave Morton alone for too long. Good luck."

"And you, too, Mr. Greene. Thank you and God bless you."

When Greene was out of sight, Jimmy gave her a wink. "I'd say that worked out well." He held up the bills and crinkled them noisily between two fingers. "For you *and* for me!"

Tied together with rope and a makeshift handle, the screens were awkward and unwieldy, and climbing on and off the trolley with Christina was more difficult than Anna had imagined; she was happy when she could give them to the boys to carry from the park to Vandam Street, even though Michael still wasn't quite as strong as usual and had to stop and rest twice a block. Still, she would have gladly carried the load on her back if that's what it had taken, and nothing could remove the bounce from her step. Screens!

The moment they turned into their block the empty chairs of the three crones told her that something wasn't right—she saw that before she saw the old horse-drawn ambulance. It was standing in front of her building and a black automobile with INSPECTOR — DEPARTMENT OF HEALTH painted in white letters on the driver's door was parked behind it. The boys ran ahead to join the crowd gathered around the stoop, but a cold bolt of panic shivered her spine and Anna felt her legs turn to water. She clutched Christina's hand and walked the rest of the way in a daze.

"Momma, momma!" John said. "They want to take Willie to the hospital!"

The hospital? Hearing the boy wasn't dead roused Anna from her stupor. "Go upstairs, now. Get your brother."

"Oh, no, ma! I want to see what's happening!"

She grabbed him roughly by the shoulder and spun him toward the front door. "I said get your brother and get inside. Here, give me the screens."

Shocked by his mother's sharp tone, the boy grabbed his younger brother by the wrist and moved quickly up the steps, following Anna as she used the bundle of screens to drive a wedge through the crowd. Crane-necked, gaping hopefully for a view into the iceman's first-floor apartment, they barely took notice of her. Anna could hear Willie's hysterical mother even before they entered the vestibule.

". . . no right! None! Don't you think I know how to take care of my son? Don't you? What kind of people are you? You come here when my husband is working and can't stop you! Bullying a woman and a sick child!"

The voice that answered was quiet and harder to hear, yet unyielding. Hurrying by the open apartment door, insistently nudging the boys with the front of the screens and hardly giving Christina's feet a chance to scrape the floor, Anna managed a furtive glance into the apartment. It was crowded: Willie's mother was surrounded by a tall, bald man in shirt-sleeves—he was the one talking—as well as two white-smocked ambulance drivers and a pair of policemen. Anna drove the boys up the stairs.

"Willard Parker? *Willard Parker?*" Willie's mother was shrieking, her voice filling the stairwell. "Why don't you just put him in the street and run him over? Better yet, put us both in the street and run us over! Can't you at least take him to New York or a decent hospital? You think I don't know what you're up to? You think I'm stupid? Why don't you take him where you take the rich kids? No, you want him to die in some filthy ward. Why? I keep telling you it's just a bad stomach! You want to stick him in a room with forty others and make sure he *does* get polio! Why are you bothering us? Why don't you leave my Willie alone? He's not the only one in the building who's been sick, you know!"

Anna, hanging out over the rail of her landing and listening, felt as if she'd been shot. Oh, God! When all she'd ever done was look out for Willie—the ungrateful witch! For a moment she thought to send Michael to the roof until they left, but everyone out front had seen them come in. She ran into the apartment, locking the door behind her.

"Michael! Quick!"

Oh, the boy was filthy! Between the afternoon in the park and carrying the screens, he looked as if he'd been rolling on the ground. She had to hurry.

"Come." She led him into the kitchen and pulled his shirt over his head. He'd lost weight and looked pale. She ran the water in the sink and, lathering a cloth with soap, scrubbed hard from the tip of his fingers up his frail arms to the top of his head all the while taking no interest in his protests. From the doorway, John and Christina watched silently. The boy's arms turned rosy from the scrubbing but his face, though clean, looked even paler than before. Without warning, she pinched each of his cheeks hard. Michael burst into tears.

"I'm sorry, Michael, but you've got to listen to me—this is very important. Very important. The men from Willie's apartment may come up here soon. They're looking for sick children. But you're not sick, are you?" Big-eyed, he shook his head. "No, you're not. And you weren't, either. Do you understand? If he asks if you were sick, say no. And if he asks you anything else, I'll answer. *Capice?*" The terrified boy nodded. "Good boy. Okay. Go put on a clean shirt. John, you help me put these screens in."

As they struggled to fit the screens into the kitchen window, Anna watched the ambulance drivers load Willie on a stretcher, his mother climbing in beside him for the ride to Willard Parker. The man in the white shirt was wearing a hat now and standing on the street alongside the policemen—maybe he wasn't coming up after all. Maybe she hadn't said anything more to them! Or perhaps it was late and he just wanted to go home! The man said something to one of the policeman, who turned and spoke to Mr. and Mrs. Rose from downstairs. Mr. Rose shrugged and the couple turned away. Then the policeman crossed the street and spoke to the chair ladies. One of them pointed up at the Altobellis' window.

Oh, God!

In the minute it took for them to come upstairs, Anna tried and discarded a half-dozen plans. Maybe she shouldn't answer the door. Should she refuse to let them into the apartment and talk to them in the hallway? Maybe they didn't know how many children were in the apartment—she could hide Michael in the closet and only let them see John and Christina. In the end, she decided to seat the boys side by side on her bed in the living room and answer the door with the baby in her arms. Nothing to hide, she thought—no one sick here. She felt confident.

Her confidence disappeared with the first knock. Anna realized she was shaking as she turned the lock and hoped her boys didn't see.

"Yes?" She made sure the man in the white shirt and the policemen saw her prop Christina on her hip.

"Mrs. Altobelli? I'm Mr. Henry from the Department of Health. I'd like to come in and have a word with you, please."

She opened the door without a word, but forced a smile. They entered, the policemen looking around the small sparsely furnished living room, Mr. Henry looking only at Anna. He was very tall and took his hat off as soon as he passed through the doorway. He looked . . . normal, like any stranger on the street. Still, Anna couldn't keep her legs from shaking and she had to transfer Christina to the other hip to hide it.

"Do you know Willie Stephens?"

"Yes, he's the iceman." She was surprised to hear how calm her voice was.

"No, I mean his son."

"Of course I know Little Willie. I know every child on this block and the next one." She smiled. "Is he going to be all right?"

"That's what we want, although his mother doesn't seem to understand that."

Anna was silent.

"I understand one of your children has been sick."

"No. Maybe somebody else."

Mr. Henry looked at the boys sitting on the sofa for the first time; John was staring straight ahead, refusing to acknowledge them, and Michael was looking at his feet.

"Son," the inspector said, pointing at Michael, "would you please come over here?" Michael didn't move.

"What for?" Anna asked.

"Please, ma'am," said one of the policemen, walking across the room and kneeling in front of Michael. Having been assigned to follow the inspector the preceding day, he knew he was going to examine the boy for weakness in his limbs. "Do y'know what this is?" he said to the boy, holding up his nightstick.

Michael nodded, big-eyed.

"Ever held one? No? I'm not surprised. Oh, boys try and steal 'em all the time but no policeman worth his salt will let anyone take his shille-lagh." He smacked it against his palm dramatically and winked. Then he held the butt-end out to the boy. "Let's see if you can get mine away from me, okay sport? Like we were having a tug-of-war."

Captivated, Michael nodded slowly and wrapped both small, thin hands around the stick. Anna shuddered.

"Got it? Good. Okay—one, two, three, pull!"

With barely a tug the policeman yanked the stick out of Michael's hands.

"That's no fair!" John yelled. "You should let him stand up! That's no fair!"

But the policeman had already turned back toward the health inspec-tor with a shrug.

"There's nothing wrong with him," Anna said, an edge coming into her voice for the first time. "He's never been very strong. He's just tired—he was out all day with me. Look, he helped carry these screens all the way from Washington Square."

For the first time Mr. Henry saw the stack of screens leaning against the kitchen window, and Anna could see that it gave him pause.

"Yes, that's right, Mr. Henry. I'm the only one in the building with screens. Do you think I want my children to get polio?"

"That's good," he said. "But the boy needs to be examined by a doc-tor. He and the other children have to be quarantined for at least two weeks if it turns out he's had even a mild bout of paralysis. Let us take him over to Willard Parker where the doctors can check him."

"No. He can't go there."

"Mrs. Altobelli, please. Don't make me insist."

"No. He was just checked at school two weeks ago."

"Mrs. Altobelli . . ."

"No! There's nothing wrong with him! He's not sick and he hasn't been sick! Look, Mister, I know what sick is. My husband—their father—just died of the influenza six months ago. Do you know where they took him? Do you know where the doctor said he'd get better? Willard Parker. Please, don't make me talk about this in front of my children. Do you want to scare them?" She looked over at the boys, who were staring at her with open mouths, and raised an eyebrow.

Henry could hear one of the cops exhaling heavily behind him. The inspector shook his head. "All right, Mrs. Altobelli. Here's what we'll do. You're going to take this boy to a doctor and have him examined. I'm going to come back next week and you're going to have a signed letter from that doctor saying your boy didn't have polio. Understand?"

"Of course I understand. But this isn't necessary—the boy hasn't been sick."

"Fine. Then it won't be a problem. Because otherwise he's going to Willard Parker and the others are going to have to be quarantined."

She gave a resigned shake of her shoulders and shifted Christina again. "I understand."

Henry put on his hat and opened the door. "Next week. Don't forget, because I'll be back." The others were out the door when the policeman who had administered the test touched his stick to the bill of his cap. "Sorry about your husband."

Anna nodded and smiled wearily. "Good night." She closed the door, leaning against it and listening. She didn't turn around until they were all the way downstairs, and then handed Christina to John and collapsed beside them on the sofa, placing an arm around Michael and squeezing until she could feel both bony shoulders dig into her flesh.

"Are you okay?" she asked him.

The boy nodded. "I'm hungry."

"Me, too. Come—I'll start dinner. What about you, John? Hungry?"

"Ma, I thought they took Papa to Welfare Island."

"That's right, hon, they did." Then, in her best Mrs. Spabari imitation: "Welfare Island, Willard Parker—is a da same place, no? No?" She gave her forehead a comic slap. "Ay! I'm such a silly old woman!"

When the mayor rubbed his right temple, Teddy cringed—it was a sure sign Mitchel was getting one of his debilitating headaches. But none of the city commissioners seated around the boardroom table in the New York Bar Association for a meeting on the crisis noticed, least of all Haven

Emerson. No, Teddy thought grimly, that knot head is in his glory. Emerson seemed to have a genius for missing the point. Mitchel wanted a presentation on concrete steps the city departments could take to combat the polio epidemic; Emerson's answer was a group of researchers from the contagious disease lab at Rockefeller Institute whose puzzlement at the cause of the malady was all too apparent. Indeed, their overarching concern appeared to be convincing the mayor to press customs authorities to release a shipment of rhesus monkeys from quarantine so the institute could study the effects of injecting the monkeys with floor sweepings from a polio ward. And Teddy saw that Mitchel had run out of patience.

"Sit down," the mayor said, interrupting a Dr. Fletcher in midsentence. "Commissioner Emerson, I take it all this ridiculous monkey business means we won't have a vaccine this summer." The other commissioners snapped to attention and looked at Emerson.

"I—that is, we—hopefully."

"Here we are beginning July. How many confirmed cases of paralysis are there?"

"Five hundred and twenty-five."

"Fatalities?"

"One hundred and twenty-six."

"That's nearly ninety fatalities in the past week alone, am I right, Commissioner?"

"Yes, Mr. Mayor."

Mitchel let out a low, appreciative whistle.

"What are our projections for this week?"

"Approximately two dozen fatalities a day."

"Two dozen a day. My, my. This certainly is an efficient little bug, isn't it? And then?"

"It will spike higher or lower on a day-to-day basis. Mostly higher. Depending probably upon the weather."

"The weather, eh? Is that important, Haven?"

Emerson made no reply. The doctors stared at Mitchel. The commissioners, all of whom had a pretty good idea what was coming, looked anywhere else.

"What can you tell me about the worst cases?"

"They're young."

"Young?"

"Most of the fatalities are under three. In the cases with resulting, lingering paralysis, the severity declines as the population gets older."

"So most of our paralysis victims . . ."

"Are under eight."

"I see." Mitchel stood up and walked slowly around the table. He seemed to be looking out the window toward Centre Street and the courts, tugging his fingers and cracking his knuckles absentmindedly. Teddy, sitting against the wall and taking notes, had seen this show before and knew Mitchel was making the sound to unnerve everyone. He also knew it was a good sign. If the Mayor was stage-managing his temper, he had it under control. Now Mitchel turned to the doctors. "This is obviously highly contagious. Can any of you gentlemen tell me how this disease is spread? How it incubates? Who the most frequent carriers are? Whether convalescent patients are dangerous? Are there incipient cases? What about doctors, nurses, health inspectors—can they be carrying it without showing the signs? What about dust? Flies? Tainted food? Don't you know anything?" Mitchel rubbed his right temple again. "Why children?" he asked.

"Certain facts suggest that adults have acquired a general immunity from previous mild polio infections which went unrecognized at the time," said a doctor sitting across from Emerson. "Therefore, to answer some of the questions you posed before, it's most likely that the virus is spread to and from those without a resistance, which is to say child-to-child, including some who are experiencing aborted or weak cases and showing few if any outward symptoms. In actuality, the number of reported cases are really just the number of severe ones and a fraction of the actual number. Conversely, it's most unlikely that adults—particularly health care workers—are acting as carriers."

"What's your name?"

"Frost. Wade Frost."

"So tell me, Dr. Frost. Why, if our water is cleaner, if our sanitation is better, if our medicines more potent, are the outbreaks growing in severity and mortality? And if it's a question of hygiene, why hasn't the epidemic remained isolated in the poorest communities? In fact, the latest reports from the health department suggest wealthier children are even more vulnerable than immigrants."

"Mr. Mayor, the polio epidemics may be growing in severity as a *direct result* of our improved sanitation and hygiene. Perhaps infants were once exposed to mild strains of the virus through unfiltered water, through other environmental factors which we've since altered and controlled, and no longer have the early opportunity to develop an immunity. It would certainly explain why this virus has cut so dramatically across class boundaries. We need a vaccine. But until we have one, I doubt there's much we can do to slow the spread of the epidemic beyond quarantine."

Mitchel returned to the head of the table and sat down heavily, staring at nothing in particular for a long, apparently unfocused, minute. Only Teddy knew he wasn't lost, knew he was in fact sifting through what he'd just heard, weighing and reorganizing the points until they suggested a coherent plan. Without moving his head, Mitchel's eyes sought out Frost. "You're saying that this outbreak of polio is truly epidemic—that virtually all children in this city are going to be exposed to poliomyelitis."

"Probably."

"And that we won't see it—that we'll just see the severest cases."

"Yes."

"But the public won't perceive it this way?"

"No. The parents of mild cases will convince themselves their children had something else."

"And what we can offer them for protection is . . . ?"

Frost offered a pair of upturned palms. "Quarantines?"

Mitchel nodded. "Okay. The first thing we're going to do is hire additional doctors and nurses to work on an emergency basis with the health department and the hospitals, and for that we'll have to release emergency funds to the Board of Health. Teddy, I want the Controller in my office in forty-five minutes.

"Now then, Haven," he said, "we're going to have to strike some balance here with the quarantines. We need to keep parents as calm as possible, to show there are things that can be done and that the city is taking every step possible. By the same token, we don't want our actions to appear draconian, otherwise we'll create panic. Every parent who can afford it is going to take their child and leave town, anyhow. There's already evidence of a mass exodus out of the city—I'm told the Long Island and Pennsylvania railroads sold a record number of children's tickets yesterday. And every one who can't afford to leave is going to fight us tooth-and-nail before they let us take their child to one of those outhouses we call charity wards."

"It's happening already," said Emerson. "One of our nurses in Brooklyn received a letter from the Black Hand after she had two boys removed to hospital."

Mitchel nodded. "No one in this room would allow their child to go to one of those wards. Look, tell your people to use some discretion. Just remove the life-and-death and severe paralysis cases. And don't insist on the 'Quarantined' signs in the wealthier neighborhoods. All it will do is make people flee."

"What about summer school?" Emerson asked. "Do we want to cancel it?"

Mitchel weighed this for a moment. "No. I'm not worried about kids panicking—I'm worried about the adults who come into contact with them. And I don't want the playgrounds closed, either, although I want Parks Commissioner Cabot to think of a few things to make them more sanitary. But are there other places we should consider closing? Places where groups of kids are highly visible and likely to make others nervous?"

"Trolleys and subways?" asked Teddy.

"Okay. No one under sixteen. Where else?"

"How about the motion pictures, open-air theaters and nickelodeons?" asked the police commissioner.

"Could we do that?"

"Why not?" It was George Bell, the commissioner of licenses. "The operators will hate it but, sure, we can do it."

"Okay. But let's close the children's reading rooms at the public libraries as well, so they can't say we're holding them to a unique standard. Haven—what else?"

"Mr. Mayor, I don't disagree with anything Dr. Frost said before. But even if poliomyelitis has nothing to do with filth and insects—and we still don't know that for a fact—it can't hurt to have Sanitation aggressively cleaning the streets and enforcing the garbage laws, especially in the immigrant neighborhoods. At the very least it will focus people and raise awareness of proper hygiene."

"You mean give 'em a big show since we don't have a clue what we're up against? Haven, you devil. Are you health commissioner or mayor?" For the first time, several of the others laughed. "Well, it's not bad health policy and it's definitely good politics, and I'll tell you why. There's another issue here, gentlemen. I want us to be seen handling this ourselves. No matter how bad things get, I don't want any department of the federal government involved in this. No outside help from national agencies or organizations—including the Red Cross. Washington is calling me every hour, and if someone down there gets the idea to quarantine the whole city, it will be an economic disaster. So, yes—by all means. If no one knows what the hell is causing this epidemic, let's at least step up street cleaning dramatically."

July 11, 1916, was an extraordinarily hot day in Brooklyn, one in which health officials would record one hundred fifty-five new cases of poliomyelitis and thirty-nine infant fatalities, the highest one-day total in the history of the borough. Anna was up early that morning: by seven o'clock she had left her sister's apartment with Christina, Michael, John, and Julietta's two eldest boys, Nick and Anthony, for the Brighton Beach public baths.

They'd been staying with Julietta for nearly a week. Although Anna knew there was nothing wrong with Michael, she just couldn't bring herself to have him examined. What if the doctor wouldn't give him a clean bill of health? Didn't the newspaper say the health department wouldn't let anyone quarantine at home without a private toilet? She didn't like Mr. Henry, certainly didn't trust him, and in the days following his first visit she'd kept the children out of the apartment until after dark. Then the police came around one night and they had to turn out all the lights and pretend no one was home. She hated the idea of Michael going to the hospital even if there *was* something wrong with him—and there certainly wasn't. So they came to Julietta's, where her brother-in-law, always sullen to begin with, retreated to the kitchen each evening to sit alone and drink beer, making Nick walk to the corner tavern several times a night to refill his empties. Julietta was just grateful for another set of hands.

Matthew and Dolly were both a good deal sicker than Michael had been, with Dolly showing enough paralysis in her legs to keep Julietta on the constant verge of tears. A doctor had been in to see the children twice and, despite a diagnosis of polio, had been convinced by Julietta not to report the cases—with a bath in the apartment and her sister to help, she would be able to see to their needs she insisted, and pointed out that there was no one to infect since all of the other families in the building with children had already left for a rooming house in Pennsylvania. In return, she was scrupulous in following the doctor's prescriptions, which included hourly peroxide rinses for the throat and mouth and keeping Dolly stationary with pillows and rolled-up blankets supporting her arms and legs. The doctor also encouraged Julietta to keep the other children outside as much as possible, so Anna often found herself back at the Prospect Park playground. But the previous day a crew had emptied the sand from the sandbox and sprayed the playground with an awful smelling oil—"to keep the dust down"—and now the children wouldn't play there. Through the smothering heat of the week a picture of the baths had shimmered in Anna's imagination like a mirage at the edge of the desert. She couldn't get used to the idea of having a bath in the apartment, wouldn't dream of lying in the tub when Julietta needed to keep it clear for Dolly and Matt. Now, with the park so unappealing, it seemed a perfect way to spend the day. She feared what the conductor or passengers would say if she tried to take so many children on the Coney Island Avenue trolley, so they walked the thirty-five blocks to the baths, Christina gripping her hand and the others holding old, threadbare towels.

"Why do we have to go to the baths?" Anthony asked. "I don't even like to take a bath at home!" John, just three months younger than his cousin, nodded his head vigorously, curious to see how his mother would answer this challenge.

"The doctors say it's particularly important now for everyone to stay as clean as possible. There are a lot of germs around."

"Why?"

"Waddaya mean, *why?*" snapped Nick. "Don't you numbskulls read the paper? There's a polio epidemic on."

"Where did you learn to talk to your brother and cousin like that?" Anna asked, squeezing his neck in mock admonition and embarrassing the older boy exactly as much as she'd intended. Nick was normally a sweet boy, but being caught between his father and an apartment full of small children was taking its toll; unlike the others, he was old enough to understand how potentially debilitating his sister's illness might be, and Anna could sense the weight of enlightenment tugging at his heart.

"Well," said Anthony, "I still don't see what's so all-fired great about bathing."

"Stop complaining," said his aunt. "At least it will cool you off."

The debate proved moot: at eight-thirty they reached the end of Coney Island Avenue to discover literally a thousand mothers and children already waiting to get into the baths, the line stretching around the corner and down Brighton Beach Avenue.

"Oh, this will never do," Anna said, biting her lip. "Come on—let's walk two more blocks to the beach."

"But we don't have suits," said Michael.

"So what? You can roll up your pants, no one will mind. And we can spend the bath money for something to eat and drink on the boardwalk."

It proved a blessing to have the baths so crowded. The boys were much happier on the beach, although Anna insisted they play among themselves and keep a distance from any other children in the throng. She relished dipping and splashing Christina in the ocean—the girl giggled more than in weeks—and was greatly relieved to see how strong and agile Michael looked diving in and out of the waves, dishing out and taking dunkings from the bigger boys in water fights and showing none of the signs of exhaustion that marked his every action of late.

At the west end of the boardwalk between Coney Island Avenue and Corbin Place was a small park with shade trees where Anna brought them for a lunch of hot dogs, corn, and peaches. The boys, even Nick, had been happy playing in the water and reluctant to leave the beach, and she was surprised at how quickly they warmed to the idea of sitting in the park. Then she noticed what they had already obviously seen: a man setting up a portable carousel.

It was old and wooden but freshly painted in bright red, cool green, and screaming yellow. Each small gondola door was painstakingly decorated with a different fairy tale: Jack and the Beanstalk, Rapunzel, Rumpelstilskin, an oversized spinning top of childhood fantasies. It was the kind of ride one saw at street fairs and feasts—whirligigs, switchbacks, and spinners, always mounted on carts and ingeniously designed to fold up and be transported on their base. Anna hadn't seen Coney Island until she was a grown woman and Vincent had taken her there for dinner, and until then she'd thought all rides were designed to be folded onto carts and taken away at night; she still maintained a nostalgic fondness for the portable amusements and their itinerant operators.

"Can we go on the ride, Aunt Anna?" Anthony was the first to ask.

"No, dear. I don't have much money."

"Well, if you'd told me I wouldn't have had a hot dog. Certainly not a peach!" The boy collapsed on the grass at her feet and sulked.

"Aw, what's the matter?" She rubbed a hand playfully in the boy's hair. "Did little Anthony want to go for a ride in Rapunzel?"

The others had wandered off across the park to watch the man finish locking the last pieces of the carousel together. Anna also saw three men approaching from a building on Brightwater Avenue. They were soon arguing animatedly with the carousel operator. She could hear them plainly long before she and Anthony had reached the others.

"I don't know what you mean," the carny said. "Look, I've got the permit right here."

"And I'm telling you I don't care what you've got," said the oldest of the men. He was small, pale and angry looking. "We don't want you here. Now pack it up and get moving."

"No, this is not right. Maybe I should get a policeman."

"You want a policeman? Here's a policeman." He pointed to the two men behind him, one of whom wore a suit while the other stood tall and heavyset and looked like a brawler. Anna doubted either was a policeman. "You're gonna need a doctor if you don't do like I say. I'm telling you one more time: knock it down."

"But I bought my permit! I got a right to be here today!"

The biggest man moved forward and, leaning down, shoved his face right into the carousel operator's. "Let me draw ya a picture, you little Guinea bastard. This is a clean neighborhood. We don't want you bringing any of your immigrant filth here and making our kids sick. Now if you don't take this thing apart, I'm going to—and you won't like the way I do it. Then I'll take you apart. You won't like that, either."

Terrified, Anna's first impulse was to grab the children and shepherd them away. She surprised herself instead. "Excuse me, gentlemen," she said in a remarkably even voice. "My children were waiting for this man to finish setting up so they could take a ride."

The big man barely looked her way. "Go away, lady."

"Hey!" said Nick. "Don't talk to my aunt that way."

For an instant the man appeared ready to strike the boy. But nothing happened and he simply glared. Instead, the man in the suit stepped forward. "We're sorry, ma'am, but we're closing him down."

"But the children are waiting for a ride."

The man thought for a minute and then threw up his hands. "Okay," he said with a smile. "Have a ride." He leered at the operator and pointed toward a bench. "When they're done we'll be waitin' right over there. Come on, boys."

"Are you all right?" Anna asked as soon as the men were seated at the entrance to the park.

"I'm sorry," he said. "I can't give your children a ride."

"Why not?"

"Because they'll destroy the carousel as soon as you go. Look, I know you're just trying to help, but believe me, I've got to go."

"Oh, but you shouldn't! It's so wrong!"

"Wrong? Yes, I know. Shouldn't?" He paused and looked at Anna and then shifted the bandanna around his neck just enough to expose part of a long, ugly red choke mark. "This isn't the first time. Or even the second." He looked at the children and patted Christina on the head before turning away and reaching a grease-stained hand for a wrench to disassemble the car arms. "Sorry, kids. If you come by the Feast of Our Lady of Mount Carmel this weekend, you can have a free ride."

That night Anna decided to leave the city. "I can't go back to Vandam Street," she told Julietta. "And I'm seeing things that make me worry for the safety of the children. Not here, I mean," she said, motioning around the apartment. "Not that. But out there. People are getting crazy. They're so afraid. Of what, they're not sure. Of whatever they don't know, of whatever is different, of anything *else*." Julietta listened but made no reply. "You remember my friend Rosemary? She and her husband have a house in Hoboken with plenty of room—I'm sure they'll let us stay. Besides, the country air will do them all some good."

The Canal Street ferry to Hoboken left every fifteen minutes. Anna always marveled at how easily it navigated the busy river, slipping between the ocean liners and tankers like a mouse skittering through a roomful of cats, and at how much cooler the air was just a few feet from shore. Like Michael and John, she always stood outside at the rail when the weather was nice. When another woman with two boys wandered past and gave Anna a smile, she eagerly struck up a conversation.

"So lovely out on the water," Anna said.

"It is, isn't it?" The woman seemed just as grateful to have someone to talk to. "I couldn't wait to get out of Manhattan! Don't go much myself—can't stand it, too busy—and I almost never take the children. But there was nothing to be done for it today. And to have to take them in the middle of this plague! Just dreadful. But that's why I had to go, you know. My husband, Tom, is a furrier. Over on West Twenty-sixth Street. Now what fur has to do with this awful disease I can't possibly tell you—I mean, wouldn't my children be sick if there was?—but the police have issued him three sanitation violations in the last week. Three! Of course, he couldn't possibly miss work so I had to take the children and go to the courthouse by the Essex Market. I can't begin to tell you what was going on there! Complete and utter pandemonium! And talk about nerve—they give out sanitation tickets like it was nothing, like we were causing this horrid epidemic—and then the judges won't allow our children in their courtrooms! How insulting can you get? As if they were saying 'it's your fault—and don't bring your filthy children in here.' Oh! I hope to God that's the end of the tickets, because I don't think I can go through that again."

Anna shook her head sympathetically. "Do you live in Hoboken?"

"Yes. On Garden. Where are you? Your younger boy looks like he and Tom, Jr., might go to school together."

"We're just visiting friends for a while."

The woman looked at her. "In Hoboken?"

"Yes."

"Honey, haven't you heard? Hoboken's been quarantined for the last two days. Unless you live here or can prove you're only passing through, they're not going to let your children off the ferry."

"What?"

"Oh, yeah. At least they're nice about it. I hear they've got shotgun quarantines over in Passaic and Paterson. Any children who don't live there are being escorted out of town. And, oh—see over there?" She pointed to a blue-and-white police boat a half-mile upriver. "That's the Edgewater police. They've closed that ferry line and they're inspecting any boats that come in the harbor." She leaned a little closer to Anna. "I hear they put the police boat out there because the locals were doing it themselves—stopping boats at gunpoint." She shook her head. "They were always a little crazy in Edgewater."

Anna didn't believe it until the ferry pulled within view of the broad wooden terminal and she saw the four policemen standing in front of the gate. Without attempting to disembark, she herded the children together and headed toward the other end of the boat for the return trip.

"Sorry," said the furrier's wife with a sad smile. "Good luck to you, hon."

The return trip was spent debating what to do; Anna didn't want to return to Brooklyn and couldn't go home. Instead, when the ferry docked in New York, she took Christina and the boys down to the subway and over to Grand Central Terminal. She had been carrying most of their money in expectation of staying several weeks in New Jersey, and now decided the best thing would be to go to Vincent's family in Providence, Rhode Island. The idea made her nervous—her husband hadn't been close to his father and brother, and his mother never really embraced Anna—but what else could she do? At least the children would be safe.

It was already late in the day when they arrived at the station and, with the retreating light barely illuminating the long, western windows high above the Vanderbilt Avenue entrance, it felt later. The station was busy with people going home, mostly businessmen in suits, but women also, well dressed with pretty hats and big shopping bags. It took Anna a long while to reach the front of a ticket line, the boys silent and taken with the movements of the crowd but Christina tired and whining through the wait. "I'd like one adult and three children to Providence, please," she told the man behind the grate.

He peered out at Christina and the boys. "Health certificates?"

"Pardon?"

"Health certificates. Don't you read the newspapers, lady?"

Anna stared at him.

"You can't buy out-of-state tickets anymore for them kids 'less they got certificates from the Board of Health saying they're healthy and there's no quarantine at their home address. Look over there, lady." He stuck a finger through the bars of the ticket window and pointed to a long disheveled line of tired women and unhappy children snaking down the corridor toward the Forty-second Street doors. "If you got a doctor's letter, they'll just check your address and give you a certificate. Otherwise there's a quack there who'll look at your kids first. You can probably get it done in time to catch the last eastbound train tonight. Hey, lady, are you listening to me?"

She wasn't.

"Lady, please! There's forty people behind you and most of 'em ain't as nice as me."

"Oh! Sorry. You said that's for out-of-state tickets? What's the last stop before Connecticut?"

"Port Chester."

"And what's the next stop after that?

"Greenwich."

"Well, how far is it from Port Chester to Greenwich?"

"You mean walkin'? Jeez, lady, how would I know? I don't lay the tracks, I just sell the tickets."

"I have a weekend house in Westport," said the man standing behind Anna. "I think it's about three miles from the Port Chester station to the one in Greenwich."

"Three miles?" she asked the stranger. "I guess that shouldn't take us too long."

"Can't take you any longer than it's taking me to buy this ticket," said someone else in line.

Anna turned quickly back to the window. "Port Chester, then."

"Seventy-five cents, lady."

The commuter train was crowded and she thought they'd have to stand until a man, seeing her with Christina, insisted she take his seat. Grateful, she sat down and gave a smile of relief to the two women facing her. Neither smiled back, but instead cast long, uneasy looks at John and Michael. After another moment, they got up wordlessly and walked to the other end of the car. "Well," Anna said to the boys as she watched the women walk away, "I guess we've all got seats."

When the train came out of the Park Avenue tunnel at Ninety-eighth Street, late afternoon had blossomed into a long crimson summer twilight, and its high, flat clouds tipped in purple and pink promised another hot day to come. As the train turned to cross the river, Anna looked away from the glow of Manhattan and saw the first star hanging in the darkening sky over the Bronx. Looking north to her left she could clearly see the silhouette of the Polo Grounds.

"Look, Michael—do you know what that is?"

The boy shook his head.

"It's the ballpark. Do you remember when Papa built that?"

He looked carefully now, as if in doing so he might see some physical evidence of his father's presence—his face perhaps, or even a handprint. But he couldn't find it and shook his head.

"I do," said John.

"I'll bet you remember when the old one burned down, too," she said, and the boy nodded. "That was a big fire. You could see the smoke just about wherever you were. That was all anyone talked about for days."

214

"How did it catch fire?" Michael asked.

Anna shrugged. "It was wooden. That's why this one is concrete and steel. It was the biggest job Papa worked on—he was there for months."

"Did Papa take you to the game when it was finished?" John asked.

"No! Who can afford such foolishness?" And though she would never have considered attending a baseball game with Vincent, she felt a pang just the same.

Riding into the darkness, each long wooden train station that came into view with its peaked roof looked the same to Anna, as did the towns. They appeared out of the black night gradually, one house at a time: spare, dimly lit, and isolated. Yet somehow, whenever the train reached a station, it would be haloed in light and surrounded by a village. The alternating rhythm of green darkness and lamp-lit streets was so different from the city; it was lulling, soothing in its inky peace. But she couldn't enjoy it. Rather, she feared missing their stop and sat nervously on the edge of her seat, searching the blackness on the other side of the windowpane.

The Port Chester station was on a raised platform overlooking the streets, and the air was cool and damp with the heavy smell of a receding tide. It was a welcome relief after the close, smoke-filled air of the train. Yet Anna felt uneasy and held the children back while the others filed out of the station. It wasn't until the train had departed and the platform was nearly empty that she could see all of the exits save one were boarded over and that everyone was exiting through the one still-open stairwell. By that stairwell stood a small man who, though drab in appearance, was nonetheless menacing in his presence; beside him stood a policeman. She suddenly feared for the worst.

"Good evening," the man said pleasantly as they approached, although he did not lift his hat to Anna. "Can I help you?"

"Yes, in fact." She smiled her sweetest smile and pointed to the road below. "Does that street go to Greenwich?"

"Yes it does. But so does the train. Why did you get off?"

"Oh, yes, well, my sister just moved there from Brooklyn and she told me her house was closer to this stop."

"I'm sorry, I can't let the children walk through town. There's a two-week quarantine for anyone under sixteen who enters Port Chester."

"But we're not going to Port Chester. We just want to walk on a public street."

"I can't let you do that unless you're going to a Port Chester destination where you will observe the quarantine."

"But that's just silly!"

"Sorry."

Anna smiled at the policeman. "Officer, is this true?"

"Yes, ma'am."

"Well, is there anything the police can do to see us to the Greenwich line?"

"Afraid not. All the cars are being used to check the roads coming into town. Besides, you're already at the train station—why don't you just get back on the train?"

"But you see, I didn't think I'd need the out-of-state health certificate since I wasn't taking the train to Greenwich!"

The two men looked at each other significantly.

Down on the street a car pulled up alongside the platform, and they all turned to watch. Without turning off the engine or the lights, the driver emerged and, slamming the door, looked up at the station. "Is there a policeman there?" he shouted.

"Yes," said the officer. "What's the trouble?"

The man took the stairs two at a time, reaching the platform quickly. In the dim light of the station, his hat brim all but hid his face. But he was big and disheveled and clearly upset and nervous, with one of his hands moving rapidly as if shaking a bottle or a thermometer. "Where's the hospital?" he asked, and something about his voice stuck in Anna's ear.

"Do you live in Port Chester?" asked the policeman.

"Why do you ask? We've been staying with friends for the last ten or twelve days," he said. "Please—my son is very sick."

Anna looked again. "Mr. Greene?"

Hearing his name confused the leasing agent even more, and he seemed unable to actually focus for the long minute he looked at Anna. Finally, it registered. "Mrs. Altobelli?" But her presence, if possible, seemed to confuse him even more.

"What's the matter, Mr. Greene? What's happened?"

"Morton. He's in the car."

"What happened to your friends? Couldn't you stay with them?"

"Huh? Oh, yes, yes. They're sick. The children are all sick. Doctor came again today. Then the hearse. Morton needs a hospital."

"Who are you staying with?" asked the man who had blocked Anna's exit.

"Owen Obeirne."

The name clearly had meaning to the man. "I'm sorry," he finally said, "but if you don't live in Port Chester, the hospital is not going to admit your son. I recommend you take him home and have his regular doctor admit him somewhere."

"Go home? To Manhattan? But he needs a doctor right now!"

"I understand, sir, but believe me, if you take him to the hospital here, they will not see him and you will just lose more time."

"Oh, God! What kind of place is this?"

But Anna saw that the men would not budge. "Please, Mr. Greene," she said. "Hurry! Do what they say!"

More confused than before, he stood with his mouth agape and seemed almost to sway, as if something within had been disconnected. Then he recognized Anna again and gave her a quizzical look. "What are you doing here?" he asked.

"Please, Mr. Greene, don't waste any time! Take your son back to New York! Hurry!"

Her words seemed to register this time, and the leasing agent nodded sharply and, without a look at the others, bounded back down the stairs to the car.

"How do you know him?" the policeman asked.

"He works for my landlord. He's a very dear man and his boy is sweet. He always helps whoever he can and you should have helped him instead of turning your back."

The man sighed. "What would you have us do? You heard him say he's been with the Obeirnes for almost two weeks? I quarantined that house three days ago, but their two little girls both died today."

Anna put a hand to her mouth. "My God! Poor Mr. Greene! And his boy! How could you make them drive back to New York?"

"Because it's essential for the health of the children of Port Chester to keep the cases as isolated as possible. What would happen if we allowed infected children from New York to come and go? Then what would happen? Would you let sick strangers into your home to be with your children?"

"Oh, but he's here! Why won't the people at the hospital show a little mercy?"

"Lady," the policeman said as he walked toward the edge of the platform and looked out at the street where the taillights of the Greenes' automobile were disappearing into the night, "they won't even take him at the village morgue."

Anna put her arms around her children and turned them toward the New York–bound track.

"Oh, Christ—not again! Every time I light a cigarette!"

Teddy, sitting in the mayor's car behind a large sanitation-department pumper parked at the corner of Fourth Avenue and Carroll Street in Brooklyn, saw the woman under the next street lamp. She was wearing a housecoat, carrying two cats in her arms, and heading straight for Mitchel, Emerson, and Sanitation Commissioner Fetherston. He sighed, took one last greedy drag on the butt, and was out of the car and intercepting her before the mayor and the commissioners even noticed her.

"Hello, dear!" he said jovially, reaching out his arms to take the cats. "What have we got here? A couple of strays, eh?"

The woman suddenly clutched the cats tightly to her breasts. "Strays?" she asked indignantly. "Do these look like filthy strays, you oaf? They're purebred Maine coons and they're positively terrified to be out of the house for the first time! I can't believe I'm doing this!" She looked like she was about to cry.

"I'm so sorry—please forgive me." Teddy used his most soothing voice, the one he'd perfected during three years of calming the outraged ward leaders who were always snubbed by Mitchel. "You're the fifth person in the last two hours to turn cats over to the mayor, but the others were all strays. Why don't you take your beautiful cats home? I'm sure they're healthy."

"Oh, I know, I know! And they do mean everything to me. But I just couldn't live with myself if one of the neighbor's children got sick. I mean, could you? Always wondering if your selfishness had brought misery and pain to a poor child and her parents? I couldn't bear it. So please, take them."

Teddy smiled sympathetically and reached for the cats. They were terrified of him and squirmed in the woman's arms, scratching his hands and drawing blood. He simply continued to smile, even as he wondered how. The sanitation worker assigned to caging any cats saw how much trouble these two were and made himself busy, obliging Teddy to load them in the carrier on the back of the pumper himself. By the time the secretary looked up, the woman had collared Mitchel. Teddy groaned and rushed over. He was never sure how Mitchel was going to react to even an innocent situation. He'd heard John casually make the most extraordinarily rude remarks and brutally berate everyone from the chief justice of the city court to the old woman who mopped his office. And Teddy thought the country would have to go to war the day the Italian ambassador took the mayor's old Columbia University fencing foil down from the wall. Teddy adored Mitchel. But he also knew that it was a miracle he'd ever been elected.

There was no reason to worry this time, though. Mitchel could see the woman was distraught, and he was solicitous in his way as she mourned her cats. Still, the mayor's patience was about to reach its limit and Teddy moved in, catching her before she could launch into a soliloquy on "The Things Children Could Learn About Cleanliness From Cats."

"You've done a marvelous, selfless thing," Teddy said as he put an arm around the woman's shoulder and began to steer her away from Mitchel. "We'd better step back, though, because they're about to wash the street."

"Don't forget," she called tearfully to the mayor.

"Got it. I'm going to make sure the commissioner looks into it," Mitchel replied, pointing to Emerson. Teddy handed the woman off to a policeman and returned to the mayor's side.

"What does she want looked into?"

"Hand laundries," said Emerson.

"Hand laundries?"

"Yeah. All that communal washing spreads germs, don't you know."

"And the Chinamen spit in the wash," Mitchel added with a roll of his eyes.

"Well, that's a new one," Teddy lit another cigarette and watched the sanitation-department pumper hook up its hoses to the fireplug. "I had her pegged as another emissary from the anti–chewing gum society. What's the winning cause of polio we've heard so far tonight?"

"Talcum powder," said Emerson.

"The Standard Oil refinery in Bayonne," said Mitchel.

"Best home remedies?"

"Alcohol rubs and chiropractors."

"Ox blood," said Emerson.

"Ox blood?" Mitchel was aghast. "What the hell do you do with that?"

"Bathe in it. Apparently it's a popular Eastern European cure—my inspectors say they're lined up every morning at the slaughterhouses with buckets. Mind-boggling what people think is good for them, isn't it? Say, Teddy—give us a cigarette."

Mitchel was no longer listening. He was watching the pumper, which was ready, and the police, who were backing all the onlookers away from Fourth Avenue. A moment later, water was flooding the sidewalk and rolling down the street, and a crew of white-suited sanitation workers with stiff push brooms went to work scrubbing from the buildings to the curb and pushing hundreds of gallons of water into the gutter and down the storm grates. They'd been doing this every night in Brooklyn and Manhattan since the meeting, and while there was no evidence to suggest it had stemmed the epidemic, the city was certainly a lot cleaner—something that Mitchel suspected gave Emerson more pleasure than a big box of tongue depressors. The mayor considered his health commissioner a strange duck. Well, he was certainly right about the public relations and morale-boosting value of the program. And those idiots from the newspapers loved it—there'd been a dozen photographers and nearly as many writers at the first stop by Grand Army Plaza earlier in the evening.

Mitchel hated the press. They were the worst part of the job, incapable of formulating an intelligent question. Worse, they were more interested in what he did when he wasn't working than when he was. As if it were any of their damn business! And behind most of his newspaper troubles lurked that weasel Hearst, always giving everything the worst spin. It was hard for Mitchel to believe the publisher had once endorsed him. God, he'd turned fast—the lousy Hun apologist. Amazing, just amazing. The man starts a meaningless war but does everything in his power to keep us out of the one that matters. Well, he was going to have to wait for some other mayor to get his damn *Maine* Memorial put up, and let him put money on *that*. But the thought didn't cheer Mitchel—in fact, it depressed him: he knew Hearst wouldn't have long to wait. Ah, the hell with them all—he'd given politics his best shot, but this just wasn't his game. He could never convince himself there was a percentage in doing the wrong thing for the right reason.

"Mr. Mayor?" Teddy considered it part of his job to bring the boss back whenever he got one of his faraway looks.

"How many more of these stops are there, Fetherston?"

"On Fourth? About ten, your honor."

Mitchel looked at his watch. "Will they be done before eleven?"

Fetherston was dubious. "I hope so."

"Well, I'm supposed to be at the Biltmore by midnight."

Teddy felt his heart sink. Those were the last words he wanted to hear. "Why don't we take a dinner break, Mr. Mayor?" he quickly asked. "I know a terrific Italian restaurant just a few blocks from here. The commissioners can meet us there."

The only way to hold Mitchel's attention and respect was to be direct, and Teddy wasted no time when they were alone in the mayor's car. "Do you really have to go to the Biltmore tonight?"

"Damn it, Teddy, don't start that again. Are you my campaign manager now?"

"But you know what's going to happen."

"Maybe."

"Maybe? *Maybe* the hotel's bell captain is going to earn himself a sure sawbuck by calling the *American* as soon as you walk in? Or *maybe* it will be the elevator operator? You don't know what these reporters will do for a tip. Believe me, I do."

"So I'm good for the economy. So what?"

"Come on, John. You're the first honest mayor in my lifetime—don't be the last. You've already accomplished more than the previous three administrations combined."

"That's not saying much."

"Stop it. I've never seen anyone who can work so long and so hard. Eighteen, nineteen, twenty hours a day—day after day, week after week. And I doubt a bullet through the brain would cure one of those headaches you get. See? I know. So how can you drive yourself—abuse yourself, even—to accomplish some good, and then invite these jackals to rip you apart?"

"Because it's no one's damn business who my friends are and where I go on the rare occasion that I'm not working. I mean, for Christ's sake, Teddy, I'm just going dancing! What the hell has that got to do with the job?"

"I know, it's ridiculous. And it's unfair. But that doesn't change the facts. And the facts are that as long as you go dancing at the Plaza or the Biltmore and get your picture taken with Mrs. Vanderbilt, or spend your Christmas vacation at Palm Beach and your summers at an Adirondack hunting lodge, Hearst is going to paint you as a society swell and every jug head who buys the newspaper is going to believe it. And you know what? If you cured polio, they'd still believe it. I know I'm overstepping my place by saying this, but do yourself a favor—do the *city* a favor—and let the picture in the paper tomorrow be you washing the streets in Brooklyn instead of dancing at the Biltmore."

Mitchel looked out the window as the car pulled up in front of a restaurant at Union and Third. "Look," he finally said. "The only thing I can do is run the city as a business, which is what it is. I got elected mayor precisely because I wasn't a politician. Right? So what good can I do if I let the job turn me into one?"

"But you're wrong, John. You are a politician—and a good enough one to beat Tammany without a machine."

Mitchel's hand hung on the door handle. He seemed unsure about whether he was getting out. "I won't do it," he said.

"You won't go to the Biltmore?"

"I mean I won't allow anyone to dictate my actions." He shoved the door open with his shoulder.

It was a modest neighborhood restaurant and, as such, the appearance of the mayor couldn't have been any more surprising to the diners had he shown up on their doorsteps. When the shock of his presence wore off, Mitchel was greeted nervously by the owner, who came out from the kitchen wearing whites, trying to wipe the sweat from his hands and face with a dish towel. It was a cozy, well-worn family restaurant, but there weren't any children there, of course.

"Mr. Mayor! Please, let us make a table for you and get you some wine."

"Thank you. Do you have a telephone I can use?"

"Oh, certainly! It's in the kitchen, I'll show you."

"No, I can find it. Teddy—you know what I like. Order for me." He walked quickly toward the kitchen, trying to avoid looking at any of the diners.

Mitchel's abruptness left the restaurateur flustered, obliging Teddy to offer a soothing smile. "Been a long day," he said. "Out washing the streets. All this worry about the epidemic, too much to do. I'm sure the wine is just what he needs. Did you make it?"

"My brother."

"I'll bet it's terrific. What's good tonight?"

"I make the best veal chop in Brooklyn! The mayor will—"

"The mayor doesn't really like veal. Too heavy. Just a little spaghetti for him. If it makes you feel any better, I want to try the veal. And I'm sure these guys will eat up a storm," he added, pointing to Commissioners Emerson and Fetherston who were just coming in.

Through the kitchen door everyone could now hear Mitchel yelling, although it was impossible to make out what he was saying. For as long as the tirade lasted, which was a good two minutes, the entire restaurant with the exception of Teddy seemed to be focused in frozen attention on the red door and the small round pane of glass through which nothing could actually be seen. The mayor's voice rose steadily in pitch and intensity. An extraordinary clatter of metal punctuated the conversation's conclusion, and Teddy guessed Mitchel had flung a pot across the kitchen. As the mayor burst through the door and stormed across the dining room, a dishwasher could be seen cringing under the sink at the rear of the kitchen. Teddy fluttered his eyes at Mitchel and nodded his head slightly in indication of their surroundings, causing the Mayor to close his eyes and exhale. He patted his hair with his palms, and turned to face the room.

"Please forgive me," he said. "I don't mean to interrupt anyone's dinner."

"Give 'em hell, Jack!" someone yelled, and the laughter and applause eased both the room and Mitchel, who waved his thanks and sheepishly sat down.

"See?" Teddy said, leaning across the table. "When you let 'em, they love you."

Mitchel only scowled and shoved a piece of bread into his mouth. "Yeah, well, that's because I take out their garbage. That was the theater operators' representative. They want the ban on kids lifted or they'll go to court. Tell Arthur Woods to put auxiliary police outside every picture house and open-air theater in the city. This thing stands."

Teddy made a note in the small book he always carried to call the police commissioner. "Is that all?" That kind of carping normally wasn't enough to get Mitchel's goat.

"No. The office also said the department store owners released a statement that they're not taking returns on children's clothing during the epidemic—"in the interest of the public health.""

"It's a canard," said Emerson. "They've been trying to void returns on children's clothing for years and there isn't a scrap of evidence that germs can live long enough on cloth to be transmitted."

"Well this is one duck that isn't flying. Haven, I want you to release a statement tomorrow slamming them down hard. Call 'em un-American if you want to—in fact, nothing could make me happier. Selfish pigs! Aside from abusing their customers, they haven't the faintest interest in how this makes the city look—and at a moment when every hotel is empty and I'm trying to talk half of Washington out of quarantining us!" He rubbed his forehead and accepted a glass of wine from Teddy.

"Mayor Mitchel?" A young man was standing nervously by the table, a woman at his side. "We're here tonight celebrating our engagement."

"Congratulations."

"Thank you, sir. Well, it's so odd that you would show up here on the night that we decided to get married, we were wondering if maybe it was a sign or something. You know, if maybe you'd be willing to marry us."

"Now?"

"Oh, no! Certainly not, sir!"

"Well, why didn't you wait a few minutes so you could interrupt my dinner, too?"

Teddy quickly jumped in. "Have you set a date yet?"

The man looked down, but the woman shook her head. Teddy could see that Mitchel, who wasn't even looking at them, had already destroyed their evening. She was shaking, her eyes brimming with tears. Mitchel was popping another piece of bread into his mouth.

"Here's my card," Teddy said, standing up. "I'm the mayor's personal secretary. When you set a date, call me. Maybe we can work something out."

"That's all right," the woman said, her voice quavering. "I'd rather get married in the church. By a real Catholic." She turned, pulling the man with her.

"That's the way it should be," Mitchel said to the table. "I'll stay out of the marrying business if the Church will stay out of the city's business." He shook his head. "A hundred-and-ten-hours a week, children are dropping like leaves, and I'm supposed to be a justice of the peace in the bargain? What the hell do these people want?" Fetherston and Emerson stared at Mitchel. Teddy lit another cigarette and focused on the kitchen door, as if it would make their food appear that much quicker.

After dinner they caught up with the sanitation crew at Sixty-eighth Street for the last three stops along Fourth Avenue. When the pumper swung back up Fifth, the mayor told his driver to head for Manhattan.

"Where do you want to be dropped?" he asked Teddy. "City Hall or home?"

"I'll go with you to midtown."

"Fine. But no more lectures."

They sat in silence for most of the ride. Mitchel's eyes were tired yet restless in their curiosity and were still managing to dart as nimbly as a bee, alighting ever so briefly but incisively on something—what? Teddy wondered, marveling one more time at the depth and selectivity of his curiosity—before they moved to the next thing and then the next thing and then the next thing.

The car slowed as it approached Grand Central Terminal, stopping in front of the Biltmore. "Sure you won't change your mind?" Teddy asked.

"Never. What about you? Care to go dancing? I'm going to go upstairs and change first—I'm sure we can scare up a tux for you."

"Nah."

"Take the car if you don't want to walk. I'll see you in the office at seven."

"Tomorrow's Saturday."

"Eight, then."

"Eight."

Mitchel stuck his head forward to his driver. "Just be back here in three hours." Then he was gone.

Teddy watched him walk into the hotel's pink marble lobby and enter the elevator. As soon as the door closed, the bell captain reached for his telephone. "You know," Teddy said to the driver as he pulled out his cigarettes, "sometimes there's no pleasure in being right."

"You can't tell that guy nothin'," the driver said. "And I mean nothin'. Where do you wanna go?"

"No place just yet. Let's see how long it takes 'em to get here."

A car with three photographers pulled up behind them fifteen minutes later, just as Teddy saw the tuxedoed Mitchel reemerge from the elevator and cross the lobby for the ballroom.

"There he is!" yelled one. "I'll go in this way, you guys take the side doors." They split up and the photographer who turned left charged straight into a woman, nearly knocking her off her feet. The woman, who wore a black scarf on her head, was walking with two boys and carrying a small, sleeping girl. "Sorry, lady!" he yelled over his shoulder, not even waiting to see if the girl, who was now crying, was all right.

Teddy was at their side immediately. "Can I help you, ma'am?"

"Oh, I can't stand it anymore!" said the woman. "The world's gone crazy! Don't cry, Christa." She rocked the girl, trying to calm her, as her two young boys looked on with a mix of exhaustion and fright. "What did I just get shoved for?"

"A picture of the mayor dancing."

"That sounds like our newspapers. And our mayor," she said.

"No. No, it really isn't. He's actually a great man who never bothered to learn how to be a good man. Besides, didn't you ever just want to do something for yourself at the end of a long, long day?"

She looked at her children and then back to Teddy. She didn't answer.

"Where are you coming from at this hour?"

Anna waved vaguely toward Grand Central but just sighed. "No-where."

"Well, where are you going?"

"Brooklyn, I guess."

"Come on," Teddy said, opening the car door and waving toward the sleepy boys. "The mayor wants to give you a ride."

8

FORTITUDE

ight-thirty!

E Attilio never slept this late, even if it was Sunday. He hadn't been to a morning Mass in the twelve years since his mother's death, but still retained the lifelong habit of rising early and the prospect of a late start annoyed him. It must be the studio. He certainly wouldn't have slept this late at home. There he could count on his wife and her sisters to disturb him. The three sirens, he called them. Not to their faces, of course. He didn't like to admit it, but his marriage was another reason he didn't go to Mass. It was Father Rinaldi who had needled him into meeting Julia. The late marriage was a mistake—some men are born to be bachelors, and he should have admitted that instead of pretending to be something he wasn't just to make them all happy. Ah, the Church was nothing but trouble. Home was nothing but trouble. The only things worth having were in these buildings.

Attilio was spending more nights here than at home, and whenever Julia made a caustic remark about it he would just wave a tired hand and mutter vaguely about a deadline on a piece. The French project had been all the excuse any man needed. But had anyone else noticed that he'd slowly been moving in? None of his brothers had said anything, but they had to know—Furio had seen one of the apprentices taking Attilio's shirts to the laundry on 138th Street. But beyond clean shirts, he really didn't need much. He was an elegant man—always meticulously groomed and still solid and trim even in his mid-fifties—but he liked to keep things simple. He only owned four suits and the two he preferred, the ones he'd had made in Milan, were almost twenty years old. Of course, a Piccirilli really didn't need many suits. At work the brothers all wore smocks over white shirts and ties. Suits were for the Donnellys. They were the Piccirilli's biggest competitors, New York's other leading stonecutting studio. They weren't sculptors, though, just businessmen. Bookkeepers, Getulio said dismissively. And while Attilio would never be that crude, he did wonder what anybody named Donnelly could possibly know about marble. But he was also the first to admit they knew the business: it always seemed to come down to the Piccirillis and the Donnellys whenever a big job was bid. Their shop, in Queens rather than the Bronx, did good work, too. They should, thought Attilio—some of their top cutters had apprenticed at Piccirilli Brothers. Oh, well, free enterprise. That's what makes America great, yes?

No one seeing this apartment could doubt the artistry of the Piccirillis. While it was lovely to begin with, with polished-wood parquet floors running from the bedroom through the rolling entrance doors and out into the music room and a living room overlooking 142nd Street, it was nearly impossible to notice anything except the enormous fireplace of white Carrara marble with *PB* carved just below the scrolled stone mantel. The mantel itself was supported by two large cherubs, while stone carvings of fruit and flowers bound with ribbons hung above the fireplace, framing a large old mirror. On the mantel Attilio kept the marble-handled brush-and-comb set he had made for his mother while studying as a boy at the Reale Accademia di Belle Arti in Rome. Just below the ceiling, a wide frieze ran the entire length of the room, a scroll done in the Renaissance style, and a large matching centerpiece hung from the ceiling. It was more like the chambers of a doge than a home, and there wasn't a living room to compare with it even in the finest buildings on the Grand Concourse.

So late, so late! Without bothering to make coffee, Attilio took his pipe from the nightstand, shoved it in the pocket of his smock and hurried down the hallway and through the door to the studios on the top floor of the adjoining building. Entering the enormous space where each brother had his own studio was always the best moment of the day, like stepping into another and better world. Even now in February, the high bank of steeply angled, staggered skylights climbing overhead spun a blanket of pure light from the hard gray wool of winter sky. The light freed Attilio like nothing else. Here there was no ceiling, only sky.

He often did his best work in the quiet solitude of Sundays. During the week, each of the one hundred coat hooks in the downstairs hallway held a jacket, and the steady pounding of pneumatic hammers, the motor of the enormous, room-sized elevator, the trucks coming and going through the main door, and the shouting of the men echoed through the attached row of buildings. But now it was silent and Attilio's footsteps were the only sound as he shuffled across the floor and automatically picked a sheet of newspaper from the pile by the door, absentmindedly folding it into a hat. There wouldn't be any marble dust today—he was putting the finishing touches to a bronze cast—but he could no more work without a hat than Father Rinaldi say Mass in pajamas. His own studio, the largest of the enormous workrooms, was in the back of the building and faced northeast over the apartment roofs and toward the green splotch of St. Mary's Park. He rarely looked out the window, though, and this morning his eyes fell to a slab of raised bronze propped against an old marble pediment by his corner tool bench.

Attilio had worked on the piece deep into the night, smoothing casting defects, removing the last traces of the vent and gate seams, and brushing on the acids that would bring out the green and blue of the metal. Normally he would heat the bronze with a blowtorch, applying the patina to the hot metal. But this was an outdoor piece, so it had been preferable to apply the acid cold, even if the results were a little less predictable. Normally he didn't like to do funereal pieces—he'd done more than his share for Adler's Monument and Granite Works on East Fifty-seventh Street when the Piccirillis first arrived in America—but this was different. He knew what a decade of winters at Woodlawn would do to this piece, had seen the weather inexorably color the *Fortitude* casting at his mother's grave, the blues and greens running across the figures like tears. Better to try and beat nature at her own game and take control. He studied the results, satisfied the color was almost right. One more application of acid. It was a good job, even if bas-relief wasn't his strength. Thea's hands were especially well done—not a surprise considering how strong and beautiful he'd always found them. He sighed, worried. What would *Avvocato* La Guardia say when he saw this?

He didn't want to think about that. Not yet. There was a small Victrola in the studio—he kept it right near his tools—and he wound the crank a dozen times, dropping the wooden needle on the thick Victor disk. Enrico. *"Tu, ca nun Chiagne."* The Neapolitan street songs had always been the singer's own favorites, the ones he sang for friends. It was all the sculptor listened to anymore. Attilio slumped down in a folding chair in front of the bronze relief and placed the brush, gloves, and can of acid on the floor. He couldn't believe he'd never see Enrico again. These deaths seemed so senseless—didn't the world need all the beauty it could get? He listened to the old folk song, motionless in his chair. And when it

was done, the last notes decaying into the air and the only sound the needle of the machine rubbing over and over against the label, he sat yet.
Only the front doorbell broke the spell. He didn't have to look out the
window to know who it was. Attilio took a small brown felt jewelry pouch
from his workbench and headed briskly down the circular stairwell to the
main floor of the studio.

The delivery boy was waiting on the front stoop of the brownstone, a
cardboard box at his feet, and he was surprised when the heavy garage
door of the next building opened instead. He saw the sculptor stick his
head out and wave.

"Over here, Gennato!"

"Yes, Maestro Piccirilli." The boy picked up the box and walked back
out the gate and around to the studio.

He'd never been in this building before and it was like none he'd ever
seen. The room was as big as a large public garage, but instead of wagons
and automobiles, enormous blocks of stone, most taller than a grown
man and some as wide as a trolley, were parked on thick wooden timbers
along the side walls. At the back of the warehouse was the largest elevator he'd ever seen: it was bigger than his parent's bakery and looked high
enough to drive a truck into. He followed the sculptor to the building's
rear corner where a door led back into the brownstone and downstairs
into the kitchen.

It was a long room with a huge marble-topped dining table, big
enough to seat a dozen men, and Attilio motioned for the boy to place his
box of groceries upon it. The walls of the kitchen were lined with cup-
boards, while below them a chair rail over narrow wooden slats circled
the room. Ground-level windows and a back door opened onto a rear
courtyard. In the yard, the boy could see still more blocks of stone along
with several carved statues of naked women in various poses, a young boy
playing with a goat, and another leaning on a stick and holding up an apple. Behind them, sprawled alongside the fence, was an enormous head
with a beard. He stopped to stare.

"Do you know who that is, Gennato?"

"Yes, Maestro. Did you carve that statue?"

Piccirilli fished his pipe out of the pocket of his white smock and picked up a box of matches sitting on a large industrial stove. Lighting the bowl, he looked through the smoke at the boy. "No. It's a plaster model. We used it to carve a giant marble statue of President Lincoln that will be unveiled in a few months in Washington, D.C. Here at the studio we sometimes carve our own statues, and sometimes we carve them for other sculptors. This one was for a friend of ours, Maestro French. We carve a lot of his statues, almost all of them. Did you know that most sculptors don't carve their own statues?"

"No, Maestro. Does that mean they're not good artists?"

Attilio smiled. "That's a good question. A very good question." He puffed on his pipe. "No. But cutting stone is a very ancient and special skill. The town where my family comes from, Massa-Carrara, and where my father used to have a studio, is world-famous for its marble and its sculptors and stonecutters. For as long as anyone can remember, sculptors have always sent their clay or plaster models to Carrara to be transferred into stone. When we came to America, the sculptors here saw they didn't need to send their work all the way to Italy anymore."

"Is the whole statue that big?"

"Nineteen feet. Including the base it is over thirty feet tall." Attilio leaned over the table to lift three loaves of bread from the box of groceries. "Gennato, your father's bread is always the highlight of my Sunday morning. Still warm, too. We're lucky to have someone of his talents in the neighborhood. And I thank you for stopping to pick up these other things at the grocery. What's this?" He lifted a small black pan wrapped in butcher's paper. "Stuffed artichokes?"

"My mother said they are for you and Signora Piccirilli. On Saturday nights she likes to stay at the bakery and make things in Papa's ovens for Sunday dinner. She was so surprised to find the artichokes this time of year at the Belmont market that she couldn't resist buying a lot of them; the greengrocer said they had come by train from California. And of course if there's one thing we've always got plenty of at the bakery, it's breadcrumbs." Throughout his reply, the boy had not taken his eyes off the bust of Lincoln. "Maestro, if the statue is in Washington, why is the head here?"

"We carved the statue upstairs. What's the matter? You look puzzled."

"How did you do that? I mean, can you really fit a thirty-foot statue in the elevator?"

"No! Do you know how much that would weigh? But you're a smart boy—how do you suppose we did it?"

He thought for a moment. "I don't know, Maestro."

Attilio opened the back door and tapped the tobacco out of his pipe and then shoved it back into his pocket. "Come," he said. "I'll show you."

Following the sculptor up the circular stairs and into one of the larger studios on the third floor, the boy once again found himself surrounded by stones. This time, however, they weren't just raw blocks. All around were plaster casts and statues—some seemingly complete, others just emerging from the stone. There were classical figures of nudes, cherubs and fawns, a small lion that looked exactly like the famous ones in front of the Fifth Avenue library, historic pieces of soldiers, statesmen, and politicians including George Washington, and several different busts of the same beautiful young girl. Toward the back, leaning against the wall, a large stone bas-relief caught Gennato's attention.

"You like that one, eh?" Atillio asked. The boy nodded. "This is my brother Getulio's studio, and that's the model for something he carved many years ago for a sculptor named John Quincy Adams Ward. The finished work is downtown over the entrance to the Stock Exchange. But come—take a look at this." Attilio led him around the workbench, which was laid out with carefully arranged sets of drills and carving tools, and past two modeling tables and a hoist. There, set off by itself, was another statue of President Lincoln, this one life-size, seated in a chair.

"This is the plaster cast we worked from. It's exactly like the finished carving except that it's only seven feet tall instead of nineteen. We measure the model with one of these." He held up a metal tool with three legs that looked like a small easel stand. "It's called a pointings gig. We use this to transfer measurements from the model to the stone and it tells us how deep or wide to cut. Now—let me show you what Getulio came up with to get the statue in and out of here." Above the sculptor's workbench a thin slab of marble acted as a shelf. Attilio reached up and took down a long cardboard tube. Inside were diagrams and blueprints.

"So, Gennato—let me ask you: how much do you think the big

statue weighs? Fifty pounds? A thousand? Five thousand? *Ten* thousand pounds?"

The boy thought about it. "Ten thousand pounds?" he ventured.

The sculptor shook his head and smiled. "Three hundred thousand pounds. Do you think we could get that up here in the elevator?"

"No, Maestro."

"No. That's right, Gennato. So what did Getulio do?" Here he unrolled the plans with a dramatic flourish. "Signore President Lincoln might have held the Union together, but we had to break him apart. The statue is really twenty-eight pieces, each one carved individually and weighing about five tons. But to look at it you would never know. Getulio figured out a way to do it so that the seams are nearly invisible and it looks like one stone."

"Like a giant puzzle?"

"Yes, just like a puzzle. Do you like puzzles?"

"Oh, yes, Maestro! I have a really difficult one with two thousand pieces. It takes me more than a week to put it together. How long did it take to make the Lincoln statue?

"Over two years, and it is not quite done yet. I have to go to Washington again with the sculptor to make sure everything is just right."

"Two years! That must be a long time to work on one statue."

"Not really. Time is different to a sculptor. Most statues take several years and I have one that I've been working on for over five. The greatest sculptor who ever lived, Michelangelo, was also the fastest. He carved many of the world's greatest statues and could finish them in just one year. You know who Michelangelo is, yes?"

The boy shook his head.

"*No?*" Although he pretended to be appalled, Attilio wasn't surprised. "You don't know who Michelangelo is? Where is your family from? Ireland?"

The boy reddened and shook his head.

"Germany?"

The boy looked down. "Lucania."

The sculptor nodded. "Oh, *Lucania!* Well, even that's no excuse!" He laughed and put a hand on the boy's shoulder to show he was only joking.

"You're a good boy, Gennato. I appreciate you coming here to bring my bread and groceries, and I see the way you help your mother and father, even when the other boys are playing. You will be a good man. Of course, I see you still have some time to play—I have seen you in the park if I am out walking in the afternoon. Maybe you can help me understand something. I see you playing a game with a circle and little round pieces of glass. What is that?"

"Why, marbles, Maestro."

"Marbles? Why do you call it marbles when you are using glass?"

"I don't know, Maestro. It does seem funny, doesn't it?"

"Do you think that a long time ago they played the game with little balls of marble?"

The boy shrugged.

Attilio reached into the pocket of his smock and took out the small felt jewelry bag. "Here," he said, handing it to the boy. "Try playing with these."

Eyes wide, Gennato turned the bag over in his hand and six smooth, round, cool marble stones tumbled into his palm. Polished to a lustrous finish, five were white and the sixth, slightly larger, was a glowing pink. "That's the queen," Attilio said. "You should try not to lose her."

"I don't want to lose any of them, Maestro! They're so beautiful—I don't know how I can risk any of them in a game. Thank you! Did they take a very long time to make?"

Attilio waved his hand dismissively. "No, it's easy. Why? Do you think you'd like to learn how to make them?"

"Me? Are you crazy? I mean, yes, of course, Maestro. Could you really teach me?"

"Sure. You know working in stone is one of the oldest and most respected professions back in Italy. If your parents say it is all right, I can show you how to make your marbles any Sunday. If you want, I can even show you how to use the tools and design and carve." He waved, as if creating the contents of the studio was no more challenging than making the simplest toy. But Attilio could tell from the look on the boy's face that the whole idea was both overwhelming and exciting—as unreal as if a subway motorman had offered to let him drive his train. "Come, I have to get back to work. But if you like, I will talk to your parents this week and see if you can't come over and study." He fished a hand into the pants of his trousers and came out with a quarter. "The marbles are a gift; this is for doing your job and delivering my groceries."

"Thank you, Maestro. Thank you."

When Attilio had let the boy out and latched the carriage door behind him, he returned to his own studio to apply the final coat of patina to the bas-relief. There wasn't much to be done other than check the color as it dried, but he had to watch it carefully because he had a specific effect in mind.

The piece should not look new but weathered, permanent—as if it had always existed somewhere out in the world. This was the impression he wanted his friend to have the moment he laid eyes on the monument. Perhaps then he could accept that things were as they were. In the nearly ten years of their friendship he had never seen *Avvocato* like this. Over Christmas he had accompanied his friend to Havana, thinking the sea and the sun (and, who knows, maybe even the women) would bring him around. But it might as well have been the Bronx: all he did was drink. Two weeks in Cuba and the only thing redder than his skin was his eyes. Attilio understood the pain, but would never have believed his friend could fall apart like this; he had always been so strong. Maybe it was because other things had been going so badly, even before this. Perhaps that was it—perhaps it was feeling like payment for a charmed life, weighing on him like an inevitable settling of a score on which there can be no appeal. When they first met in the Village, back even before the first run for Congress—when he was just *Avvocato*, the energetic young lawyer who loved nothing more than to drink and joke with artists and musicians—Attilio could tell he was special, a man destined for greatness. And even though he lost that first race he won the next, the first Italian-American congressman. When America finally joined the war, he held onto his seat while taking a commission as a major and pilot in Italy. He flew enough missions to become a hero, but it was as an unofficial attaché that he really excelled, really proved his stuff. So what does a young man with the world at his feet want? Why, he wants to be the mayor, of course. Maybe that was the mistake; maybe he should have stayed in Congress, set his sights on being Speaker. Instead, he ran for president of the board of aldermen—a nothing job but a stepping-stone to City Hall—and won easily. But then his luck ran out.

First it was that stupid fight with the city's comptroller. Regrettable, but understandable—the comptroller was an idiot. But why he'd picked a fight with Governor Miller—the man who'd sponsored him for president of the aldermen—was beyond knowing. The Republicans would never nominate him for mayor without Miller's approval. What could he have been thinking? Perhaps it had all been getting away from him—first the baby, then his wife, Thea, and of course his own bad back and painful surgery—Attilio could only guess. They'd talk and the sculptor would listen, offer another cigar, and pretend he understood his world. But he really didn't. He only knew his friend was falling apart.

By three o'clock the winter sunlight seemed already to be weakening in the Mott Haven sky. Satisfied that the patina would do, Attilio placed a cloth tarp over the piece and went back down to the kitchen and put a large pot of water on the big industrial stove. He liked to cook and he was good at it—all the Piccirilli brothers were. There was always a fight over who would get to cook lunch whenever schoolchildren came to tour the studios. What could he say? The Piccirillis just liked to make things, and Attilio had to admit that he liked to cook more than he liked to eat. The thought made him smile. Attilio's disinterest in his own cooking was fine with *Avvocato*—he could really pack it away—and Attilio would tease him that if he didn't stop eating they'd never find enough marble to build his Washington statue. But that felt like a long time ago. Attilio took a box of small cigars out of the cabinet and put them on the table. He was hoping for the best but expecting the worst when the doorbell rang. He didn't bother going upstairs. *Avvocato* had been coming to the studios long enough to know the front door of the brownstone was unlocked; ringing the bell was just to announce his arrival. The sculptor heard the front door close, the unusually slow footsteps in the hall and on the stairs, and even the labored breathing just before his friend appeared in the kitchen door.

The last six months had aged Fiorello La Guardia. When they first met, Attilio had been startled by the tiny man's power and dynamism. Though barely over five feet tall, he easily dominated any gathering with his personality, which preceded him like a gust of wind. And despite being so short, he'd still cut a striking and tough figure as a major, and Attilio recalled how dashing he'd been in his belted black leather flight jacket. As a speaker and campaigner, Fiorello could work a crowd like few others, regardless of whether he was speaking on the floor of Congress or to a group of pushcart vendors. Attilio the sculptor had always paid close attention to how a man carried himself, to the physical actions he used to express himself, and he had always believed Fiorello's power was in his dark, burning eyes and the jabbing, short-fingered hands, that he had an almost mystical ability to convey his passion and humanity through them. But there was no fire in those eyes today, and the hands hung at his side, limp and bloodless as two skinned rabbits in a butcher's window. The black wool overcoat made him look bulky and amorphous, and his blue-black hair, lank and damp, emphasized how pasty and puffy his face had become.

"*Buon giorno*, Uncle Picc," he said, the name sounding like *peach*.

"*Avvocato. Come sta?*"

"*Bene, grazie*," he said automatically. He held up a paper sack containing two bottles. "I brought some wine."

"Wine? You carried wine on the subway from University Avenue? Fiorello, are you crazy? Don't you care if anyone sees you? Don't you think the newspapers would love a picture of the president of the board of aldermen carrying liquor, even if it is just wine?

The outburst amused La Guardia, and it touched him to see his friend worry for him. "Calm down, Uncle. First of all, everyone knows how I feel about prohibition, so what's the difference? But if it makes you happy, I had my new kid meet me here with the bottles."

"What? Who? Where is he?"

"Outside on the stoop."

"What's the matter with you? It's February! You really have lost your mind, haven't you? Tell the boy to come in and have dinner with us!"

"Of course, sure. I just wanted, you know, a few minutes alone. To see the stone."

Attilio nodded. "Sure. *Avanti*. But first, give me your coat."

Trudging up the winding staircase, the sculptor wondered again if he'd done the right thing, if the images he'd selected would have their intended effect. Too late to change them now, he thought grimly. Still, his doubts made him reticent to say what he wanted to. "So who is this boy?" he asked instead.

"Marc? This one's a pip. A natural-born demagogue." He chuckled. "I heard him speak a few years ago at an assembly when he was still a student at DeWitt Clinton High School. He was already better than half those stiffs in Congress. Talked about the need for old-age pensions. Could you imagine? A little squirt like that talking about pensioners' rights! He was so good, so pressing, I had to steal it when it was my turn to speak. We stayed in touch—he's at NYU now and I want him to go to law school. He just organized a successful rent strike in East Harlem where his family lives. He's quite a boy."

As soon as they reached the top of the stairs, La Guardia saw the cloth tarp. A shiver ran through his body. Every other stone in the studio disappeared, and he felt as if his bones had turned to water, his head to light. He'd felt the same exact physical shock when he'd gone to see Fioretta at the funeral parlor and had never wanted to feel it again. When Thea died five months later, he was in the hospital for his back surgery and hadn't been able to move, let alone attend her funeral. He couldn't tell which he felt more shame over: missing it or his secret relief at not having to see his wife in her coffin. Attilio could feel La Guardia shaking and lightly put a supporting arm behind his back. Time to say something.

"You know, *Avvocato*, the piece I have made is a metal plate, just a little smaller than the headstone will be. Caterson's is going to send the stone over to Woodlawn, and we'll mount the piece on it there, okay?"

If he heard him, La Guardia made no response. He simply stared at the cloth-covered slab, and Attilio found it impossible to read his thoughts. Was he trying to make it vanish—to will it out of existence?— or was he simply steeling himself? Finally, without looking at Attilio or even taking his eyes from the cloth, he said, "Show me." Attilio gently pulled up the veil.

There were two figures. Fiorello immediately recognized the familiar, smaller one on the left. It was an infant, arms outstretched and legs planted tentatively, about to take its first step. Just three years ago, Attilio had created a small bronze statue of this baby as a wedding present for Fiorello and Thea, a sculptor's prayer for a happy marriage and a fruitful union. Fiorello kept the statue in his office. And here was the baby again, this time as his Fioretta, wobbling toward a kneeling mother with outstretched hands. Thea. He wasn't sure he could do this, could feel his knees weakening. Across Thea's lap were roses, but at her back grew lillies, the mortician's sweetly fetid bloom, and their scent, represented as a cloud, wafted crudely over them. Dead. *Dead.* Fioretta dead. Thea dead. Yet there was an infinite delicacy and tenderness in Attilio's rendition of Thea's reaching, welcoming hands, and it was this expression of her essence which proved too much. "Uncle," he sobbed, collapsing into his friend's arms. "I want my family back. Please. Please, Uncle. Please. I'll do anything. Please. Just give them back to me."

It was the moment Attilio had worked for and dreaded, and he simply wrapped his arms gently around his sobbing friend, towering over him in his white smock like an old family doctor. He knew how painful this was, knew how much Fiorello had loved Thea, had no doubt that his friend's successes in Italy and in Congress were in no small measure undertaken to spark a fire of admiration in her dark eyes. But these last few months had been unbearable. It had to stop or Fiorello would destroy himself— he was already dangerously close. And so Attilio had not missed the opportunity to use his skills not, as he usually did, to immortalize, but rather to finalize. *Look. Look! They are there, together, without us.* The only ones who get to stay in the cemetery are the dead.

"Why wouldn't she stay with me, Uncle Picc? She left me, you know. I loved her so much, but she didn't want to be with me."

"Fiorello! How can you shame her like this? Thea loved you, you know that!"

"So why did she let herself get sick? She was fine until the baby . . . and then she stopped wanting to live. She stopped wanting to be with me." At these words he collapsed again into sobs. "Why wouldn't she stay with me? What could I have done? What didn't I say? Oh, Uncle Picc! I never should have gone into the hospital for my back surgery! I should have stayed with Thea, I should have made her promise to stay . . . I should have forced her . . . I should have . . ."

"Fiorello," he said gently. "She just had a broken heart. Look how difficult this is even for a strong man like you. Forgive her. Forgive yourself."

As the winter sky above the glass ceiling darkened, the two men stood together nearly motionless. After a while, La Guardia patted his friend on the shoulder and moved back in front of the bronze slab to sit on the stool and study it. He sat there for a long time, occasionally shaking his head slowly, shivering or heaving a sigh. Piccirilli padded across the shop, wound the Victrola, and played the record again, the melody of the old folk song filling the dimming room. La Guardia snorted.

"I don't know how you can listen to this crap!"

It was an old routine with them, and it was just what Piccirilli had hoped for.

"The greatest opera singer who ever lived, and all you ever want to hear anymore are these crummy songs that every neighborhood Casanova sings at the annual church feast. Please, Uncle Picc! Don't you think I deserve something better? A little bit of 'Pagliacci' maybe? What an old wop you're turning into!"

Attilio wagged a warning finger at the insult. "So—now you know music better than Caruso, eh? It must be nice to know everything! Why don't you teach me? I'm just a simple stonecutter—an old wop."

His friend waved a hand dismissively but wouldn't rise to the bait.

"No? Not going to tell me how little Caruso knew about music? It's a good thing he's not here—I'll bet he could tell you how to fix the god-damn subways, Mr. Bigshot, president-of-the-board-of-aldermen." At this he could hear La Guardia stifling a laugh, and the sculptor dug his pipe from his smock pocket and triumphantly stuffed and lit the bowl.

"You still miss him?"

Attilio blew the smoke gently toward the skylight and turned on a small table lamp clamped to his workbench. "Sure," he said. "We always had such great fun with him, didn't we *Avvocato?* I've had three presidents in this building, but only one prince. You know what kind of man he was. A simple and beautiful man, a real man. I'll never forget the day he stood downstairs and sang for our men during their lunch break. Could you imagine it? Enrico Caruso—singing for a bunch of Bronx stonecutters! And do you know why he was great? Because it meant no less to him than singing at the Metropolitan Opera House."

La Guardia seemed to be considering this. "Funny he should die of pleurisy, huh? You would think he'd have the strongest lungs in the world."

Piccirilli eyed his friend thoughtfully over his pipe. "Sailors drown. Miners get black lung. Firemen burn. He was a singer; he used his lungs more than they were intended." He paused. "Perhaps that's why Thea died of a broken heart."

La Guardia made no reply, but continued to look at the bas-relief. After a few minutes he said, "It's wonderful, Uncle Picc, thank you. You're a hell of an artist."

"Me? I'm just an old wop."

"Aw, Christ!" La Guardia growled, rising from the stool. "Let me off the hook!" He turned and winked at the sculptor.

"Are you hungry?"

"Always."

"Good. The baker's wife sent over some stuffed artichokes with the bread. And I have homemade sausage that one of the workers gave us."

"Don't forget the wine."

Attilio shot him a look.

"Don't worry, Uncle. I feel a lot better."

"Good. Then why don't you stop being a jerk and let that poor boy come in out of the cold!"

Leaning over the stove, his head bent above a loud pan of spitting sausage, Attilio didn't hear Fiorello come back in with the boy, and he only turned around when he smelled the cigarette smoke mingling with the frying spiced pork. They were already seated at the table, Fiorello pouring three glasses of wine, the boy smoking and trying not to stare at the old, faded floral apron Attilio was wearing to protect his clothes. The boy himself had none of the sculptor's natural fastidiousness and wore the kind of cheap dark suit and blandly invisible tie worn by men who don't think about clothes. His face was thin and pale, and his small dark eyes moved in staccato fashion like the heads of two tiny birds. He was looking at the floor, and Attilio assumed the boy was just shy until he noticed both heels tapping nonstop. He was as tightly clenched as a fist, and it was taking all of his concentration to sit still. When Fiorello slid a glass in front of him, the boy's hand shot out and brought it to his lips in one swift, sharp movement. Only at the last second—when he was poised to toss the wine back in a gulp—did he catch himself and wait for the others.

"*Salute*," Attilio said, raising his glass.

"*L'chaim*," Fiorello answered, draining his. The toast seemed to catch the boy off guard, and La Guardia smiled mischievously and wagged a finger. "If you're going to be a politician in New York you're going to have to be able to drink in a dozen languages—not just Italian."

Attilio scowled. He approved of the way Fiorello took these young boys under his wing, but he didn't like his methods. He was always too quick to humiliate them.

"What's the matter, Uncle? You think I'm too rough, eh? Let me tell you something: Marc is plenty tough. Which is good, because in the world he wants to enter a man has to be able to take a punch and smile. Besides, he knows what I'm talking about. He spends too much time with *Circolo Italiano* instead of studying law."

"I'm sure you're only making trouble, but it's lost on me. I don't know *Circolo Italiano*," Attilio said. "What is it?"

Fiorello waved dismissively. "A big waste of time."

At this the boy reddened. Seeing the effect his words had, La Guardia grinned and poured it on. "It's a club. They play bocce and make wine."

The boy slammed his hand on the table. "Stop it! Why do you have to say that? Can't you see he doesn't know you're kidding?" But he quickly checked himself and appeared embarrassed by the outburst.

"Ah! Vesuvius erupts!" La Guardia cackled. "Okay, smart guy. You think my Uncle Picc doesn't know when I'm having someone on? Why don't you tell him what you do in that secret society." At this he gave Attilio a conspiratorial wink.

The boy lit another cigarette. "I live in Italian Harlem," he said, forcefully expelling a thin stream of blue smoke up toward the ceiling. "But I went to DeWitt Clinton High School over on Tenth Avenue. There were not a lot of Italian boys over there. In fact, I was the only one from the neighborhood. You know how it is sometimes with the people from the old country and school—the family comes first and you get a job as quick as you can. I had to hide my books in a candy store if I didn't want to get beat up on my block." He clenched his fist and took another drag on his cigarette. "Don't get me wrong. I don't mind fighting. I'd just rather not, and not day after day for no reason. So anyways I had a couple of good teachers there. One was my history teacher, Mr. Lefkowitz. He's running for Congress this year, Louis Lefkowitz. He opened my eyes to a lot of things. The other was Mr. Covello. He started teaching Italian as a foreign language at Clinton. Not just to see it get the same respect as French or Spanish or German, either. Mr. Covello saw that something was holding us back—something more than poverty. It was the failure of our own educated people to take pride and confront that old *contadini* mentality. So he started these student clubs, *Circoli Italiani*, to deal with this and build a path between the old ways and the American way. Now we have a circle down at NYU to tutor the high school kids. Mr. Covello also started a community center, Casa del Popolo, at a church on 118th Street near my mother's apartment."

"You know what this kid does over there?" La Guardia asked. "He teaches citizenship classes. In English and Italian."

Attilio nodded. "That's wonderful. That's how you make Americans."

"Yes, Uncle Picc. But you know what else it makes? Voters."

"You're too cynical, *Avvocato*."

"What's cynical about seeing them as voters? I'm a politician. Tell me, Uncle Picc: when somebody walks through those big doors upstairs with a huge, ugly public commission for Piccirilli Brothers from some well-connected *Artista* who isn't enough of a cutter to get hired here to sweep the floors, do you only think of the art and never the money? You have a hundred men working for you, depending on you for the support of their families. I've known you long enough to know that you wouldn't be so irresponsible as to only think of what is 'worthwhile' or 'lasting' instead of what makes money for Piccirilli Brothers. That's a luxury even an artist can't afford, and your men couldn't feed that to their families. Politics is no different. If I want to accomplish some good, I'd better find some voters, yes? And I'm certainly not going to teach this boy any different. Where are you hiding the bread?"

Attilio brought the hot artichokes to the table on small stone plates which made a clicking sound on the marble tabletop when set down. He wasn't surprised to see that the boy ate quickly and without thought, but he was pleased to see the way La Guardia dug in, rolling up his sleeves to avoid spattering them with oil and breadcrumbs, filling his wineglass

nearly to the rim. It wasn't until Fiorello was halfway through the artichoke that he even noticed Attilio had settled back with his pipe to wait
for the noodles to boil instead of joining them.

"Uncle Picc, *eat!*" he said through a mouthful of food. But this garnered only a dismissive wave, and La Guardia shook his head. "Jeez! I
don't know how you stay alive. You got statues eat more than you!"

Attilio puffed his pipe and gazed across the table. "Maybe," he said.
"But I don't think I have any that weigh more than you."

La Guardia narrowed his eyes as if about to launch an attack but instead broke into a laugh. Throughout, the boy's eyes followed the exchange, switching from face to face, his own betraying neither surprise
nor humor. His hand never stopped tugging leaves from the artichoke
and shoveling them to his mouth.

When Attilio laid the platter of spaghetti in front of them he brought
three plates. "Satisfied?" he asked, pulling the platter toward himself after the others had taken portions.

"You know, Uncle Picc, it always amazes me that you don't like to eat.
You're such a terrific cook."

The sculptor smiled but shrugged. "Mastery isn't a matter of inspiration, only repetition."

"Oh, what a load of bullshit. You've got more talent in your pinky
than most sculptors have in their entire bodies."

"Don't be ridiculous, Fiorello. But even if it was true, it wouldn't matter.
You have to be able to see it, yes, but even that is learned. What genius
would submit to spending months and months in front of a piece of rock? Is
that what you teach this boy? That he has to be 'inspired' to be successful?"

"Yes! Because he has to inspire others and make them believe in him.
Look, you remember Mayor Mitchel, right? A terrific mayor—maybe our
greatest. He was a fantastic administrator and manager and did more for
reform than anyone else who ever held the office. Just a brilliant man. So
everyone loved him, right? Wrong! He lost reelection by a huge margin to
our dopey friend Mr. Hylan—whom I need not remind you is currently
enjoying his second term. Mitchel was a jerk who acted like a bank president instead of a mayor! He wanted to believe results speak for themselves.
But they don't—especially not in politics. It's as important to be passion-

ate as it is to get results—maybe more! And the guy wasn't much of a pilot, either." La Guardia rolled his eyes. "Besides, I don't think Marc needs much tutoring in the fine art of inciting a crowd. He just led a successful rent strike up in Harlem." La Guardia clapped a hand on his protégé's shoulder. "Really, Uncle—you should hear this little bastard stir 'em up!"

"*Avvocato!* Why do you talk like this? Because he looks up to you, you have to be so rude to him? I won't have you talking like this in my house." He punctuated the words by rising from the table, although he turned out to only be going to the stove for the sausage. Having served the artichoke and spaghetti to La Guardia first, he now put the meat in front of the boy. "You know," he said, "when Fiorello first ran for Congress he wasn't much older than you. He was already the Piccirilli Brothers attorney, our *avvocato*. He came and asked us for money and advice. Well, mostly money." He looked directly at Marc but shook his finger at La Guardia. "He didn't know a damn thing about being a congressman but nobody made fun of him." As Attilio dropped back into his chair, La Guardia saw his friend really was angry.

"You know why he comes here?" Attilio asked. "He pretends it's for the food. But he really comes here to see his father." Marc could feel La Guardia shifting in the next chair and knew he was uncomfortable. But he was even more surprised that he was taking it. He'd seen La Guardia rip an alderman to shreds for not saying hello in a hallway, had heard him humiliate powerful men for the barest of provocation. Attilio relit his pipe. "Not really—I mean, of course I'm not his father. But his father was an artist, too. A musician." He paused and gave La Guardia a mild look. "He thinks he's at home so he mouths off."

"Uncle—"

"Ah, shut up. So Marc—it's Marc or *Marco?*"

He looked up from the plate of sausage. "Marc. It's really a nickname. My family's name is Marcantonio." He looked down at his plate, speared a piece of the meat with his fork, and shoved it into his mouth.

"What do they call you at home?"

He swallowed hastily. "Vito. It's just my mom and me. My dad's dead. He was a carpenter. Got hit by a streetcar two years ago." He reached for the wine bottle and poured himself another glass.

Attilio wondered how a boy with a widowed mother could afford not to work but didn't want to pry. "Your mother must be very proud of you," he offered.

Marcantonio shrugged and lit another cigarette. "I guess." He knew what Piccirilli was asking. "It's tough, though. She and my grandmother take in wash and sew lace, and I've got a job at a law firm."

La Guardia snorted. "Yeah. The firm of Lenin & Trotsky."

The other two ignored him. "It's Haile, Nelles, & Schoor," Marcantonio said. "Mostly labor law, although they represented a lot of the Palmer raid deportees like Emma Goldman."

"That's good," said Piccirilli. He tapped his pipe conspicuously to make sure La Guardia was looking at him. "I'm glad you've found a lawyer who can actually teach you something."

"Ah, shit!"

"Why do you insult me like this? How can you use such language at my dinner table?"

La Guardia raised his hands as if to animate a point, but then gave up and dropped them heavily on the table, rattling his silverware and glass. "I'm sorry, Uncle Picc." He turned to Marcantonio. "You know, this old man really is a fantastic teacher. You should see the guys that come out of here—guys who can cut anything, design anything, make anything."

Marcantonio nodded his head and took a nervous drag on his cigarette. "I don't know anything about art, but this looks like quite a place."

"Don't apologize," said Piccirilli. "Nobody in this country knows anything about art. Least of all the ones who think they do. You should see what they call sculpture now. I call it demolition."

"You don't like any of it, Uncle?"

"No."

"You don't think any of these guys know what they're doing?"

Piccirilli waved. "What they know isn't worth knowing. Some of it makes sense, but in denying the past it doesn't aim particularly high. It doesn't try to be much."

"I don't know," said La Guardia. "I saw a picture of a gravestone in Paris—it was clearly a headstone, but it was also two people kissing. It was very primitive—it looked like the guy spent about a week on it. But it caught my attention."

"Brancusi. He's clever, but again—it's not much. And pretending he's a pagan. Where's he from? Easter Island?"

"So his work would be better if he made it look like he came from sixteenth-century Florence?" asked Marcantonio.

Piccirilli considered this for a moment, turning his pipe while he thought of a reply. "I liked you better when you didn't know anything about art," he said.

"I meant no offense."

Piccirilli lit his pipe. "This is just the reason I'm starting an art school," he said.

"Hey, that's great, Uncle Picc! I might even be able to help you find some money if you want. The Piccirilli School of Art! This'll be great."

The sculptor frowned. "I think we'll call it something else. But we need to teach an appreciation for real carving before it's too late."

Marcantonio looked doubtful. "Are you talking about a technique or a style? I mean, do you want to teach the way that you work or your own notion of art?"

"Both, because they are inseparable. Look, I would never say that art should stand still or that someone can only be a real sculptor if their work looks like mine. I love Rodin. But he could never do what he did unless he knew how Leonardo worked, knew Michelangelo."

"And these other sculptors you're speaking of—they don't?"

A look of real disgust crossed Piccirilli's face. "No. It's like comparing a coloring book to the Sistine Chapel. The things some of these men are interested in—questions of material, of form, of motion—that's construction, not sculpting. Great art isn't great because it's technically proficient or clever, it's great because it uses that knowledge to convey real meaning and sentiment and subject."

"So a work of art is only great if its subject is great?"

"No, but it must aspire to convey humanity—at the very least."

Marcantonio thought about this. He wasn't sure he agreed. He saw La Guardia light a di Nobli while watching him, could sense his amusement and curiosity as to how he would fare in a debate, and how far he would push his argument. Screw him, he thought.

"Major La Guardia tells me that the *Maine* Memorial at Columbus Circle is your work."

Piccirilli nodded.

"It's quite impressive. Some of the different statues are very beautiful. I always look at the one of the widow comforting the child.

"*Fortitude*. It's one of my favorites, too."

"How did you come to do the monument?"

"There was a competition for the commission. My design won."

"Oh, yes, now I remember. Didn't Hearst sponsor the commission?"

Piccirilli nodded unenthusiastically. He knew where Marcantonio was going.

"Hearst—he agitates for the war, he gets the war, then he memorializes it in bronze and stone. Why isn't he sponsoring memorials to the victims of the Triangle Fire?"

Piccirilli poured himself another glass of wine and glanced at La Guardia, who was smiling in a guilty, almost furtive way. *Avvocato* was enjoying this—good! He gave his friend a quick wink.

"So, Vito—you are saying that art would be better if it memorialized the things you want it to rather than the things Hearst wants it to?"

"No—although I'd be much happier if the world stopped doing what Hearst wants it to. But you are celebrating an official position—one which I disagree with, one which I think has been a lie. Is that what public art is? Telling lies?"

Piccirilli shrugged. "It doesn't matter what their motives are. All that matters is what I put there, and no one has ever suggested I'm in the business of telling lies." He paused, allowing the remark to linger. "I don't care who pays, whether it is Hearst or the Medicis. If the sculpture is any good, it will be there long after the war or the king is forgotten. When you tell me that *Fortitude* speaks to you—that maybe it makes you feel something about how it has been with you and your mother—then it is doing what it is supposed to."

La Guardia saw Marcantonio's face redden and laughed. "Kid," he said, "You'll never get rich playing another man's game. That's why he's the Maestro." Turning to Piccirilli, he asked: "Seriously, though, Uncle Picc. This newer stuff, the direct carving and everything, it doesn't worry you?"

"I don't worry about garbage. It will pass. Nothing will ever knock figurative sculpting off the pedestal."

"I don't know. It might be that way with art, but in politics times change and you have to be able to change with 'em. I've been giving it a lot of thought because it's past the time for me to figure out what to do next." He paused, then added softly: "Long past." Marcantonio, who had been a tumult of movement throughout dinner, tapping his foot, drumming the table with his fingers, rolling the wineglass between his palms and lighting cigarette after cigarette, was suddenly still. "My wise and generous friends in the Republican Party think I might be able to run for Congress again. After that, who knows?"

"What about the man who has your seat now? Is he going to step aside?"

"Not my old district in Greenwich Village—uptown in Marc's neighborhood. Who knows? Maybe I'll let him be my campaign manager."

Marcantonio grinned. "I know we can kill 'em if you run as a progressive. We'll have La Guardia clubs all over East Harlem before they know what's happening."

Piccirilli frowned, but a raised eyebrow from La Guardia cut him short. "The kid's on the level, Uncle, and a born organizer. I swear to God, he could sell horseshit at Belmont."

"But why would you run as a progressive? You were elected last time as a patriot and a war hero—no one is going to forget that."

La Guardia weighed his answer. "We've passed the time when an Italian has to prove he's as much a patriot as other Americans in order to hold office—at least I hope we have. And I think you know how I feel about the American Legion and some of these other things that are being done in the name of patriotism. There's never been a military caste in America and we shouldn't start one now. I don't want any American Mussolinis." He paused. "That's how I feel now. The world is changing."

"Really? The world? Or just your district?"

"Now who's being called a liar? Look, Uncle Picc, I'm just like an artist or a sculptor. I can see New York as it should be. But I feel like a man who has a conception of what he wants to carve or paint, who has the model before him, but no chisel or brush! The only way I can get that tool in my hand is by being pragmatic enough to win office. Then I get the chance to stand in front of that marble or canvas."

Attilio gazed steadily over his pipe at Fiorello. "Are you sure you're not abandoning your principles for a commission?"

La Guardia shook his head. "The world really has changed since the war. The problems are different problems and they need different solutions. I think that's really all intelligence is in the end—how well you change to handle what the world throws at you."

The older man shrugged mildly. "There are never new problems, only the same old ones." He tapped his chest for emphasis and smiled. "So I don't think I'm going to change. But I'm glad to hear you talk like this, *Avvocato*. I wasn't sure if you were . . . coming back to us."

Fiorello looked down and sighed. "Believe me, Uncle Picc, I didn't want to." Then, softly, he added: "And really, I still don't." The room was quiet and La Guardia's eyes took on a glassy, far-off look, making the sculptor worry once again over where his friend's heart and mind wandered. It wasn't until Marcantonio struck a match for another cigarette that La Guardia came out of his reverie and looked at Piccirilli. "You know, for an old stonecutter you do passable metalwork. Thea's hands . . ." He shook his head and then held his own hands up in front of his face, clenching and unclenching them as if discovering them for the first time. Seemingly satisfied, he grinned and reached across the table for the last piece of bread. "So what d'you think, Uncle Picc?" he asked, shoving the bread in his mouth and garbling his words. "Do I have good enough hands to be a stonecutter?"

Piccirilli grimaced and shook his head. "You? Never."

"Never? What the hell are you talking about?" He shot Marcantonio a sly wink. "Christ, Picc, there's nothing to it! I was at the zoo last week and I even saw a couple of monkeys banging on rocks. Are you telling me there's something a monkey can do that I can't?"

The sculptor lit his pipe, squinting through the smoke. "Yeah. He can keep his hand out of his mouth long enough to pick up a chisel."

9

ACCOLADES

Seated on the floor of his suite at the Delmonico Hotel in nothing but underwear, stockings, and garters, Finley Peter Dunne had a sudden flash of clarity and saw at long last what had held him back for sixty-two years: his fingers were too damn short.

Like so many of the most inspired ideas, this one had appeared halfway through Dunne's third scotch, tapping him unexpectedly on the shoulder like an old friend at a party. Grinning, wet eyes shining, he stood up and greeted the idea with good-natured, conspiratorial glee, waving his glass unsteadily to the empty hotel room.

"Yes! Too small—how could I have missed this? No good for grasping, don't you see?" He held his glass up and shook his head at the three-inch gap between the tips of his thumb and middle finger. Pathetic! "I've no respect for a man who can't hold his liquor properly." Then, with a grin, he remembered the scissors he'd packed with Philip's old Harvard chemistry books, intending to razor out the section on Joseph Priestley.

He rose and picked his way through the litter of wadded paper surrounding the dark mahogany desk, the usual result of a morning spent in the unproductive quest for a *Collier's Weekly* essay, this one on the stock market. *Collier's*. Dunne shook his head. Amazing that he now had so much trouble producing *Collier's* columns. He had been writing there just a few weeks shy of forever. Been its editor once, even owned it for a minute when Bob Collier died and bequeathed it to him and Frank Garvan and Payne Whitney. They didn't keep it, of course; Bob's wife needed it far more than they did. Well, far more than Frank and Payne. He never grieved for the money, though, just the sorry state of the publication. The perfect example of the descent of man. How did something so vital become so . . . vapid? He sighed. Magazines were like people. They shouldn't live beyond their time.

Of course, he wasn't helping the *Collier's* cause any by writing about the stock market and pretending he knew something about it. While every other idiot and his driver had made money, he'd lost it. And how! God, he thought, as he picked up the scissors, *everyone* had better information than he did. Well, that wasn't quite true. How about when Payne tailored that little manipulation for their benefit? What was it, a rubber company? Glass? Can't even remember anymore, but the way he'd loaded up on it would've made Morgan green with envy. Buy at 25 and sell at 50, Payne had instructed him. *Instructed him!* Like he was a kid! To hell with that crap. When it shot to 50, Dunne knew it couldn't miss going to 100. A week later his broker sold him out at 18.

He put the scissors back down and gave himself another splash of scotch, then placed an outstretched hand palm-down on a piece of paper and traced the outline. The drawing had comically elongated fingers. A witch's claw. He did the same with his other hand, then cut both tracings out and laid the results against his palms, holding them in place with four rubber bands fished from the desk drawer. He walked to the mirror on the bedroom door to see how they looked hanging at his side. Suitably ridiculous, he decided with satisfaction, and imagined himself walking down Fifth Avenue to the Waldorf-Astoria in a few hours, dressed for dinner with his new hands flapping at his sides. "But," he asked the empty room, "can they pass the true test? Are they, in fact, *actually* useless? Or is this just one more inflated hope?"

It was with some disappointment that Dunne discovered he could, in fact, still hold a pencil and a lit cigarette. "Still disgustingly competent," he said with a shake of the head. No problem holding the glass, either, although the paper stuck to the wet sides. Dissatisfied, his eyes searched the room until they lit upon a three-foot curtain rod hanging above the window. He climbed the desk and grabbed the rod easily and was soon busy collecting wadded sheets of writing paper from the floor.

"Sure, you can reach around the glass now," he said, holding the mitts in front of his face. "But can you play golf?" He nodded, as if giving the paper hands a moment to let the idea sink in. "That's the true test because it's such a noble game, a gentleman's game. Did you know that golf is Scotland's greatest gift? Of course, it's Scotland's *only* gift. Well, not counting the theory of infant damnation, naturally." He kicked a ball of paper to a clear spot and used the curtain rod to sight-line a shot at the toilet through the open bathroom door. After a few tentative half-swings, he drove the paper wide right and it landed on a large green sofa. "Oh, in the rough! What's that?" He held a paper hand to his ear. "No! No mulligan! A man can play as poorly as he wants with no fears, provided he's rich enough or quick-witted enough. I should know—I used to be the highest-paid writer in the country. It's true. But that was never my strategy for the game, and I played with them all. Do you know who shot a good round of golf? Harding. Surprisingly good. Much better than Teddy, if you can imagine that. What? Betting? Of course." Dunne lined up another ball of paper, wrapped the floppy hands around the curtain rod, and this time succeeded in banging the wad off the frame of the bathroom door. "Closer. Maybe you've got promise. I used to say that to Philip before the little ingrate forgot I was his father and commenced to beating me without fail. You know, there was a time not so long ago when we used to place friendly wagers on our games. But as his play improved it became necessary for his moral upbringing to point out just how shallow betting makes one appear." He grinned and whacked another ball of paper, this time hitting a table clock. "Good lord! Is it really after five o'clock?"

Dunne pulled the rubber bands off his wrists, dropped the mangled hands in the bathroom wastebasket, and filled the tub with hot water. He returned briefly to the desk, thought about taking the bottle, but instead picked up the chemistry book and his cigarettes. He lit one of the smokes, then balanced the pack and the book on the lip of the tub. When the water was high enough, he stripped and lowered himself into the hot bath, which fogged his pince-nez. He took the spectacles off and dipped them in the hot water, then dried them and put them back on before reaching for the book.

"Priestley, huh?"

Dunne liked to think it a vestige of his unpretentious Chicago upbringing that he felt somewhat ridiculous walking the streets in formal dinner wear. Still, the mild temperature and lingering sunlight of the early September evening had put him in mind of the sundowns out at the Hamptons, leaving him oddly sentimental and mellow. He'd long held the second and third weeks of September to be the most beautiful in New York, and he was unwilling to let a top hat and a pair of tails get in the way of a memorable twilight stroll. Indeed, he barely felt a breeze as he stepped out of the hotel at Park and Fifty-ninth, and the air was almost palpably soft against his freshly shaven cheeks. The last full sunlight of the early autumn day fell in a clear and golden slant against the upper reaches of the concrete and cut-stone cliffs of the Manhattan canyons, making the highest windows glitter.

Strolling had long been one of Dunne's favorite New York activities, especially in Mr. Dooley's glory days. His own face was well known back then, and he had to listen to at least a half-dozen yobs a day express amazement at the discovery that the Irish bartender's creator didn't speak in the same illiterate cartoon brogue. On the contrary, Dunne spoke with little trace of the rough-and-tumble Chicago newsrooms that had produced him, and sounded more like a typical member of the exclusive gentleman's clubs he'd come to love. That was where he most liked to be recognized—settling into a chair at the clubhouse out at the National or sitting down to a game of poker at the Racquet Club, an open bottle and bucket of ice on the sideboard, the blue smoke of good, rich-smelling cigars shifting lazily above, knowing by the nods and furtive glances that other men took him seriously. Rich men, powerful men. Men who recognized that, like them, he was the best in his business. Of course, it wasn't as lucrative as manufacturing steel or cornering the sugar market. But everyone checked in with Mr. Dooley, from the man in the White House on down, and that was a finer sort of currency. Wasn't it? It bought as many drinks and as much companionship as the other kind of success. Unfortunately, it had a way of depreciating with time; you couldn't bank it or will it to your children now, could you? That was the rub, and the thought left him painfully aware of his mortality. Walking down Park in the last hour of daylight he looked, as casually as possible, for an old familiar face. But he had no luck and was glad to reach the sanctuary of the Waldorf, turning the corner just in time to see the doorman helping Margaret, fresh in from the Hamptons, alight from a taxi. His wife was wearing Dunne's favorite blue satin evening dress, and she looked particularly handsome standing on the red runner that the hotel placed out to the curb. He was about to compliment her when the doorman, trailing Margaret back toward the hotel lobby, caught a heel on the edge of the carpet and pitched forward, just missing bowling her over. "Good Lord, man," Dunne said, rushing to assist him to his feet. "Are you all right?"

The doorman was clearly more flustered and embarrassed than anything. "Fine, sir. Fine. Thank you." Then, to Margaret: "Sorry to give you such a start, ma'am."

"Frankly, I'm more surprised to see this man standing than you falling," she said, giving Dunne a wink and offering him her arm. He took it and pretended to be hurt by the remark.

They walked the corridor known as Peacock Alley together and Dunne was relieved to reach the Waldorf lobby, which was dark and quiet with thick, worn rugs and dim lighting. "I know it sounds silly, but I'm going to miss this filthy place," Margaret said as they turned into the long and equally dim thoroughfare connecting the Waldorf to the old Astoria Hotel. "You must have passed the new site on the way down. Have they begun yet?"

Dunne shook his head. "They're still clearing the property."

"Are the towers really going to have the most expensive apartments in the city?"

"I shouldn't be surprised. Rumor has it that Hoover will be one of the first tenants.

Margaret giggled. "Doesn't he already have a place to live?"

"It's not due to be completed until '32, and that's an election year. If he can't figure out how to cure the stock market of these jitters, he'll need an apartment."

"Has he really got that kind of money?"

"I'd be surprised if he was paying. Wouldn't you?"

She considered this and then smiled. "I'm sure Al Smith would put in a good word to have him living in New York."

"Well, maybe not New York but certainly anywhere but the White House."

"I expect we'll see him tonight."

"Hoover? God, no!"

"Oh, don't be dense, Peter. Al, of course!"

"I'd think so. He and Frank are thick as thieves. And speaking of thieves, here we are."

They heard the orchestra before they turned the corner and saw the dancing couples and milling men in the Astoria Ballroom. By the entrance, a carefully lettered placard stood on an easel.

THE AMERICAN CHEMICAL SOCIETY

Honoring

FRANCIS PATRICK GARVAN

with

THE JOSEPH PRIESTLEY MEDAL

IN RECOGNITION OF HIS OUTSTANDING

CONTRIBUTION TO CHEMICAL RESEARCH

September 12, 1929

A portrait photo of Frank—impeccably groomed in a businessman's white shirt, tie, and dark jacket, his expression tight-lipped and unreadable behind rimless spectacles, looking every bit the prosecutor he'd once been—was tacked to the placard.

They entered the ballroom and a white-jacketed waiter immediately approached with a tray of cups.

"What's this? Punch? You've got to be joking. Do I look like a seven-year-old girl?"

"Oh, be quiet, Peter, and let the poor man do his job."

"Yes, the world is full of men who are just doing their jobs—and the women who put them there."

"Oh, not that again! Why are you preaching to me? When was I ever a dry?"

"You know damn well we'd never have the Eighteenth Amendment if the Nineteenth wasn't marching in line behind it."

"Yes, well, if you've finished blaming me for prohibition, I'm going to say hello to the Sabins." She was really angry and Dunne watched her walk away with regret. He'd been acting a jerk. "Absurd times and stupid laws will do that," he said aloud, heading toward the far end of the bar.

"Ginger ale," he said, raising a finger toward the bartender.

"Like it's lonely or like you want to drink it?"

"Drink it? Ginger ale? What do you take me for, mister?"

The bartender grinned and filled a glass with ice, adding just a few fingers of soda. Dunne nodded appreciatively and took it to a quiet corner of the ballroom, shaking several ice cubes out of the glass as he went. Turning his back on the room, he furtively topped off the soda with scotch from a tarnished silver flask in his jacket pocket and took a quick gulp. "You know," he said to himself, "it's actually not so bad as long as you don't stir it."

"I believe I overheard Mayor Walker make exactly the same remark just a few days ago," said a voice behind Dunne. "But I'm almost positive that he was discussing the electorate." Appreciative howls greeted the joke.

Peter recognized the voice before he'd even turned: former district attorney William Travers Jerome. He was flanked on his left by a short, lumpy fellow with tousled dark hair and darker eyes wearing an ill-fitting double-breasted suit with a small but freshly shining food stain on the lapel; on Jerome's right was an older but tall, athletic man wearing the dark suit and white collar of a Catholic priest. It took Dunne just an instant to recognize Father O'Hara, the president of Notre Dame. The other required a moment longer, but he was no less pleased when he had the name for the face.

"Congressman La Guardia?"

"Guilty!" The small rumpled man smiled and stuck out a hand. "Good to see you again, Mr. Dunne."

"Please, my friends call me Peter. And although we've only crossed trails once or twice, I've been reading enough about your work in Washington to know that we are friends and kindred spirits."

"A little early for you to be waxing so eloquent and full of cheer, isn't it, Peter?" asked Father O'Hara. He looked pointedly at Dunne's glass. "It must be a very good year for ginger ale."

"Believe me, John, it's never a good *day* for ginger ale."

The men chatted and exchanged political gossip as the orchestra played and the room, which was set about the dance floor with tables, filled. When Garvan entered the ballroom from a side door a few minutes later, it was with his wife, Mabel, on one arm, and a phalanx of elegant tuxedoed men, most of whom could no longer be described as middle-aged, escorting women dressed in what appeared to be extraordinarily expensive gowns.

"Geez," said Dunne, "When did being a chemist become so lucrative?"

La Guardia snorted. "It's been a long time since those guys were chemists—the ones that ever were. See the one with the red boutonniere? That's Willard Dow. The old geezer monopolizing the guest of honor? Mr. Alfred I. Du Pont. No, they aren't chemists. They're the chemical *business*."

"And grateful they should be to Frank for helping them to become one," said Dunne. "Instead of being rich as the Rockefellers, the Du Ponts would still be working for the Germans."

"Well, I'll say this for our Francis," said Jerome. "He's sure come a long way in this world. It's a far cry from prosecuting fraud and murder cases."

"No, he wouldn't see it that way," said Dunne. "It's all of a piece to him. Say, who's that queer duck? The one by himself? Should I know him?" He indicated a short, pudgy, and somewhat younger man at the back of the group trailing the Garvans.

La Guardia chuckled. "That's Washington's other Mr. Hoover."

"Frank's kid from Justice? I met him once. Quiet, hard to get a fix on. Frank said he was extraordinarily efficient, though. Put together all of the alien files practically by himself."

"I wouldn't call him a kid anymore. He holds a lot of the enforcement strings at Justice now. Came in with the Democrats, but he's in his third Republican administration."

Dunne noted with some amusement that Hoover, like them, was standing back from the general hubbub in order to assess the knot of well-wishers and favor-seekers drawing around Garvan. It was quite a group: Dunne recognized more than a dozen prominent New York attorneys, and almost as many bankers. Aside from Father O'Hara, he saw Father Duane, the president of Fordham University, Mother Angeline, who was both president of St. Joseph's College and Frank Garvan's sister, and Jim Angell, the president of Yale. The horsey set wasn't Dunne's crowd, but he knew several of Frank's friends from Saratoga, and some of the less familiar faces he took to be footsoldiers in the small army of art, furniture, and antique silver dealers constantly tramping in and out of Frank's office and homes. Toward the back of the crowd he spied Al Smith and John W. Davis, the last two Democratic candidates for president, politely waiting their turns to congratulate Frank. Dunne smiled, wondering what a professional survivor like Hoover made of *that*. For his part, Dunne believed Frank's far-flung contacts to be the natural product of a life lived with courage, vigorous morality, unwavering patriotism, and intellectual clarity.

The orchestra ceased playing and dinner was announced. Peter hustled to the bar for another setup and took it with him to the dais, where he found himself seated between the president of the chemical society, whom he did not know, and Joseph Tumulty.

"Joe! Been a while! No, please—don't get up. I'm dying to sit down."

Dunne liked Tumulty, had liked him the first time Frank brought him to Tumulty's White House office. Frank was alien property clerk then, and lobbying Wilson for support on setting up the Chemical Foundation; he knew Tumulty to be a lifelong admirer of Mr. Dooley, and brought Dunne along hoping to get on Tumulty's good side. The moment they'd met, Dunne had no doubts Tumulty would get the foundation approved. It wasn't simply that Joe, who was Wilson's private secretary, had enormous influence with the president on all issues ranging from policy to patronage, but that Dunne could feel the way they all understood each other. Take away the White House, strip away the prestige and power, and the man seated across the desk was a plain-speaking Irish Catholic attorney from Jersey City. Tumulty had ultimately proven a great advocate for Palmer and Garvan within the White House, and he and Frank had remained close in subsequent years.

"You're looking superb, Peter. I've been needing to get your advice— I'm out of things to read. What's on your night table?"

Dunne had once told Tumulty about his lifelong insomnia, confessing that he considered it a blessing in disguise to be able to spend most nights sitting up in bed, smoking and reading. "Nothing that you don't already know. Montaigne's *Essays*. Boswell's *Life of Samuel Johnson*. Burton's *Anatomy of Melancholy*. I guess I've reached the age where I'd rather sit with my old friends than go out and meet new ones." He smiled. "And stop flattering me. I should be asking you what to read. Which reminds me—when are we going to see another book from you?"

Tumulty shrugged. "I've said what there was for me to say about my experiences in Washington. Writing was never my avocation. Now, you don't have that excuse. Come on, Peter, don't you think we could use Mr. Dooley right about now?"

"Ah, everybody wants to bring back Mr. Dooley, but I'll tell you something, Joe. Mr. Dooley wouldn't fit in anymore. Look at us. We're all rich and connected. We don't need a beard to speak plain."

"It was more than plain speaking. There was a humor and a warmth and a love for the country in even the most deflating and devastating of Mr. Dooley's rambles. There aren't any editorialists who write like that anymore—they're all pamphleteers. That's the part I miss."

Peter looked into his highball glass. "There's a reason newspapers no longer sound like that, don't you see? That's precisely the part that's gone out of the world. That's why it wouldn't work anymore."

Before dinner was served, a Marine color guard entered the banquet room and everyone rose, first for the Pledge of Allegiance and then for the orchestra's rendition of "The Star-Spangled Banner." The waiters placed shrimp cocktails before the guests and Father O'Hara said grace. As he finished, Dunne slipped off to the bar for another soda and ice, mixing in the scotch surreptitiously beneath the dais tablecloth. Tumulty, ever courteous, focused on his shrimp; the society president on Dunne's other side, however, was just as pointed in observing the clandestine operation, and Peter smiled at him.

"I believe in your business mixing two solubles is called a solution," Dunne said. He held the glass up and took a drink. "I don't know what kinds of problems chemists encounter, but many of the writers I know believe this to be our best solution." If the chemist found this funny, he didn't show it, and Dunne mentally dismissed him and looked down at the plate of graying roast beef and parsleyed potatoes the waiter set in front of him. He took two forkfuls but found it as bland as his companion. Dunne put the silverware down and lit a cigarette, enjoying the look of annoyance it produced in the chemist, who was methodically consuming his dinner. Dunne took his pen and the notes for the speech from his pocket and began fiddling with them, squinting through the smoke. He was pretty happy with the results by the time Al Smith, who proved to be the master of ceremonies, called him up, and even happier with the long, warm applause that greeted him as he shook Smith's hand and placed his drink prominently upon the podium.

"Good evening, ladies and gentlemen. They tell me this is a very prestigious award and a solemn occasion, so I'll try my damnedest not to embarrass the honoree." With an exaggerated flourish, Dunne took a sip from his drink and leaned across the podium to look pointedly at Garvan. The crowd, noting how Garvan remained immobile and stone-faced, laughed as it was meant to; only those sitting closest could see the quick wink Garvan gave back to Dunne.

"Normally I detest these dinners. They're nothing but an opportunity for me to make a fool of myself. I have a god-awful memory for names and I always seem to be seated next to someone who has the advantage over me. I remember a number of years ago being seated next to a handsome woman whose face was perfectly familiar, but whose name just wouldn't come. For the better part of an hour we sat and chatted amiably, and all the while I was trying desperately to steer the conversation to a point where I might glean a clue as to who this damn woman could be! Finally, I saw my opening when she remarked that she'd seen her brother the prior week and that he'd sent his regards. As cool as could be, I said, 'Oh, yes, your brother. Tell me, what's he doing these days?' The woman stared at me blankly. Then she said: 'He's still the president of the United States.' The lady was Mrs. Douglas Robinson, Theodore Roosevelt's sister.

"So I'll try to stow my discomfort and be entertaining. Certainly, there's nothing undignified in being entertaining. For many years Francis and I were privileged to call America's greatest writer, Mark Twain, our good friend. But as frequently happens to those of us who practice the craft, Mark met for a while with serious financial reversals. He was forced to earn a living as a performer on the lecture circuit. It changed him not a wit. He was as grand and marvelous when diverting an audience as he was when brandishing his awesome pen. So I find no disgrace in providing a little levity between dinner and coffee.

"Perhaps it's the presence of all these priests and nuns, but before I go any farther I need to make a confession: when it comes to chemistry I know less than anyone in this room. However, I am a newspaperman, so I have cultivated a professional skill wherein a little research allows me to sound authoritative on virtually any subject no matter how little comprehension I actually possess. For starters, I've learned a bit about your Mr. Priestley and why he's the Chemical Society's patron saint. It was, I've discovered, an 1884 colloquium marking the centennial of Priestley's discovery of oxygen that provided the impetus for the formation of this august group, and any chemist would certainly be hard-pressed to find a more deserving or inspirational bit of work to celebrate. But I've also discovered a few other things about Joseph Priestley that, as a journalist, I feel I must share with you. Unsettling things. Dark things.

"For starters, Priestley was indeed priestly—he was a Presbyterian minister and a bit of a rabble-rouser. I've got nothing against Presbyterians myself, mind you, although I hear they cheat at bridge and golf. More than a part of me admires the fact that the Reverend Priestley's views were so anathema to the Anglican Church that it all but ruined his chances as a scientist. To put it bluntly, he was persecuted and run out of town on a rail for his religious views. His enemies within the government and Church of England were legion, and he was repeatedly denied opportunities and appointments, including the chance to sail to the Pacific as Cook's science officer. Eventually, Priestley's home was burned by a mob of religious bigots, and he and his sons obliged to flee the country for Pennsylvania where, among other things, Priestley founded the Unitarian Church of America. Now that's all good and admirable, but I must say, I'm always a bit leery of a man who's overly religious. If I can paraphrase my friend, Mr. Dooley, I have never known an unworthy clergyman—but the less you have to do with them, the better.

"Now, my wife is here and she can attest that I'm a tolerant man." At this he smiled his sweetest smile and looked downward at the table in front of the dais where Margaret sat with Mabel Garvan and the rest of

Frank's family. Margaret rewarded him with a smirk and a roll of the eyes, producing the intended effect from the crowd, and Dunne pretended to be taken aback. "But even my tolerance has limits."

"In 1767, in a beautiful demonstration of the benevolent way in which God smiles on the righteous, Priestley assumed a ministry based near a Leeds brewery. But note the way such good fortune can be lost on the overly religious. What did Priestley find noteworthy? The conviviality and love of one's fellow man to be discovered in that golden brew? Its miraculous wealth of vitamins and nutrients? No, my friends. He was not a convivialist, nor was he a nutritionist. He was a chemist, and he became fascinated with the unique ability of beer and sparkling wines to capture carbon dioxide through fermentation and, as he put it, 'fix air.' There's every evidence that this was the moment when Priestley became enamored with the chemistry of gases and started down the road that would lead to so many important discoveries, yet its first milestone would prove one of the darkest moments in human history. What was this monstrous deed?" He paused, leaning across the podium, then lifted his glass high and shook his head gravely. "Soda water. *The man invented soda water!* Oh, then did the angels cry at humanity's wretched insistence on so poorly mimicking the God that creates ale and champagne! Priestley? Beastly is more like it!"

Dunne paused and removed his pince-nez to prolong the moment, milking the laughter and scattered applause. "I understand that the Priestley Medal has, until tonight, been awarded exclusively to chemists and that Francis is the first layman to be so honored. This, of course, makes it all the more special. But with due respect to your field, I propose that Francis Garvan may well be the most apt recipient ever chosen for this medal because, like Priestley, he is a man of omnivorous and extraordinary reach. Your group, like history, remembers Priestley for his scientific contributions. But history doesn't always tell us how people lived. It's clear that Joseph Priestley relied upon his heart and soul as much as his extraordinary brain. As an Englishman, he was an outspoken defender of both the American and French revolutions, a stance that earned him as much enmity in his homeland as his religious beliefs. But he found new friends in his new country, and counted both Franklin and Jefferson in that group.

"Everyone in this room is aware of all that Francis has done for manufacture and research in chemistry, knows that there would be no modern chemical industry without him. In 1917, when the United States entered the war, there were six chemical plants in this country and no research laboratories. The business—to the extent that it could even be called one—and our entire nation were captives of a predatory German chemical cartel. It was Frank Garvan, in his role as the alien property clerk, who hit upon the idea of placing seized German patents in a cooperative trust and creating the Chemical Foundation to administer them, thus breaking the German stranglehold. Today, there are two hundred American chemical plants equipped with research laboratories, and the American chemical industry produces 96 percent of the United States' chemical products and does a robust export business.

"Ten years ago, when Frank helped start the Chemical Foundation, he had no intention of turning it into his life work, yet that is what it has proven. And through it all he somehow found the energy to also serve as the Dean of the Fordham Law School, to remain an active member of the New York bar, to argue his own case in front of the Supreme Court, and to become one of the country's preeminent scholars and collectors of American arts, crafts, and furniture. The sense of duty and patriotism that Frank brought to his work with the chemical industry can be found in his approach to all things. I hope the Garvans will forgive my stealing a little of their thunder by revealing that they have just agreed to donate their famous collection to Yale University." At this, James Angell, who was seated on the dais, rose and began applauding, a move that forced the rest of the crowd to its feet. Garvan, who'd sat impassively throughout the speech, dropped his chin to his chest and shook his head, but acknowledged the applause with a quick and sheepish wave.

"My God!" Dunne said with a triumphant laugh. "I've made Francis blush!" He fished out his cigarette case, tapped the end of one on the thin silver box, and lit it, waiting until the diners had settled back into their seats before continuing. "There's one more salient similarity between

Priestley and Garvan that I'd be remiss in passing over. I've mentioned how Priestley numbered such giants as Franklin and Jefferson among his confidants. More even than a great scientist, Priestley was a great *mind* and humanitarian, and he sought his own level. Looking around this room, I see the most accomplished men in industry, science, politics, law, education, and religion. This, more than anything, is the ultimate testimony to a life. I am pleased and proud to stand here tonight and help recognize and pay tribute to the life Francis Garvan has led, and to see him honored with the Joseph Priestley Medal. But more than anything, I am grateful for the chance to stand before you all and say he is my friend."

Dunne turned away from the podium toward Garvan and, amidst applause, touched a hand to his forehead in salute. Then, suddenly remembering something, he held up a finger and turned back toward the hall.

"By the way," he said. "I need to warn all you swells against stealing the flatware. Frank promised that to Yale, too."

A succession of handshakes and backslaps attended him as he stepped down and gave the podium over to the dour president of the society, who was to make the formal presentation of the medal. Dunne, riding a cloud of elation, floated straight for the bar and another setup, then on to the men's room to collect himself. The lounge had a large sitting area with telephones as an anteroom, and he plopped himself down in a red plush chair. His blood was racing. God, that had gone well! The queasiness Peter had felt in recent meetings with old acquaintances, especially Frank, was gone, and he felt more his old self than he had in months. He doctored his drink, lit a cigarette, and settled into the chair. Frank would be speaking soon, but there was still enough time to savor the moment. He smiled, satisfied. When he needed it, he still had it.

". . . his sister, you dolt, not his mother . . ."

He could hear the voices vaguely from behind the washroom door. At first it was only bits and pieces of conversation and laughter. But they grew louder, apparently as the men moved to the sinks and the attendant's station by the door.

"Mother, daughter, sister. What does it matter? I'm sure he knew Roosevelt's grandmother, too! Probably remembers her as a little girl. Took her to the village square dance or something."

The other laughed. "When I was a kid, my old man used to read Dooley twice a week like religion. Frankly, you've got to feel for him. They say he can't write anymore."

"Why should he? Do you know how much money his buddy Payne Whitney left him?"

"No, how much?"

"I don't know, but I heard it was a fortune. More than even he can drink up."

"Jesus."

"Yeah. Seems a waste, doesn't it?"

The door opened and the laughter was immediately louder. The two men were in their late thirties; Dunne had noticed them earlier and pegged them as lawyers. One was holding a hand towel.

"Sorry, Rastus," he said as he tossed the towel back through the door and patted his pockets. "I don't have any change."

Both flinched when they saw Dunne. The one who'd been doing most of the talking pretended he hadn't recognized him and looked straight ahead toward the outer door; the other nodded quickly before looking away. Dunne gazed at the ceiling and took a drag on his cigarette as they crossed the lounge.

"Five hundred thousand dollars."

"What?" asked the man who had nodded.

"Five hundred thousand dollars. That's how much Payne left me."

The man who was looking straight ahead continued quickly out the door, but the other stopped. "Look," he said. "We really—"

"Progressive enfeeblement isn't the worst of old age. I'd spite Payne's generosity in a second for the chance to spend another day with him."

"I'm sorry."

"Who cares? You're a numbskull and a bore." Dunne stood up and crushed the cigarette in an ashtray. "I'll bet your father had a lot more insight into human nature. Or at least he knew where to borrow it twice a week." He left the highball glass on the side table and exited the lounge.

Dunne passed the next hour wandering the hotel corridors. When he heard Frank's voice, he snuck back into the ballroom to listen to the acceptance speech, but even that didn't really register beyond the fact that

Frank, as usual, managed to sound simultaneously low-key and confidently forceful. It wasn't until Margaret appeared at his side that he realized the dinner had ended.

"You were marvelous," she said, taking his hand.

"Naturally."

"Naturally." She smiled warmly. "Come. We're expected upstairs."

"Must we?"

"What's the matter? Had your fill of accolades?"

"Yeah."

She looked at him closely. "Do you feel all right, Peter?"

He nodded heavily. "Tired."

"We won't stay long. But we do have to congratulate Mabel and Frank. He'll be looking for you."

Dunne had always liked the suites on the Astoria's upper floors, but the twinkling view they afforded up Broadway didn't rate a second look tonight, and the churning, smoke-filled room, normally his preferred element, felt like a foreign country, the cocktail chatter a strange language. Frank was off to one side of the room talking earnestly to his Mr. Hoover. Peter recognized the look on Frank's face: he invariably wore it when delineating the reasoning behind his interest in one particular piece of silver or pewter over another to a dealer, or when telling a young colleague why a strategy was unlikely to work at trial, or when instructing his children in "The Facts of the World." Hoover, clearly, was an apt pupil; whatever the specifics of the lesson, his expression said that he was getting it all. Dunne, watching them and patting his jacket pockets for his cigarettes, didn't notice Mabel Garvan until she was nearly upon him.

"That was a marvelous speech, Peter—Frank loved it." She gave him a warm smile. "Someone has asked to meet you."

Dunne sighed. "Not a lawyer, I hope."

"No, a history professor at Columbia."

"Good Lord! How did he get dragooned into this? Are you and Frank giving something to Columbia now, too?"

"Don't be silly. I gather that he is here with his brother, a chemist."

The historian, a man named Sterne, was tall and thickly built, with thinning hair, and looked a good deal more like a fighter or a football player than an academic, and he proved a tonic to Dunne. His area of specialty was French colonialism, but he was keen on American history as well and clearly could have taught it just as easily. He had the historian's eye for the parallels and threads joining seemingly disparate events into a meaningful continuum, and Dunne enjoyed talking to him immensely, particularly regarding events for which Dunne could offer personal recollections. He was intrigued by some of Sterne's ideas, especially the suggestion that the single greatest event in the formation of Wilson's character had been Reconstruction, which the president had lived through as a boy in Georgia. It was the hardship and humiliation his family had suffered during that era, and not any sense of altruism or a sophisticated view of the evolving world gleaned at Princeton, Sterne argued, that had made Wilson such a staunch advocate of peace and globalization over retribution and factionalism.

"I can't say I knew Wilson well," Dunne said. "But based on what I do know about the man, it would make sense. Funny Joe Tumulty never suggested that. Hey! You should run this by him. He's here, you know."

Sterne shrugged. "History has already embraced Tumulty's version of events. He's not likely to welcome an amendment."

"Oh, no! He's not like that at all."

"Come on, Mr. Dunne. You're going to tell me only academics attack any new idea that might challenge an assumption that made their reputations?"

"No, of course not. But Joe is a good man."

"This room is filled with good and decent men. Sometimes good and decent men commit crimes. I can't imagine you need me to tell you what it takes to assemble an industrial giant like Du Pont. But as the brother of a chemist, I can assure you that no one in the head office is thinking about the Nobel Prize. They're thinking about how to ensure that things like their proprietary process for manufacturing lead-based gasoline becomes the world standard."

"You're preaching to the choir, brother. Just steer clear of the kind of campus sophistry that says behind every great fortune lies a great crime and we're in complete agreement."

Sterne nodded. "It's all too gray for that. Which brings me to what I'm really curious about. Your remarks tonight—I realize he's being feted, but how should we really judge your Mr. Garvan?"

"Pardon?"

"What was it you said earlier of Priestley? 'Even the greatest man has his dark deeds'?"

"Listen, Frank has never—and I mean never—had any interest in the chemical industry beyond freeing it and seeing that research is encouraged."

"I'm well aware of that. I have a niece with a Garvan fellowship at Cornell."

"And Du Pont's gasoline be damned! Frank has personally funded research in manufacturing ethanol from corn as a farm and engine fuel."

Sterne chuckled at Dunne's dudgeon. "I didn't hear you say anything tonight about the Palmer raids."

The anger slipped from Dunne's face and his florid color wilted. "I didn't say anything about it then, so who am I to talk now?" he asked softly. He looked carefully at Sterne. "You're old enough to remember those days—what the country was like, how scared everyone was. I'd say Palmer was the most reluctant avenging angel I've ever seen. The patriotic fervor of the moment was mass hysteria. Everyone was calling for alien expulsion, for the suppression of foreign agents and sympathizers. Yet Palmer wasn't so sure—the public and the papers had to drag him to it. After he'd finally given the *New York Times* just what they'd been demanding, they became embarrassed and hung him out to dry. The poor bastard."

"No one had to drag Francis Garvan to it, though, did they? He seems to have had a much easier time with the idea than Palmer."

"Frank is a patriot, not a fanatic. Look, the Garvans were starving in Ireland. Should he forget what America has done for his family in just two generations? That's what he's grateful for, that's what he wants to protect."

"And how far would the Garvans have gotten if subjected to the kinds of abuses of law he engineered? Mass arrests without warrants. Illegal detentions. Denial of counsel. Wholesale deportations. Guilt by inference and nationality. How do you protect freedom by denigrating it?"

"It was war! The country was under siege and the threat was real."

"But they didn't stop there. The true number of bomb throwers was minuscule—did they actually ever even arrest and convict any of them? Garvan and his friends exploited the panic, trying to kill whole flocks of birds with the stone of national security. The conscientious objectors, the socialists—they were hardly alien agents. They were just as American as Garvan."

"Look, you can't pretend these events happened in a vacuum. It was what the country demanded. Christ, even Wilson—the peace candidate!—couldn't pardon the socialist Debs. Under those circumstances, with the country under attack, no one has the kind of backbone you're talking about."

"Assistant Labor Secretary Louis Post did. He had the guts not to sign off on the Palmer crowd's deportation orders."

"Post was unique. And I thank God he was."

"Really? Will you be waiting and praying for someone unique to step up again if the Klan and other God-fearing citizens convince folks that the Garvans and the Dunnes and all the other Catholics have to go because their true allegiance is to the Pope in Rome? It can't happen here? Too many good and decent men like Hoover and Palmer and Garvan? History doesn't operate with a scalpel, it hacks with a broad ax. Not because it has to but because it requires a good deal less thought and skill to be a lumberjack than a surgeon."

"This isn't a perfect world filled with perfect people. Good and decent men? Your standard is impossible. I've spent my whole life battling demagoguery and delusion, even in people I admired. *Especially* in people I admired! We all believed in preparedness—hell, I wouldn't even vote for Wilson because I couldn't pretend the war wasn't coming. Then, as it drew closer and closer, you could see preparedness become a tidal wave of nationalism, rising wildly from a raging sea of public opinion. It was enormous and it carried a lot of ugly flotsam and garbage, and everyone knew it was going to knock over anything in its path. And when it finally broke, no one could stand in its wake. No one. It was a war, it had to be that way. The Palmer raids were a combination of fear and unspent passion, a hangover from the zealotry of the war."

Sterne nodded. "So you can live with that standard?"

"Live with it? Yes. Approve of it? No."

"And Mr. Garvan? A good and decent man?"

"That's not even up for grabs."

"Would you be as forgiving of a stranger?"

Dunne lit a cigarette. "I can't say. I don't know them. I know Frank."

"Well, his own survival has been impressive. The raids destroyed Palmer and here's Garvan, a prime architect, celebrated as the patron saint of an entire industry."

"You say 'saint' the way an atheist would."

"I see a lot of very rich men in this room. Rich because of Francis Garvan."

"Is that why you think he set up the Chemical Foundation? Because he's the lickspittle for a bunch of dye makers? Frank Garvan?"

"The Alien Property Office seized German goods and land and patents, supposedly for the defense of the country and the welfare of the American people. I don't doubt for a moment that the German chemical cartel was working hand-in-glove with the military, that their business practices were inseparable from the German government's prosecution of the war. So why did Garvan just give these men the German patents at a fraction of their value?"

"First of all, he didn't give them anything. The Chemical Foundation is a public trust and anyone can license its patents."

"Anyone the board approves. And these men—and not the United States government or its people—are the board. It's all pretty cozy."

"You son of a bitch. You think he did this for money? To hoodwink and rob the American citizenry? You know nothing. Frank and Mabel have six children. They had seven. Patricia. She came down with strep when she was five. Frank was told that a German synthetic chemical, un-available in the U.S., might have cured her. Who the hell besides the companies that sit on the board of the foundation could have gotten that drug into the market quickly? Jesus! Tell all the taxpayers whose daughters didn't die of a sore throat this year how Frank Garvan fleeced them!"

"Who am I fleecing now?" asked a voice at Dunne's back. "Good Christ, Peter—you're not talking about that card game in Palm Beach again, are you?" Garvan, immaculate in a new tuxedo with shiny silk lapels and matching tie and cummerbund, the Priestley medal hanging from his neck on a thick rope of purple satin, had slipped up alongside them. Just slightly taller than Dunne, his straight-as-a-beam bearing showed none of Dunne's slouch, nor did he carry any of his friend's extra weight. Up close, Garvan's skin was whiter than his still-stiff shirt, and his eyes were hard pinpricks of clarity behind gold-rimmed spectacles. His eyebrows were raised in an odd way that somehow managed to convey both amusement and something else, something that definitely was not amusement.

"Fleecing?" asked Dunne. "Francis, you've had so much baloney poured into your ears this evening that you can't even hear anymore. The professor was just telling me how proud he is to have a niece as a Garvan fellow."

"Yes? What's her name?"

"Sterne."

"Oh, Sandra. She's doing colloid chemistry research at Cornell Medical School. Hell of a chemist. I'm surprised they took her there, though. They're usually a bunch of anti-Semitic bastards."

"We're not Jewish."

"Well, there you have it."

"I've got to be going. Congratulations on your award. Thanks for the conversation, Mr. Dunne."

Peter grunted and watched Sterne beat a retreat to a far corner of the suite, scanning the crowd for his brother as he went.

"What the hell was that all about?"

"What it's always about. *Nothing.*" Along with his anger, Dunne felt mortification. He had betrayed the Garvans by speaking to Sterne of Patricia. It was nobody's goddamn business, least of all a jerk like that.

"You were in rare form downstairs tonight, Peter."

"I'm afraid that's true."

Garvan gave him a puzzled look.

"I'm rarely in form these days."

"Oh, for Christ's sake! Save that woe-is-me routine for someone who wasn't there. You never liked writing! It wasn't as easy or as much fun as anything and everything else in the world. You want to pretend you lost it? Dandy—but you never had it. They tied you to your desk twice a week just to get the goddamn Dooley column and a monkey could have written half of them. Have you really forgotten what hell it was?"

"Was it?"

"A wise man once said the past always looks better than it was, that it's only good when it's gone."

"No, I said 'it's only pleasant because it isn't here.' Let me polish the pearls of wisdom and you stick to the silver and pewter, okay Garvan?"

"You know, I should have made you kiss my rump on that dais. Now that would be a night to remember. Are you staying in town or out at the Hamptons?"

"I've been in town, trying to work. Margaret came in tonight."

"I've got to keep moving around the room, Peter. Can we see you next weekend?"

Dunne nodded, then clapped a hand heavily on Garvan's shoulder. "Get back to it. We'll see you then."

Garvan turned and was immediately engaged by Frances Perkins, who was there as Governor Roosevelt's emmisary. Then Jim Angell introduced him to John Marshall Phillips, who would be curating the Garvan collection for Yale. Garvan listened, polite and seemingly intent, as Phillips twittered on about his plans for cataloging and exhibiting parts of the enormous collection. Without moving or even seeming to stop looking directly at Phillips, Garvan caught Hoover's eye and the FBI man came over swiftly and cut through the crowd.

"I'm sorry to interrupt," Hoover said officiously, "but I've just received an urgent message for Mr. Garvan." He quickly steered Garvan toward a corner and looked up at him expectantly.

"Thanks. I couldn't take five seconds more of that claptrap. Does anybody really care what color velour provides the most suitable backdrop for a goblet?"

Hoover snickered. "What do you expect from an Ivy League fruit like that?"

Garvan, who had starred in baseball and run track for Yale, ignored the remark. He had a deep respect for Hoover's focus and unique ability to stay on top of Washington; he had learned to simply stop hearing the doltish remarks. Instead he asked: "Have you ever heard anything about a Columbia history professor named Sterne?"

Hoover shook his head. "No. But if he teaches at Columbia I can guess. Is he here?"

Wordlessly, Garvan turned and looked in Sterne's direction. When he was certain Hoover had him in his sights as well, he nodded once. "Got him," Hoover said, and Garvan pretended not to hear. "Hey—didn't I see him with your friend Dunne?" At this, Garvan raised an eyebrow and Hoover answered with a toothy aw-shucks smile. "I know a lot of people liked that column of his, but its charm always escaped me. That whole newspaper crowd is nothing but second-guessers and drawing-room pantywaists." He spit this last word as if it were something bitter on his tongue, and Garvan's gaze narrowed. Hoover took it as a sign of anger or impatience. "Well, I guess it hardly matters anymore," he said, seemingly obsequious. "You don't really see his name these days."

Garvan gave a noncommittal grunt, but the dig hit home. He pulled a handkerchief from his pocket, removed his gold-rimmed spectacles, and polished the lenses slowly, thinking of what Peter had said earlier about rarely being in form anymore. He *was* worse. But what would anyone expect after all that booze? It had drowned Peter's fire. That was all it was, he told himself. Still, he felt uneasy when he recalled Peter's speech— he'd never seen Dunne act the clown before! That couldn't just be the booze—was it for his benefit? Garvan held the polished lenses up to the light and, satisfied, put them back on. He looked at Peter, sitting alone on a couch with a highball, and had to turn away immediately. Instead, he glanced at Hoover, who stood silently at his side scanning the faces at the party, straining for snatches of conversation. He was waiting like some kind of hunting dog to see what was next. It was funny, Garvan thought: two men as different as Hoover and Dunne, both totally dedicated to him. Normally he didn't care—not about admiration or medals or endowments or any other kind of accolade. He always saw it for what it was: grease on the wheels, the impersonal masquerading as the personal, but really just the cementing of business arrangements and the way things got done. Why was Dunne the only one he still cared about? He was hardly a sentimentalist. Yet somewhere, somehow—God knew why—he felt he'd done Dunne wrong. Had he expected more than he should have? Ignored the weaknesses—or worse, counted on them?

Without a word to Hoover, Garvan strode across the room and found Mabel. She and his sister, Mother Angeline, were talking to Father O'Hara.

"Can't we find someone to talk to Peter?" he asked.

"Of course, dear. I'll go over there in a minute."

But by the time she'd shaken loose, the Dunnes were gone.

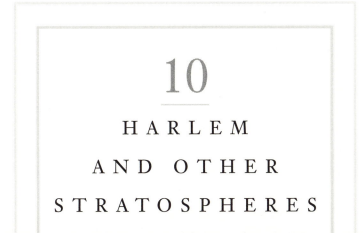

10

HARLEM
AND OTHER
STRATOSPHERES

Not long ago I cracked open the *Daily News* to discover one of Woodlawn's residents, Julius Langbein, had taken a walk. Langbein, who died in 1910, was a successful attorney and a New York state legislator, achievements that no one with the possible exception of his direct descendants are likely to remember today. Yet Langbein's name remains meaningful among Civil War buffs. As a fifteen-year-old drummer for the 9th New York Volunteers, Langbein risked his life to save an officer shot in the head at the Battle of South Mills in Camden, North Carolina, an act of bravery for which the boy was awarded the Congressional Medal of Honor. Indeed, while Admiral David "Damn the torpedoes!" Farragut and several Civil War generals are buried in Woodlawn—a surprising number of Confederate officers among them, including General Archibald Gracie, Jr., a northern businessman who married a Richmond woman and fathered the Gracie who barely survived the sinking of the *Titanic*—it's the former drummer boy's mausoleum that is a popular meeting place for Civil War societies and reenactment groups. The most prominent feature of Langbein's crypt is a four-foot marble statue depicting him in uniform and holding a drum, and it was this seven-hundred-fifty-pound marker that went strolling one sunny summer lunch hour. Apparently bound for the collection of a Civil War aficionado, the statue was recovered three days later when a cabbie recognized it on the street in front of an antique and salvage store in Manhattan and phoned police.

Ghoulish as it is, there is a national market for stolen cemetery decorations, including headstones and the iron fences and gates that enclose them. In one of the more ignominious cases of recent years, a gang of thieves in New Orleans swiped cemetery statues to order for antique dealers, who, in turn, shipped the pieces to Los Angeles for sale as "garden ornaments" at flea markets. Since Woodlawn's four hundred acres encompass a world-class trove of statuary, stonework, and architectural accents—and some, such as stained-glass mausoleum windows by Louis Comfort Tiffany or bronze monuments by Gertrude Vanderbilt Whitney, are quite valuable—it's perhaps encouraging that the Langbein statue was the first major theft of Woodlawn art in over ten years.

Of course, arrivals are much more frequent than departures at Woodlawn and that's as true for statuary as it is for bodies. Despite the passing of the era when New Yorkers spent their Sunday picnicking and gamboling amidst the greenery of a cemetery and thus an investment in a personal shrine was a smart way to lobby history and the affections of the public, new and unusual funerary work still pops up at Woodlawn.

The most celebrated recent addition is *Memorial to a Marriage*, a seven-foot sculpture by Brooklyn artist Patricia Cronin. The statue depicts Cronin and her life partner, Deborah Kass, naked in bed and, perhaps more surprisingly, the actual Cronin and Kass are still very much alive. While they plan to be cremated and have their ashes stored alongside the statue, the compelling thing about Cronin's work is the way it uses cemetery art to comment on an ongoing condition of life: the statue celebrates a marriage in death that the law won't allow to exist in life. It's intriguing to wonder if Cronin hasn't hit on a significant idea, i.e., that cemeteries are an untried canvas and that art employing death to deal directly with the issues of the living could reinvigorate graveyards as popular destinations rather than just the shunned green squares between city blocks or suburban development tracks. Perhaps that's the explanation for why *Memorial to a Marriage* has quickly become one of the most visited sites in Woodlawn, although I somehow doubt it. I also trust that most of those already interred don't object to the statue's subject. If there is an afterlife, it's a safe bet that the fantasy of every dead man is to see two dead women together in bed.

Using Woodlawn as a gallery would be simple enough; the cemetery has already played host to visiting pieces related to people buried there. Not long ago a statue of the Harlem Renaissance poet Countee Cullen was temporarily displayed at Woodlawn. Created by Meredith Bergmann, the piece beautifully conveys the creative and personal dilemma at the core of Cullen's life and work by employing two busts of him. One, in white marble, portrays him in the classic Greek style of the laurel-crowned poet; the other, cast in bronze, shows a darker, modern Cullen contemplating his white ideal. The piece was particularly welcome since Cullen, a prodigy who'd flared brightly in his youth but sputtered in his thirties and drifted far from the public eye even before his death in 1946 at the age of forty-two, is buried in an extremely modest plot in one of Woodlawn's more anonymous and unlovely sections.

As his statue suggests, Cullen's artistic slide likely owed a great deal to

the unrealistic role he was shoved into. An outstanding and justly celebrated young talent, Cullen aspired solely to being a poet, but had to
shoulder the immense burden of being a symbol for all that African Americans might achieve if given the chance. The adopted son of the minister
Frederick Asbury Cullen, who held the pulpit at Salem Methodist Episcopal Church on 127th Street, one of Harlem's leading congregations,
Cullen won literary prizes as a student at DeWitt Clinton High, attended
NYU on scholarship, earned a masters at Harvard, and was recognized as
a leading poet by the time he was twenty-one. Even his first marriage was
freighted with enormous public expectations: before three thousand guests
skimmed largely from the cream of the Talented Tenth he was regally married in his father's church to W. E. B. Du Bois's daughter, Yolande, with
Langston Hughes acting as an usher. It was billed as the ultimate merger
of intellect and beauty yet proved a brief and possibly even unconsum-
mated marriage. Yolande was widely rumored to be in love with the bandleader Jimmy Lunceford, while Cullen's own sexual preferences, like those
of his adopted father, were the subject of more than a little speculation. Yet
whatever public indignities Cullen suffered throughout his life from rumors, he was not afraid to take his most crushing personal weight and lay
it bare in his work, perhaps most famously in "Yet Do I Marvel":

I doubt not God is good, well-meaning, kind,
And did He stoop to quibble could tell why
The little buried mole continues blind,
Why flesh that mirrors Him must some day die,
Make plain the reason tortured Tantalus
Is baited by the fickle fruit, declare
If merely brute caprice dooms Sisyphus
To struggle up a never-ending stair.
Inscrutable His ways are, and immune
To catechism by a mind too strewn
With petty cares to slightly understand
What awful brain compels His awful hand.
Yet do I marvel at this curious thing:
To make a poet black, and bid him sing!

During the 1920s, Cullen was smack in the eye of the artistic and so-cial hurricane roaring through Harlem. Among his friends was famed Harlem hostess A'Lelia Walker, whose popular literary salon, "The Dark Tower," was named for Cullen's column in the National Urban League's magazine, *Opportunity*. Walker, along with her mother, the entrepreneur Madame C. J. Walker, is also in Woodlawn. And while the plot and pol-ished black headstone they share is a good deal nicer than Cullen's, it's nowhere near as opulent as might be expected for someone believed to be not just the first African-American woman to make a million dollars, but the first self-made American millionairess, period. Perhaps Madame Walker, who earned her fortune teaching a generation of black women how to operate their own beauty parlors, was careful with her money. It's also equally likely that her daughter just had better things to spend it on: A'Lelia's parties enjoyed a storied reputation even in an era famous for good parties. Poetically, the lasting physical proximity of Cullen and the Walkers extends beyond Woodlawn and is etched in Manhattan concrete: the Countee Cullen branch of the New York Public Library on West 136th Street in Harlem is built on the former site of the Walkers' side-by-side townhouses and A'Lelia's "Dark Tower." The library is now also home to Bergmann's matched busts of Cullen.

On the summer Saturday of the Harlem Book Fair, I stopped in at Woodlawn to see Countee Cullen and then bicycled Jerome Avenue down to the Grand Concourse and over the 145th Street bridge into Harlem. The bridge puts you on the thoroughfare variously known as both Lenox Avenue and Malcolm X Boulevard just a few blocks north of Harlem Hospital and the Schomburg Center, Harlem's principal library. And with the Cullen library located just around the corner, Harlem is likely the only New York neighborhood that can boast back-to-back pub-lic library branches. All that Saturday a gentle summer breeze was rip-pling through Harlem, rustling the trees in front of the townhouses up on Sugar Hill and ballooning the tents at the book fair down on the flats of West 135th Street, providing an extra little come-on to buyers by flipping open the covers on the paperbacks.

The book business, which in all manners of marketing can be counted on to be far behind the film and music industries, has finally gotten around to trying to cater to African-American readers. Mimicking the record business, most of the leading publishers have instituted black imprints, and the Harlem fair also boasted an encouraging number of small, independent African-American houses offering everything from radical political tracts to bodice rippers. There are enough exhibitors showing enough books at the fair for it to take an hour or two to travel from one end to the other. What I don't find, however, is anything by Countee Cullen. The only consolation I can take away from the display tables is the continuing popularity of Cullen's student, James Baldwin.

It was, in fact, just four blocks up Lenox Avenue at PS 139 that Cullen spent the second half of his too-short adult life teaching French and English to Baldwin and others at the very junior high school where not long before Cullen himself had been the star pupil. Whether he was depressed by his reversal of fortune I can't say; but it's clear that the burdens Cullen shouldered as a young man were unwanted and that he was an excellent and dedicated teacher. Although Cullen never had any children of his own, he remarried later in life and wrote a pair of children's books, neither of which is currently in print. Both are ostensibly credited to Cullen's cat, Christopher, and one, *My Lives and How I Lost Them*, is the animal's autobiography. The other, *The Lost Zoo*, is a collection of poems describing the fanciful animals who either refused or missed getting onto Noah's Ark. Both books were written with his students in mind. As a teacher, Cullen also recognized Baldwin's exceptional mind and talents—and, perhaps, a little more: like Cullen, Baldwin was the sensitive adopted son of a preacher, and he took the less privileged youth under his wing. Along with his academic and artistic example, the hand of Cullen is evident in the younger writer's lifelong Francophilia.

PS 139 is gone; there's now a park, a senior citizen's home, and an elementary school on the block. I pedal west up the rise across Adam Clayton Powell Boulevard to the area officially named the St. Nicholas Historic District but far better known as Striver's Row (which, by the way, is the name of one of the big publishing companies' new African-American imprints). Built in the 1890s as middle-class housing, the two-block development includes a row of neo-Italian houses designed by McKim, Mead and White, and became one of the most sought-after addresses in Harlem by the 1920s, when its residents included professionals like Vertner Tandy, the first African-American architect licensed by the state of New York, the entertainers Ethel Waters, Eubie Blake, and Fletcher Henderson, and, most notable for me, the heavyweight boxer Harry Wills.

Wills, who left Striver's Row for Woodlawn in 1958, was known as the Brown Panther. He fought over a hundred times in the course of a twenty-one-year career and was a big-time contender forced to spend six frustrating years hounding Jack Dempsey for a title bout that he couldn't get. Leading promoter Tex Rickard, mindful of the riots that had attended his Jack Johnson–Jim Jeffries fight, reportedly feared mounting a "mixed match," to say nothing of the prospect of another black champion. Rickard apparently wasn't the only one with those fears: the New York Boxing Commission stonewalled the fight, and in 1925 the match was finally made for July 4 in Indiana. But even that fell apart and Wills— who was gracious enough to say he believed Dempsey wanted to fight him—had to be satisfied with pocketing a fifty-thousand-dollar guarantee. The Panther, who was rumored to have carried some of his white opponents in a bid not to scare off Dempsey, beat several of the top white heavyweights of the era, including Willie Meehan (who beat Dempsey twice), Gunboat Smith, and Charley Weinart, and earned his biggest payday (one hundred fifty thousand dollars) fighting the Argentine boxing star Luis Firpo to a draw. Still, Wills spent most of his career battling other black boxers and had at least eighteen fights against the great Sam Langford (who didn't have as much luck as Wills in the nickname department and was marqueed as the Boston Tar Baby). Unlike so many other fighters, Wills ended his career in good financial shape and later used his ring earnings to amass a sizable Harlem real estate portfolio.

I ride down Frederick Douglass Boulevard, past the Lionel Hampton Houses, the low-and-middle income enclave built by the vibraphonist, and pick up St. Nicholas Avenue—known among bicyclists as the St. Nick Expressway because it cuts a nearly uninterrupted path from Central Park through upper Manhattan to the George Washington Bridge— turning off on 116th Street east of Fifth Avenue. This street is now named Luis Muñoz Marín Boulevard, in honor of the first elected governor of Puerto Rico. But since everyone else in New York seems to be lobbying to have a street renamed for someone, I'm going to say that this one should be Vito Marcantonio's. I've come to have a look at 116th and Lexington, which Marcantonio called his "lucky corner." Like so much in the congressman's career, the corner was inherited from Fiorello La Guardia, and it was the spot where both men went to deliver important speeches and hold election-night rallies.

Although the stores and the names of the doctors and dentists and lawyers and accountants operating businesses in the second-floor offices of the brownstones are different, the corner itself seems to have changed very little. After World War II, East Harlem became Spanish Harlem, and only the faintest echoes of the Italian Harlem that Marcantonio grew up in can be found, most notably in the handful of remaining neighborhood restaurants like Andy's Colonial, Patsy's Pizzeria, and the now-exclusive Rao's. Rao's is a big hangout for A-list politicians nowadays, so I can't picture the proletariat's representative eating there. But I can easily imagine him at his lucky corner, his banners strung from the upper windows of the brownstones, the rolling stage set up in the middle of the intersection, the kleig lights, the band, and the tumultuous crowd hanging on his every word. Marcantonio was a histrionic speaker who understood rallies as theater. Rocking back and forth on his heels, pounding his palm, his voice rising and face turning red, Marcantonio had a trick of stamping his feet in a building cadence matched to his words that reminded some of a flamenco dancer. Nor did his theatrics omit props. In 1948, when he was facing John Ellis, a silk-stocking district Republican with a Sutton Place address, Marcantonio hired the ventriloquist Paul Winchell to pull up to rallies in a limousine and emerge dressed in a top hat and formal evening wear and carrying a bag. Whenever Winchell's entrance made its inevitable stir, Marcantonio would call him up to the stage and ask where he was from. "I'm from Wall Street," Winchell would reply, and when Marcantonio would then ask what was in the bag, Winchell would pull out a dummy that looked like Ellis.

Such stunts were indicative of the real and deep animosity between Marcantonio and many of the city's more mainstream politicians. Beloved in his district, Marcantonio was also a brilliant organizer who built on his earlier work as La Guardia's campaign manager by creating a powerful and truly independent political machine for himself on the American Labor Party line. And while both Democratic and Republican candidates often sought the ALP's endorsement, Marcantonio's leftist views increasingly excited attackers (including the *New York Times*). Yet he never moved to the middle, even as the McCarthy era unfolded, and remained at all times a street-tough tactician in the hardball worlds of New York and Washington politics. On the eve of Marcantonio's 1946 election, a Republican district captain with strong anticommunist views named Joseph Scottoriggio was beaten by four men on his way to an East Harlem polling place and subsequently died without regaining consciousness. The Manhattan district attorney, Frank Hogan, appeared convinced the Marcantonio camp was responsible for Scottoriggio's murder, and the resulting grand jury investigation lasted three years—reportedly the longest-sitting grand jury in New York city history—and included interviews with one thousand three hundred area residents, including two of Marcantonio's own district captains who were held as material witnesses. Although quickly released, one, Anthony Langana, disappeared and was later found in the East River. Marcantonio, who immediately waived immunity and testified before the Hogan jury, steadfastly maintained that neither he nor any of his associates had anything to do with the beating. The police eventually declared Langana's death a suicide and the grand jury never returned any indictments.

At his lucky corner, Marcantonio exhorted his crowds with a kind of street-corner demagoguery now so far out of fashion as to be considered tasteless. Perhaps more to the point, it's become ineffective and superfluous in an era of multimillion-dollar PAC war chests. Though it happened only a lifetime ago, imagining a maverick neighborhood politician with a "lucky corner" is already as quaint a picture as that of the first meeting of the New York Stock Exchange being convened under a tree. I wish the rabble-rouser Marcantonio—who cast the sole vote against United States involvement in the Korean War, who refused to support Chang Kai-shek and the Chinese Nationalists, who lobbied for social welfare and equality, who fought relentlessly against poll taxes—was around today. I so long to hear not just what he would say about the current administration, but to hear him take on its bully surrogates, those men and women so eager to live in a world without dissent and so insecure with democracy as to label any who might disagree with them traitors. The absence of a Marcantonio does not speak well of our own time. When dissent is political suicide the body politic is already in the ground.

Before leaving the neighborhood, I feel compelled to mention that every so often I come across something claiming jazz singer Billie Holiday is buried in Woodlawn. It isn't true and the confusion very likely comes from the fact that she is buried in the Bronx, although at St. Raymond's. Her musical soul mate, the great and enormously influential tenor saxophonist Lester Young, is buried in Brooklyn's Evergreen Cemetery, but the other tenor giant of the era, Coleman Hawkins, is in Woodlawn. Or so they tell me. Weirdly, I've gone over and over the section he's listed in with everything short of a Geiger counter and I can't find his grave. I even conned a groundskeeper into helping me, but to no avail. I'm sure there's a simple explanation—a redrawn section border, a typo in the record, some miscalculation on my part—but I find his elusiveness unsettling. If you can't count on a cemetery for an answer, what can you count on?

As I discovered during my earlier run-in with the wrong Henry Bergh, Billie Holiday isn't the only figure mistakenly said to be in Woodlawn. The comedian Fatty Arbuckle has been erroneously buried here by one author, and planted in Hollywood's Forest Lawn by another biographer. In fact, the now-obscure silent film stars Pauline Hill and Digby Bell are in Woodlawn but Arbuckle, who died in New York, was cremated in Queens and had his ashes scattered on the Pacific by his widow. Famously victimized by a scurrilous, career-destroying scandal in which he was accused of raping and mortally injuring a woman during a party in his San Francisco hotel suite, Arbuckle, when ultimately acquitted after three trials, was still blacklisted by the Hays Office and died of a heart attack at forty-six. But then, Arbuckle got off to a bad start from the very first moment of life. His actual name was Roscoe Conkling Arbuckle—a cruelly derisive name bestowed on him by an embittered father who believed the boy was not his own and so named him for the famous

Casanova of the Senate. When Roscoe's mother died twelve years later, his father simply abandoned him.

It's hard not to gape in the presence of such senseless cruelty. Perhaps I've simply become more attuned to the notion of legacies during my walks around Woodlawn. As the preferred planting ground of the Gilded Age, one is surrounded by Goulds, Guggenheims, Vanderbilts, Whitneys, Huntingtons, Baches, Harknesses, Havemeyers, Helmsleys, Lamonts, Lehmans, and Woolworths—including the legendarily unhappy heiress Barbara Hutton, who had seven husbands (one of them Cary Grant) and supposedly transformed a $50 million Woolworth fortune into three thousand dollars. I've come to realize that bequests, like everything else, have a fashion: today we discern the hand of an egotist in the last will and testament of Woodlawn's Henry Francis Shoemaker, a Civil War hero and tycoon who left his grandson, Henry Barclay Perry, $2 million on the condition that he change his name to Henry Francis Shoemaker. Yet that wasn't an uncommon condition of inheritance in the nineteenth century. Unfortunately, the kind of cruelty shown to Arbuckle has so far proven immune to fashion.

One Woodlawn family with a very good name and a complex emotional legacy caught my attention, and I have repeatedly found myself drawn to the family's plot in Woodlawn's quiet and heavily shaded Oakhill section. Their name is Nichols, and, although I suspect some of the family is still living in the New York area, I was taken with Ruth Nichols, a pioneering female pilot born at the turn of the twentieth century. Through her father, who claimed direct descent from Leif Eriksson (and was himself named Erickson Nichols), Ruth inherited the commingled birthright of entitlement, adventure, and noblesse oblige that came with being a member of New York's privileged Four Hundred. Her father, one of Roosevelt's Rough Riders and a successful stockbroker, sent his daughter first to Miss Master's School and then to Wellesley. And when the seventeen-year-old Ruth was bitten by the flying bug after a ten-dollar ride with World War I ace Eddie Stinson at an Atlantic City aviation show in 1919, he encouraged her to become the first licensed female pilot in New York. In later life Erickson suffered serious business reversals, shattering both the family's economic standing and his health.

But in Ruth's mind he remained the towering taskmaster of her girlhood: dashing, determined, but above all demanding; the sportsman of spartan standards who ever and always insisted that, while everyone gets thrown once in a while, a Nichols always gets back on his horse.

Her sense of what it meant to be a Nichols propelled Ruth to become a trailblazer. A contemporary and rival of Amelia Earhart, with whom she was a cofounder of the still extant flyers' sorority known as the Ninety-Nines, she tested the boundaries of a newly opened sky that was sometimes a playground, sometimes a nascent industrial zone, and always dangerous. Nichols walked away from two fatal crashes, could boast more broken bones than a member of the Hockey Hall of Fame, and achieved dozens of firsts in both stunt and commercial flying over the course of four decades. She crashed in a bid to become the first woman to fly solo across the Atlantic, but could still lay claim to being the first female pilot for a passenger airline. And although Nichols probably reached the apex of her fame in 1931, when she used the same plane to break the women's speed, altitude, and distance records, her desire to push the boundaries of space never flagged: she was piloting subsonic jets and still breaking altitude records in 1958 at the age of fifty-six.

Yet the need to lead was only half of Nichols's inheritance. Her mother's family, the Rowlands, were Quakers with a long tradition of service and pacifism. Nichols was profoundly influenced by her devout and doting aunt, whom she variously called "Angel" and "Aunty," and beside whom she is buried. Like her, Nichols never married and became an avowed pacifist who yearned for a religious calling. She eventually found a mission by creating flying ambulance programs and in her later life mounted a global fact-finding and publicity flight to help launch UNICEF.

Still, there was in Nichols a soul-deep and unfulfilled longing and a nearly morbid fear that she could never do justice to either her father's swashbuckling, frontier spirit or her aunt's puritanical altruism, divergent American impulses hot-wired into her genetic code. Lonely and apparently depressed in her later years, Nichols was nonetheless still stirred by the dream of going into space. In 1959, she sought entrance to what would become the Mercury program. Although given a tryout, it's unlikely the military viewed her bid as anything other than a photo op for the program.

Indeed, the managers of the early space program misled dozens of female pilots, all of them a good deal younger than Nichols, into believing they had a shot at going into space. Sexual discrimination has a particularly strong tradition in aviation: the union of commercial pilots barred licensed female flyers beginning in the thirties and most male pilots simply refused to team with a woman in the cockpit. Nothing really changed at the airlines until the 1970s, and the sight of a woman at the helm of a commercial flight is still a rarity. For Mercury, more than a dozen women were selected for training and one of them, Jerrie Cobb, finished all three phases of physical training. Cobb, who came into the program boasting ten thousand hours of flight time—more than Alan Shepard and double that of John Glenn—was bounced along with the rest of the women when the military, apparently facing the prospect that Cobb would qualify and that they'd never really seriously considered the possibility of women pilots in designing and testing any phase of a space flight (nor, obviously, considered the possibility that women might be more suitable), decided it would only accept flight hours accrued in the military. It was a nifty trick: regulations forbade women from piloting military aircraft.

Like Nichols before her, Cobb—who is now in her seventies—remained a professional pilot. Spurned by NASA, she also echoed Nichols by turning to humanitarian projects, flying medicine into the Brazilian jungle. Cobb, whose cause has been taken up by the National Organization of Women, was lobbying for a chance to go into space on the shuttle before John Glenn's celebrated curtain call; she was still waiting when the *Columbia* explosion put the program in limbo.

Nichols never saw manned space flight. On the night before the first Nixon-Kennedy debate, she took her own life with an overdose of pills. Her long-out-of-print autobiography, *Wings for Life*, offers no hints to help predict or understand the coming cataclysmic act, the only intimations of trouble being awkward evasions on personal matters, her silence suggesting a solitary life. In every other way, it is the memoir of a woman who, in her day, would have been hailed as a game gal with a social conscience and sense of responsibility toward life. Her ultimate despair arrests my graveyard stroll.

From the surface, Nichols's grave is like thousands and thousands and thousands of others, sharing its stone with that of beloved "Aunty," who lived to be 103. (Was *that* it? The unbearable prospect of another forty lonely years?) Is suicide something different? Or is depression no less corrosive than lymphoma? Why recoil at a handful of barbiturates when we shrug at acute alcoholism? Perhaps the moment is just too stark in its fierce desperation and her repudiation of life rattles around in our hearts like a bone in a box. Will giving her flesh unfreeze her tongue and silence death's rattle? Or are we simply upset when someone refuses to join us in clinging desperately to this beloved gift of a brief, sweaty, elbow-throwing subway ride through the city?

11

THRENODY

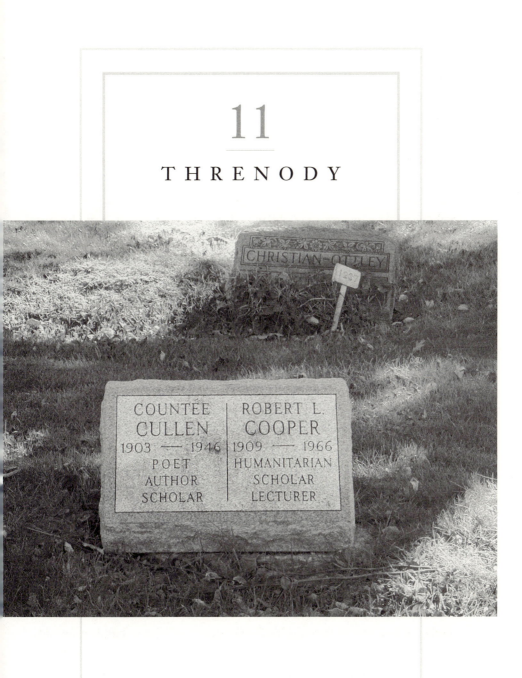

Jimmy felt sick and dizzy and he blamed his father.

He was standing on the platform of the Tuckahoe train station under the clear blue of a crisp Thanksgiving Day sky, waiting for his former teacher, Mr. Cullen, but all he could think about was the old man's stormy rage. What in God's name was wrong with him? They'd exchanged angry words (nothing new!) about Jimmy's trip, but the shouting match had left him so angry that he'd spent the entire twenty-five-minute ride from 125th Street chain-smoking Chesterfields—and he was now as nauseated as a twelve-year-old who'd just taken his first puff. Jimmy sucked a deep, biting lungful of the cool autumn air, trying to shake the feeling. He would never fathom the source of his father's bitterness, never understand why it was invariably directed at him. Didn't he help support the family? Didn't he watch the little ones? And what could his father possibly have against Mr. Cullen! Not for the first time Jimmy wondered if the neighbors were right and his father really and truly was insane. He also felt a sudden and secret flash of relief at the recently gained knowledge that he was actually only his stepfather. But just as quickly as the thoughts occurred to Jimmy he felt shame rising hot in his cheeks. Whom else should he call his father—some stranger who'd passed along his genes before disappearing into a neighborhood bar to sit day after day forever before a half-empty beer glass, hat pushed jauntily back on his head? Still, he felt only confusion and shame at the thought of his father and there was no denying the relationship was a burden—an irrational, jealous, raging, embittered, intolerant and intolerable burden. What bothered Jimmy most about today's fight was that he'd been looking forward to this trip for weeks—obsessing on it, really. Why wouldn't his father let him be happy, just for a day?

It had to be jealousy—Jimmy had always adored Mr. Cullen. Six years earlier, when Mr. Cullen was his French and English teacher, Jimmy had taken a special pride in being the most outstanding student. But now, at eighteen, he knew a great deal more about his teacher's career—knew who he *really* was—and had very nearly come to worship him. He'd spent all of last week's lunch breaks at the defense plant rereading *Color* and *Copper Sun*. Along with his cigarette-induced nausea, Jimmy felt an icy pang of fear in his stomach that said just how much the man's opinion mattered to him. Perhaps he feared his father would prove right when he ranted that accepting the invitation was a terrible mistake.

"Jimmy!"

Mr. Cullen, wearing a brown cardigan instead of his usual jacket and tie, was waving from alongside a green Pontiac parked toward the end of a row of idling cabs. There was a broad smile on his face, and Jimmy instantly felt better. He crossed to Mr. Cullen at a barely contained trot and shook his hand warmly.

"How was the ride? I always worry about the trains on holidays."

"Oh, just fine, Mr. Cullen! I can't imagine what it would be like to ride it everyday."

"Tedious."

"You can't mean that! I wish I could be so blasé! Perhaps it's just today—all the children with balloons coming from the parade—but it really was quite festive, you know." He looked down and was surprised to see Mr. Cullen wearing bedroom slippers instead of shoes, but of course said nothing. Instead, he took his first good look at the brick-and-brown of the imitation gingerbread English country town that was Tuckahoe and asked: "What's it like to live in paradise?"

"Paradise?" Cullen laughed good-naturedly. He was a small, prematurely balding man with a paunch and looked best when laughing. "Five miles north of the Bronx would be a strange place to build paradise." He shook his head and chuckled. "The house is about a mile from here in Yonkers."

"Well, Yonkers might as well be the Yukon to me," the boy said with an embarrassed but earnest smile. "It's all so beautiful. And I'm honored that you've invited me. Oh, here." He proffered a small, paper-wrapped bouquet of flowers. They'd been sweet and festive in the window of the florist's shop a block from the Harlem station but now felt shoddy and past their prime in his sweaty grip, and he feared the stale, heavy smell of tobacco that tainted his breath and hung on his skin and clothes had infected the bouquet as well. "These are for Mrs. Cullen."

"She'll love them. But why don't you give them to her yourself?"

Jimmy rarely rode in cars and he enjoyed the short trip to the house. His eyes darted back and forth between the automobile's spotless interior with its brown-and-white dashboard and chrome and cream-colored plastic knobs and the endless green swatches of lawn and trees that rose on either side of the road just a block from the train station. The car climbed a brief, twisting rise and came to a stoplight where the road crossed a parkway before continuing up a long, steep hill. Shifting down, Cullen stole a look at Jimmy and smiled at his continuing rapture. "We're almost there," he said, cocking a finger toward the top of the ridge. "That's Grandview Boulevard, our street."

Long and narrow, it was hardly as wide as a city street let alone a real boulevard. On either side were brick and clapboard colonials, two-story stucco haciendas, and small English Tudors, each set well back from the sidewalk in a manicured lot. Architecture had always registered with Jimmy. He loved to wander Striver's Row and Sugar Hill, to gaze in unvarnished admiration at the splendor and integrity of the bold brick-and-stone buildings and let his imagination conjure the extraordinary lives that had to transpire behind such opulently leaded windows, solid wrought-iron balconies, and silent oak doors. And although he'd never been in the suburbs before he immediately recognized it as something other, something closer in spirit to his own modest neighborhood than the majesterial road of country estates it pretended to be. It was—what? Not unreal, but not entirely real, either. Modest homes putting on airs, as transparent as a bellman trying to pass as a cavalry officer. Not the genuine article, not Convent Avenue. They drove past a man walking an old swaybacked dog. The man stared hard at them—unfriendly and as if he somehow didn't trust his eyes. Jimmy knew that look too well, and it made him think of his job and the fight he'd just had with his father.

And yet, the fantasy neighborhood had a certain allure, and he wanted desperately to give himself up to its seduction. Mostly it was the gardens and the trees. Clumps of big, leather-leaved shrubs (he'd later learn they were rhododendrons), carefully shaped geometric evergreens, sweeping willows, old oaks, paper-barked white birches, and a towering chestnut tree, its long leaves twisting half-golden in the clear autumn sun, nuts dropping and bouncing on the pavement with a hop whenever the wind shook the branches.

"It's fantastic!" Jimmy exclaimed, rolling down the window. He wanted nothing to interfere with the sights and smells, and was seized with an impulse to get out, to lay facedown on a lawn or let his fingers read the bark of a tree. He wished to stay here—away from his father, away from the awful factory—forever. "It's so verdant and still! The Garden of Eden with a train station."

Cullen laughed and shook his head.

"No? Am I being too romantic? It just seems the perfect place to write. So much solitude."

"Is that what a writer needs, solitude?"

"Yes, isn't it?"

"I knew a poet who did his best work in a nightclub. There is no secret to success except hard work and getting something indefinable which we call 'the breaks.' If you want to succeed as a writer, I suggest three things—read and write . . . and wait." He slowed the car and turned into the pebbled driveway of a white Dutch colonial. "Solitude has its good side and its bad side. Yes, you need to concentrate if you wish to write, but life is with people. If you pursue solitude, then solitude is what you'll end up writing about. Of course, that's done quite a bit." At this, he cut the engine and, looking out at the quiet street, recited:

"O solitude! if I must with thee dwell,
Let it not be among the jumbled heap
Of murky buildings; climb with me the steep,
Nature's observatory—whence the dell,
Its flowery slopes, its river's crystal swell,
May seem a span; let me thy vigils keep
'Mongst boughs pavillion'd, where the deer's swift leap
Startles the wild bee from the fox-glove bell.
But though I'll gladly trace these scenes with thee,
Yet the sweet converse of an innocent mind,
Whose words are images of thoughts refin'd,
Is my soul's pleasure; and it sure must be
Almost the highest bliss of human-kind,
When to thy haunts two kindred spirits flee."

Flattered to be thought a kindred spirit, Jimmy flushed simultaneously with pleasure and embarrassment. "When did you write that, Mr. Cullen?"

"When did I write it? Good Lord, boy, what did they teach you at Clinton? I'll tell you this: if I had been your high school English teacher, you'd recognize John Keats."

Jimmy smiled sheepishly, his large doe eyes lidded in an only half-mock mortification. "Well, at least there's nothing wrong with my French."

"Damn right!" He slapped a hand on the boy's shoulder. "Come on, let's go see the ladies."

Standing in the driveway of the white colonial, Jimmy let his gaze climb the lavishly pintoed old plane tree that dominated the front yard, blotched branches pushing up against the house and hovering high above its roof. He could see now that the house itself was actually much larger than it appeared from the road—he guessed it had at least four bedrooms. There was an elegant center entrance with a brass door knocker leading to a small vestibule, but his eyes locked on the two tiny windows on the third floor. They were nestled side by side under the curved roof and positioned directly above the entranceway. He felt a jolt at the realization that this would be Mr. Cullen's private study.

Jimmy remembered his first day in Mr. Cullen's class. Back then he didn't know that the short man in the generously tailored brown suit was famous, just that he was a special teacher. He loved the way Mr. Cullen threw himself into teaching, the way he managed to be more engaging and alive than the others, dominating a classroom from the second he slid his leather book bag across the teacher's desk and sternly clapped his hands for the class to come to order. Like most of the seventh graders, it took Jimmy a while to discover Mr. Cullen's other life. *His other life*—that was the way he thought of it, then and now. He still couldn't reconcile Mr. Cullen, teacher of French and English at Frederick Douglass Junior High, with Countee Cullen, Harvard graduate, Guggenheim Fellow, poet laureate of the Harlem Renaissance, author of *Copper Sun, Heritage, Yet Do I Marvel*, and *Incident*, and winner of nearly every major poetry prize. Looking up into the window of his study, Jimmy wanted more than anything to see it, to sit at the desk and put his fingers on the type-writer. He wouldn't dare punch the keys—touching them would be enough.

A smiling woman stood in the doorway, watching, her arms folded. She was a good deal younger than he'd imagined. Well, that was often the way it was in second marriages. Jimmy walked up to the house and held out the flowers. "Good evening, Mrs. Cullen. Thank you for having me."

She spurned the flowers and gave him a dirty look. "Mrs. Cullen?" She ran a hand through her hair for effect and turned to Cullen. "I told you I needed to get my hair done."

"This is my stepdaughter, Mrs. Nimmons," he said to Jimmy. "Her husband is in the Marine Corps, stationed at Camp Lejeune." He shook his head and placed an arm around his guest's shoulder. "Son, I think you need to get out more often."

"Got that right," she said, although it was obvious that the insult was being exaggerated as a tease. "You think I'd have that tired old man's name? I don't want anything from him."

"Except maybe a kiss?" Cullen asked.

"Well, maybe." They embraced and then she turned toward the house, pushing the door open. "Momma," she called, "there's a good-looking young man here to see you and he's got flowers. But be careful—Countee's coming in right behind him."

Ida Mae Roberson Cullen was not the kind of woman to greet a guest in an apron, and it was a moment until she was sufficiently satisfied with her appearance to push open the swinging kitchen door and join them in the dining room. She was a large, middle-aged woman, not heavy but solidly substantial and homey in a formal, nearly elegant sort of way, like a grandfather clock. She was well dressed in a blue flower-print dress with delicate yellow and red blossoms—far from expensive but absolutely tasteful and certainly selected with much more care than her husband would ever muster for his wardrobe. She wore an unusual onyx necklace and large, black frame eyeglasses. "You must be Jimmy," she said, smiling warmly and wiping her already clean hands with a spotless white dish-towel before extending one. "It's such a pleasure to finally meet you after hearing Countee speak of you all these years."

Jimmy could feel the blood rising in his cheeks, and he had to summon all his courage not to look down as he took her hand. "*Enchanté*."

"Oh, I like that! You hear that, Countee? How come the only time you speak French in this house is when you're bothering me to make coq au vin?"

Cullen raised an eyebrow to the boy and pointed at his wife. "I think she's the one who gets the flowers." Jimmy looked down to see the forgotten bouquet hanging limply at his side. "He's been trying to give them away since he got off the train."

"Don't razz the boy, Countee." She took the finally delivered flowers and held them to her face to bask in the bouquet's aroma, just as she sensed the boy wanted her to. "Thank you, dear, it was very thoughtful of you. Let me go put them in a vase right away. Are you thirsty?"

"No, ma'am."

"I am," said Cullen.

"Yes, of course *you* are. But you're not a guest here, so why don't you get what you want while I tend to these lovely flowers?" She didn't wait for an answer but disappeared back into the kitchen.

Cullen gave a big mock sigh. "You know, I think I get even less respect at home than I do at school."

"Well, you can always make her conjugate a dozen irregular verbs." It was Cullen's favorite punishment for poor classroom behavior.

"Oh, yeah. I can see you know a lot about women."

Jimmy blushed again. He knew nothing about women. Well, not nothing. As a thirteen-year-old preacher in the Pentecostal Church the women in the congregation had doted on him—"*And a child shall lead them*"—it was like having a dozen adoring mothers. But the other stuff? He'd idolized Mr. Cullen since the first day of class six years ago, although he was hardly the only teacher to recognize Jimmy's talents and potential. Still, he was the only one who seemed to instantly know who he was and how he felt and thought. At first, Jimmy had romanticized the relationship, believing it was an artist recognizing a young but nonetheless kindred soul. Now that he was out in the world he wondered if the bond wasn't due to a recognition of a different sort.

He'd always ignored the cruel and ignorant things he'd heard said of

Mr. Cullen in Frederick Douglass's halls and cafeteria. And why not? Those idiots were wrong about everything else and they certainly had no feel for the sensitivity and temperament of an artist. Nonetheless, his curiosity had led him to the periodical room in the new 136th Street library, where he'd dug through the yellowed and already crumbling copies of the *Amsterdam News* from 1928 until he found the accounts of Mr. Cullen's wedding to W. E. B. Du Bois's daughter, Yolande.

It had been the social event of the year in Negro New York: three thousand guests—the cream of the Talented Tenth—at Salem Methodist Church where Mr. Cullen's renowned father was pastor. He'd married the couple, of course, and both Langston Hughes and Arna Bontemps had been ushers. A few weeks later, Guggenheim in hand, he'd sailed for Paris with his father and a close friend, Harold Jackman. Yolande was to join them a little later, but the marriage lasted just slightly longer than the honeymoon. There were all kinds of stories, and everything depended on whom one spoke with. Some said Yolande was in love with Jimmy Lunceford, the bandleader. But there were also rumors about Cullen and his friend Jackman, who had been quite the dashing and scandalous figure uptown and a model for the main character in novels by Carl Van Vechten and Wallace Thurman. One story had it that after one of Cullen and Jackman's parties, Yolande had stormed out of their Paris quarters with the crank to her husband's Victrola. And for that matter, there was no shortage of tales about Reverend Cullen, either! Jimmy's own father was a storefront preacher who couldn't latch on with a congregation, and even so fleeting a thought of him and his personal demons made Jimmy flush with anger again. But he couldn't imagine what it must have been like for Mr. Cullen to grow up the son of a pastor with a reputation for chasing choirboys! The most colorful stories had Reverend Cullen enjoying his evenings at home in a dress and makeup. Of course, he hadn't learned that at the library—he'd heard those stories from a friend in the Harlem numbers racket over drinks at Connie's Inn. That was right after Jimmy decided he definitely was *not* born to be a preacher. No, what Mr. Cullen had said was true: he had never been particularly interested in learning about women. He couldn't help wondering just how much Mr. Cullen really knew about them.

"We've got a while before dinner. Come, I'll show you around if you'd like."

"Yes, please. I'd like that very much."

They began in the living room, done in French farmhouse furniture including what appeared to be a very old hand-hewn hutch. Two of the walls were taken up by floor-to-ceiling bookshelves, full but neatly arranged. There was little in the way of bric-a-brac save for a small hand-painted metal cast of the *Ile de France*, the ship Mr. Cullen had sailed for Paris on in 1928 and nearly every summer after until 1939, and a bronze bust that proved to be of Baudelaire. A side window was swaddled in delicate old, ivory-colored lace curtains and gave out onto a partial view of the yard, a hedge, and the next house. But more engaging views were to be found in the numerous framed photographs of Parisian scenes hanging on the side wall itself, including one of Mr. Cullen seated with a white couple at an outdoor café. They were smoking and drinking wine and smiling for the camera. Mr. Cullen was wearing a beret and his Phi Beta Kappa key was plainly visible on his vest.

"Those are my friends the Greens," he said. "They gave me a quiet place to work when I needed it in their home near Montsouris Park. Of course, they had to come back when the war started." He looked long and longingly at the photo but said nothing more. "Enough of that. We've done the French room, now let's see the American one, shall we?" He pushed through a white swinging door at the back of the room.

It was the library. The walls were darkly muted with books and the room felt as warm and snug to Jimmy as a nest. There was a worn, brown leather couch, an enormous radio in a walnut cabinet, and an end-table with an old RCA Victrola, complete with a shiny black metal horn. Jimmy craned his head to see if it still held a crank—it did—and his eyes skimmed over a large white-and-orange cat curled up on a sagging old green settee in the corner. Then he turned and saw the fourth wall.

Unlike the rest of the library, which was as brown and mellow as a row of cigar boxes, this last wall was chaotic, like a child's tub of crayons. Paintings of glaring yellows, late-night blues, shocking reds, and a dozen different shades of glowing browns hung side by side, frames abutting, the top of one resting on the bottom of the next, each fighting for space, for the ownership of Jimmy's eye and heart. An elegant couple dancing to a jazz band. Four rakish and worldly Negroes playing poker. An old woman mending socks. A deep and fertile coffee-brown nude lounging on a whiter-than-white sheet. A simple watercolor of a lonesome country shack. An oil of the cathedral at Notre Dame. Directly below the paintings stood a long-legged rolltop partner's desk with a high stool. It was all but obliterated by the drama of the paintings and looked very uncomfortable.

"Is this where you write?"

"No! That's Mrs. Cullen's desk. I work upstairs. But I love to read on that couch. Sleep on it, too, sometimes—depending on what I'm reading." He smiled, then glanced over at the cat. "Of course, I'm not the only sleepyhead around here. Isn't that right, Christopher?"

If the cat recognized its name, it made no sign. But Jimmy did.

"The famous author? I should have brought my copy of *The Lost Zoo* for an autograph!" He leaned toward his host, and added in a mock-hushed tone, "Or do you suppose he would have found that hopelessly gauche?"

"Nooo—he's a pussycat." He ran a hand under the cat and picked him up. "Aren't you, Christopher? Aren't you, my baby?"

The old cat barely opened his eyes and Jimmy could hear him purring like an engine in low gear. The boy reached out to rub him behind the ears, but the cat surprised him by quickly batting his hand away.

"A pussycat, huh? Seems he's got an artistic temperament."

"The truth is, he's just a lazy, neutered ex-tom who hasn't been out of the house since the day we brought him home. Just wants to eat and sleep and be left alone." He placed the cat back on the chair and, pretending he didn't want the animal to hear what he was about to say, put a hand on Jimmy's shoulder and spoke directly into his ear. "I wouldn't want this to get around—he's very vindictive and can be as petty as the next cat—but I had to write almost all of those books myself. He was damn near useless. And of course he became just impossible to live with when the first one got such good reviews. No more cold milk, won't eat tuna unless it's presented *à la salade niçoise*." He rolled his eyes in mock disgust and Jimmy chuckled. "Time was he simply said '*meow, meow, meow*.' Now it's nothing but '*me, me, me*.'"

"First book? Is there another?"

"Haven't I told you? Yes, Christopher has a new book coming out next year. *My Lives and How I Lost Them*. Something of an autobiography intended to correct the misconception that it's only a fable cats have nine lives. As told to yours truly, naturally."

Jimmy forced a wide smile. In truth, he didn't particularly like *The Lost Zoo*. Mr. Cullen had once confided that he'd written it after years of hearing his students say they couldn't understand any of his poems, and he couldn't possibly let him down by admitting that he hadn't found it as charming as he was meant to. Indeed, he thought it rather flat and ordinary. More troubling, he couldn't reconcile the intense, famous young Countee Cullen who had dared to wonder what kind of insane God would *"make a poet black and bid him sing"* with the middle-aged schoolteacher standing before him, a roly-poly man who preferred to spend his energy signing a cat's name to children's doggerel about imaginary animals left behind by Noah's Ark. It was best to simply change the subject. "Are you working on anything else?" he asked hopefully.

"Arna Bontemps and I are adapting his book into a musical, *St. Louis Blues*."

This was more to Jimmy's liking and a good deal more encouraging. Cullen and Bontemps had been friends since their Harlem days, and he was certain the project would prove a good deal more dignified and appropriate. "A musical? It must be fun to try your hand as a lyricist."

"We're not working on the lyrics or music, just the book. Harold Arlen and Johnny Mercer are handling the songs."

Jimmy was dumbfounded. He thought himself rather sophisticated when it came to the inner workings of the theater. Why would someone hire a great poet to work on a musical and not have him write the lyrics?

"I'm enjoying collaborating with Arna," Cullen said. He tilted his head toward the settee and gave a self-deprecating shrug. "I guess it's a lot healthier than writing with the cat."

Jimmy giggled. "I'll bet that you have a lot to talk about. You and Mr. Bontemps, of course. Did you spend a lot of time together back then?"

"You mean during the Harlem Renaissance?" Cullen intoned the words with mock gravity. "That's what they're calling it now, right?"

"You say that like it was nothing."

"Oh, it certainly wasn't nothing. It was every bit as vibrant and exciting as you imagine. I just . . . look, it was a great time and I'm glad to have been part of it. But it wasn't Shangri-la on the Harlem River. Some of it was embarrassingly pretentious and misguided. And I never want to overlook the fact that there's also this moment, this life, being a teacher—I've been teaching French and English at PS 139 for ten years and that's much longer than I was a columnist for *The Crisis*. I guess I'm saying that it's all good, that it's all important." He could tell his answer was disappointing Jimmy, that the boy was too young to really understand. He tried again. "Do you know what the Harlem Renaissance did for me? It gave me something poets almost never get: a moment in the sun, a moment when I had everyone's attention. It wasn't anything I created—I was lucky enough to happen along just when the literati were desperately searching for a bright black boy. No poet can expect the world to be waiting for him—I've spent the rest of my life trying to remember that. And I've succeeded. You know, Jimmy, with or without the world's ear, I'll never stop being a poet, never stop writing."

"But you're writing children's books—and sharing authorship with a cat, to boot! Doesn't that make you angry?"

Cullen laughed. "Why should it? You might not like *The Lost Zoo*, but most of my students do and that's who it was written for." He could see Jimmy was embarrassed at having his feelings so easily guessed. "Don't worry, that's not all I write. I've got almost enough good new poems to fill a volume. Maybe you'd like to read some of them after dinner."

"I'd be honored. God, I'm an awful guest! You invite me to holiday dinner and I talk like—like I don't know what. I guess because I didn't live through that time I feel as if I've shown up at some fabulous parade just in time to watch the last float go by. Harlem has been terrible since the war started—it feels . . . angry and desperate and combustible and awful. All these incredible paintings on your wall glow—it just seems like everyone was more alive then and they needed brighter colors to paint their world."

Cullen wagged a finger. "You've fallen into the trap. Just about every one of these artists is still alive, still painting. Can you tell me which of these paintings were done in Harlem in 1928? Or in Paris in 1932? Or in

South Carolina or Florida five years ago? Or just last month in a West-chester studio overlooking the Hudson River? We had the world's atten-tion, and it gave us focus and the courage to take ourselves seriously. Now that that unique moment is gone and things are back to normal, it's up to every artist to keep that faith on his own. That's what the legacy of the Renaissance means to me."

Jimmy nodded thoughtfully. "Why do you suppose it ended?"

"The crash. We didn't think so at the time—the energy was high and we were running on a lot of momentum so it really took a while before we realized the money tap had been shut off. But that was really it. When the market tanked, the white folks went back downtown. And I don't just mean the nightlife, although no one really had the money for clubbing anymore; I mean *they went back downtown.* A lot of artists depended on white patrons, and even if you didn't there just wasn't as much work or as many places to write. Of course, it wasn't just white money. Does the name Casper Holstein mean anything to you?"

"Wasn't he a gangster?"

"The king of the Harlem numbers rackets. At least until Dutch Schultz kidnapped him and muscled in. Yeah, Holstein used to get the number every day indexing the race results. If you had that number—hey, you hit. The black penny game, that's what they called it."

"It's still around," Jimmy said, although he didn't tell Mr. Cullen about his friend.

"Oh, I know. But Holstein was an unusual fellow—from the Dutch West Indies and something of a Robin Hood. He used to send a lot of money back home, especially when there was a storm or some other calamity. And he underwrote an annual poetry prize with a two-thou-sand-dollar first prize."

Jimmy smiled conspiratorially. "What did you do with the money?"

Cullen waved dismissively. "I wrote." But he couldn't suppress his grin. "Of course, whenever I looked out the window over my desk I saw Paris. Which reminds me—I want to show you something. Grab your jacket."

Cullen led him through the kitchen, where Ida was spreading orange icing on a large angel-food cake, and out a back door into a small yard. There was a tiny patch of lawn close by the house and stone walkways wending through carefully planned beds which, although already cleaned out for winter, were well tended and ambitious. Jimmy also noticed a tiny slate patio with a wooden lawn chair piled with a large mound of blankets in a sunny corner by the driveway. At the back edge of the yard stood a whitewashed stone wall. Directly in front of the wall was a row of four pear trees, each pruned flat like an extended candelabra with six arms. From the way Cullen was smiling and watching him it was obvious that this was what he wanted Jimmy to see.

The boy looked hard at the shaped trees. "Good Lord!" he exclaimed. "They're attached! The lower branches are contiguous!"

Cullen laughed. "Fantastic, isn't it? That's espalier, a medieval technique that's still popular in France. It was originally developed to grow fruit trees in the limited space of a walled garden. Also, by growing them flat against the warm southern garden wall it was possible to extend the range of many trees north where the seasons were short. I'm sure pruning to maximize the exposure of the branches to sunlight helped as well. Now, of course, it's done for ornamental reasons and that's what I love about it. Who but the French would raise something so practical to an art? This particular design is called a palmette verrier espalier."

Jimmy walked over to the trees. He saw wires had been used to train the branches to travel horizontally before turning up at ninety-degree angles into upraised arms. He was particularly impressed by the symmetry of the four separate trees, which had been painstakingly pruned and directed to assure that each one's six branches sprouted at almost exactly the same height on each tree. The coup de grace was the way the bottom branches of each tree had been grafted to a neighbor, forming one living wall with four trunks. He shook his head and looked at Mr. Cullen, who was clearly delighted to see Jimmy nonplussed. "It must be an incredible amount of work."

"You have to be attentive, yes. But serving beauty isn't work."

"What a load of junk! What kind of nonsense are you filling that boy's head with?"

The voice was muffled and Jimmy thought it came from the kitchen until he saw the mound of blankets on the wooden lounge chair shift. An arm appeared from under the blankets and the whole pile heaved forward as it grabbed on to the side of the chair for leverage. Twisting under the weight of the blankets, a torso pushed its way forward and sat up. Whoever it was was still covered with a mustard-yellow blanket and reminded Jimmy of a ghost in a Little Rascals short.

"You sure do like to hear yourself talk, Countee. And runnin' on about Espalier like he was a tree instead of a singer. It's a miracle any of your students can still talk let alone think when you get done with them."

The arm pulled the blanket forward, revealing an old, wiry man incongruously dressed in a thick, regal blue angora sweater and a floppy red wool knit woman's hat with a big yellow flower crocheted onto the front. He pointed at the hedge. "You're not Espalier! Espalier is the great champion of *chansons françaises!*" He spread his arms and began to sing.

If the nightingale
could sing like you
they'd sing much sweeter
than they do
For you've brought a new kind of love
To me . . .

"That's Chevalier, Pop—not espalier."

"Ce n'est pas la même chose?"

"I don't think he gets the joke, Pop."

"The Marx Brothers," said Jimmy. "*Monkey Business.*" He stared warily at the old man in the woman's hat, not sure what to make of him.

"That's the ticket, young man! Don't let this fellow snow you. *'Beauty isn't work.'* Not work? Take it from me, being beautiful is lots of work! Tons of work! A life's work!"

"Yeah, Pop," said Cullen. "We love your hat."

The old man put a hand to the hat and turned sheepish. "Forgot all about that!" He took it off quickly and waved it at Jimmy. "It's Ida's. Thought I'd take a little snooze out here in the sun and it was the warmest cap I could find. Don't worry, young man—I'm not crazy." He looked at his son. "*Yet.*"

"Yet? You've been crazy your whole life!" Cullen managed not to break up for another couple of seconds. "Jimmy, this is my father, Reverend Cullen. But you've probably surmised that from his contemplative, spiritual manner."

Reverend Cullen waved a hand. "Don't listen to him—I'm just trying to keep the boy in line. Lord knows someone has to." He extended a hand in greeting. "Frederick Cullen."

"Jimmy Baldwin."

"Pleasure."

Jimmy shook his hand and smiled although he couldn't help thinking about the stories he'd heard. Worse, he had the feeling that Reverend Cullen knew what he was thinking. He wasn't sure about the way the old man was smiling at him. Was he just being friendly or was that bemusement in his eyes? He suddenly wanted a cigarette and reached into his inside jacket pocket for the Chesterfields.

"Mind?" he asked the Cullens, holding up the pack.

"Knock yourself out," said Mr. Cullen. "Just don't throw the butt in the garden. And don't smoke in the house—it makes Duane sneeze."

"Who's Duane?"

"My step-granddaughter. She's been napping but she'll be down for dinner."

"You've got a crowd even without a guest," Jimmy said.

"Wish it was just *a* guest," said Reverend Cullen.

"Come on, Pop."

"What?"

"Mrs. Morrison is a lonely old woman."

"It's no wonder the way she talks. I never heard so much nonsense in my whole life. And I mean never."

"Pop, please. Let her have a nice Thanksgiving."

"Oh, you know I'll behave. But I don't have to pretend to like her, do I?"

They were quiet for a moment, both eyeing each other. "Our neighbor," Cullen finally said to Jimmy. "She's a widow and her sons are in the Navy. The least we can do is have her over for Thanksgiving."

"Oh, I don't know if it's the *least* we can do. Admit it, Countee—you don't even like her yourself."

"Enough!" He smiled uneasily. "You're being ridiculous. Of course I like her. Besides, what's Jimmy going to think? He'll be wondering the whole way home what we're saying about *him* behind his back."

"Aw, that's not true," said Reverend Cullen. "Don't worry, young man. I like you well enough to cuss you to your face!" He glanced down the driveway toward the street. "Uh-oh. Speak of the devil. Here she comes now." He slumped back down in the chair, grabbed the yellow blanket and pretended to be asleep just as Mrs. Morrison's high heels carefully picked their way up the gravel driveway. She was a large white woman, matronly but not heavy and a bit dressier than Jimmy had expected a widow with sons in the service to be. Her hair was cut fairly short and dyed a lustrous black. She wore pointy, green-framed eyeglasses on a chain and was clearly primped for the holiday in a tan suit with a cameo broach pinned to the jacket and a fox stole over her shoulders. She carried a bakery box tied with string in one hand. Jimmy immediately lifted his left foot and stubbed the cigarette out against his heel, pocketing the butt.

"Good afternoon, gentlemen!" The greeting was delivered with an exaggerated, melodious lilt, as if Mrs. Morrison were on the verge of singing the words. "You don't have to stop smoking on my account, young man. Don't smoke myself, but I just love the smell. Reminds me of when my house was full." She smiled sadly. "You must be a Cullen."

"No, ma'am. But I wish I was."

"This is one of my former students, Jimmy. We reconnected last year when he interviewed me for his high school newspaper. He's working in a defense plant now."

"Isn't that marvelous?" She extended a hand. "I'm Mrs. Morrison."

"Yes, ma'am. Delighted to meet you." He could smell that his hand, which had been in the pocket with the cigarette butt, reeked of tobacco; he felt dirty and was embarrassed.

"Can I take your package, Mrs. Morrison?" Cullen asked.

"Oh, that's all right, Countee. I'll take it in to Ida."

"Well, she'll be furious if I let you come in through the back door. Let's walk around to the front." He reached into his back pocket and took out a pair of gardening shears, which he handed to Jimmy. "Why don't you check the espalier for stray buds and see if there are any ripe pears to put on the table?"

"I'm looking forward to hearing all about your job during dinner," Mrs. Morrison said. She turned and walked up the driveway toward the front. Without turning around, she added: "Don't think I didn't see you pretending to be asleep, Reverend." She leaned conspiratorially toward Countee, who laughed.

Reverend Cullen pulled the blanket up around his chin. He didn't speak until he heard the front door open and close. "Catch that?" he asked Jimmy, the twinkle in his eye replaced by a steely gaze. "That man is one of the most celebrated poets of his day, a Guggenheim recipient. But she's 'Mrs. Morrison' and he's 'Countee.'"

"Does it bother him? Do you think he even noticed?"

"It's part of a writer's business to notice. Do you think he's a good writer?"

"He's a great writer."

The old man shrugged. "Then I guess he noticed."

Jimmy began examining the pear branches. He'd never actually seen fruit growing on a tree before. What was left this late into the autumn proved slim—hard, immature fruits that would never ripen before the frost set in, and Jimmy found only a few pears suitable for picking. "Do you think Mrs. Morrison actually reads poetry?" he asked over his shoulder. "Not many people do. Perhaps she's not really familiar with Mr. Cullen's work."

"Don't you read poetry?"

"Sure."

"So do I. Oh, she knows who he is, all right. There was an interview with Countee on the front page of the Yonkers newspaper when we moved in. She came over and introduced herself the next day."

"But you have to admit that Mr. Cullen is pretty low-key. I mean, considering all he's done." Jimmy turned to face Reverend Cullen. "I wish I was around then. But he acts like it never happened."

The old man snorted. "It happened."

"You officiated at the wedding."

Reverend Cullen looked at him for a long minute then nodded. "Yep. And at the one that mattered."

"You think I'm shallow. Starstruck."

"No. No, I think you're a bright young man who's trying to figure something out."

"Why would an artist want to be overlooked?"

"That's not what he wants—not at all. But what he had wasn't what he wanted, either."

"What do you mean?"

"Countee never wanted to be a Negro poet. He is a poet. He has more in common with Edna St. Vincent Millay and Edward Arlington Robinson and Keats, all of whom he adores, than he does with Langston Hughes. But you'll never convince the world of that."

"But what of all the powerful poems he's written about race and racism like *Color* or *Yet Do I Marvel* or *Incident*?"

"What do you expect him to write about? The tea parties he attended at Harvard? I mean, he went to them—is that what he should write about?" The old man chuckled. "Look, Langston Hughes set out to be the poet of his race. But Countee certainly didn't. He always tried to write about love and death, which are the things most worth writing about. He's written dozens of memories and threnodies. He takes life as he finds it and writes. As for those 'race' poems you mention, well, it just so happens that his life is . . . colored by color."

Jimmy nodded and lit another cigarette. He took a few drags and waved at the yard. "I don't know what to make of this. It's like he's buried himself out here. And not just here, but . . . don't misunderstand me, Reverend. I'm grateful that Mr. Cullen was my teacher. He's changed my life. But a junior high school teacher! No offense, but most junior high school teachers are idiots, second-rate civil servants trying to put in enough time for a pension. Why?"

Reverend Cullen smiled. "Don't you think you've answered your own question?"

Jimmy smiled and bobbed his head, a cloud of smoke enveloping him and then dissipating. "Yeah, I guess."

"Plus, a very good friend of Countee's was a junior high school teacher."

"Harold Jackman?"

The old man gave him an odd look—Jimmy couldn't tell if it was new-found appreciation or apprehension. "Do you know him?"

"No. I've heard he was quite the roué. A real Harlem legend."

"Oh, he is that. And a good deal more. He can be full of the devil."

"And a schoolteacher in the bargain. Are they still in contact?"

"We'd better go in. I need to change for dinner. I'd be taking my life into my hands sitting down at Ida's table for holiday dinner without a tie."

In the dining room, the long wooden table was already set with holi-day china and a sideboard held the orange-iced cake Jimmy had seen Mrs. Cullen preparing. To the left of the cake stood an uncorked bottle of red wine and Mr. Cullen, seated in a chair with Christopher cradled in one arm and a small girl on his lap wearing a white party dress with red rib-bons in her hair whom Jimmy took to be Duane, motioned for him to help himself. Jimmy wasn't normally one for wine, although he knew the beverages the boys on his neighborhood stoops favored had little in com-mon with whatever was in the dark, slender French bottle. He read the la-bel, making a note of the name, and poured a glass. It wasn't sweet—in fact, it was a little acidic and gave him an odd tingle in his cheeks toward the top of his mouth. He wasn't sure he liked it, although he had the im-mediate thought that it would pair well with a cigarette and had to fight the urge to light up.

"Did you see that beautiful fox stole that Mrs. Morrison was wear-ing?" Cullen was asking the little girl. She nodded seriously. "Is it alive?" She shook her head. "That's right, Button, it's not alive. But did you know that Grandma is the only woman with a live fur wrap? It's true! Some-times, when she has a very fancy party or dinner to attend, she'll call Christopher up to her bedroom and when she's all done putting on her dress and makeup and fixing her hair and putting on her long, golden ear-rings, she'll say, 'Come, Christopher! Let's go to the party!' And Christo-pher will climb right onto her shoulders and curl around her neck. And of course, everyone can see that Christopher is a real, live cat and all the ladies are just beside themselves with admiration and envy at such a beau-tiful and well-behaved cat. Isn't that right, Christopher?" He held the cat's muzzle up to his face and nuzzled him, then brushed his whiskers across the little girl's nose to make her giggle.

The kitchen door swung open. Mrs. Cullen emerged carrying a bowl of soup in each hand; she was followed by her daughter and Mrs. Morrison, also with bowls. "Oh, Countee! Please don't bring that cat to the table! Are we all here? Where's Dad? Is he still sleeping out back?"

Cullen shook his head and pointed upstairs. "Just cleaning up. He'll be down in a minute." He put the cat on the floor and looked at Duane. "Are you ready for a bowl of Grandma's famous split pea soup?"

She shook her head and wriggled her nose. "I don't like peas."

"I want you to try a little," said her mother. "Did you touch Christopher?"

She nodded solemnly.

"Then go wash your hands again."

Countee stole a glance at his wife. "Well?" she asked. "What are you waiting for?" He got up and followed Duane. She shook her head. "Enough with the cat," she muttered. Then, as if rediscovering Jimmy, she looked him up and down. "What about you, young man? Have you been messing with that cat?"

"No, ma'am."

"And how does your mother feel about you smoking and drinking?"

"To tell you the truth, I don't recall her saying anything to me one way or the other unless it was to warn me not to steal her cigarettes." He smiled. "I'm not really much of a drinker. Although I'm beginning to suspect I haven't had the opportunity to taste anything worth drinking. I must say I kind of like this wine."

"That will make Countee happy. I'm sure he brought this bottle out for your benefit. It's from his dwindling stock downstairs."

It hadn't occurred to Jimmy that the war must have made the wine precious, and he looked ruefully into his glass. "It's wasted on me. Who knows when Mr. Cullen will be able to procure more?"

"Don't be silly—he's delighted to share it with you. And as for wartime sacrifices, going without your favorite margaux hardly qualifies, does it?"

"No, ma'am. I suppose not."

Reverend Cullen could be heard clopping down the stairs just as Countee and Duane returned. "Oh, good," said Ida. "Come on, everyone! The soup is getting cold." Cullen stood behind his chair at the head of the table, while his father gravitated to the opposite chair. "Mrs. Morrison, why don't you sit on Countee's left, and I'll sit on this side so I can be near the kitchen." Jimmy took the seat on Reverend Cullen's right, opposite from Mrs. Nimmons and Duane, and they all sat. "Dad, are you ready to say grace?"

"I think I'll leave that to our young guest. Excuse me," he quickly added, looking at Mrs. Morrison, "our *younger* guest." She smiled appreciatively and nodded. "He's a preacher, too, you know."

"No," Jimmy said quickly. He didn't want to have to explain how he'd lost his faith and why he hadn't set foot in church in nearly a year. Instead, he said, "Reverend, I couldn't possibly presume to preach in your presence any more than I would dare recite poetry in your son's. And please— I never had the chance to hear you in the pulpit at Salem."

The old man looked at him as if weighing his response, then bowed his head and folded his hands.

"Dear Lord," Reverend Cullen said. "This is the day we set aside to give thanks for your bounty. Sitting here, safe and secure in our nice home with this marvelous meal we're about to enjoy, surrounded by friends and family, we know how truly blessed we are. Every year we give thanks, and every year the changing season spurs us to ask that you help us to change the things in this world that need changing. And as always, we ask that you look over us. But this year we also ask your special blessing on our loved ones so far away. Help them pursue justice and bring peace to this world and keep them from harm as we keep them always in our thoughts and prayers. Amen."

"Amen."

"Thank you, Reverend," said Mrs. Morrison. "You know, I could just about die with pride for my boys, but it's so hard to be having Thanksgiving without them. So thank you for those words. And thank you for inviting me."

"It's our pleasure," said Countee. "Are you ready for a little wine, Mrs. Morrison?"

"You know, I think I am, thank you." She turned and looked down the table. "Jimmy, are you really a preacher?"

"I was, yes."

"How old were you when you started preaching?"

"Thirteen. My father—my stepfather, really—is a Pentecostal preacher."

"And a very fine one, too," said Reverend Cullen. "I've heard him preach a number of times—got that burning spirit." He smiled slyly at Jimmy. "As I recall, he has a special passion for preaching Revelations."

"When he's even got a church," Jimmy grumbled, embarrassed that Reverend Cullen had heard his father. "Which he hasn't for some time."

"Don't need a church to have a congregation and you don't need a congregation if you can touch a heart and mend a soul. Jesus never had a church or a congregation. He had disciples, though."

"I assure you, my father doesn't have any disciples."

"No? You followed in his path to the pulpit."

Jimmy shuddered. "I don't preach anymore. I don't feel the spirit."

"Oh, don't say that!" said Mrs. Morrison. "It sounds awful to hear someone so young say they've lost their faith!"

"To be honest, ma'am, I'm not sure now that I ever really had it."

"But surely you must have if you were able to preach."

"I don't know. I wonder if instead of the spirit I wasn't filled with a desire to deny some truths about myself—to hide in the Church and God and the physical release of holy rolling rather than look in the mirror."

"But you can't mean that! You're simply too young to say such things!"

"I often wonder these days if youth isn't a more natural companion for insight than maturity," said Countee. "The older I get, the less I can see beyond what my heart desires."

"And what's that, Mr. Cullen?" asked Jimmy.

"Another glass of wine. Can't carve the turkey without it."

"I'll bring it out," Ida said. She rose and collected the soup bowls, motioning for Mrs. Morrison to remain when she made a move to assist. "You stay put. Have you had any letters from your boys lately?"

"Not in a couple of weeks." She did a poor job of sounding casual. "And of course, the letters I do receive have very little in the way of real information. I don't even know where they are, although the tone of one of Bobby's last letters led me to believe he hadn't been far from the action at Midway. Is it awful for me to say that I hope they're stationed somewhere out of harm's way?"

316

"Certainly not," said Cullen. "Although I doubt any place is really out of harm's way. Look at this ridiculous riot they had yesterday between Australian and American servicemen."

"Where?" asked Jimmy.

"Australia."

"Over what?"

"Near as I can tell? Women."

"Now *there's* something worth fighting about!" said Reverend Cullen.

"No, seriously, Pop! MacArthur's headquarters are in Brisbane, and there's a huge contingent of American servicemen stationed there. Apparently the Americans are paid about six times what the Australian soldiers and sailors receive, and the local girls only want to go with the Yanks!"

Reverend Cullen laughed. "This is a story as old as war. You've got to admit, though, it's a damn site funnier than what's happening in France."

Cullen nodded. "Has there been anything more on the radio regarding Toulon?"

"Not that I've heard."

"What's going on in France?" asked Mrs. Morrison.

"The Nazis have most of the French fleet bottled up in Toulon," said Cullen. The table was silent. He sighed. "Well, we can at least thank God that we pretty much know where ours are and that they're all right."

"Yes," said Mrs. Morrison. She turned to Ida's daughter. "Where's your husband, dear? Have you heard from him?"

"Not lately," Mrs. Nimmons said, "although he sends Duane a postcard every week. He's stationed in North Carolina."

"Camp Lejeune," said Reverend Cullen.

"The marines?" asked Mrs. Morrison.

"Yes."

"You know, I'm not sure I've ever seen a Negro marine."

Ida came back through the swinging kitchen door carrying a large turkey on a scalloped white serving platter. Cullen rose and took it from her and placed it by his seat for carving.

"That's because there haven't been any," Reverend Cullen said. "Arthur is one of the first. They finally inducted about three hundred of 'em back in August as a result of 8802. Fifty-first Battalion."

"Well, that's marvelous! A battalion of Negro marines! That should scare the daylights out of Tojo!"

"Probably not as much as it would scare you and your two little navy peckerwoods," Reverend Cullen mumbled, just loud enough for Jimmy to hear.

"Excuse me, did you say something, Reverend?"

"Oh, just that you never know what's gonna peak out of the woods, Mrs. Morrison."

Cullen paused in his carving and shot his father a deadly look, but Reverend Cullen returned it with his sunniest smile. "Just dark meat for me, son. That white stuff is too dry. You know how it makes me choke. Jimmy, why don't you get the wine off the sideboard and pour a little more for Mrs. Morrison and Mrs. Nimmons?"

"Oh, that would be lovely," said Mrs. Morrison. "Thank you, Jimmy. Tell me, Reverend, what's this 8802 you mentioned?"

Instead, Jimmy, who was leaning in to refill her glass, answered. "An executive order signed by President Roosevelt forbidding discrimination in the war effort." Jimmy sighed, but Mrs. Morrison didn't notice. He was thinking about the grief he took every day as the only Negro on the line at his defense plant job in New Jersey. Ostracized? The stupid crackers wouldn't even sell him lunch in the cafeteria! They'd tried to get rid of him twice already and it was only a matter of time before they made it stick. "I understand 8802 hasn't been particularly welcomed by the military brass."

Mrs. Nimmons snorted.

"What's the matter, dear?" asked Mrs. Morrison.

"As soon as he completed basic, Arthur began training as a noncom. He joined the marines because it's the toughest outfit they have going and he wants to fight. But I'm not sure that's ever going to happen."

"What do you mean?"

"Well, obviously there are no Negro officers. And with the exception of one master sergeant who came over from the navy, all the drill instructors at Lejeune are white. That means the commissioned and non-commissioned officers are all white, and the soldiers in the battalion are Negro. Arthur said a lot of the DI's made it clear they weren't happy about training Negroes. You can imagine the tension."

318

"Oh, how awful!"

"So what the marines need most are Negro drill instructors. And that's what they've got Arthur training for."

"Well, what's wrong with that?"

She sighed. "For starters it means he'll probably never see combat—although there's already a rumor that the 51st is never getting combat designation, anyway—because he'll always be Stateside doing basic training."

"Oh, honey—you should be glad! Arthur couldn't have a better posting during the war than Camp Lejeune!"

"Really?" Her voice had turned noticeably icy. "You know, it's bad enough that these men come and say they are ready to die for their country and are told in return that the best way they can serve the Marine Corps is as stevedores and stewards. And of course, Arthur is being trained specifically to be a drill sergeant for Negro marines—if he turns out to be the greatest DI in the history of the corps, he will never instruct a white marine. Do you know that he's not even free to come and go on the base? The 51st is barracked separately at Montford Point, and no Negro can set foot anywhere else in Camp Lejeune unless accompanied by a white marine."

In the uncomfortable silence that followed, Reverend Cullen watched his son with amusement, waiting to see how he would handle it. Finally, Countee shook his head and began to laugh. "Look at it this way, hon," he said to his stepdaughter. "Camp Lejeune is probably the only place in North Carolina where whites *want* Negroes walking with them." Even Reverend Cullen laughed, and Countee didn't miss the opportunity to steer the conversation back to the mundane. "That's about it for this turkey—I think we can eat as soon as Ida brings out the other dishes."

"You look to have a real talent for carving that bird, Countee," said Mrs. Morrison. "I don't think there's a mouthful of meat left on that frame!"

"Thank you."

"No, really! I haven't seen a carving job like that in I don't know how long! It reminds me of one time when I was a little girl, taking the train with my father to Chicago. He ordered fish for me in the dining car and when they brought it to the table, it had been prepared whole—head and all! Well, of course, I was very young and didn't know what in the world to do with it. And this nice Negro waiter carved it for me. He did such a beautiful job—you would have thought he was a surgeon! Can you imagine that? Oh, he did such a marvelous job—I didn't find a single bone in my dinner!" Cullen smiled blandly and Mrs. Morrison plowed on. "I'm so looking forward to Ida's meal! I've had her apple pie and it's just luscious! She's a good cook, isn't she?"

"Excellent."

"Oh, I knew it! The best cook was my aunt's maid, Bitsy. They lived in Baltimore and I used to look forward to visiting just for those meals. Have you ever been to Baltimore, Countee?"

The table was suddenly very quiet. Mrs. Nimmons and Mrs. Cullen seemed simultaneously to put down their forks and gaze into their laps.

Jimmy was thunderstruck. He stared at Cullen who, guessing what the boy was about to say, shook his head and closed his eyes. "Yes, Mrs. Morrison—I've been to Baltimore," Cullen said. "I don't think I know Bitsy, though."

Reverend Cullen drew in a sharp breath as if he'd been hit in the gut, and Jimmy turned and looked at him. The Reverend's face was contorted and one of his eyes was twitching. He looked for all the world as if he were about to howl or stamp out of the room or bury his face in his hands and weep, and it scared Jimmy. It scared him because he looked like no one so much as his own father.

"Bitsy?" asked Mrs. Morrison. "Of course I don't imagine you know Bitsy . . . Oh, my goodness! Countee, I've insulted you somehow, haven't I?"

Cullen looked at his father, then shook his head. "Not at all. Ida, why don't you pass the sweet potatoes and string beans."

The rest of the meal was eaten without incident, although Duane proved impervious to all entreaties to eat anything other than dinner rolls, and Reverend Cullen was unable to keep from nudging Jimmy under the table nearly every time Mrs. Morrison spoke. When Ida and her daughter rose to clear the table for dessert and to make coffee, Jimmy excused himself, following them into the kitchen and out through the back door and into the yard for a cigarette. The cat slipped out with him, tearing off for a patch of garden where Jimmy assumed Mr. Cullen had grown catnip.

He lit a cigarette and sucked the smoke down hard. Reverend Cullen had been right, of course, he thought, exhaling. She was a stupid woman who hadn't bothered to read any of his poems. The ignorance of whites never surprised him—growing up he'd felt sorry for them. But that had begun to change when he went to work in the factory. He had always detested the obvious bigots in their evil and small-minded stupidity; now he was less patient of those like Mrs. Morrison who craved the sleepwalk of sweet ignorance—all the nice white people who'd never dream of calling anyone a nigger and were quite certain that was more than enough. Well, what about *his* hate? Did he deserve this pain and anger? To hope the world is a decent place and therefore feel it must hate him for a *reason*? That was the worst of it, he thought as he took another drag, the cigarette tip glowing hot in his cupped palm. The bitter, ever-present bile of self-hate. That's what the Mrs. Morrisons of the world were guilty of fostering when they twittered and pretended that everything was a-okay. He wasn't willing to forgive them anymore, not after what he'd seen on Reverend Cullen's face. He'd seen much more than anger: he'd seen the gut-tearing deep down self-loathing of a black father who knows he has proven impotent in failing to prepare and protect the person he loves most in the world, who sees only too clearly that everything he had to give—every lesson, every encouragement, every prayer, *everything*—could not spare his beautiful son the poisonous birthright of undeserved anger and pain that he inherited with his father's skin. Jimmy took one last drag and ground his cigarette out angrily, forgetting to pick it up.

And what of Mr. Cullen? Jimmy looked at the stripped-down back-yard in the late-November afternoon light. Was that what he was doing out here? Hiding? Was that why he preferred to deal fairy tales instead of thunder? Was it too hard? Too much? Or had he figured something out—something to keep the poison away? He looked at the half-frozen ground and suddenly thought of one of Mr. Cullen's couplets:

Let me be lavish with my tears,
And dream that false is true,

Though wisdom cometh with the years,
The barren days come, too.

When Jimmy returned to the dining room, the cake was in the center of the table and neither Duane nor Mrs. Morrison seemed able to take their eyes off it. Jimmy came up behind Duane's chair and leaned over the girl, as if helping her reconnoiter the cake.

"Think you can eat all of that?"

She tilted her head back, examining and assessing the cake's size. She shook her head.

Cullen laughed. "Forget the bellyache—she'd have a fight on her hands. That's my cake."

"Yours?" asked Mrs. Morrison.

He nodded. "Ida and I met at a party where they served a layer cake with orange icing. She usually just makes it on our anniversary."

"Well, isn't that sweet! Where did you meet?"

"At the home of a friend of mine named A'Lelia Walker. She was something of a famous hostess in Harlem. Perhaps you've heard of her mother, Madame C. J. Walker."

"Of course! The woman who trained all the Negro beauticians! She was very wealthy!"

"Yes, that's right. She made a fortune in beauty and hair-care products—enough to make her the first self-made female millionaire, Negro or white. And part of it came from teaching other women how to operate their own beauty parlors. But A'Lelia had none of her mother's discipline, and her sole ambition was to give the best parties in town. Which, I must in all fairness say, was a goal she attained."

"The Dark Tower," said Jimmy.

"Yes. The Dark Tower." Cullen looked at Mrs. Morrison and smiled. "That's what she called the literary salon she held in her mother's Harlem townhouse. Well, at least it had pretensions to being a literary salon. It was really an excuse for her to throw parties."

"My son is too modest to tell you where the name came from," Reverend Cullen said. "It was the column he wrote in *Opportunity*."

"Really? Isn't that marvelous!" Mrs. Morrison smiled, and Jimmy knew she was doing her level best to look appropriately impressed while having no idea what *Opportunity* was. He gave her a thin, impatient smile.

"Now that woman knew how to set a table," said Reverend Cullen. He grinned playfully.

"What do you mean, Reverend?" Mrs. Morrison asked.

The Reverend leaned back in his chair and for a second Jimmy saw what he must have looked like in the moments before he preached a Sunday sermon to a full house at the Salem Methodist Episcopal Church. "She had one party—her black and white party, I think they called it—where she invited all the folks and patrons from downtown to a formal affair with the folks and artists from uptown. You know, there was quite a vogue for Harlem back then. Negro music. Negro dancers. Negro women. Negro poets. It was all . . . exotic. In any event, Miss Walker had this one particular party where she served champagne and caviar—but only to the Negro guests. All the white people could get was chitterlings and hog maws. That one broke up kind of early, didn't it, Countee?"

Mrs. Morrison wrinkled her noise. "I think I'd rather eat this cake."

Cullen laughed. "I'm with you."

"I've always wondered where the Dark Tower was," Jimmy said.

"Just a couple of blocks from the school. But it's not there anymore—they tore Mrs. Walker's houses down to build the new public library at West 136th Street."

"But I go there all the time!" He didn't mention that he had recently researched Mr. Cullen's first marriage in its stacks. "I can't believe it's gone!"

"Believe me, it's a better use of the space."

"What became of Miss Walker?"

"She's still around—lives up here in Westchester now. We see her from time to time."

"Who are you talking about, dear?" Ida had returned from the kitchen.

"A'Lelia."

"Oh. Yes, she introduced us," she said to Jimmy. Then, turning to Cullen, she added somewhat wearily: "The giblets are ready."

He smiled. "Thank you. Time for Christopher's Thanksgiving." He rose and went out to the kitchen. Mrs. Morrison and Duane were heartbroken, seeing they'd have to wait for cake. Mrs. Cullen just looked annoyed.

"I don't know what would have happened to him without us," Ida said. She held two fingers up. "He was that close to becoming one of those people who can only talk to their pets." She shook her head. "Sometimes I still wouldn't mind seeing America's newest feline literary star doing an extended book signing down at the Yonkers' pound."

"*Chris, Chris,*" Cullen called from the kitchen. "*Where's the puss? Here, Christopher.*" He waited a moment. "*Here, puss.* Gee, that's odd. He always comes as soon as I put the turkey down for him."

"Oh," said Jimmy. "He went out in the yard with me before."

"*WHAT?* Cullen was back in the dining room before he'd finished saying the word. "Christopher can't go outside! He's never been outside—the old tom down the block will kill him! Oh, my God!

"I had no idea . . ."

"Ida, Dad—let's scour the block. Honey, maybe you and Duane can check the yard. Jimmy, up in my office on the third floor is a travel valise for Christopher. It might prove useful." And with that he was out the front door, not bothering with a coat.

Ida looked at Mrs. Morrison and shrugged. "I'm sorry. Hopefully this won't take more than a minute or two."

"Don't be silly. I'm right behind you."

"What have I done?" Jimmy asked Reverend Cullen. "This is terrible!"

Reverend Cullen stood and put a hand on his shoulder. "Don't worry. I've got to admit, though, Ida's right. Countee is a little nuts when it comes to that damn cat. Maybe it wouldn't be such a bad thing . . ."

Jimmy was horrified.

"Ah, that cat is too lazy to get itself killed. Go see if you can find the carrier. I'll keep an eye on Countee."

Even agitated and guilt ridden, Jimmy couldn't suppress a feeling of excitement as he mounted the narrow, twisting stairs to Mr. Cullen's private study. *What's wrong with me?* he wondered as he gripped the knob.

Paradise had proved to be just like everywhere else, only with greener grass. Yet Countee Cullen, if still as vulnerable as any other dark-skinned man, seemed at peace in his tiny world. Had he found a way to live in the world, or just a way out of it? Did he win or just give up? The questions burned in Jimmy, who could feel a hate and fear of the world growing in him like a cancer and knew now that he would pay any price not to be destroyed by it like his father. If the answer was in this room, he'd find it. *I'm a guest in this man's home—have I no shame? No decency?* He pushed the door open and the voice fell silent.

It was a low attic room with sloping, uneven rooflines. There was a row of filing cabinets against one wall and a sagging old pink love seat with a floor lamp and side table against the other. Over the couch hung a charcoal portrait of an extremely handsome man signed by Richmond Barthé. Somehow he knew it was Harold Jackman. By its side was a large frame containing a prize, the Harmon Foundation's award in literature, and a copy of the work for which it was given. The poem, "Incident," was one that Jimmy knew by heart. Still, he couldn't keep from reading it.

> *Once riding in old Baltimore,*
> *Heart-filled, head-filled with glee,*
> *I saw a Baltimorean*
> *Kept looking straight at me.*
>
> *Now I was eight and very small,*
> *And he was no whit bigger,*
> *And so I smiled, but he poked out*
> *His tongue, and called me, "Nigger."*
>
> *I saw the whole of Baltimore,*
> *From May until December;*
> *Of all the things that happened there*
> *That's all that I remember.*

He sat on the couch in the dark. He saw Christopher's carrying case on top of the filing cabinets. He also saw the desk.

It was an old plain, wooden desk, exactly like the kind used by the teachers at Frederick Douglass, and it took Jimmy a moment to realize that it was probably a school castoff. It sat beneath the two small windows and was neatly arranged with a Remington typewriter, a blank notepad, and a row of framed pictures. He crossed the room for a better look. The photos were of Ida with her daughter, son-in-law, and granddaughter; Reverend Cullen and his wife with Mr. Cullen at his Harvard commencement; and an old photo of a woman whom he took to be Mr. Cullen's grandmother. He picked this picture up and the thought of touching something private, something unknown about Mr. Cullen, gave him a deliciously forbidden thrill. When he put it down, he touched the typewriter keys, closing his eyes and lightly touch-typing *Once riding in old Baltimore*. He sat down in the chair. There was nothing else to see on the desk—the pad was disappointingly fresh and unused. He couldn't resist trying the handle on the deep filing drawer. There was a large manila envelope with a string marked *Correspondence–1941*. He closed the drawer and tried the one above it. Letterhead, pads, typing paper, and carbons. The long, thin pencil-drawer remained. It was locked. With a flush of excitement and shame, he picked up a letter opener sitting by the typewriter and ran its tip in the space between the desktop and the drawer, looking for a catch. He felt something above the lock and wiggled the blade, twisting it until he felt it gouging the wood. He loosened his grip, mortified at what he was doing. He looked up and saw two eyes watching him.

"God Almighty!"

Jimmy jumped up and Christopher arched his back. The cat was on a branch of the plane tree, watching him through the window.

When his heart stopped hammering, Jimmy grabbed the travel valise and opened the window. The cat crouched, just out of reach, and Jimmy leaned across the sill. "Nice puss, good Christopher," he cooed.

On the lawn, Reverend Cullen saw Jimmy lean out of the window, saw the cat back away. "Don't do anything foolish, boy!" he called. "Wait! I'll go get a ladder!"

"Nice Christopher. Got a story you want to tell me? I'll write it down for you, just like Mr. Cullen." He climbed across the desk and put his knees up on the window, reaching out for the branch. As soon as he leaned his weight onto it, the cat shrank into a deep crouch.

"Jimmy!" It was Mr. Cullen, who had come running over and was now under the tree. "Be careful! Christopher—hold still!"

Jimmy was now almost completely out of the window, his feet alone dangling on the inside of the sill, his knees trying to balance on the flexing tree branch, his hands clawing toward the thicker part of the limb. "Good cat. Good cat. Good cat." It was a prayer now, recited for his own benefit. He barely saw Christopher, just felt the branch swaying up and down and heard his blood pounding in his ears as he lifted his feet beyond the window and put all his weight on the branch.

"Jimmy! Stop! There'll be a ladder here in a minute."

The branch held. *It held!* Jimmy caught his breath and felt a surge of confidence. He was splayed across the branch, his open jacket draping down, his tie hanging like a rope for a child's swing. "Don't worry, Mr. Cullen! I'll get him back for you!"

Jimmy pushed up from the branch, spread his knees, and sidled toward the cat, who was backed up as close as he could get to the plane tree's trunk. "Good Christopher. Good boy." He leaned toward the cat and moved to wrap a hand around his midsection.

In a flash, the cat shot across Jimmy's shoulder and down his back, pushing off in one leap for the open window. Surprised, the boy forgot himself and made a twisting lunge for the cat. The last thing he saw was Christopher's tail inside the window, the cat ambling past its valise. The ground spun up toward Jimmy in a flash.

The back of his head felt huge and his right elbow stung. They were all standing above him when he opened his eyes. Duane was looking at him with big eyes.

"Are you dead?" she asked.

"I think that's up to Mr. Cullen." He sat up and touched the back of his head. He wasn't bleeding but he felt dizzy. He looked at his host. "I'm sorry."

Cullen stared at the boy. "For what?"

"For letting your cat out. For violating your house and hospitality. For the pain, the pain. I'm so sorry. I just wanted to *know*."

"Countee," said Ida, "get this poor boy inside—he's talking gibberish. Can't you see he's hurt himself?"

Cullen leaned over and extended a hand to Jimmy. "Come on, m'boy. I think a little cognac will clear your head." He put an arm around Jimmy's waist and placed the boy's good arm around his own shoulder.

"I'm sorry. I'm sorry."

Cullen ran his hand gently across the boy's hair and spoke fiercely into his ear.

"No. Don't ever be sorry."

12

CRYING
SESSION

APRIL 6, 1947

G oddamn wine. After a lifetime of Saturday night bull sessions he should know better by now.

Vito Marcantonio put his leg up on the bowl of the commode, lifted his undershirt, and jabbed the syringe into his side, spiking the plunger with his thumb. Immediately the nausea he'd anticipated ran through him in a sickening wave. Fearing he'd retch, he clutched the enamel towel rack on the wall with one hand and placed the other on the edge of the sink. He closed his eyes briefly, then looked in the mirror of the medicine chest. His skin was sallow and felt clammy and his dark eyes were rimmed with red. No good. He turned on the cold tap and flicked the chain and plug into the basin, which quickly filled. Plunging his face into the frigid water, he felt the shock drive the sickness back down his throat and his head clear and he came up inhaling wetly, like a fish in the bottom of a boat. But he felt better—much better. He pushed his lank, wet hair back from his forehead, yanked the plug by the chain, and turned the hot water tap. Swinging the medicine chest open, he saw that his eyes were already clearer, his cheeks pink with the cold. He put the needle on the top shelf and moved on to his razor and shaving soap.

Within twenty minutes he was dressed in a clean white shirt, red cotton tie, and freshly pressed dark, three-piece suit and seated in his chair by the table in the big front window of the Fiorello H. La Guardia Political Club that looked out onto 114th Street. He scanned the stack of Sunday newspapers, searching for stories about the Scottoriggio case, and found three. The articles in the *Times* and *World Telegram* contained no new information; there was yet another unctuous editorial in the *Journal American*, this one charging that the grand jury's failure to hand up any indictments was due to a massive railroading job engineered by "a polluted pot of punks and political gangsters, some of them imported" rather than a lack of evidence. Christ, how long would this go on? They couldn't beat him in the election booth, so now they were bleeding him to death with slander! Marcantonio's mood was black when he heard his assistant, Delores, arriving from seven o'clock mass at Our Lady of Carmel, unlocking the club's front door.

"Congressman! You're getting an early start!"

"More like a late finish," he replied, grateful to have something else to think about. "I was playing cards and eating pizza in the back of Luigi Albarelli's until almost five o'clock. It didn't seem to make much sense to wake Miriam and my mother, so at that point I stopped off for the papers and came here. And who is this young man? Is this really Crescenzo?"

The boy, tall and gangly in the unique way of fifteen-year-old boys and wearing a white shirt and tie, looked down in embarrassment as his mother beamed and grabbed him by the forearm. "He won't stop growing!" She gave him a shake that made him blush that much deeper. "I hope you don't mind, but he's interested in politics. Go ahead—tell Congressman Marcantonio, Chris." She nudged the boy and he looked up and nodded.

"Yes, sir."

"Yes sir?" his mother repeated. "That's a conversation? He's only a sophomore and already the student council treasurer at Benjamin Franklin."

"Treasurer?" Marcantonio asked. "Treasurer is good. We like treasurers. How do you get along with Principal Covello?"

"Fine, sir. I'm not sure how well he knows me, though."

"Oh, believe me, he knows you. He knows every student in that school. The fact that you think he doesn't is a good sign—it means you're not on his radar." Marcantonio smiled. "He was my teacher, you know."

"Mr. Covello? He was a teacher at Franklin?"

"No! At DeWitt Clinton. There wasn't any high school in East Harlem when I grew up. Do you know who built your school? Mr. Covello and I did, that's who." He paused for a minute and looked out the window. There was a dark blue Pontiac parked across the street with two men in it, and the sight made Marcantonio frown. "So tell me, Crescenzo. Do you like being treasurer?"

The boy shrugged. "It's okay. I'd like to run for vice president next year and president when I'm a senior."

"A man with a plan. I like that! What kind of a campaigner are you?"

"Okay, I guess."

"See, that's no good. But you've come to the right place. Because as your mother can tell you, I know as much about campaigning as any man in New York City—and more than most men in Washington, even. Do you know what campaigning is?"

"Telling people what you believe and what you'll do if elected?"

"No. That's just talking. That's only the surface. If you do it right, if you really serve, then campaigning and carrying out the duties of the office are the same thing. I have been elected to work for the people of East Harlem. If I'm a strong advocate and represent their interests, they will continue to support me. No matter what anyone says, there's nothing wrong with being a politician. In fact, I do more for them than anyone and it's as honorable as any other job. Every minute that I'm working and using the power of my office, I'm campaigning. And every minute that I'm campaigning, I'm seeking to deliver the power of that office to my people. Do you want to learn how to campaign? How to *really* campaign?"

"Yes, Congressman. Definitely!"

"Good. In the room behind the kitchen are folding chairs. Bring about seventy or eighty out and set them up in rows facing this table. You'll also find a voting machine back there. Bring it out and put it against that wall. And come here a minute. Marcantonio dug into his pocket. "Here's two bucks. When you're done with the chairs and that booth, get us all coffees and bring me a quart of orange juice. And you see the two men in that blue Pontiac on the corner?" Marcantonio, who now had his back to the window, pointed his thumb casually over his shoulder. "They're detectives from District Attorney Hogan's office. Get them coffees, too. And make sure you speak to them with respect, *capice?* I don't want your mother to have to go downtown and get you out of jail." He winked at Delores.

"No, sir. Yes, sir."

In the time it took Crescenzo to handle his assignments—forty-five minutes to set up the chairs and move the voting booth, an additional twenty to pick up coffee and drop two cups with the detectives who, while somewhat taken aback, took them nonetheless without comment—the room had filled with people. The congressman's two other secretaries, a tall, stately Negro woman named Roberta whom everyone called Bobbi and an older Jewish lady named Emma, had been the next to arrive. They were followed by the lawyers, Leonard Fink and Congressman Marcantonio's partner, John Pizzo. Because it was the first Sunday in April, there were also a pair of accountants, sent over as a favor to the congressman by the Workers Alliance to help people prepare their income taxes, and they were set up at a special table at the back of the room. There were already about two dozen people seated in the front few rows waiting to see Marcantonio. Whenever someone came in, they were greeted by one of the secretaries, who wrote down their name, address, and reason for coming, and directed them to a seat. Although Crescenzo's mother spoke Italian and a little of the Spanish she'd learned since marrying his father, there was a special clerk, Manny Medina, to help Puerto Rican constituents. He, along with two other clerks, sat at the window with Marcantonio. A young Negro man was just being seated at the table when Crescenzo approached with the congressman's juice and coffee.

"What can I do for you, Mr. Williams?" Marcantonio was asking.

"Maybe you can help put an end to the runaround I'm getting from the hack bureau, Mr. Marcantonio." He pronounced it as if the congressman had two names. *Mister Mark and Tony.*

"Do you need a license?"

"Got one. I need medallions so I can put my own cabs on the street."

"What are the cops telling you?"

"That the medallions are maxed out. Now, I know it's true that there's a fixed number of medallions issued in the city. But I also know that the West Side company that sponsored me for my license gets new medallions for the asking. I got the money to buy a couple of cabs—earned it during the war driving trucks from Calais to Berlin for Uncle. And I even got a line of credit for more cabs if I can make it work. But I get the feeling that I ain't gonna see no medallions unless I grease the wheels, which is just a load of BS, if you'll pardon my French, Congressman."

"No—you won't have to do that. It's shameful that a man serves his country, risks his life in a war, and comes home to a shakedown just because he wants to make a living. We're not greasin' any wheels for this." Marcantonio spoke to the clerk sitting next to him. "Give this one to Leonard. He'll know who to call." He turned back to Mr. Williams. "Sir, someone from my office will contact you within the week and tell you where to pick up your medallions. You have my word. Anything else I can do for you today?"

"You mean it'll get done? Just like that?"

"Just like it *should've* been in the first place."

"No. No! Nothing else." Williams rose and offered his hand. "Thank you for your help, Congressman."

Marcantonio took the proffered hand without rising. "That's what you pay me for, Mr. Williams." Then he noticed Crescenzo, seemingly for the first time. "Wadda ya doin'? You waiting for this man to get his medallions so he can drive you somewhere? I see dozens of people looking for help—go make yourself useful." Stung, the boy put the coffee and juice down and turned to go when he felt Marcantonio grab him by the arm. "Wait a minute." The congressman was motioning for a stooped old lady sitting in the front row to come up to the desk. She had a casserole pot nestled on her lap and wore big, heavy, old-fashioned black shoes with buttons. Her legs were so short that the shoes barely reached the floor. She had on stockings, but Crescenzo couldn't help noticing as she moved to stand up that they were only rolled to just above her knees.

"Mrs. Jeske—how are you today?" Marcantonio asked. "Did that *go-niff* landlord fix the hot water?"

"He did, thanks to you and no thanks to him, may he rot in hell. Here, Congressman. I made you a nice *tsimmes*."

"You shouldn't have, Mrs. Jeske. You keep feeding me like this and I'll never eat anything my wife cooks."

"No disrespect, Mr. Congressman, but everyone knows your wife isn't even Italian. I mean, she's a wonderful woman and they say Haarlem House couldn't run without her, but isn't she from Utica or Syracuse or some place like that?"

"New Hampshire."

"New Hampshire? Do they even have food in New Hampshire? What kind of place is that to be from? You take this *tsimmes* and eat it. And if Mrs. Marcantonio wants the recipe, I'm only too happy to give it to her."

Marcantonio took the pot, looked under the lid, and gave Mrs. Jeske the appreciative roll-of-the-eyes she wanted. "Thank you, Mrs. Jeske. Here, Crescenzo, take this and have your mother show you where to put it in the kitchen. Now, Mrs. Jeske, I hope you didn't come here just to give me a *tsimmes*. Do you really have enough hot water?"

"Believe it or not, yes—thanks completely to you. Only now that *momser* won't pick up the garbage!"

Crescenzo didn't want to hear any more. He took the casserole dish to the back of the room and began searching for his mother. Before he could find her, Bobbi intercepted him.

"What's in the pot?

"Beats me," he said, holding it out for her inspection.

The secretary lifted the lid and made a face. "Ugh! *Tsimmes!* I didn't see Mrs. Jeske come in."

"How often does she bring this?"

"Too often. Nasty stuff, ain't it? Even Emma won't eat it. Mr. Fink loves it, though. What did she want today?"

"The landlord isn't picking up her garbage. Is that really a problem for a congressman?"

"Oh, if it's got anything to do with a landlord, Marc is the man. Honey, there's more fresh paint gets slapped onto apartment walls in this district than the rest of Manhattan combined. Come on. I'll show you where to put this mess."

The kitchen was a small, narrow galley alongside the room where the chairs and voting booth had been stored. He found his mother there, making a pot of coffee. "How does it look out front, Bobbi?" she asked.

"Oh, it's gonna be busy today. Your son wants to know why you never make him a *tsimmes*."

Delores rolled her eyes. "Put it over there," she said, indicating a counter with two other dishes, one containing sausage and peppers and the other a peach cobbler. "Do I have time for a cigarette?"

"Probably not," said Bobbi. "I thought I saw the literacy worker from the teacher's union getting out of a cab a minute ago."

"Damn! I forgot about her! Chris, there's a folding table under the stairs. Put it by the voting booth. Also, we'll need five or six more chairs." She turned the fire off under the coffeepot and left it to finish brewing. "Come on, Bobbi. I don't want Emma to blow a gasket."

By the time the boy had set up the table and chairs, a young, well-dressed woman whom he took to be the literacy worker was standing in the voting booth. She was extremely attractive and had long, dark, wavy hair. She wore a tight blue suit that came just below her knees as well as stockings and black high heels. Crescenzo couldn't stop stealing glances at her. She was speaking Spanish to a couple, pointing at the levers and demonstrating how to open and close the curtain. Meanwhile, his mother and Bobbi had joined Emma at a table set up near the door, beneath a framed letter. They took turns greeting people as they came in, inquiring in English, Italian, Spanish, and Yiddish as to the nature of the problem. It soon fell to Crescenzo to steer them where they needed to go. Anyone wanting to speak with the congressman was shown to a seat, while those needing income tax assistance were taken over to the accountants' table. Crescenzo couldn't help remarking to his mother on the amazing number of people, mostly recent arrivals from Puerto Rico, who'd come for tutoring on the voter registration literacy test. She just smiled and pointed to the ledger in front of her where every newcomer's name was being entered.

"Most of them have been here before or have family who have been helped by Marc. We use the ledger primarily for tracking cases and making sure everything has been taken care of. But a couple of times a year, Marc's political club sends its volunteers to visit people who have been in with problems to make sure everything is okay or see if anything needs to be done. They also ask them if they're registered to vote."

When she turned away to help a young mother with three children, Crescenzo read the framed letter hanging over the table. It was a carbon, but typed on congressional stationery.

July 24, 1945

My Dear Senator Bilbo:
I have before me a letter which you sent to Josephine Piccolo, 93 Garfield Place, Brooklyn, N.Y., addressing her as "My dear Dago."

It may be of interest to you to know that this lady had three brothers in the armed forces of the United States, and that one of them lies buried in Germany.

If you have any shred of decency left in you you would apologize.

Very truly yours,
Vito Marcantonio

"Hey, kid!"

Crescenzo looked up to see a burly man in a heavy, battered coat standing in the doorway. He wore an old applejack cap and had a pair of workman's gloves in his hands. "I got a delivery that needs unloading and you're it." Crescenzo followed him outside and down the brownstone steps to the street, where a truck was idling. The teamster put on his gloves, threw the latch on the back, swung the doors out, and jumped into the back of the truck. It was filled with all manner of goods: coats, dresses, and bolts of material mostly, but there were also two cardboard crates holding slabs of beef, five cases of Canadian Club, and several hundred cartons of cigarettes.

"What? You takin' inventory?"

Crescenzo looked down. "There are two detectives sitting in a car across the street."

"Yeah, I seen 'em. I got receipts for everything, so fuck 'em. Worst that'll happen they'll bust my balls for a couple of cartons of smokes. You smoke, kid?"

"No. My mom does, though. Philip Morris."

"Hey, what do I look like? A candy store? You want a *Daily Mirror* and an egg cream, too? Here—closest thing I got are these Chesterfields. And take this shit, too." The trucker handed down an enormous, unwieldy floral arrangement made of several dozen roses and an armful each of snapdragons and irises. It was ghastly. Then he pushed forward a rack of men's suits. "Hang on, junior. Don't try and take that down yourself or we'll be picking gabardines out of the gutter." He hopped down and helped Crescenzo muscle the metal rack onto the sidewalk. "You take the front. I'll take the back and carry the flowers."

The trucker lifted the flowers in one arm and bent down to grab the base of the clothes rack with his free hand. When he looked up, Crescenzo was still trying to figure out how to carry the two cartons of cigarettes while lifting the metal rack."

"Jee-zus H. Christ!" groaned the man. "Where you from, anyway?"

"108th and First."

"Yeah? Come here." The trucker whirled Crescenzo around by his shoulders, lifted the back of his jacket, and shoved the two cartons into the waistband of his pants. "You tryin' to tell me you ain't never boosted nothin'? Livin' in this neighborhood? *Marone!*"

Crescenzo thought the rack was heavy, but he found all he had to do was guide it and lift it high enough to clear the brownstone's concrete steps. He wheeled it into the main room.

"What the hell is this?" asked John Pizzo, the congressman's law partner. He was standing by the front table and eating what appeared to be a plate of rice balls.

"Compliments of Mr. Lucchese," the driver said, placing the flowers alongside the table. "If the suits don't fit or the congressman don't like the colors, just let us know."

"The suits are great," said a voice behind Crescenzo, who turned around to see Marcantonio approaching from his window perch. "Nice to see you again, Charlie," he said, extending his hand to the driver. "Please tell Tommy this was totally unnecessary but greatly appreciated."

"He's the one who's appreciative, Marc. They're all real, real proud of the kid, and I know Tommy ain't gonna forget this."

"Just doing what I'm here for. Now you tell Tommy that I'm going to put these suits to good use and I look forward to seeing him real soon."

When Marcantonio walked back to his table, Crescenzo saw that Mr. Pizzo was looking at the flowers and frowning.

"Are these from Tommy Lucchese? The gangster?"

"Do you know something the cops don't?" asked Pizzo. "Last time I heard, he was in the trucking business."

"What did the congressman do for him?"

"Wrote a letter of recommendation to West Point for his son."

"Did he get in?"

"Of course."

"Why did he do it?"

"Because he was asked to."

"Do you mean he had to?"

Pizzo looked sideways at Crescenzo. He seemed to be weighing whether he was going to reply. Finally, he said, "Yeah, he had to. But not for the reason you think, and shame on you. You go to Franklin, right?"

"Yeah."

"I'll bet you go to school with some pretty tough guys."

"Sure."

"Maybe you hang out with them, maybe you don't. But you know 'em, right?"

"Yeah."

"Perhaps one or two of 'em lives on your block or you know 'em from the park or the playground since you were a kid or maybe you see their parents or their sisters at Our Lady of Carmel. I mean, these guys ain't your best friends but you see 'em on the street you say hi, right? And definitely you say hi if you run into 'em somewhere outside the neighborhood, like say at a movie in Times Square on a Saturday night, right?"

"Yeah, right. Of course."

"Because they're from the neighborhood and you know 'em. It would never occur to you to do anything else, would it? To insult somebody that way? When Marc was growing up, there were just as many tough guys, maybe more. You know he never left the neighborhood—he doesn't even know how to drive let alone own a car. He's spent the better part of the last fourteen years down in Washington every week when Congress is in session, and he still ain't got his own place down there—he rents a hotel room and walks to work. He comes home every weekend where he still lives in a third-floor apartment two blocks from here with his mother and his wife and her mother and his sick brother. He's a neighborhood guy who's seen the same guys every week of his life and you could never convince him that the sun doesn't rise and set in East Harlem. Now, do you think he's gonna turn down Tommy Lucchese or anybody else from the neighborhood who wants help?"

Crescenzo, feeling an odd stab of pain in his back as an old man brushed past him, remembered the cigarette cartons. Without taking his eyes off Mr. Pizzo, he reached around and pulled them out of his trousers.

"What the hell is that?"

"Cigarettes. For my mom."

"What a nice boy! Fell off a truck?" Crescenzo blushed and Pizzo laughed. "Ain't you one to talk!"

Crescenzo put the cigarettes on the table in front of his mother, who was busy adding a young couple's information to the ledger. When she gave him a quizzical look he just pointed at the suit rack and shrugged. She smiled. "Thank you," she mouthed.

"Hey, kid." It was Pizzo again, and Crescenzo cringed, hoping to avoid a continuation of their conversation. "Marc wants you."

Marcantonio was finishing up with a gaunt but smiling young man to whom he'd been speaking Italian. "Chris, this is Mr. D'Noffrio. He's got an immigration hearing coming up next week and he needs something to wear. Help him pick out whatever suit he wants. Then I want you to do me a favor. The flowers? Take them over to Mt. Sinai on Lexington and have them sent up to room 526. Yes? Good, thanks. Tell them . . . he thought for a moment, then smiled. "Put a note with them saying 'Big flowers to inspire a little flower.' Sign it 'The Errant Son.' Got it? Good. Here's five bucks for cabs. Don't dawdle—I want you around this afternoon. And I expect some change this time!"

Crescenzo, who spoke passing Italian, helped Mr. D'Noffrio select a dark blue suit. They left the La Guardia Club together, and when Crescenzo discovered they were both heading west, he offered to share his cab. Climbing into the backseat with the flowers and the suit, the two made an unusual pair.

"Been to see Santa Claus, huh?" asked the cabbie, hiking a thumb toward the club.

"Saint?" asked Mr. D'Noffrio with some confusion. "Yes—Marcantonio saint!"

"Whatever, pal. Saint Ivan, most likely. At least he'd be wearin' a red suit."

"How's that?" asked Crescenzo.

"Come on! Marcantonio's the best man the Kremlin ever had in Washington. He's as red as they come. I'll say one thing for the guy, though: he sure knows how to spread the sugar around. They love him to death up here, brother. To death."

A red? Congressman Marcantonio? Crescenzo wasn't exactly sure what that meant, just that it was bad. He hurried through his errand as he'd been told, dropping the flowers with the hospital receptionist and taking another cab back to 114th Street, but his mind was in a ferment. There was a history teacher at his school, Mr. Weiss, who was a communist. Or at least that's what people said. He'd been arrested at a march somewhere upstate and had his picture in the paper. Some kids from Yorkville had been suspended for throwing snowballs at him, and someone had even tried to drop a brick on him from a rooftop while he was walking to the subway. Whenever Mr. Weiss came into the cafeteria, someone would yell, "*Commie! Traitor! Go back to Russia!*" Never so they could be identified, but it got so bad that Mr. Covello took to accompanying Mr. Weiss on the lunch line. Congressman Marcantonio couldn't be a communist! His mother would never work for someone evil, for a traitor. She said Marcantonio was the best congressman in Washington, that he was a real man who spoke for the people no one else spoke for: miners, the unemployed, labor, slum dwellers, Puerto Ricans, the Negro people down south who weren't allowed to vote, immigrants. Crescenzo's father wasn't so sure, but even he knew better than to question his mother's faith in her boss. Still, he wouldn't help her when she went out every night before an election to coordinate campaign workers for the congressman's American Labor Party.

It was after one o'clock when he got back to the office, and the bustle of the morning had graduated to full-blown pandemonium. Nearly every seat he'd set up was filled. A young mother in the back of the hall was trying without much success to mollify a pair of infant twins, who took turns wailing. Between the aisles, a game of tag was being played by a half-dozen young children, who squealed and yelled in Spanish and took a special delight in running around the voting booth, grabbing its weighted curtain. The accountants' table was swamped—Crescenzo's mother had settled in alongside them to help people put their work stubs and receipts in order and fill out the top of the tax forms so the accountants could concentrate on running figures through the adding machines and tallying the returns. Leonard Fink, who'd been working earlier at the congressman's table, was now at a separate desk handling welfare applications and complaints. The din was constant, like a church social or market, and a blue haze of cigarette smoke hung just below the ceiling.

Thirsty, Crescenzo wandered back into the kitchen. He found Emma there, along with an older woman. Although they were both eating pound cake off napkins and laughing, it was obvious that the woman had been crying, and Crescenzo looked away in deference to her red-rimmed eyes, his own gaze falling instead on the counter, which was now packed end-to-end with all manner of homemade food, from coconut layer cake to lasagna, mofungo, arroz con pollo, banana pudding, macaroni and cheese, stuffed peppers, potato kugel, pineapple upside-down cake, fried chicken, several dishes of pasta, and three or four more casseroles that he couldn't identify. He took a plate from a stack on the drain board and quietly helped himself to a tray of sausage and peppers, pretending he wasn't hearing the women's conversation.

"Believe me, Lillian, if Marc says he's going to handle it personally, then it's as good as done. I've been with him ten years and I can't remember the promise he didn't keep. Your niece will get her refugee visa and be in New York before you know it."

The other woman sighed deeply. "I hope to God you're right." She began to quiver, her tears once again close to the surface. "Poor Hannah! Seventeen years old and the only one left. A family of eight. *Eight!* Oh, so foolish! I can't tell you how many times I wrote and begged them to leave Poland, but would my sister listen? Not her! And now look! Oh God, if she were alive I'd kill her myself!"

The woman burst into tears and collapsed against Emma, who wrapped her in her arms. "Please, Lillian—this is doing you no good. Go home and get some rest. Marc will take care of everything."

Crescenzo shoveled the untouched food back into the serving dish and went back into the main room to see if his mother needed any help. Along the way he passed a short man with an ecstatic grin leaving with another of the suits. At the door, the man passed a tall, well-dressed middle-aged Negro man who, unlike the other visitors who all went straight to the desk of secretaries, sidled up against the wall near the front of the room, obviously waiting for someone to notice him. Whether by signal or accident—Crescenzo couldn't tell—it didn't take Leonard Fink more than thirty seconds to come over and warmly shake the man's hand. When the Negro leaned over and whispered something in Mr. Fink's ear, Crescenzo saw him slump and rub his forehead, as if Mr. Fink had suddenly developed a crippling headache. The two continued whispering and trading serious looks for a moment, and then Mr. Fink took the larger man by the shoulder and led him to the back of the room, leaving him at the foot of the stairwell to the second floor. Combing his hair nervously with both hands, Mr. Fink walked rapidly to the front of the hall and stood motionlessly alongside Marcantonio's table. The congressman, who was talking to a young couple waving a letter, took no notice of Fink and, for a moment, Crescenzo had the odd sensation that he was the only person in the bustling room to see Mr. Fink or suspect something out of the ordinary was going on.

"What you lookin' at?" He hadn't heard Bobbi come up alongside him.

Crescenzo nodded his head toward the back of the room. "Do you know who that man standing by the stairs is?"

"Mm-hmm. That's Jim Pemberton. He's the Democratic district leader."

"Why would he come here?"

Bobbi gave Crescenzo a funny look, as if the question made no sense. "Why wouldn't he?"

"Isn't Congressman Marcantonio a member of the American Labor Party?"

"Honey, Congressman Marcantonio *is* the American Labor Party. But he got more votes as a Democrat this year and Mr. Pemberton had a lot to do with that."

"He ran as the nominee of two parties?"

"Hell! He's run on all three parties some years! And you know what? If a Martian spaceship landed on 116th Street tomorrow, I guarantee you he'd be out there first thing trying to get them to organize a Martian party to give him another line to run on!"

"But why would the Democrats and Republicans nominate him if he's in another party?"

" 'Cause can't nobody beat Marc in East Harlem, that's why. The Republicans in Albany keep trying—they gerrymandered the district and redrew the lines to include Yorkville, but he still wins. Now the Republicans up there are trying to pass a bill making it illegal for any party to endorse any candidate who isn't a member, a bill intended solely to stop Marc. Yeah, they try all kinds of schemes but can't nobody beat him. *Can't.*"

Marcantonio had finished with the couple, and Fink leaned in, placing a hand on his shoulder and whispering in his ear. Crescenzo saw Marcantonio look at Pemberton, but his face betrayed no emotion. The congressman turned briefly to the clerk on his left, and then stood up. He stopped to shake hands with the young mother who was next in line to see him, and led her up to the clerk. Then Marcantonio walked to the back of the room where Pemberton was waiting and the two went upstairs. Fink didn't go with them.

"What do you suppose he wants?" Crescenzo asked.

"I don't do no supposin' and neither should you. When Marc is here, this is a congressman's office and all kinds of people come in for all kinds of reasons."

"Even communists?"

"All kinds of people."

"Is it true that the congressman is a communist?

"No."

"Then how come people say he is?"

"You know, long as I known your momma she's been braggin' on you. So I *know* you can't be that big a chump. How the hell should I know what makes a no-nothin' talk a lot of trash? I only know what I see—do you know what you've been seeing all day? Looks like democracy to me. Nobody takes care of their constituents like Marc. And it ain't just the people of this district. He's been the best advocate for Negro rights in Congress— sometimes the only advocate. He's been fighting southern poll taxes since he got to Washington and he made himself a pest during the war with his 'all-Harlem rider,' insisting that all defense contractors hire Negroes.

"Look," she continued, "do communists come in here? As often as Pemberton. Sure, there are communists in the ALP, and they're some of the hardest-working canvassers in the party—Marc makes sure of that. But that don't make him a communist any more than running on the Republican ticket makes him a Republican, or running on the Democratic ticket makes him a Democrat. No matter what line he gets the most votes on, he always lists his congressional affiliation as American Labor Party. Now, if Marc was a Republican, he'd say it. If Marc was a Democrat, he'd say it. And if he was a communist, believe me, he'd say. Because that man ain't never been afraid to say what he is or who his friends are."

"Then why does he have communists in the ALP?"

Bobbi gave a snort. " 'Cause he ain't a phony like the rest of 'em, that's why. You're probably too young, but do you know who started the ALP? President Roosevelt. That's right. His political people were looking for a way to get some of the socialists who wouldn't vote Democratic to back him. Then Marc stepped in on the local level. He was always a great one for believing in having his own machine, in not being beholden to Tammany or Albany. Don't forget—he was Mayor La Guardia's campaign manager and they saw early on that you didn't need either party to win in the city, that you could do it on your own with the right coalition. And the reason I say he's not a phony like all them other politicians is 'cause Marc won't apologize for what he believes in or who the ALP has ringing doorbells on election eve. Man, the other politicians all talk about the communists and socialists like they were roaches—but they're mighty happy to have all them roaches scurrying about their districts knockin' on doors the week before election, you can bet on that. And *that's* why the Democrats and even some of the local Republicans either endorse Marc or run some turkey against him. They want Marc's machine. And the price for that is staying out of East Harlem."

"Where'd they find Tony?"

Pemberton didn't want to answer. He was seated in front of Marcantonio, who was standing and leaning on a desk. Instead, Pemberton fiddled with his cigarettes, stuck one in his mouth, and gazed steadily at the floor. Finally, after lighting it and taking a deep tug, he sighed. "They fished him out of the East River about five or six this morning."

"Oh, Christ." Marcantonio rubbed his face. "Does the family know?"

Pemberton shrugged. "I only heard about it an hour ago from one of our guys down at the morgue."

Marcantonio shook his head. "At least now I know why those pricks from Hogan's office are sitting on the corner." He knit his brow. "Your man say what kind of shape he was in?"

"Yeah. Dead."

"Hey—that's still Anthony Langana you're talking about. The man

345

was my clerk, I've known him my whole life! Do they know how long he's been dead? Did he die in the river, or . . . ?"

"They have him listed as a drowning. I take that to mean there's no evidence that he was knifed or shot or roughed up. And how long he was in, I couldn't say. I suspect my guy would've said something if Langana was ripe—I mean, you, know, if he was floating for a while. It's cold, but I doubt they would have recognized him if he was in long. The bodies swell up. And then the fish and crabs and whatnot. I hear they go for the eyes first."

Marcantonio held up a hand. "Who do I call to get his body released?"

"Oh, come on, Marc! Don't do that!"

"Don't do what? The man's been missing for three months! Hasn't his family suffered enough?"

"And what do you think Hogan is gonna do when he hears you signed for the body?"

"Tony worked for me!"

"That's exactly right—Tony worked for you. And as far as Hogan is concerned, that was enough to make him a suspect in the Scottoriggio case."

Marcantonio stiffened. "The suggestion that Tony Langana or anyone else who was an ALP captain would have beaten that red-baiting Republican bastard to death is so blasphemous, so vile, so indefensible that they wouldn't dare make it to my face. I told that grand jury—with Hogan sitting right there!—that I don't know who attacked Scottoriggio and that's the truth. I mean, just the notion that we'd have to resort to something like that to win an election is outrageous! But because it's Harlem, the papers all talk like we're a bunch of animals!"

"Marc, you know I'm not gonna argue with you about any of this 'cause I don't know who did Scottoriggio, either. The guy was obviously looking for trouble and found it, period. I just don't wanna see you do the same. Can't somebody else call the morgue?"

Marcantonio sighed. "I'll have someone at Giordano's Funeral Home call in the family's name."

"We'll split it with you. But please, Marc—have them send the bill to me."

He nodded and pursed his lips. "Thanks."

Pemberton looked at Marcantonio carefully. "What do you think happened?" He said it in a manner that made it clear that he felt he had to ask.

A long minute passed in which Marcantonio twice appeared on the verge of speaking but didn't. Finally, he scratched his chin and sighed. "Tony was very depressed. He was a hardworking family man. To be picked up by the police, scandalized and defamed in the newspapers— he'd never been through anything like it. He wasn't a public figure, he wasn't used to it like you or me. He loved his job and the thought that he'd become a liability rather than an asset—that he'd never be able to come back to work or be useful to the ALP—was crushing. Crushing. Of course, when he's arrested it's on the front page and when the charges are dropped it's buried on the bottom of page thirty-nine. They ruined him. A man who did nothing, who knew nothing, and they ruined him." He paused for a minute and looked directly at Pemberton. "The last time I saw him was in February. He didn't know what he was going to do."

"So you think he was suicidal."

"I didn't at the time, but . . ." he exhaled heavily. "Obviously, I was wrong."

Pemberton nodded and stubbed out his cigarette. "Who knows?" he asked, rising. "A tragedy like this, it might make Hogan think twice about his next move."

"A silver lining, huh?"

"Something like that."

"Nothing like that—and I don't wanna fucking hear it again, okay?"

"Take it easy, Marc! I'm just trying to help."

"By suggesting I should use the death of a friend and associate to make political hay? That's being helpful? What do you think I am?"

"A man with a lot of enemies who want to bring him down. And I shouldn't have to remind you that I'm not one of them."

"I might not be able to pick my enemies, but I can certainly pick my friends. It's your call, Jim."

The two men glared at each other. It was Pemberton who broke the gaze, shrugging.

"Look. This Scottoriggio shit isn't going away. You know it and I know it. I also know your boy didn't know anything about it because there isn't anything *to* know about it. We're not Republicans and Scottoriggio was a loose cannon on a Republican ship, so what the fuck do we know about it except that the guy was a son-of-a-bitch and got his ass kicked for it, right? But as long as Hogan's grand jury drags on and on we're as dead in the water as Tony. Look at Mayor O'Dwyer: he courted the ALP endorsement in the last election but now he don't know you. How do you think that's gonna shake out for me in '48 when I say I want you to be the Democratic candidate from East Harlem again? We gotta make this Scottoriggio shit go away, and the sooner the better. All I'm suggesting is that if the callous, headline-hunting tactics of an overzealous, politically motivated district attorney led to the suicide of an innocent man, then that's a card we need to play. I didn't invent this game, Marc, and neither did you. I'm just not used to seeing you fold a winning hand when there's a big pot on the table."

Marcantonio bit his lower lip and rubbed his chin. It was his turn to shrug now. "I can't do it," he said. "I'm sorry for what I said before—you've been a real friend for a long time. But I can't. I won't. The man still has a family. I'm not gonna kill him twice. Nobody really knows what happened to Tony, so let's just leave it that way."

Pemberton gave a halfhearted nod. "You're the boss."

"Sorry. I know I'm not making things easier for you."

"Hey, you never do." Pemberton grinned. "You got big ones, Vito. I never saw any man who could go it alone like you."

Although meant to cheer him, Marcantonio dismissed the comment with a waved hand. "Ah, it's always something with those bastards. If someone should break ranks with the bosses and vote for the people instead of the real estate kings and the landlords and the bankers and the utility companies and the insurance combines and the rest of Wall Street's racketeer friends, then he's gotta be taken down!" He was working himself into a lather, his voice rising in pitch and growing louder just as it did when he was exhorting a crowded rally on 116th Street at his lucky corner. "What's un-American about slum clearance and low-rent housing and adequate health and welfare benefits for the working man and woman? I make no apologies for the way I vote! I vote for the people and I vote my conscience!" He stamped his foot. "Why do they need to get rid of me so bad? Just so the next time they vote the Marshall Plan or aid to Chang Kai-shek the vote is 435–0 instead of 434–1?"

"Or the next time they vote on an anti–poll tax measure," said Pemberton.

Marcantonio nodded. "They all know they're living on borrowed time." He smiled—a tightlipped, I-don't-really-feel-happy smile. "Come on. I want to tell my people about Tony so they don't hear it somewhere else."

Before they'd even reached the bottom of the stairs, a woman with a twelve-year-old daughter in tow had grabbed Marcantonio by the hand.

"Look, Congressman!" she exclaimed, pulling the child forward. "Don't they look beautiful?" She pronounced the word *bu-tee-full*. Marcantonio looked blankly at the girl, then gave a questioning look to her mother. "The glasses! The glasses you gave us the money for last month! Doesn't Theresa look beautiful?"

The eyeglasses, which were a dull brown plastic with drawn-up, pointed corners, did very little for Theresa's looks, and her red-faced scowl said she knew it.

"Can you see the blackboard now?" Marcantonio asked, recalling at last the original conversation.

"Yes, sir."

"Then I want you to come in here with your next report card and show me, *capice?*"

The girl nodded.

"I promise we'll pay you back," said the mother. "I thought you might be able to help us get welfare to pay for them. I didn't want you to spend your own money, Congressman! How can I thank you?"

"I hope you'll remind your friends to vote in the next election. And Theresa—don't forget that report card." Marcantonio noticed Crescenzo across the room looking his way and motioned for the boy to come over. "Excuse me," he said, winking conspiratorially to Theresa and her mother. "I've got to put this lazy boy to work."

Crescenzo looked up nervously and cast a quick, apprising eye at Pemberton, as if hoping to deduce what the congressman would say.

"Tell your mom and the other ladies that I need to talk to everybody when we're done for the day." He reached into his pocket and pulled out a small leather wallet, which proved to contain business cards. "You know Agnelli, the florist on Second Avenue? Good. I want you to give him my card and say I need flowers for a condolence call. Lilies and whatever he recommends. Don't let him scrimp. I want a big one. Bring it back here, okay?"

Crescenzo nodded and turned to go, but another thought appeared to occur to the congressman, and he stopped. "Hey," said Marcantonio, "remember those detectives you brought coffee to this morning?"

"Yes, sir?"

"How'd they treat you? Decent?"

Crescenzo shrugged. "I think you surprised them."

Marcantonio nodded. "Take 'em a couple plates of food on your way out. A little bit of this, a little bit of that, some cake. Really mound it up."

"Okay."

"Make it nice, right?"

"Sure."

"But whatever you do, make sure you get rid of as much of Mrs. Jeske's *tsimmes* as earthly possible."

Sunday visiting hours at Mt. Sinai ended at nine o'clock, but the receptionist at the main desk recognized Marcantonio and just smiled. "Room 526," she reminded him, and he removed his brown fedora and bowed, even as he continued past the desk to the elevators.

There was an empty chair outside the room where a cop was supposed to be and, despite the hour, he had expected to see Marie as well. But when he entered, La Guardia was alone and asleep, half-propped up in bed with his reading glasses on, his mouth open, and a piece of the Sunday *Daily News* folded across his belly. The Lucchese bouquet was tucked along the wall with a dozen others. A radio on the windowsill was tuned to a Sunday opera broadcast. Marcantonio removed his coat and hat, picked up a copy of the *Post* from the tray table, and sat in the chair at the foot of the hospital bed. He thumbed to the editorial page to see what the letters were about. Nuclear test controls. Subway fare. Puerto Rican im-migration. A call for more public housing. He read them all, then an ed-itorial calling for a reform of the law giving borough presidents the power to appoint civil court judges. Ha! Fat chance of that! Those were just about the juiciest plums those guys had to give out.

"Ah—the errant son! I must be sicker than I thought." Except for the fact that his eyes were open and peering over his reading glasses, La Guardia hadn't moved.

"Sorry if I woke you, Major."

La Guardia frowned. "No, you're not. Besides, that's all there ever is to do in this place."

Marcantonio pointed a thumb at the wall of flowers. "Looks like you haven't been hurtin' for company."

"Aah!" He waved his hand. "Mostly deliveries. That was a mighty spiffy bouquet you sent up. You steal it from a wedding or something?"

Marcantonio grinned mischievously. "Nah. It's from Tommy Lucchese."

"That *delinquente!*" He put a hand to his forehead and made a face of mock outrage. "It's not bad enough I got you here? How'd you get past the cop? Wait—don't tell me. No cop, right?" He shook his head. "Ah, Vito. Don't ever lose an election."

Marcantonio shrugged. "I'm not gonna. But you can have my cops if you want. I got two from Hogan's office parked downstairs. Fat bastards are probably too full to move."

"Still with the grand jury?"

Marcantonio sighed heavily. "Tony Langana finally showed up today. In the East River."

La Guardia whistled softly. "Suicide?"

"Gotta be."

"Are his people religious? Will there be a Mass for him if it's a sui-cide?"

"I think so. I was just over at the apartment and they were waiting for the priest."

"What a tragedy. I'll have Marie write the family a letter." La Guardia looked at Marcantonio. "And what about you?"

"Me? I'm not the one in the hospital."

"You know what I mean. This Scottoriggio business."

"I've told Hogan everything I know about it, which is a lot less than the cops. You know I voluntarily waived immunity the second the grand jury was impaneled. I've got nothing to hide."

"What about congressional hearings?"

"They've been put on hold pending any indictments from the grand jury. Until then—*niente*."

"Then it's a dead end because Hogan is never going to indict anyone. I knew Scottoriggio. Not well, but well enough to know he was a real stiff-neck. Not real popular with the Republicans downtown."

"Yeah, I know. It could've just as easily been their people getting carried away as anybody. But try getting a reporter to write that! Freedom of the press. There's as much freedom as the owners of the press and their financial overlords will permit."

"Now that sounds like the Vito Marcantonio I know! Tell me—where did I go wrong with you?"

Marcantonio snorted.

"No, really! I should have put you over my knee years ago."

"You put me over *your* knee? You're forgetting who put your machine together."

"And you're great at it. You're also the best congressman this city has by a mile. But if you'd stuck a little closer, if you hadn't drifted so far to the left and relied so heavily on all your fellow travelers, I could have turned the reins over to you. I gave you my congressional district. I could have given you City Hall, too."

Marcantonio shrugged. "Who knows? I might get it yet. O'Dwyer is corrupt and he's weak."

"Sure. You've got a shrinking party whose name is becoming poison, and your friends are dwindling as your enemies increase. Not to mention that there's a grand jury and an unsolvable murder hanging around your neck. You were the best I ever saw and you played yourself onto the margins."

"No. I just wouldn't be their dog. No one can make me forget who I am or where I come from because I don't want to. And I'm not done."

La Guardia began to say something but then thought better of it. Finally, he just shrugged. "Maybe you're right. Besides, the days of me telling you what to think or do are long gone." He grinned. "If they ever existed at all." He looked down at the newspaper in his lap and raised his eyebrows, as if discovering it for the first time.

"It's Sunday," he said. "It doesn't feel like Sunday anymore without dinner at Uncle Picc's." La Guardia looked out the window at the city. "You remember Uncle Picc? He liked you. God knows why." He kept his eyes on the window as he spoke, and followed the movement of the traffic below. In the growing dark of the evening, cars and cabs were heading steadily uptown on Lexington Avenue toward Harlem and the Bronx. "Hey," La Guardia finally said, "how's your diabetes?"

"A pain in the ass. Especially after a night of drinking and playing cards in the back of Albarelli's."

"I ask because my daughter, Jean, has it, too."

"Oh yeah? Just tell her not to drink too much homemade wine."

La Guardia laughed. "Not too much chance of that." The two men looked at each other and smiled, but didn't say anything more. La Guardia went back to looking out the window, and they sat in silence together for a long time in the fading light. Finally, Marcantonio said: "I remember your Uncle Picc always had a good glass of homemade wine around."

But La Guardia was asleep.

13

C. A. V. U.

RUTH ROWLAND
NICHOLS

Second month, 23rd.
1901

Ninth month, 24th.
1960

BELOVED BY ALL

MARY ROWLAND
HAINES

Eleventh month, 11th.
1860

First month, 31st.
1963

"ANGEL"

No matter how far she walked, Ruth could still look back and read the unsteady, shimmering numbers on the Rearwin's cloth wings, taunting her as she trudged heavily through the white light and smothering heat of the desert. From the air, the terrain had not looked cruel, especially after the fright of the storm over the Chuckwallas. But on foot it was endless. Spotting the small cabin from the sky, she had estimated its distance at three miles, yet she'd been walking the better part of the afternoon beneath a relentless sun—*an Icarus sun*, she thought grimly—and seemed no closer. The loose sand sucked at her boots and even the hard-pack along the old, wind-eroded rain gullies frequently crumbled and gave way, tossing her ankle or pitching her sideways. The straps of the emergency knapsack cut into her shoulders with the weight of a three-day supply of compressed food, and she could feel something metal, either her flashlight or automatic pistol, banging unsteadily into the small of her back. She had barely missed stepping on a tarantula and kept her eyes fixed on the ground, as she was deathly afraid of rattlesnakes. She carried her leather flight jacket in a sweating hand as a hedge against the possibility of a cold desert night. Though Ruth prided herself on being prepared, there was only the one canteen and she was loath to do more than wet her lips as infrequently as possible; instead she used the trick her father had taught her of keeping a pebble in her mouth. She looked up. The cabin was no closer. The sun raked angrily at the back of her neck, the bridge of her nose, her scalp. Once she made the mistake of brushing the hair out of her face with her jacket, and the zipper across her cheek was hot as an engine block. The stifling air was thick in her mouth and heavy in her nose and when she inhaled her nostrils burned. She was tired, so very tired, but there was no place to wait out the heat and she walked on, her only diversion cursing first the Albuquerque mechanic who had failed to properly tighten her oil valve and then herself for not taking care of it personally. She noticed a small Gila monster at the bottom of a gully, but it was the wrong color. She blinked and looked again but couldn't find it.

And then she was standing in front of the cabin. A thin, brown mutt with prominent ribs growled halfheartedly, a lowered tail betraying disinterest in defending her turf. The one-room cabin was as poor as the dog: there was no porch and the door hung unevenly and the windows had no glass, just flat, wide boards strung up with rope serving as shutters. Heavy with fatigue, Ruth stepped closer and a young woman with dark skin and a frizzy black halo of hair suddenly appeared at the threshold.

"*¿Como está? ¿Quién está?*"

"I'm a pilot. I've got to get to Santa Monica for a race, but I've lost all my oil and my engine seized so I put down in the desert. Do you have a telephone?"

"*¿Qué?*"

"A telephone." Ruth pantomimed listening to an earpiece and cranking a phone.

"*Ah! No, no!*" The woman smiled and pointed west. "*En Coachella.*"

Ruth looked to the horizon and saw nothing except more desert. The fatigue she'd fought all the way to the cabin came rushing back, and she was suddenly lightheaded and unsure of her feet. Now the woman was standing by her side, supporting her. "Are you my angel?" Ruth whispered, as she was led out of the sun and into the cool shadows of the cabin. The woman guided Ruth to a rough wooden bed with a corn husk mattress and made her lie down. Ruth saw that the cabin was as crude inside as out with orange crates nailed to the wall for cabinets and a rough-hewn, lopsided table but no chair. The young woman stooped at a bucket of water, dipped a cloth, and gently wiped Ruth's face. They smiled at each other. Up close like this, Ruth could now see that the woman was beautiful, and she was surprised and somehow embarrassed to notice how she smelled cleanly of fresh sage. Then Ruth closed her eyes, and held the woman's strong thin hand with the cool, damp cloth right on the bridge of her sunburned nose. It was delicious. She heard a distant ringing. "I thought you didn't have a telephone," she said. She wasn't angry, though, and she said it playfully. She wanted to hold that hand and cloth across her brow forever.

She heard the ringing again, closer this time, and moved her head. The hand disappeared. Another ring. She opened her eyes to a white stucco ceiling and the metal vent of an air-conditioning duct and remembered the motel room in Dayton. The phone was ringing and she answered it.

"Ruth Nichols."

"Will you be ready in fifteen minutes, Miss Nichols?" It was the officer from the Aero Medical Laboratory at Wright. She couldn't remember his name and didn't like him. She was embarrassed to feel so uncharitable but detested his patronizing tone. "A driver will meet you by the front desk."

She washed and ran a stiff brush roughly through her gray hair. She still wore it short, in the same cut fashionable in her youth. It wasn't nostalgia that kept it short but the invective-laced drilling she'd taken from Harry Rogers when her hair got in her eyes during her very first flying lesson nearly forty years ago. They'd be giving her a jumpsuit at the lab to wear during the tests, but she had laid out travel clothes—her most severe dark suit and a white silk blouse—the night before. She'd already affixed her small, square-cut Ninety-Nines pin to the jacket lapel. The gold pin had a spinning propeller with a diamond in its hub and a *25* on the chain guard. When she'd dressed, she slipped into a pair of black flats, picked up a small flight bag containing a pair of tennis sneakers, and went downstairs.

The driver was a young, vacant-looking corporal, and they rode to Wright Air Force Base in silence, going past the sentry gate with barely a nod, but stopping to show identification at the enclosed area around the Aero Medical quad. The buildings themselves were all new and ugly in the overcast morning, either a dull rust brick or gray concrete, and the scurrying uniformed officers only added to the sense of anonymity. They entered through the administration building, the only structure with windows. Ruth soon discovered all of the buildings were connected by a warren of tunnels, some for pedestrians and some wide enough for vehicles. Many of the laboratories and facilities were completely underground and, after five separate hallways and two elevator rides, even she couldn't say which direction she was headed. The gray metal doors were all exactly alike, although she heard dogs barking behind one. The door her escort finally stopped beside had a small sign marked "Astronaut Program."

The room itself was a huge white box, about twice the size and height of a high school gymnasium. There were several enormous machines, one of which Ruth recognized as a centrifuge, and a large steel track suspended from the ceiling. A group of men comprised of uniformed officers and civilians in white lab coats, including the information officer (whose name tag identified him as Captain Horn), were waiting. She noticed that the highest ranking officer was a colonel, and winced to see that the group included an Air Force photographer. Horn introduced her around, but she wasn't really listening to the names. She was given a beige jumpsuit and escorted to a small locker room. "Of course we've got your exam and medical records from New York, Miss Nichols," Horn said once she'd changed, "but we're going to need to take your blood pressure before we start and then take it again after each test." She rolled up a sleeve and one of the civilians applied the cuff, squeezing the bulb until she felt the pressure constricting in her arm. He deflated the cuff and read the meter. "ninety-eight over sixty-eight."

"You must be a cool customer," said the colonel.

"My Quaker upbringing." She smiled thinly. "What's on the agenda? I'd love to get cracking."

"We have three initial tests to administer as part of the astronaut screening program," the colonel said. "It doesn't make any sense to train a candidate unless they can demonstrate a physical aptitude in certain required areas. Let's try this one first." Nichols and the rest of the group followed the colonel to a large platform that appeared to be made of sandwiched rubber. "This machine simulates weightlessness. I want you to stand on it while holding this sphere." He handed Ruth a clear plastic globe about the size of a basketball with a large custom gyroscope mounted within. "Now, once we turn on the simulator, the platform will seem to go soft and cease to support you. Actually, it will support you—if you can balance. But you won't be getting any information from the platform via your feet to help you do that. The only way to keep from falling is to watch the gyroscope and make certain it remains balanced. Understand?"

"Seems straightforward."

The colonel just smiled thinly.

Mounting the platform, Ruth was directed to stand within three feet of its front, and two lab-coated technicians came right up to the edge, resting their arms on the platforms. She had to admit she was nervous and grateful to have the spotters. But then, when she was about to smile at them, she saw they were staring intently at the gyroscope. She could feel her backbone stiffen and couldn't resist casually spinning the globe between her hands. One of the technicians took a sharp breath and leaned forward. "Is this expensive?" she asked innocently.

"Very," he said with no trace of humor. "And it's quite delicate. Please don't do that. And if you feel yourself falling, try to push it toward one of us."

Ruth looked down into the globe, centering the gyroscope. She took a deep breath and relaxed her neck and shoulders. "Ready," she said.

The loss of the floor gave her an instantaneous shock, but Ruth successfully fought the urge to stiffen her legs and instead focused her eyes on the gyroscope while centering her weight in her middle. She leaned precariously for just a moment but was never really in danger of slipping. Instead, she brought all her concentration to bear on the globe and discovered that the sensation was one she'd actually experienced before. She kept her elbows loose, rolled her neck, and tried to make every move come from her spine. At the ninety-second mark, when there was no longer any doubt that she was in complete control of her body and the gyroscope, she felt the platform stiffen beneath her feet.

"Bravo!" said the colonel, a zealous smile plastered across his face. "You were as comfortable as anyone I've ever seen with this test."

Ruth handed the globe casually to one of the technicians, then made a point of hopping down to the floor without any of the proffered hands, despite the fact that the sudden return of gravity made her legs leaden. "We used to get the same sensation in the early days with airboats," she said. "Not that we went particularly high, obviously. But the planes were very light and just conveyed that same sense of nonsupport. You really felt like you were floating."

"How high did you fly?" The question came from a captain. Ruth could tell by reading the ribbons over his left pocket that he was a serious pilot; she recognized several honors and qualifications that had also been awarded to her brother, Erickson, the Air Force attaché stationed with the embassy in Cuba.

"Well, naturally we flew open cockpits back then, regardless of whether it was an airboat or a Jenny. And when I qualified for my first international license in 1924, we stayed low because there weren't any air charts or even beacons. You planned your flight with road maps and followed ground markings. Rivers, train tracks, post roads—whatever made the most sense. I copiloted the first nonstop airboat flight from New York to Miami and we tried to stay in sight of the shoreline the whole way. But I've flown high; I own several height records." She smiled. "I'd like another one."

A technician checked her blood pressure again and pronounced her ready and able for the next test, which proved to be a centrifuge. It looked like a sleek bathysphere, except for a protruding bar that acted as a counterweight. The pod was mounted on a small circular track.

"I've been in one of these before, at Hamilton."

"What for?" asked Horn.

"I took a prototype of a subsonic to fifty-one thousand feet last year." She began to climb into the seat without prompting and buckled herself in.

The captain whistled. "What'd you think?"

"Well, naturally I was impressed. I can't believe the level of coordination and training you fellows need for something like that. But the flight sensation at that speed was really surprising. Like sitting in your living room."

"You didn't find it jarring?"

"No, quite the contrary." The motor on the centrifuge was ratcheting up and she had to talk in an increasingly loud voice. "My first altitude record was in 1932 in an open cockpit. I went over thirty thousand feet."

"In an open cockpit? You must have had an oxygen mask, though."

"No!" She had to shout now to be heard. "I had a tank with a rubber hose that I could put in my mouth. Stupidly, we strapped the tank to the wing."

"Ouch!"

"Indeed! The thermometer mounted alongside the tank shattered at forty-below. We're pretty sure it was twenty degrees colder than that."

"What happened?"

"The oxygen froze my tongue solid." She shrugged as the lid on the centrifuge was locked down.

Ruth had found the pressure in the Hamilton centrifuge unpleasant but bearable, and she had an uneasy suspicion they weren't going to turn it up as high this time. She gave a thumbs-up through the hatch and the centrifuge began spinning slowly to her right. Beyond the test machines there were few distinct points in the lab, and she settled for watching the group of officers and technicians disappear and reappear with each revolution. As the centrifuge gained speed and their features grew indistinct, she had the illusion that she was the one rooted to the ground and they the ones moving. Now they were just a brief smear in her vision. What was that story? About the boy and the tigers? Chase around the tree and turn into butter? Aunty would know. Little Black Sambo, right? Confusing—can't tell if he's African or Indian. Been to Africa, been to India. UNICEF. Saw lots of children. Never saw any butter. Lots of butter in Wisconsin. The Dairy State. Forty-six states. Remember? What year? 1928? No. Twenty-nine. Remember the plane? Yes. Curtiss Fledgling. Stick like this one. But open cockpit. Yes. Not closed. No. Double wing. Struts. Nice. Aviation clubs. Too bad. Crash. Not mine that time. Stock market. Too bad. Open sky. Don't look out. No headache. Watch hand. Open sky. No. Hand. Watch hand. No headache. Watch hand. No headache. Watch hand. No headache. No headache. No headache. No headache. No headache. Spot. No—watch hand. Dizzy. Watch hand. There! Again! No headache. Again. Again. Again. Lake? No—them. Watch hand. Slowing. Breathe even. Stiff neck. Okay. Don't look. Stick. Hold the stick. Watch your hands. Don't look out or you'll get dizzy. Breathe. Don't look. Okay. Stopping. Wait, don't move. Let them move. Let them come. Let them pop hinges. Breathe. Okay. Smile.

The centrifuge lid slipped back and Ruth reached up for the harness buckles. A flashbulb popped and she looked at the colonel. She was very dizzy and her temples throbbed and she hoped no one would notice that she was still seated.

"Why did you stop?" she demanded.

"It's a limited test."

"You mean you got your pictures, don't you?"

"Excuse me?"

"Look, Colonel, I'm a little too old to be so easily snookered. I came here because I want to go into space. I had to test longer than that at Hamilton just to qualify for subsonics."

If the outburst surprised the colonel, his face didn't betray him. "There's no need to go further, Miss Nichols. We have your Hamilton results and, frankly, we're still not sure what G-force someone in a rocket will have to withstand. So why overdo it?"

He was lying—she had only to glance at the captain's expression to be certain. Well, she'd fight this battle from back in New York. Ruth stood up resolutely, her anger a crutch against the dizziness. "What's next?"

The final test, isolation, was in a separate room off the lab and required her to change again, this time into a rubberized suit with a helmet. She was secretly grateful for the break, which gave her a few minutes to shake the lingering sense of nausea from the centrifuge. But as the lab technician led her up the stairs, Ruth realized the isolation test wasn't going to be at all as she'd envisioned. It was a room-sized water tank. An air line was attached to her helmet, which she now saw had no window and would be perfectly dark. For the first time she felt panic.

"Please sit on the lip of the tank," the lab coat said. "Have you ever done this?"

Ruth shook her head and sat down uneasily.

"This is a sensory deprivation tank. It's meant to simulate the experience of being alone in space in just a pressurized suit. We do this because we anticipate astronauts will have to leave their crafts for repairs at some point or deal with power failures within the total dark of an enclosed space. Part of the training program is getting acclimated to the lack of sensory information. After that, we're going to work on coordination and simple motor functions. But for now we want to see how you react to total isolation. I'll attach the helmet and help you slip into the tank."

She wanted to ask how long the test ran but knew she couldn't. Instead she simply nodded and sat still while he attached the metal helmet to the suit. The darkness was all-encompassing and the silence complete—she couldn't even sense the perimeter of the helmet; the air tube kept the pressure even. She felt the technician pushing her forward, but had no sensation of moving into water. Indeed, there were no sensations at all, save for an initial feeling of being gently pulled. She surmised they were using the air hose to position her in the middle of the tank where she couldn't bump against the walls. Then there was nothing. Absolutely nothing. The suit was slightly weighted to keep her feet and arms down so she wouldn't even drift. She didn't like it. She didn't like it at all. *This isn't flying. This is the opposite of flying.* She hummed, needing to hear the proof of her existence. *I know what alone is. Alone is to be alone in the world, not alone without a world. This is death. No. This is worse than death. This is consciousness and the knowledge of the absence of life.* The humming gave her no comfort and she stopped. Instead, Ruth imagined she was asleep and dreaming. She flashed on her father, standing with her by a hangar at Mitchel Field. He was holding her thermos of coffee and paper sack of caviar sandwiches while she climbed into the cockpit of *Akita*. The morning sun was in his hair and he was still strong and healthy and he had that great smile, that old Rough Rider smile that he always had for her before a flight. Daddy handed up the thermos and sandwiches and reached out to rub her leather cap for luck. *"Make sure you come back to me, Rufus."* Then she was flying. She could see the boats on the Sound, the water green and blue and sparkling. With the wind in her face she could even smell it. Oh, it was glorious! *What would it be like,* she wondered, *to break through the atmospheric barrier and swing free into limitless space, at one with the whirling spheres?* Not today, though. Harry and the Chamberlins are waiting at Jersey City. Oh, but won't the city be magnificent! Still unrestricted air! She decided to fly across Long Island City and up the East River to Central Park. Back over the farms of Queens, following the railroad. A village. Cows. Those new Tudor apartments. What was it called? Jackson Farms? No—something like that, though. Now she could see the Manhattan skyline in the distance, bold and sharp and alive. She'd be there soon. Except . . . it was getting farther away. Why? It couldn't be a head wind. The sky was smooth and soft as Aunty's hand on her cheek. Why couldn't she reach it? Now there was a wind, and it pushed the nose of *Akita* straight up. Makes sense—global winds blow out of the west. She felt herself rising. Coat stuck? Something under her arms. Angry. *Why won't they let me fly?*

She heard the helmet being twisted off and came back.

There was a formal lunch with the base commander, a two-star general, but Ruth hardly paid attention. Still, she didn't want to cause any problems for Erickson, and she smiled for all of the pictures.

"I'll bet Miss Nichols put down here when the Air Development Center was just tiny little Wright Field," said Horn.

"Actually," she said, "I can remember when it was called McCook Field. They renamed it for the Wrights in 1924."

"Well, those boys put Dayton on the map," said the general.

"They put us all on the map, didn't they? You know, I came out here once to visit Orville Wright. He was an old-fashioned sort. Very much the gentleman. Dressed to receive me in his own home."

"What was the occasion?" the captain asked.

"I was trying to interest him in procuring peaceful international relations. It was very interesting. You know, the first man to develop the airplane in this country wanted it to be used for peaceful purposes rather than for the military. He was quite a pacifist. He wanted to use every single means possible to avoid war."

"Don't we all," said the general.

When lunch was finished and the last picture taken and Ruth about to be handed back to her driver, the captain spoke up. "Miss Nichols, if you're not too tired, I've got to go over to Aero Design and Engineering to look in on a project. Perhaps you'd like to see what they've got over there."

"Well," said Horn, "I'm not really sure that's such a good idea."

"Actually, I'd love to," said Ruth. "Any objections, General?"

He shook his head. "I'm sure they won't let you go anywhere they don't want you."

"Well, I'm certainly used to that, aren't I?" She smiled, pleased by the embarrassed looks the remark produced. "Thank you for an enlightening morning, gentlemen."

The Aero Design plant and hangars abutted the opposite end of Wright. Ruth, who could remember when this section of the airport had been cornfields, shook her head as the acres of tarmac and buildings rolled by. The captain, who drove them in his own car, looked bemused but well pleased with himself, and it made Ruth curious about what he might be up to.

"I don't think I've ever flown anything built by Aero Design," she said. "My brother got to fly the L-26 they built for Ike and said it was a nice little twin-engine. I could really use something like that. What do you think? Consolation prize for not going into space? Or maybe a little thank-you for being the main attraction in that little sham back there."

"I'm sorry about that," the captain said. "It was inexcusable."

Ruth eyed him. "Okay. So then what's *your* excuse, young man?"

"Me? I'm not part of Horn's PR team, Miss Nichols. I heard you were coming and I pulled a few strings to tag along."

"Why?"

"Because I know someone who needs to meet you."

They parked behind a long, narrow, one-story building at the rear of Aero Design and slipped in a side door. Row after row of men in white shirts hunched over drafting tables announced the brightly lit room as engineering. From the casual waves, Ruth surmised her escort was a regular visitor. They walked back a few rows and stopped at a table along the aisle.

She was young and the only other woman in the room. Her golden hair was cropped short and like the other engineers she wore dark trousers and a white shirt and tie. There was a jacket hanging over the back of her chair and Ruth saw the Ninety-Nines pin.

"Miss Nichols," said the captain, "I'd like to introduce Ginny Hart." The girl shot out of her chair, one hand extended in greeting, the other in front of her mouth.

"Ginny Hart? The girl with all the new altitude and distance records? But what are you doing here?"

"Wasting her time," said the captain.

"Earning a living," said Ginny. "Oh, Miss Nichols! What are you doing at Wright?"

"Wasting her time," he deadpanned again.

"I'm afraid he's correct this time. I came out under the mistaken notion that they were admitting women to the astronaut training program."

"But they are! I'm going with twelve other girls to Lovelace in Albuquerque next month for the physical!"

The captain closed his eyes and placed his fingers on the bridge of his nose.

"Oh, Jeez! Didn't they tell you? We were picked months ago! They even asked me to make some recommendations. I'm really sorry, Miss Nichols. I'm sure I would have thought of you but, you know, they set an age ceiling of thirty."

Ruth could feel her right leg throb. She offered a weak smile. "Well that's wonderful, dear. Congratulations."

"Oh, this is terrible! I'm so sorry!" She shot the captain a look of daggers. "You couldn't tell me, right?"

Ruth held up a hand. "Please. Your friend is the only real flyer I've met all day—present company excluded, of course. He thought we should meet. And I think he was right." She gave the captain her warmest smile. "Thank you."

"You're welcome."

"Now shoo." She twined her arm with Ginny's. "We need to talk. Just girls."

Beyond the parking lot was a large chestnut tree. Ginny tried to bring a folding chair but Ruth wouldn't hear of it. Instead, Ruth simply plopped herself down in the shaded grass and leaned her back against the tree. "I've never seen a Ninety-Nines pin quite like that before," Ginny said, sitting down next to her. "With a diamond in it, I mean."

Ruth looked down at her lapel. "It's a founder's pin."

"You were one of the original Ninety-Nine?"

"I helped organize the first meeting at Curtiss Airport. There were about two dozen of us there. And Amelia Earhart and I traded letters about it for years before that. I've still got them, somewhere."

"Oh, God! What was she like?"

"Competitive. But then, of course, so was I. We were constantly going after the same records and she somehow always seemed to have more money. She soloed the Atlantic the week before I was set to go."

"That's not fair."

"Of course it is. Besides, I had a shot before that but crashed. In St. John. I was flying a heavy, modified Lockheed Vega, and the plan was to stop in New Brunswick to take on a last load of fuel. The airfield was too short."

"Were you all right?"

"Broke my back in five places. Had to fly with a steel corset for the next two years."

"What about the Vega?"

Ruth smiled. The question said everything she needed to know about the young woman. "Luckily, it didn't burn. I had it taken apart and brought back to New York and rebuilt." She looked across the airfield. "I never did solo the Atlantic. I guess that one had Amelia's name on it. She was a heck of a pilot and a good girl." Ruth pointed at Ginny's shirt. "She liked to wear a man's necktie, too."

Ginny blushed. "What do you think happened to her?"

"I hope she sank quickly and cleanly into the deep blue sea."

"Oh, you can't mean that! Don't you think she could have put down somewhere?"

"Well, given the chance she certainly would have. But have you ever flown that part of the Pacific? I think it would be hard enough to find the Howland Islands now if you lost radio contact, let alone back then. It's so easy to make a miscalculation, and I always picture her running out of gas. But I envy her—it's a fitting end to a flyer's career. Disappearing at the peak of fame. On a final, glorious attempt to conquer new frontiers of the sky. To never know the erosions and disappointments of age." She watched a large transport circling for an approach and rubbed her right leg absentmindedly. "Do you have any aspirin?"

Ginny fished a bottle of Bayer out of her handbag. "You take them dry?"

"Just constantly." She tossed three in her mouth and chewed them. "Obviously, I didn't want to bring anything into the lab, even something as innocuous as aspirin." She sighed. "I've been put back together once too often."

"Your back still bothers you?"

"Not too much. In '37 I was copiloting a Condor biplane that crashed and burned. Working as a commercial pilot back then. I was the first woman to pilot a commercial flight, you know."

Ginny looked down in her lap. "I thought Helen Ritchey was."

"You know about Helen? Actually, she was the first to be hired full-time. I was already working as a sub for a friend who owned a small regional carrier, New York and New England. You know what happened to Helen, of course—how they wouldn't let her in the union and none of the men would fly with her." She shook her head. "Here it is, twenty-five years later, and there *still* aren't any women flying for the airlines." She wagged a finger at the younger woman. "And shame on you for thinking I was lying! Never be afraid to claim a first or advertise your achievements, even if it makes you sound like a records hog. If you don't shove it right in their stupid faces, they'll ignore you." She looked out at the runway, where the transport had just landed. "They'll still ignore you, anyway." Ruth smiled grimly. "So what was I talking about? Oh—'37. I was thrown through the windshield of the Condor, seat and all, and landed face-down on the tarmac. My nose was like a pancake but they rebuilt it. I still have headaches, though. Shattered my leg, too—broke it in nine places. Heel, ankle, knee—what a mess." She slapped her thigh, then rubbed it. "That's my buddy. My constant companion. I came out better than the pilot, though. He died. Which maybe wasn't so bad. The fire blinded him."

Ginny shook her head. "I don't know how you guys did it. Some of those planes were so . . ."

"Flimsy? Some of them were, sure. But that was the job—testing the limits. It still is. And at least back then when something went wrong you always believed you had a chance to walk away. That's not going to happen when you're flying at the speed of sound. Tell me: how much flight time do you have in?"

"Seven thousand hours." She said it as casually as she could, but it was impossible to suppress her pride.

"My Lord! How old were you when you started flying?"

Ginny grinned. "I was about fifteen. Hanging around the local air-field, sticking my nose into the engines, always pestering somebody to take me seriously. Finally someone did and, you know, it's like that. Since then, I've flown everything from Boeings to bombers—anything short of a dirigible."

Ruth grinned and nodded. "I've piloted a dirigible. You're not missing much. And I won't fly a bomber."

"I read about your worldwide flight for UNICEF."

"Now that was an experience."

"How did you come to do that?"

"We're Quakers. At least my mother and my Aunty. She's something, Aunty. Still calls me 'thee.' I wouldn't have become a pilot without my fa-ther. He was a direct descendant of Leif Eriksson and an outstanding horseman. Went to Cuba as a Rough Rider. And I've always had these two, I don't know, antagonistic impulses? Between my mother and my fa-ther. I mean, I love flying but I was always looking for something, some meaning. Some calling that combined the two. Aunty used to always say, 'it will come to thee, dear.' And I guess it did."

"You're lucky."

"Do you think so? I'd give everything to go into space." She stared so intently at the younger woman that Ginny squirmed, and when Ruth fi-nally spoke again her voice had an uncomfortable edge to it. "You've got to make it, you've just got to. I can tell that you have what it takes, but promise me you won't let them stop you. Promise me. Because they're going to keep trying. Just when you think you're in they'll change the rules on you. I'm the living proof of that. But whatever happens, don't ever let them get you thinking that because it's been this way it's always got to stay this way. None of us can afford that. Father used to say you can get used to anything—even hanging, if you hang long enough. I didn't believe him when I first started to fly. Now I know he was right."

That evening Ruth sat in the First Class section of the flight from Wright to La Guardia, the pain in her leg beating time with the throb of the engines through takeoff. She swallowed two Percodans and some-where over the Alleghenies, as the twin-engine jet bucked and jumped a thunderhead, she slipped back into uneasy dreams. This time she was in Louisville, tired after just breaking the women's distance record, but taxiing *Akita* down the runway for the flight to New York and her victory celebration. Suddenly the cockpit was full of smoke. She put her head down and felt for the ignition switch but couldn't find it. She'd have to jump. Ruth tried to stand but felt a sudden shiver of panic as she realized she was wedged into the seat by her parachute and steel corset. *"Get out!"* a voice called from the tarmac, *"She'll explode!"* She couldn't move. Ruth felt the heat of the flames from the Wasp engine pushing through the instrument panel, the hot fingers seeking her eyes and mouth. She choked and began to swoon. But two firm hands grasped her under the arms and yanked her forcibly upward. Woozy, she could feel her body sliding over the hull, bouncing off the wing like a rag doll and flipping onto the tarmac. She looked up through the smoke to see *Akita* spinning lazily down the runway in a curlicue pattern. A mechanic with a fire extinguisher was chasing madly alongside, looking like a circus clown in a fireman's skit as he tried to douse the engine with a white foam. Kneeling on the hull above the cockpit in an old reindeer flying suit and matching leather cap was Ginny Hart. She flashed Ruth a thumbs-up.

It was dark and drizzling when she landed in Queens, the city gray and subdued through the cab ride to East 49th Street. She'd only been gone two days, but the apartment smelled musty and unlived in and her footsteps came back as a hollow echo off the hardwood floors and bare plaster walls. There was no mail; the only messages at the answering service were from her brother, Billy, inviting her to join them in Plainview some weekend, and Dr. Fisher, calling to reschedule her weekly appointment and say he had phoned her prescription to the pharmacy on First Avenue. Nothing from Jane or Mercedes. She took down a cup, rinsed it, and made tea while glancing superficially through the *Herald-Tribune*, lingering only over the obituary page in her daily check for familiar names. She wasn't hungry, but her head hurt and she took a few aspirin with her tea. Tired, she knew better than to try and go to sleep, and the thought reminded her of Dr. Fisher's call. The pharmacy, catty-corner from the United Nations, was open all night and the pharmacist's mother, a sweet, nearly serene woman named Mrs. Engle, frequently took the late shift. There was always the chance of meeting someone interesting from the UN—she'd bumped into the Israeli envoy getting cough medicine for his daughter one evening. Ruth described her visit to the Catholic orphanage in Haifa for UNICEF, and how the nuns had had to bury their own dead in the courtyard during the Arab-Israeli war. Another time she'd met an Irish trade delegate attending a conference and fighting a bad flu. He'd had a nasty sneeze but listened nonetheless as she told him of being the first American woman to pilot the Irish Sea. She grabbed an umbrella and her father's old oilskin raincoat from the closet and went out.

Hardly anyone else was walking in the rain; even traffic was scarce. She used to like this time of year, late September, when the last few days of summer were holding on by a fingernail. It took a rain like this to announce the arrival of autumn. No summer thunderstorm but something windswept, something cold and stiff enough to rip those first leaves off the trees and fling them into the gutter. She'd always noticed little changes in the weather like that, and it gave her an uneasy feeling to realize that the end of summer had slipped past her this time. She looked up at the concrete-and-glass pillar of the Secretariat, a dark, solid wall against the rainy night. She loved the building, loved it almost more than the idea of the United Nations itself, which made her feel shallow and guilty. Still, looking at it was one of her secret pleasures, and she had taken her apartment largely for its proximity. The communality of the all-night neighborhood drugstore was a pleasant little bonus.

The fluorescent ceiling lights of the pharmacy were harsh and gave out an annoying hum. Yet the shop itself was warm and snug, its cluttered shelves a seemingly infinite catalog of the complaints and comforts of the body and Ruth, whose own apartment was so spartan, could spend an hour wandering the aisles and vacillating over whether their contents were a revelation or rubbish. She'd seen so much privation and her reaction had been to feel anger and shame rather than blessed. She had come to take a dim view of the Manhattan in which it was essential for a decent store to offer a dozen brands of hand cream. But no pilot was cut out to be a Luddite. Nor could Ruth deny the pang she felt when she thought of her younger sister, Betty, and her unnecessary death from pneumonia.

Ruth heard Mrs. Engle laughing. Curious, she edged toward the front of the store and saw her leaning her body across the counter, conversing with a youngish man whom Ruth could only describe as funny looking. He was short and fair and soft in the way of someone who had never done a day of physical labor, and she could see that, while he was already losing his hair and gaining a double chin, he had extraordinarily delicate features which still hinted at what must have been an arresting face as a youth.

"Oh, *Nixon*," he was saying in a comically high-pitched voice shot through with a southern drawl. "Vote for him? I can't even *look* at him! Doesn't he just make your skin crawl?"

Mrs. Engle giggled. "You're terrible! Well, I don't really know much about Kennedy and I'm curious to see what he has to say." She noticed Ruth and waved over the man's head. "Your doctor phoned in your new prescription, dear. Hold on, I'll get it."

Ruth stepped up to the counter and gave the man a cursory nod. He looked vaguely familiar and she assumed she'd seen him in the neighborhood.

"Are you going to watch the debate tomorrow night?" His accent shortened "tomorrow" to *ta-mah*.

Ruth cocked her head. "I haven't really thought about it."

He drew in a sharp breath. "Don't you care who our next president is?"

"I never miss an election," she said, miffed by the question. "I'm just not much of a television watcher. Never developed the habit. I prefer getting my news from radio and newspapers."

"*Please*—don't talk to me about newspapers! I've been standing here for the last half-hour making Mrs. Engle plum crazy just waiting for the late edition of the *Times*. You'd think they were driving it across the country instead of across town."

"I was the first person to fly the *Times* from New York to Chicago, you know."

"Excuse me?"

"When they began shipping the paper by air. That was me. I did that."

"Miss Nichols is a famous aviatrix," said Mrs. Engle, placing a pill bottle on the counter.

"*Really!* Where's your whip?"

Ruth and Mrs. Engle looked at him quizzically, but the funny-looking man only made himself look funnier by raising his eyebrows and stifling a chuckle. "Don't mind me. I shouldn't tell such awful jokes, but I lack *discipline*." He glanced down at Ruth's prescription and his expression changed. "Librium! Good stuff."

Ruth, who hadn't been offended at being the butt of a joke she didn't understand, was offended now. "I was always led to believe there was a premium on manners in the South."

"Why do you think they shipped me north? I'm sorry. I meant no harm."

Ruth acknowledged the apology with a stiff nod, but that was all. She wouldn't look at him as she fished a ten-dollar bill out of her purse and paid Mrs. Engle, who promptly punched the cash register and gave back change. Rebuffed, the man slunk to the front of the store, ostensibly to keep a vigil for the *Times* truck.

"He's a funny one but really very sweet," Mrs. Engle confided. "Just . . ." she pantomimed taking a drink, giving Ruth a meaningful look. But drinking was something Ruth had never seen as an acceptable excuse for failure or foolishness, and she simply let the information hang without reply. Instead, she glanced around the pharmacy.

"It's quiet tonight."

"Mm. The rain, I imagine. I'm not sorry—it's been gangbusters in here every day."

"Why are you so busy? There isn't a flu or one of those children's epidemics going around, is there?"

"Oh heavens, no." The woman leaned across the counter and lowered her voice a notch. "It's these birth control pills. We can't get enough to fill the prescriptions!" She ran a hand through her gray hair and smiled mischievously. "I don't blame these girls, though. I love my six kids to death, but I won't lie to you—there were a few surprises in the bunch. Wouldn't it have been marvelous to be able to pick when you wanted to stop?"

"Or when you wanted to start," said Ruth. "I can't tell you how many girls I knew who had to give up their careers to have a family. Or," she added with the faintest tremble in her voice, "who kept waiting and waiting and waiting until it was too late for that." She felt a sharp pain in her leg and took a deep breath. "But you know what, Mrs. Engle? This is really what I've been praying for my whole life. Freedom. Or at least freedom from the smirking idiots who say they won't hire you because you're going to get pregnant on 'em." She fished around in her purse until she felt the bottle of Percodan.

"I don't know, dear. Women are still going to want to have children."

"Well of course they are!" She pulled the bottle out, shook two pills into her hand and popped them in her mouth and swallowed. "But the lie that a woman can't be trusted with a job because she can't even be trusted to control her own body—that pretense is out the window. Oh, think of it, Mrs. Engle! It's not just family planning, it's career planning, it's life planning. It's equality!"

"What did you just take? That wasn't one of my bottles."

"That? Oh, it's just a painkiller I get from my family doctor in Rye. I've been taking it longer than I care to remember."

"Did Dr. Fisher know you were taking something else when he prescribed Librium?"

Before she could answer, a middle-aged man shuffled over to the counter. He was wearing an expensive suit and raincoat, but was quite disheveled. He wasn't wearing a hat and his dark, thinning hair was wet from the rain. His collar was open and his tie loose, and there was some sort of stain on his shirt. He smelled strongly of cigarettes and alcohol, and Ruth noticed that one of his shoes was untied. All in all, he was a mess.

"I don't feel so good," he announced.

Ruth arched an eyebrow toward Mrs. Engle, but the shopkeeper played it straight.

"Could you be more specific, sir?"

He clutched his shirt and tie near the top of his stomach and closed his eyes. "Too much."

"Upset stomach?"

He nodded. "Yeah."

"We have several kinds of bicarbonates over in the next aisle. "There's Eno, Bromo-Seltzer, Brioschi, Alka-Seltzer . . ."

"What do you recommend?" He was swaying slowly in place.

"I like Bromo-Seltzer," volunteered Ruth.

"Oh yeah? Why 'zat?"

She was going to tell him it was because of the old Bromo Tower in Baltimore—how the five hundred lights and twenty-five-foot blue Bromo bottle that once crowned it had been a beacon on her early mail flights down the coast to Florida with Harry—but for some reason his drunken face froze her tongue and made her think of the isolation tank at Wright. *This is consciousness and the knowledge of the absence of life. Oh, Rufus! For shame!* She felt as if her skin were burning and smiled weakly. "It works," she said.

Ruth said a quick goodnight to Mrs. Engle and headed back to her apartment, stopping briefly at the all-night grocery store on the corner of Forty-eighth Street for a loaf of bread and a can of coffee. Her leg was still hurting when she got to her building and she had to take the elevator. Ruth didn't bother to turn the lights on in the apartment and sat on the sill with her back to the window for a long time, staring absently at her rooms without looking at anything in particular or even feeling anything in particular. Eventually, she stood up and rummaged through her purse for the two pill bottles and placed them on the night table in her bedroom. Then she went into the kitchen. She opened the can of coffee and measured eight tablespoons and six cups of water into the pot and set it on the stove. While it perked, she found her thermos and opened a tin of caviar and made three sandwiches, which she placed in a brown paper sack. She wrote brief notes to Billy and Erickson, but not to Aunty, and sealed each in an envelope. Then she addressed an envelope to Ginny Hart at Aero Design and Engineering in Dayton and put her Ninety-Nines pin in it. She turned the fire off under the coffee and poured as much as she could into the thermos along with milk and sugar. Milk. She'd forgotten the milkman. She scribbled another note and dropped it in the silvered milk tin outside the apartment door. *"No milk today, please. Gone flying."* She placed the thermos and bag of sandwiches on the night table and picked up the pill bottles.

The early morning sun shone dappled through the trees as she drove her car west on King Street to the Armonk airport where she kept the Cessna. Then she was in the air, the thermos and sack of sandwiches on the empty passenger seat. She had been so very tired but now felt light as a cloud, as if someone strong whom she could always sense but never see was holding the plane aloft, cradling her across the sky. C.A.V.U.: ceiling and visibility unlimited. First she was over the Sound, where Harry had shown her how to fly his seaplane. She looked at the water and thought for a second of Amelia and disappearing beneath the waves. But that wasn't right for her. Then Ruth was above the beautiful city, flying low over the Brooklyn Bridge. The sun glinted on the bridge's steel support cables, making them shimmer like the strings of a giant harp while the cars on the bridge came and went from the earthly paradise beneath her just like yesterday and tomorrow, back and forth and back and forth and back and forth unchanging. Oh, it was all so exquisite! Her people, her family, her poor, beloved city! *But what would it be like,* she wondered, *to break through the atmospheric barrier and swing free into limitless space, at one with the whirling spheres?* Ruth Nichols, holder of the women's open-cockpit altitude record, pulled back her throttle and pointed her plane straight for the heavens. The sky opened to take her and she felt the blue grow fainter and the air grow colder. It was harder to breathe and she reached for the rubber tube and felt the cold shock her tongue. *I can do this—just a little more.* She breathed one more deep breath as the blue of the sky turned to the limitless black of space. *Tongue frozen. Tongue frozen.*
Tongue frozen.

POSTSCRIPT

I can't really say whether I'm sleeping better again these days, but my late-night rides have grown less frequent. Still, there will always be nights when my bedsheets feel as rough and ungiving as a patch of hard-baked earth, and I am as uncomfortable and agitated as a living man can be. Then I take out my bicycle and ramble.

My last trip to the Bronx is under a full spring moon. West on the Pelham Parkway bike path, the soft, scented night air of late May hinting at the approach of another summer. Riding elegant and silent Mosholu and then north under the elevated tracks of the IRT Number 4 on Jerome Avenue. *Last stop! Woodlawn! All off!* I want to check on something I noticed during a recent stroll through the cemetery: a gap where the bars in the iron fence along 233rd Street have been bent back and the grass is worn away. I cross the moonlit street and lean the bicycle against a tree and sprawl across the dark grass at the edge of Van Cortlandt Park. And I wait.

Save for the distant, steady hum of the Major Deegan the night is quiet and I hear them before I see them. They are young, as I knew they'd be. Neighborhood kids, young lovers mostly, but also knots of teenage boys, laughing and talking. The guys carry the beer in plastic bags and take the empties out with them later; the girls hold the boys' hands or lean against them or sometimes just float behind. Under a full moon this is their own private preserve, a little piece of teenage heaven on earth, and they wander Woodlawn in the illuminated night, sitting against the headstones and gathering in the wooded sections off the main roads where the night watchmen rarely venture. They appear at the gap in the fence from time-to-time, coming and going like bees at the entrance to a catacombed hive. At 4 a.m., when the moon and all the kids have gone, I ride home and go to bed. I feel good.

Woodlawn. Whatever else it is, its four hundred fertile acres and three hundred thousand stone sentries provide a final accounting of death. Here moulder the bountiful fruits of illness, war, and epidemics, the desiccated husks for which pain and pleasure and work and children have as much meaning as they do for a rotting ear of corn or a spent and skeletal shad at Hudson River run's end. Here, too, the fading remains of the drowned, electrocuted, poisoned, and incinerated; the mangled victims of horse, carriage, automobile, train, plane, and subway accidents; the crushed and battered casualties of cave-ins and scaffold collapses, of digging, demolition, and construction—the rising up and the coming down of the living concrete body. A fifteen-year-old office boy from the Metropolitan Life company who, running to avoid a half-dozen laughing secretaries determined to give him a birthday kiss, tripped and impaled himself upon a fountain pen. Childbirth, infant deaths. Murder. Old age. Yeah—especially old fucking age.

Middle age yips put me on a bicycle. *"Something startles me where I thought I was safest"* says Walt Whitman, poet of the enduring body of New York City, celebrant of the corruption of the corporeal. Until today *"the summer growth is innocent and disdainful above all those strata of sour dead."* Only now comes our September, and those jet engines of death hum in our ears and the once pure Hudson winds carry the most acrid and terrifying vapors. On the branch the fruit is still luscious, but its soft brown flecks foretell the future. Welcome to history.

Woodlawn itself will be turned under someday. Whatever is left of the earliest arrivals, already disinterred once from the foreclosed and gerrymandered graveyards of Manhattan, will be on the move again, to sweeten the soil of Westchester or New Jersey or Pennsylvania. Should that bother me? It doesn't. It is enough to stand here today, in a circumscribed place where time outruns me, and feel both grounded and eternal. I have a piece of the city I can wrap my mind around, a home base for rides out and among the centuries of stone markers comprising my five boroughs.

I walk among the forgotten, and I know I will be forgotten.

I animate the dead and find them just like me.

Does it matter to Ruth Nichols that she is with a stranger all these years after her death? I doubt it. But I hope the thought could have effected her actions. What about Finley Peter Dunne? Would he have stayed silent on the Red Scare if he could foresee internment camps and McCarthyism and the vile-named Patriot Act, or even just that I might lament his failure of nerve? Will remembering Vito Marcantonio give me the courage of my convictions? Can I be inspired by Attilio Piccirilli's gentle but unswerving belief in the value of his work against all fashion?

They were alive and now they are dead; they were forgotten but now they are remembered. They are as real to me as my own thoughts.

Think of me riding.

SUGGESTIONS

FOR FURTHER READING

This book mixes real people with characters and situations that, while researched and fact-based, are fanciful. In every case, the fictional was created solely to highlight what I perceived as a key issue or event in a real life. And where creative liberty was taken, the aim is always to get at something true about that person and to suggest just what it is that I find so resonant in their lives at this particular moment.

The following books provided valuable information in the researching of this work and are recommended to anyone wishing to learn more about the events and people portrayed. Although I have tried to compile this list with an eye toward more readily available work, the nature of the subjects didn't always make this possible. Public and university libraries are, of course, the best repositories of older titles and periodicals and, for those who wish to obtain out-of-print titles, my personal experiences with locating and procuring these books through online rare and used-book dealer megasites such as Alibris, Abebooks, and Bibliofind have been very positive. For subjects such as John Purroy Mitchel, for which there aren't even out-of-print biographies, I have tried to recommend material that an interested reader can find with a little digging.

PLEASE SUPPORT YOUR PUBLIC LIBRARY.

WOODLAWN

Woodlawn Remembers: Cemetery of American History, by Edward F. Bergman (Utica: North Country Books, 1988). A guide to the history of Woodlawn with special focus on the architecture of its tombs (Bergman is a professor of architecture at Lehman College in the Bronx). Highly informative and lavishly photographed.

Permanent New Yorkers: A Biographical Guide to the Cemeteries of New York, by Judi Culbertson and Tom Randall (New York: Chelsea Green Books, 1987). Biographical sketches of many of Woodlawn's most notable personalities make up several of this book's chapters. Presented as cemetery walking tours.

More on New York cemetery architecture can be found in the essay "Visible City," by Kevin Wolfe in the September 1985 issue of *Metropolis*.

WALT WHITMAN AND THE FOWLERS

Walt Whitman's America: A Cultural Biography, by David S. Reynolds (New York: Vintage, 1996). As the title suggests, Whitman in his era. Outstanding.

Leaves of Grass, by Walt Whitman. I recommend the Norton Critical Edition, edited by Sculley Bradley and Harold W. Blodgett.

The Octagon House, Orson Fowler's 1853 bestseller, has just been republished by Fredonia Books. Other titles by Orson and Lorenzo Fowler such as *Phrenology: A Practical Guide to Your Head* and *Amativeness (Free Love in America)* can also be found. Also out of print but highly informative is *Heads & Headlines: The Phrenological Fowlers* by Madeleine B. Stern (Norman, Oklahoma: University of Oklahoma Press, 1971). Oddly enough, Stern, a well-known New York book antiquarian, is also the author of a book on Miriam Leslie, the femme-fatale-turned-publisher discussed in Chapter 6. That book, *Purple Passage: The Life of Mrs. Frank Leslie* (Norman, Oklahoma: University of Oklahoma Press, 1953) is both highly entertaining and out of print.

For those seeking something a little more tangible, an outfit called the London Phrenology Company sells reproductions of the phrenological bust mapping "the phrenological organs" created by Lorenzo Fowler and sold at Fowlers & Wells. I found mine between the pentagrams and dragons in a Wiccan store in Jim Thorpe, Pennsylvania (don't ask).

HENRY BERGH

Angel in Top Hat, by Zulma Steele (New York: Harper and Brothers, 1942). As noted in Chapter 2, the Steele biography is very well done but out of print. For those with access to a decent research library, I also recommend the following magazine articles: "The Cost of Cruelty," by Henry Bergh in *North American Review*, July 1881; "Henry Bergh and His Work," by C. C. Buel, *Scribner's Monthly*, April 1879; and "Riddle of the Nineteenth Century: Mr. Henry Bergh," by Clara Morris, *McClure's Magazine*, March 1902.

Most of my portrayal of the younger Henry Bergh, who was treasurer of the SPCA until his death in 1924, is extrapolated from his *New York Times* obituary. It can be found in the paper's May 25, 1924, edition.

AUSTIN CORBIN, CHESTER A. ARTHUR, AND ROSCOE CONKLING

The Long Island Railroad: A Comprehensive History (seven volumes), by Vincent F. Seyfried (Garden City, New York: published and copyright by Vincent F. Seyfried, 1961–75). The best single source of information on Austin Corbin, the bulk of which can be found in volume 6, "The Golden Age: 1881–1900." Difficult to find.

Stanley McKenna was an actual reporter for *The New York Herald*. I don't know if McKenna was present for Arthur's trip to Long Island. However, he did interview Corbin for a July 21, 1879, article in the *Herald* entitled "Jewish Patronage Not Welcome at Manhattan Beach—Mr. Corbin's Denunciation—The Distinction of a Past Saratoga Season Re-made." All of Corbin's remarks on this topic appearing in Chapter 5 are reproduced from this interview.

"Austin Corbin and the Manhattan Beach Hotel," in *Brooklyn's Gold Coast: The Sheepshead Bay Communities,* by Brian Merlis, Lee A. Rosenzweig, and I. Stephen Miller (Brooklyn: Sheepshead Bay Historical Society, 1997).

Austin Corbin's obituary appeared on the front page of the June 5, 1896, edition of the *New York Times*.

Roscoe Conkling of New York: Voice in the Senate, by David M. Jordan (Ithaca, New York: Cornell University Press, 1971).

During the writing of this book, two other writers referenced Conkling in works of fiction. He is a major character in *Two Moons*, by Thomas Mallon, and an obvious point of inspiration for William Kennedy in his novel of Albany politics, *Roscoe*.

JOHN PURROY MITCHEL AND THE POLIO EPIDEMIC OF 1916

There is, unfortunately, no biography of John Purroy Mitchel, although his impact as a reform mayor and model for Fiorello La Guardia has been noted by that mayor's biographers as well as historians specializing in the government of New York City and the reform movement. To get a balanced assessment of Mitchel's strengths and weaknesses, I suggest two articles: "Being Human: A Great Mayor and What Happened to Him," by Emanie N. Sachs, *The Century Magazine*, February 1926, and "John Purroy Mitchel," an essay and appreciation immediately following his death written by Oswald Garrison Villard for *The Nation* on July 13, 1918.

For a good overview of both the etiology and public politics of the polio epidemic, I recommend *Dirt and Disease: Polio Before FDR*, by Naomi Rogers (New Brunswick, New Jersey: Rutgers University Press, 1992).

ATTILIO PICCIRILLI AND FIORELLO LA GUARDIA

Attilio Piccirilli: Life of an American Sculptor, by Josef Vincent Lombardo (New York: Pitman Publishing, 1944). Written during World War II, this is a worshipful and somewhat stilted biography. Lombardo's unstated but still obvious wartime concern was that Piccirilli would be derided simply for being an Italian American. While that seems ridiculous now, I also came across an article from the era insinuating that the Da Vinci School, the program begun by Piccirilli to teach classic art and sculpting to children, was some kind of warren of fascist ideology, so it's hard to dismiss Lombardo's worries. Difficult to find, but it contains many black and white plates of Piccirilli's own pieces including Thea La Guardia's head-stone and the small statue of a baby he made for La Guardia.

I am personally indebted to Bill Carroll, a Bronx high school teacher and history buff who is seeking to have East 142nd Street in Mott Haven renamed for the Piccirillis. Mr. Carroll shared his knowledge with me, and introduced me to Jerry Capa, a former student of Attilio. Mr. Capa was kind enough to speak with me and share his privately printed booklet, "A Friendship with Attilio Piccirilli." Mr. Carroll, along with his wife, Mary Shelley, has published several articles including "The Piccirilli Studio," in *The Bronx County Historical Society Journal*, Spring 1999, and "Carving America's Monuments: The Piccirilli Brothers of the Bronx," in *The Bronx Times* on July 15, 1999. Also helpful is "Making a Great Statue: How French's Lincoln Was Put into Marble," by W. M. Berger, *Scribner's Magazine*, October 1919.

Much is available on Fiorello La Guardia. Two of my personal favorites are *When La Guardia Was Mayor: New York's Legendary Years*, by August Heckscher with Phyllis Robinson (New York: Norton, 1978), and *Life with Fiorello*, by Ernest Cuneo (New York: Avon, 1955). The latter, though out-of-print, is a chatty first-person account by a newsman–turned–La Guardia–associate and worth looking for to gain a sense of the unique personality of the man friends called "the Major."

FINLEY PETER DUNNE AND FRANCIS GARVAN

The only collection of Finley Peter Dunne's Mr. Dooley essays currently available is a reprint of *Mr. Dooley in Peace and War* from the University of Illinois Press (Champaign, Illinois, 2001). I am also fond of an easily found Dover paperback, *Mr. Dooley on Ivrything and Ivrybody*, which culls *Peace and War* and several other out-of-print Dooley compendiums. Also out of print but worth locating is *Mr. Dooley Remembers: The Informal Memoirs of Finley Peter Dunne* (New York: Atlantic Monthly Press, 1963). The memoir, which Dunne never finished, was edited and effectively completed with extensive commentary by his son, Philip Dunne. Philip was also a fine writer, penning the screenplay for John Ford's version of *How Green Was My Valley* and speeches for Adlai Stevenson. A successful director in his own right and active in politics, Philip's memoir, *Take Two*, published by McGraw-Hill in 1980, is hard to find but worth the search.

Very little has been written about the life and career of Francis Garvan. However, good sources for information on the Palmer raids include *A. Mitchell Palmer: Politician,* by Stanley Coben (New York: DaCapo Press, 1972); *Red Scare: A Study in National Hysteria, 1919–20,* by Robert K. Murray (New York: McGraw-Hill, 1955); and *Crusade Against Radicalism: New York During the Red Scare, 1914–1924,* by Julian F. Jaffe (Port Washington, New York: Kennikat Press, 1972). A nice overview can be found in "The Great Red Scare," by Allan L. Damon, *American Heritage Magazine,* February 1968.

COUNTEE CULLEN

An excellent omnibus of Cullen's work—including selections from his newspaper essays and novels as well as his poems—is *My Soul's High Song: The Collected Writings of Countee Cullen, Voice of the Harlem Renaissance,* edited with an insightful introduction by Gerald Early (New York: Doubleday, 1991). The book also contains seventeen-year-old James Baldwin's interview with Cullen for the De Witt Clinton High School newspaper.

Both of Cullen's children's books, which are co-credited to "Christopher Cat," *The Lost Zoo* and *My Lives and How I Lost Them,* are out of print. The originals were published by Harper and Brothers in 1940 and 1942 respectively; both have been republished by other houses several times and can be readily found through used-book dealers.

For information on the young James Baldwin, see the early chapters of *James Baldwin: A Biography,* by David Leeming (New York: Alfred A. Knopf, 1994). Baldwin's own *The Fire Next Time* (New York: The Dial Press, 1963) and the essays "Autobiographical Notes" and "Notes of a Native Son," appearing in *Notes of a Native Son* (Boston: Beacon Press, 1955) were important source material for me.

VITO MARCANTONIO

I Vote My Conscience: Debates, Speeches and Writings of Vito Marcantonio, selected and edited by Annette T. Rubinstein (New York: Vito Marcantonio Memorial, copyright 1956). Exactly what the title suggests, organized chronologically with an unsigned and unapologetically biased appreciation of his career as an introduction. Great pictures, too, including Marcantonio and Paul Robeson at a "lucky corner" rally and Marcantonio's funeral procession through East Harlem.

An outstanding critical discussion of Marcantonio's career can be found in Gerald Meyer's *Vito Marcantonio: Radical Politician: 1902–1954* (Albany: State University of New York Press, 1989). Meyer, a superb researcher and student of city politics, really gets it all, from the rough-and-tumble street politics of the era to an insightful analysis of how the maverick congressman managed to balance political realism with his ideological beliefs.

For divergent views on Marcantonio, you can read the positive take of Richard Sasuly's "Vito Marcantonio: The People's Politician" in *American Radicals: Some Problems and Personalities*, edited by Harvey Goldberg (New York: Monthly Review Press, 1957). Or, you can find unflattering portraits in the essay "Vito Marcantonio: New York's Leftist Laborite," part of *American Demagogues*, by Reinhard H. Luthin (Boston: Beacon Press, 1954), and Richard Rovere's article "Vito Marcantonio: Machine Politician, New Style" in the April 1944 edition of *Harper's*.

RUTH NICHOLS

Wings For Life: The Life Story of the First Lady of the Air, by Ruth Nichols (Philadelphia: J. B. Lippincott, 1957). Out of print but available.

A transcript of an interview with Nichols conducted by Kenneth Leish in June of 1960, just a few months before her suicide, can be found in the collection of the Columbia University Oral History Project. Like the autobiography, it gives no hint of what was to come, but it was here that I learned of Nichols's trip to Ohio to audition for the space program.

FRED GOODMAN is the author of *The Mansion on the Hill: Dylan, Young, Geffen, Springsteen, and the Head-on Collision of Rock and Commerce,* which received the Ralph J. Gleason Award for best music book of 1997. A former editor of *Rolling Stone,* he writes for a wide range of national publications. He lives with his wife and sons in White Plains, New York.